# WOMEN POETS
## OF THE
# RENAISSANCE

# WOMEN POETS OF THE RENAISSANCE

SELECTED AND EDITED BY

MARION WYNNE–DAVIES

ROUTLEDGE
NEW YORK

Published in 1999 by
Routledge
29 West 35th Street
New York, NY 10001

Originally Published in Great Britain in 1998 by

J.M. Dent
Weidenfeld & Nicolson
The Orion Publishing Group Ltd
Orion House
5 Upper Saint Martin's Lane
London, WC2H 9EA

10 9 8 7 6 5 4 3 2 1

Library of Congress Cataloging-in-Publication Data

Women Poets of the Renaissance / selected and edited by Marion Wynne
–Davies.
     p. cm.
  "Originally published in Great Britain in 1998 by J.M. Dent"—T.p.
verso.
   ISBN 0-415-92350-6 (alk. paper)
   1. English poetry—Women authors.     2. English poetry—Early modern, 1500-1700.
   3. Renaissance—England.     I. Wynne-Davies,
Marion.
PR1177.W64  1999
821'.30809287—dc21

                                                                98-52072
                                                                CIP

# CONTENTS

# NOTE ON THE EDITOR

Marion Wynne-Davies teaches English literature at the University of Dundee. She is the author of *Women and Arthurian Literature: Seizing the Sword* (London: Macmillan, 1996), and the editor of *The Bloomsbury Guide to English Literature* (London: Bloomsbury, 1989 and 1995) and *The Tales of the Clerk and the Wife of Bath* (London: Routledge, 1992). She has also co-edited with S. P. Cerasano *Gloriana's Face: Women, Public and Private, in the English Renaissance* (Hemel Hempstead: Harvester Wheatsheaf, 1992), *Renaissance Drama by Women: Texts and Contexts* (London: Routledge, 1995) and *Renaissance Drama by Women: a Reader* (London: Routledge, 1998).

# CHRONOLOGY

| Year | Literary Dates | Historical Events |
|---|---|---|
| 1485 | | Henry VII |
| 1492 | | Columbus discovers America |
| 1498 | | Erasmus in England |
| 1509 | | Henry VIII succeeds as king of England on death of Henry VII |
| 1513 | Gavin Douglas: trans. of Virgil's *Aeneid* (written; printed 1553) | |
| 1514 | Barclay: *Eclogues* (completed) | |
| 1516 | Sir Thomas More: *Utopia* | |
| 1517 | | Luther's 95 'Theses'; start of the Reformation |
| 1520 | | Meeting at the Field of Cloth of Gold between Henry VIII and Francis I |
| 1521 | | Henry VIII Defender of the Faith Luther appears before the Diet of Worms |
| 1525 | Tyndale: trans. of the New Testament | |
| 1526 | | Burning of Tyndale's trans. of the New Testament |
| 1531 | | Henry VIII declared Head of the Church in England |
| 1532 | | Submission of the clergy (to Henry VIII; begins English Reformation) |
| 1533 | Skelton: *Magnificence* (posthumous) | Jan. Henry VIII secretly married to Anne Boleyn |

| Year | Literary Dates | Historical Events |
| --- | --- | --- |
| | | Apr. Divorce of Henry from Catharine of Aragon |
| | | June. Coronation of Anne Boleyn |
| | | July. Henry VIII excommunicated by the Pope |
| | | Sept. Birth of Princess Elizabeth to Anne Boleyn |
| 1534 | | England's final break with Rome |
| | | More's refusal to take oath to the succession |
| | | Parliament passes Act of Supremacy: Pope's powers in England taken over by Henry VIII |
| 1535 | Coverdale: trans. of the Bible | Henry VIII named 'Supreme Head of Church' |
| | | Trial and execution of Sir Thomas More |
| 1536 | | Execution of Anne Boleyn |
| 1539 | | Act of the Six Articles passed, 'abolishing diversity of opinions' |
| | | Marriage treaty between Anne of Cleves and Henry VIII |
| 1540 | | Annulment of Henry VIII's marriage to Anne of Cleves |
| | | Marriage between Henry VIII and Katharine Howard |
| 1542 | | Execution of Katharine Howard |
| | | Mary Queen of Scots accedes on the death of James V of Scotland |
| 1543 | | Marriage of Catherine Parr and Henry VIII |
| 1545 | Sir Thomas Elyot: *Defence of Good Women* | The Council of Trent: beginning of the Counter-reformation |
| 1547 | | Death of Henry VIII: succeeded by Edward VI (aged 4) |
| | | Repeal of the Six Articles (1539) |
| 1548 | *Book of Common Prayer* | |
| 1549 | | New *Book of Common Prayer* to be used from this date |

| Year | Literary Dates | Historical Events |
|---|---|---|
| 1553 | Gavin Douglas: trans. of Virgil's *Aeneid* (written 1513) Wilson: *Art of Rhetoric* | Death of Edward VI Lady Jane Grey proclaimed queen, later executed Mary I proclaimed queen in place of Lady Jane Grey |
| 1554 | | Roman Catholicism re-established in England by Parliament |
| 1554 –5 | Elizabeth I: 'Woodstock' poems | Elizabeth I imprisoned in Woodstock |
| 1556 | | Anne Cecil de Vere born |
| 1557 | Earl of Surrey: trans. of Virgil's *Aeneid* (Books II and IV) *Tottel's Miscelleny* (poems by Surrey, Wyatt, et al.) | |
| 1558 | Knox: *First Blast of the Trumpet* | Death of Mary I; accession of Elizabeth I |
| 1559 | *Mirror for Magistrates* (first edition) | Coronation of Elizabeth I Act of Supremacy and Act of Uniformity |
| 1561 | Thomas Sackville (and Norton): *Gorboduc* (acted) | Mary Sidney born |
| 1563 | Foxe: *Acts and Monuments* (Foxe's Book of Martyrs) | The Plague in London kills many thousands |
| 1565 | Golding: trans. of Ovid's *Metamorphoses* (Books I–IV) | |
| 1566 | | Birth of James VI of Scotland |
| 1567 | Whitney: *The Copy of a Letter* | Abdication of Mary Queen of Scots |
| 1569 | | Aemilia Lanyer born |
| 1570 | Ascham: *The Schoolmaster* Elizabeth I: 'The Doubt of Future Foes' | |
| 1572 | | St Bartholomew's Day massacre in Paris |
| 1573 | Whitney: *A Sweet Nosegay* | |
| 1577 | Holinshed: *Chronicles* | Francis Drake begins his circumnavigation of the globe |
| 1578 | Lyly: *Euphues, the Anatomy of Wit* (Part One) | James VI takes over government of Scotland |

| Year | Literary Dates | Historical Events |
|---|---|---|
| 1579 | Whitney, *The Lamentation* <br> North: trans. of Plutarch's *Lives* (from French) <br> Spenser: *Shepheard's Calender* | |
| 1580 | Lyly: *Euphues and his England* <br> Sidney: *Apologie for Poetrie* | Performance of plays on Sunday forbidden <br> Francis Drake returns to England |
| 1581 | Joseph Hall: *Ten Books of Homer's Iliads* | Laws against Roman Catholics passed |
| 1582 | Elizabeth I: 'On Monsieur's Departure' | |
| 1583 | | Discovery of the Somerville plot to assassinate Elizabeth I <br> Discovery of the Throgmorton plot for Spanish invasion of England |
| 1584 | Anne Cecil de Vere: sonnets <br> Greene: *Mirror of Modesty* <br> Knox: *History of the Reformation in Scotland* <br> Peele: *Arraignment of Paris* | |
| 1585 | | Ralegh establishes his first colony at Roanoke, Virginia |
| 1586 | Camden: *Britannia* | The Star Chamber condemns Mary Queen of Scots to death <br> Philip Sidney dies |
| 1587 | Marlowe: *Doctor Faustus* (acted; published 1604) | Mary Queen of Scots executed <br> Mary Wroth born |
| 1588 | | 19 July. Spanish Armada sighted off the Cornish coast <br> 29 July. The Battle of Gravelines: The Armada defeated |
| 1589 | Anne Dowriche: *The French History* <br> Puttenham: *Arte of English Poesie* | Anne Cecil de Vere dies |
| 1590 | Marlowe: *Tamburlaine* (Parts I and II printed: Part I acted 1586–7) <br> Sidney: *Arcadia* <br> Spenser: *The Faerie Queene* (Books I–III) | |

| Year | Literary Dates | Historical Events |
|------|----------------|-------------------|
| 1591 | Sir John Harington: trans. of Ariosto's *Orlando Furioso* Shakespeare: *Henry VI Parts II and III* *The Two Gentlemen of Verona* Sidney: *Astrophil and Stella* (posthumous) Spenser: *Complaints* | |
| 1592 | Shakespeare: *Henry VI Part I* Mary Sidney: *A Discourse* (trans.) Marlowe: *Edward II* (acted) | Establishment of the Presbyterian Church in Scotland |
| 1593 | Henryson: *The Testament of Cresseid* (published) Shakespeare: *The Comedy of Errors* *Richard III* (acted) *Venus and Adonis* Mary Sidney: begins work on *Psalms* | |
| 1594 | Hooker: *Ecclesiastical Polity* (Books I–IV) Shakespeare: *The Rape of Lucrece* *Titus Andronicus* | |
| 1595 | Shakespeare: *Love's Labour's Lost* *A Midsummer Night's Dream* (acted) *Romeo and Juliet* Mary Sidney: *The Tragedy of Antonie* Spenser: *Amoretti* *Epithalamion* *Colin Clout's Come Home Again* | Death of Sir Francis Drake |
| 1596 | Jonson: *Every Man in his Humour* (acted) Shakespeare: *The Merchant of Venice* *King John* | |

| Year | Literary Dates | Historical Events |
|------|----------------|-------------------|
| | Spenser: *The Faerie Queene* (Books IV–VI) *Four Hymns* | |
| 1597 | Bacon: *Essays* Joseph Hall: *Virgidemiarum* (Books I–III) Shakespeare: *Richard II and III* | Rachel Speght born |
| 1598 | Chapman: trans. of Homer's *Iliad* (Books I–II, VII–XI) Marlowe: *Hero and Leander* Shakespeare: *Henry IV Parts I and II* | |
| 1599 | Jonson: *Every Man out of his Humour* Shakespeare: *Julius Caesar* (acted 21 Sept.) *Henry V* *Much Ado About Nothing* | Birth of Oliver Cromwell |
| 1600 | Dekker: *The Shoemaker's Holiday* (first quarto) Fairfax: trans. of Tasso's *Jerusalem Delivered* Shakespeare: *The Merry Wives of Windsor* *As You Like It* *Twelfth Night* Mary Sidney: *Triumph of Death* (trans.); completes *Psalms* | |
| 1601 | Shakespeare: *Hamlet* | The execution of the Earl of Essex |
| 1602 | Marston: *Antonio's Revenge* Shakespeare: *Troilus and Cressida* | Bodleian Library founded Re-conquest of Ireland begun |
| 1603 | Jonson: *Sejanus* Shakespeare: *All's Well That Ends Well* | Queen Elizabeth dies and is succeeded by James VI of Scotland as King James I of England and Ireland |
| 1604 | Marlowe: *Doctor Faustus* (earliest surviving edition) Shakespeare: *Hamlet* (second quarto) *Othello* (acted) | The Hampton Court Conference: James supports new translation of the Bible James VI and I proclaimed king of 'Great Britain, France and Ireland' |

| Year | Literary Dates | Historical Events |
|------|----------------|-------------------|
| 1605 | Drayton: *Poems* <br> Jonson: *Volpone* (acted; published 1607) | The Gunpowder plot |
| 1606 | Shakespeare: *King Lear* (acted) <br> *Macbeth* (probably written by this date) | Suppression of Roman Catholics by English Parliament |
| 1607 | Shakespeare: *Antony and Cleopatra* (probably written; Stationers' Register 20 May 1608) <br> Tourneur: *The Revenger's Tragedy* | English colony founded in Virginia |
| 1608 | Thomas Heywood: *Rape of Lucrece* <br> Shakespeare: *Coriolanus* (probably written) <br> *King Lear* (two quartos) <br> *Timon of Athens* (probably written) | |
| 1609 | Jonson: *Epicoene: or, the Silent Woman* (Stationers' Register 20 Sept. 1610) <br> Shakespeare: *Pericles* (Stationers' Register 20 May 1608) <br> *Sonnets* <br> *Troilus and Cressida* (two quartos) | |
| 1610 | Beaumont and Fletcher: *The Knight of the Burning Pestle* (? acted) <br> *The Maid's Tragedy* (probably written) <br> Chapman: trans. of the *Iliad* (Books I–VII) <br> Jonson: *The Alchemist* (Stationers' Register 3 Oct.) <br> Shakespeare: *Cymbeline* (perhaps written) <br> *The Winter's Tale* (perhaps written) | |
| 1611 | Authorized Version of the Bible <br> Chapman: trans. of the *Iliad* Books XIII–XXIV | The colonization of Ulster |

| Year | Literary Dates | Historical Events |
|------|----------------|-------------------|
| | Aemilia Lanyer: *Salve Deus* | |
| | Shakespeare: *Macbeth* (first recorded performance 20 Apr.) *The Tempest* (perhaps written) *The Winter's Tale* (acted by 15 May) | |
| 1612 | Drayton: *Poly-Olbion* (Part One) Webster: *The White Devil* (printed) | Anne Bradstreet born |
| 1613 | Shakespeare: *Henry VIII* (acted 2 July) | Globe Theatre burns down Poisoning of Sir Thomas Overbury |
| 1614 | Chapman: trans. of the *Odyssey* (Books I–XII) Jonson: *Bartholomew Fair* (acted; published 1631) | 'The Addled Parliament' |
| 1615 | Chapman: trans. of the *Odyssey* (Books XIII–XXIV) | |
| 1616 | Jonson: *The Devil is an Ass* (acted) *Underwoods* Webster: *The Duchess of Malfi* (acted; printed 1623) | Elizabeth Cavendish born |
| 1617 | Rachel Speght: *A Mouzell for Melastomus* Joseph Swetnam: *Arraignment of Women* | |
| 1618 | | Start of the Thirty Years' War Execution of Sir Walter Ralegh |
| 1619 | Drummond of Hawthornden: *Conversations with Ben Jonson* | |
| 1620 | Mary Wroth: *Love's Victory* | Freedom of worship granted to Roman Catholics in England in terms of marriage treaty between England and Spain Pilgrim Fathers depart from Plymouth, England, in *Mayflower* |

| Year | Literary Dates | Historical Events |
|------|----------------|-------------------|
| 1621 | Mary Wroth: *Pamphilia to Amphilanthus, Urania* | Mary Sidney dies |
|      | Rachel Speght: *Mortality's Memorandum* | Jane Cavendish born |
|      | Burton: *Anatomy of Melancholy* | |
| 1622 | Drayton: *Poly-Olbion* (Part Two) | |
|      | Middleton and Rowley: *The Changeling* | |
| 1623 | Shakespeare: *Comedies, Histories and Tragedies* ('The First Folio') | |
|      | Webster: *The Duchess of Malfi* (printed) | |
| 1624 | Middleton: *A Game at Chess* (acted 6 Aug.) | |
| 1625 | | Accession of Charles I |
|      | | Marriage of Charles I and Henrietta Maria |
| 1626 | Sandys: trans. of Ovid's *Metamorphoses* | |
| 1630 | Diana Primrose: *A Chain of Pearl* | |
| 1631 | Herbert: *The Temple* | |
|      | Jonson: *The Devil is an Ass* (printed) | |
|      | *The Staple of News* (printed) | |
| 1633 | Donne: *Poems* (posthumous) | William Laud appointed Archbishop of Canterbury |
|      | Ford: *'Tis Pity She's a Whore* (printed) | |
| 1634 | Alice Sutcliffe: *Meditations* | |
|      | Milton: *Comus* (acted) | |
| 1637 | Milton: *Lycidas* | |
| 1638 | | Anne Dowriche dies |
| 1641 | Milton: *Of Reformation Touching Church Discipline in England* | |
| 1642 | Sir Thomas Browne: *Religio Medici* | Civil War begins |
|      | Denham: *Cooper's Hill* | Battle of Edgehill |
|      | Milton: *Apology for Smectymnus* | |
| 1644 | Milton: *Areopagitica* | |
|      | Jane and Elizabeth Cavendish: *Concealed Fancies* and poems | |

| Year | Literary Dates | Historical Events |
|---|---|---|
| 1645 | | Prohibition of the Prayer Book by Parliament |
| | | Execution of Archbishop Laud |
| | | Aemilia Lanyer dies |
| 1646 | Vaughan: *Poems* | |
| 1648 | Herrick: *Hesperides and Noble Numbers* | |
| 1649 | | Execution of Charles I |
| | | Abolition of the monarchy |
| | | Declaration of the Commonwealth |
| 1650 | Anne Bradstreet: *The Tenth Muse* | |
| 1651 | Cleveland: *Poems* | Battle of Worcester |
| | D'Avenant: *Leviathan* | Mary Wroth dies |
| 1653 | Izzak Walton: *The Compleat Angler* | Long Parliament expelled by Cromwell |
| | | Establishment of Protectorate: Oliver Cromwell Lord High Protector |
| 1654 | | Union of England, Scotland and Ireland |
| 1656 | Cowley: *Works* (includes 'Davideis' and 'Pindaric Odes') | |
| 1657 | Middleton: *No Wit, No Help Like a Woman's* | |
| | *Two New Plays* (includes *Women, Beware Women*) | |
| 1658 | | 3 Sept. Death of Oliver Cromwell: succeeded by Richard Cromwell, his son, as Lord Protector 1660 |
| | | 16 Mar. Dissolution of the Long Parliament |
| 1660 | | Restoration of Charles II |
| 1661 | | Corporation Act: magistrates' oath of allegiance |
| 1662 | | Act of uniformity: revises Prayer Book: Licensing Act forbids import of anti-Christian literature |

| Year | Literary Dates | Historical Events |
|------|----------------|-------------------|
| 1663 | Jane Cavendish: 'On the Death ...' | Elizabeth Cavendish dies |
| 1665 | | The Great Plague |
| 1666 | | 2 Sept. Great Fire of London |
| 1667 | Milton: *Paradise Lost* | |
| 1669 | | Jane Cavendish dies |
| 1671 | Milton: *Paradise Regained* *Samson Agonistes* | |
| 1672 | | Anne Bradstreet dies |
| 1674 | | Rebuilding of the Theatre Royal, Drury Lane |
| 1678 | Bunyan: *Pilgrim's Progress* (Part One) Anne Bradstreet: *Several Poems* | The Popish Plot: the Pope, France and Spain are accused of conspiracy to defeat Charles |
| 1681 | Marvell: *Miscellaneous Poems* (posthumous) | |
| 1683 | | Rye House plot to kill Charles II and his brother, James, Duke of York |
| 1684 | Bunyan: *Pilgrim's Progress* (full text, including Part Two) | |
| 1685 | | Death of Charles II; succeeded by James II |

# INTRODUCTION

And in oblivion bury me
And never more me name.

These words are taken from Isabella Whitney's *The Manner of Her Will
… to London* (lines 267–8), where she asks the city to bury her without
show or ostentation. They could apply as succinctly to the body of her
work as to her own mortal remains, for, after the first publication of her
poem in 1573, the text was buried in oblivion until the late twentieth
century, and Whitney's 'name' ceased to be recorded in the annals of
English poetry. Nor is such obscurity confined to Whitney (the first poet
in this anthology), for, with the exception of Queen Elizabeth I, none of
the women represented here is well-known or widely published. Even
Elizabeth is recognized more as an icon and a symbol of English heritage
than as an author in her own right. This lack of contextual and
interpretative information raises some basic questions. To begin, we
need to ask: 'Who were these women poets and what were they writing
about?'

It has often been assumed that in the early modern period it was only
noblewomen, having greater access to education, space and economic
security, who were able to venture into the realms of creative writing or
scholarly translation. It is unsurprising that several of the poets
anthologized here fall into this category: Elizabeth I, Anne Cecil de Vere,
Mary Sidney, Mary Wroth, and Jane and Elizabeth Cavendish all had
academic and material support, which ensured that they had the time
and encouragement to write poetry. Yet three of these women, perhaps
fearing the censure resultant upon female authorship, chose primarily to
translate rather than originate material (Elizabeth I, Anne Cecil de Vere
and Mary Sidney). What is particularly unexpected is that the remaining
writers could not have relied upon such provision. Instead they must be
allocated to two lower rank or class groups: the gentry and the
bourgeoisie. Those in the first group, Anne Dowriche, Aemilia Lanyer
and Diana Primrose, were all in some way attached to the court, but
remained distinctly on the margins, more in need of patronage than in a

position to offer it. The remaining women, Isabella Whitney, Rachel Speght, Alice Sutcliffe and Anne Bradstreet, seem to have had more or less adequate financial resources, but from what little we know of them – and this in itself is an indicator of status – they belonged to the bourgeoisie and were mostly involved in some sort of domestic employment. In these two latter groups Whitney specifically complains of penury: 'I whole in body and in mind, / But very weak in purse' (*The Manner of Her Will ... to London*, lines 1–2), while Lanyer regrets the passing of a secure period of patronage in 'The Description of Cooke-Ham', where she writes:

> Farewell (sweet place) where virtue then did rest,
> And all delights did harbour in her breast,
> Never shall my sad eyes again behold
> Those pleasures which my thoughts did then unfold.   (lines 7–10)

Both poets stress their lack of material security and use their texts expressly to enhance their position: Whitney through the remuneration ensuing from publication, and Lanyer in the hope that Margaret Clifford, the Countess of Cumberland, will renew her assistance. Rather than being an obstacle to their literary activity, their lack of status and wealth appears to have been an important impetus, suggesting that Renaissance women poets, like their male counterparts, increasingly regarded their literary skills as a saleable commodity. Thus, although it is undoubtedly true that women writers of the early modern period did not have the same opportunities as men, they did not always form a separate and distinct group on the basis of their sex. Instead, they correspond quite closely to the same economic and rank divisions as male authors, and the resemblances are clearly apparent in each category, nobility, gentry and bourgeoisie. For every Mary Sidney there is a Philip Sidney; for every Aemilia Lanyer there is an Edmund Spenser; and for every Isabella Whitney there is a Thomas Dekker. Two conclusions may thus be drawn from this initial enquiry: firstly, class was an essential factor in determining the female poetic subject during the English Renaissance, and, rather than privileging the nobility, it allowed a fairly broad cross-section of women to become poets. Secondly, male and female poets cannot be treated as disconnected groups, since they were clearly both integral parts of the same social and economic system.

While rank and money were key factors influencing literary productivity in the early modern period, location and familial associations were equally important for women writers. In Lanyer's poem 'The Description of Cooke-Ham' the country house from which she has been exiled is as important to her security as the support of the Countess of Cumberland, although both are of course inextricably linked. Lanyer's vision of a pastoral idyll in which poet and patron co-exist in perfect harmony is quite possibly the first example of a country-house poem in English (the other contender being Ben Jonson's 'To Penshurst'), but she is not alone amongst the women represented here in focusing upon her environment. For example, the 'Penshurst' lauded by Jonson is also a key site for the two Sidney women included in this anthology: Mary Sidney and Mary Wroth both refer to the estate, and particularly to the flooding of the River Medway, which runs through Penshurst's lower meadows. In *Pamphilia to Amphilanthus* Wroth's poetic second-self, Pamphilia, uses the image of the river to compare fickleness with steadfastness in romantic love, 'you do well, lest staying here might breed / Dangerous floods, your sweetest banks t'o'er-run' (P51, lines 5–6). By contrast, Mary Sidney uses the flooding river as a metaphor for the instability of human existence:

> Rivers, yea, though rivers roar,
>   Roaring though sea-billows rise
> Vex the deep, and break the shore   (Psalm 93, lines 10–12)

which she rejects in favour of the truth and constancy of God: 'Stronger art thou, Lord of skies. / Firm and true thy promise lies' (lines 13–14). These themes of mutability and firmness, which are related to secular and spiritual love respectively, commonly recur in early modern poetry, but the specific locational imagery is particular to the Sidney family; indeed, Philip Sidney, Robert Sidney and William Herbert all use exactly the same trope drawn from the Medway's propensity to flood. Yet women poets are not confined to a pastoral vision of their environment: Whitney's vision of London in 'The Manner of Her Will ... to London' is acutely satiric; Jane and Elizabeth Cavendish acknowledge in their play *The Concealed Fancies* that their home, Welbeck Abbey, has become a prison during the Civil War; and Anne Bradstreet draws a dramatic vision of the hardships of life in the New World when her house burned down ('Verses upon the Burning of Our House'). In each instance the home of the female poet is a site of security and stability, but, tellingly, in each instance that protection has been destabilized through betrayal, death, poverty, war or destruction.

In her justly famous account of a Renaissance woman dramatist, 'Judith Shakespeare', in *A Room of One's Own*, Virginia Woolf pointed out that women writers need economic and locational security in order to write; however, for the early modern period she could well have added 'familial support'. Almost all the poets collected here benefited

from the support of their families in the pursuance of their literary
careers. The most famous family groups are the Sidneys (Mary, Philip
and Robert Sidney, together with Mary Wroth and William Herbert)
and the Cavendishes (Jane, Elizabeth, William and Margaret Cavendish), but Anne Cecil de Vere belonged to the illustrious Cooke family (all
four of her aunts were authors), and Elizabeth I benefited from a
programme of humanist education condoned by her father, Henry VIII,
and actively encouraged by her stepmother, Catherine Parr. These
groups are, however, all aristocratic to a certain extent, and so close
familial bonding might well be expected. What is particularly interesting
is that the gentry and bourgeoisie produced similar literary families.
Isabella Whitney had a brother, Geoffrey Whitney, who published a
book of emblems; Anne Dowriche's husband wrote at least one extant
work, to which she added dedicatory verses; Rachel Speght had a
number of literary connections, including her father and husband; the
most likely candidate for identification as Diana Primrose's father also
published his own work; Anne Bradstreet's family produced other
writers; and even Aemilia Lanyer belongs to the scholarly Clifford group
through her childhood associations. Of all the poets in this anthology,
only Alice Sutcliffe appears to have had no relatives who were writing
and publishing their own works, and this might well be explained by the
fact that we know so little about her life. Moreover, an analysis of a
similar group of male poets would not reach the same conclusion,
although the function of literary, non-blood kinship was arguably as
important for men as actual familial ties were for women. Nevertheless,
while class and money were equally important elements in male as well
as female creativity during the early modern period, women were more
inclined to focus upon environmental security and were uniquely reliant
upon family support.

In the above analysis of the personal context of the poets in this
anthology, there is a tacit acceptance of the autobiographical nature of
their writings. This affiliation between women writers and autobiogra-
phy has been thoroughly excavated since the advent of feminist criticism
in the 1970s, so it is no surprise that women Renaissance poets
drew upon personal experience rather than scholarly authority. For
example, one of Elizabeth I's Woodstock poems derives from her
imprisonment by her sister, Mary I, on the grounds of her possible
implication in a plot to overthrow the queen:

> Much suspected by me,
> Nothing proved can be;
>     Quoth Elizabeth prisoner.   ('Woodstock: the Window Poem')

Similarly, Whitney in her assertion of penury, Lanyer in her account of her youth at Cooke-Ham, the Cavendish sisters in their account of the Civil War, and Bradstreet with her evocations of the New World, all refer to their individual circumstances at the time of writing. However, there are two particular genres that seem to reveal more about the private self of the women poets than any others: love poetry and elegies.

The elegies are perhaps the most poignant of all the poems in this collection. Mary Sidney continued the Psalm translations begun by her dead brother Philip and prefaced them with a dedicatory poem clearly depicting her grief:

> To which these dearest offerings of my heart
>    (Dissolved to ink, while pen's impressions move
>    The bleeding veins of never-dying love)
> I render here: these wounding lines of smart,
>    Sad characters indeed of simple love
>    (Not art nor skill which abler wits do prove)
> Of my full soul receive the meanest part.
> ('To the Angel Spirit ...', lines 79–85)

Jane Cavendish offers a similar eulogy to her sister, Elizabeth, with whom she was involved in literary collaborations in a manner not dissimilar to that of Mary and Philip Sidney:

> And when Death's heavy hand had closed her eyes,
> Me-thought the world gave up its ghost in cries.
> ('On the Death of My Dear Sister', lines 7–8)

These expressions of sibling closeness are, however, rivalled by the grief of mothers and grandmothers at the death of children: Anne Cecil de Vere's four epitaphs upon her dead son repeat her grief continually: 'With my son, my gold, my nightingale, and rose, / Is gone,' (Epitaph 2, lines 5–6); while Anne Bradstreet recounts sadly of her grandson, Simon, 'No sooner came, but gone, and fall'n asleep' ('On ... Simon Bradstreet', line 1). These personal statements are the most overtly autobiographical of all the poetry collected here and show that, while familial relationships might have enabled women to write, they were regarded as far more than an advantageous encouragement to literary productivity.

Perhaps the most personally revealing examples of love poetry come from Mary Wroth's sonnet sequence *Pamphilia to Amphilanthus*, in which she adopts the persona of Pamphilia (all-loving) and endows her cousin and lover William Herbert with the character of Amphilanthus (lover-of-two). Much of this sonnet sequence may be read as a close familial allegory which recounts the narrative of Wroth's love affair with Herbert, but at the same time the poems participate fully in the courtly-love discourse of the period and could easily be interpreted as general rather than particular in their allusions. Exactly the same may be said for Elizabeth I's poem 'An Answer', which was directed to Walter Ralegh; its specific references are easily balanced by the focus upon more comprehensive themes such as the fickleness of fortune. Even Elizabeth Cavendish's personal avowal of love, 'I love thee, ever have, and still shall do' ('Spoken Upon Receiving ... a Heart', line 5), and Anne Bradstreet's address to her absent husband, 'My head, my heart, mine eyes, my life, nay, more' ('A Letter to Her Husband', line 1), are couched in the language and metaphors of courtly love. Unlike the elegies, which are intensely personal, the love poems are more open to a general interpretation, perhaps echoing the dominance of the latter genre in early modern poetry. What is unexpected, however, is the distinct lack of love poetry in this collection. It was not a genre generally adopted by Renaissance women poets; although their writing is strongly autobiographical, this is more often expressed in conjunction with their political and religious beliefs rather than the private concerns of love.

In discussing elegies and love poetry we have gradually been moving away from the question, 'Who were they?' to the interrogation 'What did they write?', and, in recognizing the widespread absence of intensely private material, we have also shifted from the personal to the public sphere. Yet, with a sharp sense of introspection, the most recurrent political topic utilized by women poets of the time is the life and reign of one of their own number: Elizabeth I. Perhaps her popularity as subject-matter rested on the fact that, in issues of government and national policy, Elizabeth offered the unique combination of absolute power and female gender. Allusions to the queen often take the form of brief references found in a number of poems: for example, Anne Dowriche praises the queen as the upholder of England's religious and political security ('Lord, long preserve and keep / That noble queen, Elizabeth, chief pastor of thy sheep', *The French History*, lines 2247–8); Mary Sidney combines panegyric with tacit Protestant advice in '[To Queen Elizabeth]'; and Aemilia Lanyer refers to 'great Eliza' (*Salve Deus Rex Judaeorum*, 'To the Queen's Most Excellent Majesty', line 110). Two texts, however, focus solely on Elizabeth I: Diana Primrose's *A Chain of Pearl* takes the queen as an exemplar of moral virtue, beginning in eulogistic style:

> Thou English goddess, empress of our sex,
> O thou whose name still reigns in all our hearts,
> To whom are due our ever-vow'd respects;
> ('The Induction', lines 13–15)

while Ann Bradstreet's 'In Honour of that High and Mighty Princess Queen Elizabeth of Happy Memory' similarly presents Elizabeth as divine:

> So great's thy glory and thine excellence,
> The sound thereof raps every human sense,
> That men account it no impiety,
> To say thou were a fleshly deity.   (lines 5–8)

In all these instances the references to Elizabeth do not initially appear to be gender-specific; indeed, the numerous panegyrics written to Elizabeth during her own lifetime, together with the nostalgic allusions to her after her death, are as frequent with male as they are female poets. Her political significance was also manipulated by both men and women; the Protestant ideology of Dowriche and Mary Sidney is easily identified in their male counterparts such as Spenser and Philip Sidney; while the romanticizing of the Elizabethan age in order to criticize the Stuart monarchy was as present in the works of authors such as Primrose and Bradstreet as it was in the writings of Jonson and Ralegh. For women writers, however, Elizabeth's gender was important, and several of the poets mentioned above combine a comment upon the idealized power of the queen with a resolute defence of their common sex. Before returning to this self-conscious identifying of gendered subjectivity, however, it is important to acknowledge that the political framework of the verse in this collection extended beyond such singularity towards a broader treatment of national and religious concerns.

The political poetry which treats non-gendered subject-matter deals with material as diverse as Dowriche's historical narrative of the persecution of the Protestants in France, or Bradstreet's account of English history in several poems, including that addressed to Elizabeth I. While not an overtly stated concern, Mary Sidney in her Psalm translations, and the Cavendish sisters in their Civil War writings (especially their play *The Concealed Fancies*), notably display an interest in politics of their time, from the externalized threat of Catholicism to the internal schisms of the English Civil War. There is, however, one overriding factor – religion. Radical English Protestantism is one of the most powerful unifying forces evinced by the poets in this collection: Dowriche, Sidney, Speght, Primrose, and Bradstreet are all forceful in their defence of their Church and virulently anti-Catholic. For example, Dowriche introduces Satan as one of the characters who advises the Catholic forces in her poem *The French History*. The majority of the remaining poets, Isabella Whitney, Elizabeth I, Anne Cecil de Vere, Lanyer, Wroth and the Cavendish sisters, are non-committal in the verses included here, but their Protestant affiliations are quite clear from other texts and their biographies. This leaves only Alice Sutcliffe, whose poetry suggests a possible Catholic sympathy, although such a religious link was still dangerous enough in 1634 for the text to be ambiguous about any specific faith. There can be no doubt that the women writers of the early modern period felt that their literary activities, even the publication of their works, was completely justified by the dominant concerns of their faith. If patriarchal authority on earth prohibited female expression then the greater authority of God could be invoked to counteract such an earthly prohibition.

The behaviour of early modern women was carefully policed by the dominant male hierarchy of their age: the ideal woman was chaste, silent and obedient. The act of writing was clearly an impingement upon 'silence', since the written word was a material validation of female articulacy, but to go further and publish their works also laid women open to charges of immoral behaviour in that, by allowing all men to see/hear their words, they came to be regarded as unchaste. These condemnations explain why many women of the period chose to allow their works to exist only in manuscript form and to be read privately by their own families – certainly not to be displayed in printed form for the general public. Beyond the breaches of female self-containment offered by writing and publishing lay the still worse transgression of writing and/or publishing material to be acted. Quiet reading of a female-authored text at least retained the 'words' within the boundaries of private contemplation, but any work which contained or facilitated dramatic structures inevitably drew the female voice into the public arena, even if the works were never intended for public performance. It is important to note that in England no early modern woman had her plays performed on the stage, although evidence from manuscripts suggests that private readings or performances took place. It is clear from the extant plays written by women of the period that they had envisaged such productions. Consequently, plays written by Renaissance women writers should be considered as part of their public voice rather than the private discourses of love poetry and elegies. There are two poetic extracts from plays in this anthology: Mary Sidney's *The Tragedy of Antonie* and Jane and Elizabeth Cavendish's *The Concealed Fancies*. The former work is considered to be a closet drama, written to be read aloud by a small family group or cultural coterie, and certainly not to be acted in one of the large London theatres. The speeches chosen, however, have more in common with the powerful language and acute characterization of plays by Shakespeare and Marlowe than with the formal style of Mary Sidney's French original. Antonius' speech might easily have been written by a male tragedian of the period:

> Since cruel heaven's against me obstinate;
> Since all mishaps of the round engine do
> Conspire my harm; since men, since powers divine,
> Air, earth, and sea, are all injurious;
> And that my queen herself, in whom I lived,
> The idol of my heart, doth me pursue:
> It's meet I die. (I.1–7)

The Cavendish drama is very different in tone. Aside from being a light romantic comedy, it is uniquely situated between the courtly discourse of Ben Jonson's masques and the witty interchanges of Restoration theatre. However, since much of the comic material is found, as might be expected, in the prose speeches of the play, the poetic extracts included here have more in common with the nostalgia of Primrose than with the sharp dramas of Aphra Behn. While these are the only two plays I have included, the dramatic form adopted by Anne Dowriche in her poetry signifies that her writing must be considered as accessing the public voice of literary performance. The speech given by Catherine de Medici in *The French History* is the most interesting and bears comparison with some of the well-known parts given to villainesses, such as Lady Macbeth, in male-authored plays of the period. The introduction immediately makes us aware of the text's dramatic potential:

> But here the prologue ends, and here begins the play,
> For bloody minds resolved quite to use no more delay.
> The Mother Queen appears now first upon the stage,
> Where like a devilish sorceress with words demure and sage . . .

and Catherine goes on to plot the massacre of the Protestants on St Bartholomew's Day:

> What though ye do forswear? What though ye break your faith?
> What though ye promise life, and yet repay it with their death?
> Is this so great a fault? Nay, nay, no fault at all,
> For this we learn we ought to do, if such occasions fall.... .
> What shame is this that I (a woman by my kind)
> Need thus to speak, or pass you men in valour of the mind?
> For here I do protest, if I had been a man,
> I had myself before this time this murder long began.
> (lines 1393–6, 1421–4, 1433–6)

This combination of a self-aware use of dramatic discourses, and a focus upon a strong female character, makes Dowriche's poem an important example of how women adopted a public voice during the early modern period, and it is particularly fitting that the formal aspects of the text exactly mirror its political content.

The speech quoted above is notable not only for the early use by a woman of a semi-dramatic form, but also in its comment upon gender roles, specifically a female character's powerful assertion of equality. Dowriche is not alone in this self-aware construction of a gendered authorial subjectivity: each of the women writers anthologized here makes specific reference to her sex. The most radical choose to invert traditional patriarchal expectations: for example, in *Salve Deus Rex Judaeorum*, Lanyer completely overturns Biblical convention and the orthodoxies of the Church, when she claims that the fall from grace was man's fault and not woman's: 'Her fault, though great, yet he was most to blame' (line 778). Similarly, Rachel Speght and Anne Bradstreet confound those who would detract from women's achievements. In *Mortality's Memorandum* Speght makes a direct allusion to the controversial debate about women, and attacks Joseph Swetnam (who wrote the misogynistic *The Arraignment of Women*) as a 'monster or a devil [who] on Eve's sex ... foamed filthy froth' (lines 242–3); while in 'In Honour of That High and Mighty Princess Queen Elizabeth of Happy Memory' Bradstreet notes:

Now say, have women worth? or have they none?
Or had they some, but with our Queen is't gone?
Nay masculines, you have thus taxed us long,
But she, though dead, will vindicate our wrong;
Let such as say our sex is void of reason,
Know 'tis a slander now, but once was treason.   (lines 95–100)

In parallel, Primrose, Wroth and the Cavendish sisters all choose to invert the accepted dialectic of virgin/whore by demonstrating that women could be honourable in love and that men were not always the innocent victims of feminine wiles. Thus, Diana Primrose in *A Chain of Pearl* challenges the usual representation of women as leading men astray with sexual allurements by referring to 'men's siren-blandishments, / Which are attended with so foul events' ('Temperance', lines 5–6). Similarly, Mary Wroth's sonnet sequence *Pamphilia to Amphilanthus* presents women as constant and men as fickle in love, and Jane and Elizabeth Cavendish point out that male lovers 'profane' women by suggesting that they are 'wantonly fair' (*The Concealed Fancies*, lines 2–3). Although not overtly defending the female sex, Elizabeth I's lyrics, Anne Cecil de Vere's elegies and Mary Sidney's introductory poems all positively and openly acknowledge women's virtues. This leaves only Whitney's satiric mocking of her own sex by referring to women as 'foolish' ('A Communication', line 7) and Alice Sutcliffe's more conventional surprised tone when suggesting that 'Ought good [may be] expressed by our sex's act' (*Meditations of Man's Mortality*, 'An Acrostic upon the ... Earl of Pembroke', line 13). From the above evidence it seems that women writers of the early modern period felt compelled to confront the issue of their sex in some manner and that the majority of them did this in a positive manner, many actively working to overturn the conventional gender identities of their day. It is, therefore, all the more ironic that the voices of these women have been silenced over the centuries, brought once more into the oblivion they strove so hard to evade in their own lifetimes.

This Introduction began with a bleak recognition of the oblivion that awaited so many women writers not only of the early modern period, but of all prior generations. Inevitably, therefore, the critical and editorial work undertaken on these female authors must provide the basic materials for, and undertake the initial excavations necessary to, the pursuance of more complex and extended scholarship. This edition of Renaissance women poets participates in the common project to make the works of female poets readily available to students and the general reader. The extracts chosen are all intended to make previously obscure texts understandable and enjoyable to a new readership. It is to be hoped that this will encourage further editions of individual writers, and new critical investigations into the authors and themes I have addressed. Indeed, even though over the past two decades research into early modern women writers has become increasingly common, providing us with excellent editions and criticisms (many of which are referred to in the Select Bibliography), there is still an enormous amount of work to be done. Therefore, in conclusion, I should like to turn to the last poet in this collection, Anne Bradstreet, and rehearse her lines, with their invocation not to forget the names and works of early modern women poets, but to respond to them with the articulation of our own critical and editorial 'sighs':

> And if chance to thine eyes shall bring this verse,
> With some sad sighs honour my absent hearse.
> ('Before the Birth of One of Her Children', lines 25–6)

# ACKNOWLEDGEMENTS

An anthology such as this inevitably depends upon the scholarship of numerous writers and critics over the centuries. I have consulted works which range from George Ballard's *Memoirs of Several Ladies of Great Britain* (1752), which remains an extraordinary path-breaking listing of early modern women authors, to the Brown Women Writers Project home page via the Internet, where a wealth of editorial and critical material is made available in seconds. I have attempted to acknowledge all these works and their respective authors, and I wish to emphasize here that this book would simply not have been possible without such generous and erudite support. In addition, I have received assistance from numerous people, both lecturers and students, with whom I have discussed these poems, particularly my colleagues at Keele and Dundee Universities, Susan Bruce, Roger Pooley and Victor Skretkowitz; those with whom I have been or am publishing related material, especially Hero Chalmers, Danielle Clark, Elizabeth Clarke, Stephen Clucas, Alison Findlay, Elaine Hobby, Rebecca de Monte, Miriam Plantinga, Nicole Pohl, Diane Purkiss, Julie Sanders, Sophie Tomlinson, Helen Wilcox, Gweno Williams, Sue Wiseman and Stephanie Wright; the library staff who have given me so much help over the course of this project, at the Bodleian Library, the British Library, Dundee University Library, Keele University Library, Nottingham University Library and St Andrews University Library; and the secretarial assistance generously given by Gwen Hunter and Ann Bain. In addition, I should particularly like to thank Susan Cerasano, with whom I have edited three books; this edition could not have existed without the benefit of our collaborative projects, and her influence is manifest throughout my work on Renaissance women writers. I am also deeply grateful for the patient and sustained enthusiasm demonstrated by Hilary Laurie, my editor at Everyman; I wish that the women poets included here could have benefited from such stalwart support during their own age, even though that would have made my own work redundant. Finally, I wish to acknowledge the debt to my family: to my husband, Geoff Ward, who has listened with interest to each new editorial 'discovery', however small, and to my sons, Richard and Robert, who have played and slept quietly as I completed this book.

# WOMEN POETS
# OF THE RENAISSANCE

# ISABELLA WHITNEY

## A Communication Which the Author had to London Before She Made Her Will*

The time is come I must depart
    from thee, ah, famous city:
I never yet to rue* my smart*
    did find that thou hadst pity.
Wherefore, small cause there is that I        5
    would grieve from thee [to] go,
But many women foolishly,
    like me and other mo,*
Do such a fixed fancy set
    on those which least deserve        10
That long it is ere wit* we get
    away from them to swerve;
But Time with pity oft will tell,
    to those that will her try,
Whether it best be more to mell,*        15
    Or utterly defy.
And now has time me put in mind
    Of thy great cruelness,
That never once a help would find
    To ease me in distress.        20
Thou never yet wouldst credit give
    To board me for a year,
Nor with apparel me relieve
    Except thou payed were.*
No, no, thou never didst me good        25
    Nor ever wilt, I know.
Yet am I in no angry mood
    But will, or ere* I go,
In perfect love and charity
    My testament here write,        30
And leave to thee such treasury
    As I in it recite.

Now stand aside and give me leave
  To write my latest* will,
And see that none you do deceive                    35
  Of that I leave them till.*

### The Manner of Her Will, and What She Left to London and to All Those in It, at Her Departing

I whole in body and in mind,
  But very weak in purse,*
Do make and write my testament
  for fear it will be worse;
And first I wholly do commend                    5
  My soul and body eke*
To God, the Father, and the Son,
  So long as I can speak;
And after speech, my soul to him
  And body to the grave,                    10
Till time that all shall rise again
  their Judgement for to have;
And then I hope they both* shall meet
  to dwell for aye* in joy,
Whereas* I trust to see my friends                    15
  released from all annoy.
Thus have you heard touching my soul
  and body what I mean:
I trust you all will witness bear
  I have a steadfast brain;                    20
And now let me dispose such things
  as I shall leave behind,
That those which will receive the same
  may know my willing mind.
I first of all to London leave,                    25
  because I there was bred,
Brave buildings rare, of churches store,*
  and Paul's* to the head.
Between the same, fair streets there be
  and people goodly store;                    30
Because their keeping craveth cost,*
  I yet will leave him* more.

First for their food, I butchers leave,
    That every day shall kill;
By Thames you shall have brewers store        35
    And bakers at your will.
And such as orders do observe*
    And eat fish thrice a week,
I leave two streets full fraught* therewith;
    They need not far to seek.        40
Watling Street and Canwick Street*
    I full of woollen leave,
And linen store in Friday Street,
    If they me not deceive.
And those which are of calling such        45
    That costlier they require,
I mercers* leave, with silk so rich
    As any would desire.
In Cheap,* of them they store shall find,
    And likewise in that street,        50
I goldsmiths leave with jewels such
    As are for ladies meet,*
And plate to furnish cupboards with
    Full brave* there shall you find,
With purl* of silver and of gold        55
    To satisfy your mind;
With hoods, bongraces,* hats or caps
    Such store are in that street
As, if on t'one side you should miss,
    The t'other serves you feat.*        60
For nets* of every kind of sort
    I leave within the Pawn,*
French ruffs, high purls, gorgets, and sleeves*
    Of any kind of lawn.*
For purse or knives, for comb or glass,        65
    Or any needful knack,*
I by the Stocks* have left a boy
    Will ask you what you lack.
I hose* do leave in Birchin Lane
    Of any kind of size,        70
For women stitched,* for men both trunks*
    And those of Gascoyne guise.*
Boots, shoes, or pantables* good store
    St Martin's hath for you;

In Cornwall,* there I leave you beds     75
    And all that longs thereto.
For women shall you tailors have,
    By Bow* the chiefest dwell;
In every lane you some shall find
    Can do indifferent well.*     80
And for the men few streets or lanes
    But body-makers* be,
And such as make the sweeping cloaks
    With guards* beneath the knee.
Artillery at Temple Bar     85
    And dags* at Tower Hill;
Swords and bucklers of the best
    Are nigh the Fleet until.*
Now when thy folk are fed and clad
    With such as I have named,     90
For dainty mouths and stomachs weak
    Some junkets* must be framed.
Wherefore I 'pothecaries* leave,
    With banquets* in their shop,
Physicians also for the sick,     95
    Diseases for to stop.
Some roisters* still must bide in thee
    And such as cut it out,*
That with the guiltless quarrel will
    To let their blood about.     100
For them I cunning* surgeons leave,
    Some plasters to apply,
That ruffians may not still be hanged
    Nor quiet persons die.
For salt, oatmeal, candles, soap,     105
    Or what you else do want,
In many places shops are full
    I left you nothing scant.
If they that keep what I you leave
    Ask money when they sell it,     110
At Mint* there is such store it is
    Unpossible to tell it.*
At Steelyard,* store of wines there be
    Your dulled minds to glad,
And handsome men* that must not wed     115
    Except they leave their trade.

They oft shall seek for proper* girls
  And some perhaps shall find
That need compels or lucre lures*
  To satisfy their mind.                          120
And near the same I houses leave
  For people to repair*
To bathe themselves, so to prevent
  Infection of the air.*
On Saturdays I wish that those                    125
  Which all the week do drug*
Shall thither trudge to trim them up
  On Sundays to look smug.*
If any other thing be lacked
  In thee, I wish them look,                       130
For there it is (I little brought
  But nothing from thee took).
Now for the people in thee left,
  I have done as I may,
And that the poor, when I am gone,                135
  Have cause for me to pray,
I will to prisons portions leave
  (What though but very small),
Yet that they may remember me,*
  Occasion be it shall.                            140
And first the Counter* they shall have,
  Lest they should go to wrack,*
Some coggers* and some honest men
  That sergeants draw aback.*
And such as friends will not them bail,           145
  Whose coin is very thin,
For them I leave a certain Hole*
  And little ease* within.
The Newgate* once a month shall have
  A sessions* for his share,                       150
Lest, being heaped,* infection might
  Procure a further care.
And at those sessions some shall 'scape
  With burning near the thumb,*
And afterward to beg their fees*                  155
  Till they have got the sum.
And such whose deeds deserveth death,
  And twelve* have found the same,

They shall be drawn up Holborn* hill
  To come to further shame.     160
Well, yet to such I leave a nag*
  Shall soon their sorrows cease,
For he shall either break their necks
  Or gallop from the press.*
The Fleet* not in their circuit is,     165
  Yet if I give him nought,
It might procure his curse ere* I
  Unto the ground be brought.
Wherefore I leave some Papist* old
  To underprop his roof,     170
And to the poor within the same,
  A box* for their behoof.*
What makes you standers-by to smile
  And laugh so in your sleeve?
I think it is because that I     175
  To Ludgate* nothing give.
I am not now in case* to lie,
  Here is no place of jest;
I did reserve that for myself
  If I my health possessed     180
And ever came in credit so
  A debtor* for to be.
When days of payment did approach,
  I thither meant to flee,
To shroud* myself amongst the rest     185
  That choose to die in debt
Rather than any creditor
  Should money from them get
(Yet 'cause I feel myself so weak
  That none me credit* dare),     190
I here revoke and do it leave
  Some bankrupts to his share.
To all the bookbinders by Paul's,*
  Because I like their art,
They every week shall money have     195
  When they from books depart.
Amongst them all my printer* must
  Have somewhat to his share;
I will my friends these books to buy
  Of him, with other ware.     200

For maidens poor, I widowers rich
  Do leave, that oft shall dote,
And by that means shall marry them
  To set the girls afloat.*
And wealthy widows will I leave          205
  To help young gentlemen,
Which when you have, in any case,
  Be courteous to them then,
And see their plate* and jewels eke
  May not be marred with rust,         210
Nor let their bags* too long be full,
  For fear that they do burst.*
To every gate under the walls
  That compass thee about,
I fruit-wives* leave to entertain         215
  Such as come in and out.
To Smithfield* I must something leave,
  My parents there did dwell;
So careless for to be of it
  None would account it well.         220
Wherefore it thrice a week shall have
  Of horse and neat* good store,
And in his spital,* blind and lame
  To dwell for evermore.
And Bedlam* must not be forgot,         225
  For that was oft my walk;
I people there too many leave
  That out of tune do talk.
At Bridewell* there shall beadles be,
  And matrons that shall still         230
See chalk well chopped,* and spinning plied,
  And turning of the mill.
For such as cannot quiet be
  But strive for house or land,
At th'Inns of Court I lawyers leave         235
  To take their cause in hand.
And also leave I at each Inn
  Of Court or Chancery,
Of gentlemen, a youthful rut*
  Full of activity;         240
For whom I store of books have left
  At each bookbinder's stall,

And part of all that London hath
 To furnish them withal.
And when they are with study cloyed,*    245
 To recreate their mind,
Of tennis courts, of dancing schools
 And fence,* they store shall find.
And every Sunday at the least,
 I leave, to make them sport,*     250
In divers places players,* that
 Of wonders shall report.
Now London have I for thy sake
 Within thee and without,
As comes into my memory,      255
 Dispersed round about
Such needful things as they should have
 Here left now unto thee;
When I am gone, with conscience
 Let them dispersed be.       260
And though I nothing named have*
 To bury me withal,
Consider that above the ground
 Annoyance be I shall.
And let me have a shrouding sheet*    265
 To cover me from shame,
And in oblivion* bury me
 And never more me name.
Ringings* nor other ceremonies
 Use you not for cost,       270
Nor at my burial make no feast;
 Your money were but lost.
Rejoice in God that I am gone
 Out of this vale* so vile,
And that, of each thing left such store   275
 As may your wants exile,
I make thee sole executor
 Because I loved thee best,
And thee I put in trust to give
 The goods unto the rest.     280
Because thou shalt a helper need
 In this so great a charge,
I wish good Fortune be thy guide, lest
 Thou shouldst run at large.*

The Happy Days and Quiet Times*                    285
  They both her* servants be,
Which well will serve to fetch and bring
  Such things as need to thee.
Wherefore, good London, not refuse
  For helper her to take.                   290
Thus being weak and weary both
  An end here will I make.
To all that ask what end I made
  And how I went away,
Thou answer may'st like those which here            295
  No longer tarry may.
And unto all that wish me well
  Or rue* that I am gone,
Do me commend and bid them cease
  My absence for to moan.                      300
And tell them further, if they would
  My presence still have had,
They should have sought to mend my luck*
  Which ever was too bad.
So fare thou well a thousand times,                 305
  God shield thee from thy foe;
And still make thee victorious
  Of those that seek thy woe.
And though I am persuade* that I
  Shall never more thee see,                   310
Yet to the last I shall not cease
  To wish much good to thee.
This 20 of October, I,
  In Anno Domini
A thousand five hundred seventy three,              315
  (As almanacs descry*),
Did write this will with mine own hand
  And it to London gave
In witness of the standers-by;
  Whose names (if you will have)                320
Paper, Pen, and Standish* were
  At that same present by,
With Time who promised to reveal
  So fast as she could hie*
The same, lest of my nearer kin*                    325

From anything should vary.*
So finally I make an end;
No longer can I tarry.

(1573)

# ELIZABETH I

## Woodstock: the Window Poem*

Much suspected by me,
Nothing proved can be;
 Quoth Elizabeth prisoner.

(1554)

## Woodstock: the Shutter Poem*

Oh Fortune, thy wresting, wavering state
Hath fraught with cares my troubled wit,
Whose witness this present prison late
Could bear, where once was joy's loan quit.*
Thou caused'st the guilty to be loosed                    5
From bands where innocents were enclosed,
And caused the guiltless to be reserved,
And freed these that death had well deserved.
But all herein can be nothing wrought,
So God send to my foes all they have taught.          10

(1554)

## French Psalter Poem*

No crooked leg, no bleared eye,
No part deformed out of kind,
Nor yet so ugly half can be
As is the inward, suspicious mind.

(Undated)

## The Doubt of Future Foes*

The doubt of* future foes exiles my present joy,
And wit* me warns to shun such snares as threaten mine
   annoy;
For falsehood now doth flow, and subjects' faith doth ebb,
Which should not be if reason ruled or wisdom weaved the
   web.
But clouds of joys untried do cloak aspiring minds,                5
Which turn to rain of late repent by changéd course of
   winds.*
The top of hope supposed the root upreared shall be.
And fruitless all their grafted guile, as shortly ye shall see.*
The dazzled eyes with pride, which great ambition blinds,
Shall be unsealed by worthy wights* whose foresight
   falsehood finds.*                                              10
The daughter of debate* that discord aye* doth sow
Shall reap no gain where former rule still peace hath taught to
   know.
No foreign banished wight shall anchor in this port;
Our realm brooks not* seditious sects, let them elsewhere
   resort.
My rusty sword through rest shall first his edge employ         15
To poll their tops* that seek such change or gape* for future
   joy.

                                                    (1570)


## On Monsieur's Departure*

I grieve and dare not show my discontent,
I love and yet am forced to seem to hate,
I do, yet dare not say I ever meant,
I seem stark* mute but inwardly do prate.*
   I am and not, I freeze and yet am burned,*               5
   Since from myself another self I turned.

My care is like my shadow in the sun,
Follows me flying, flies when I pursue it,
Stands and lies by me, doth what I have done.
His too familiar care doth make me rue it.                   10
   No means I find to rid him from my breast,
   Till by the end of things it be suppressed.

Some gentler passion slide into my mind,
For I am soft and made of melting snow;
Or be more cruel, love, and so be kind.                    15
Let me or float or sink, be high or low.
   Or let me live with some more sweet content,
   Or die and so forget what love ere meant.

                               (1582)

### *An Answer**

Ah silly pug,* wert thou so sore afraid?
Mourn not, my Wat,* nor be thou so dismayed;
It passeth fickle Fortune's power and skill
To force my heart to think thee any ill.

No fortune base, thou sayst, shall alter thee,                    5
And may so blind a wretch then conquer me?
No, no, my pug, though Fortune were not blind,*
Assure thyself she could not rule my mind.

Ne* chose I thee by Fortune's foolish rede,*
Ne can she make me alter with such speed;                    10
But must thou needs sour Sorrow's servant be?
If that to try thy mistress* jest with thee.*

Fortune, I grant, sometimes does conquer kings,
And rules and reigns on earth and earthly things;
But never think that Fortune can bear sway,                    15
If Virtue watch and will not her obey.

Pluck up thy heart, suppress thy brackish* tears,
Torment thee not, but put away thy fears;
Thy love, thy joy, she loves no worthless bands,*
Much less to be in reeling Fortune's hands.                    20

Dead to all joys and living unto woe,
Slain quite by her that never gave wise man blow,*
Revive again and live without all dread,
The less afraid, the better shalt thou sped.*

                               (1587)

## *Now Leave and Let Me Rest\**

Now leave and let me rest,
Dame Pleasure be content;
Go choose among the best,
My doting* days be spent.
By sundry signs I see      5
Thy proffers are but vain,
And Wisdom warneth me
That Pleasure asketh* pain.

And Nature that doth know
How time her steps doth try*      10
Gives place to painful Woe
And bids me learn to die.
Since all fair earthly things
Soon ripe will soon be rot,
And all that pleasant springs      15
Soon withered, soon forgot.

And youth that yields new joys
That wanton lust desires
In age repents the toys
That reckless youth requires.      20
All which delights I leave
To such as Folly trains*
By pleasure to deceive
Till they do feel the pains.

And from vain pleasures past      25
I fly and fain* would know
The happy life at last
Whereto I hope to go,
For words or wise reports
Or yet examples gone      30
Can bridle youthful sports
Till age comes stealing on.

The pleasant courtly games
That I delighted in,
Mine elder age now shames      35
Such follies to begin,
And all the fancies strange*
That fond* delight brought forth

I do intend to change
And count them nothing worth.                                    40

For I by process worn
Am taught to know the skill
What might have been forborne
In my young reckless will.
By which good proof I fleet*                                    45
From will to wit again
In hope to set my feet
In surety to remain.

                                                    (Undated)


## When I Was Fair and Young*

When I was fair and young, then favour graced me.
Of many was I sought their mistress for to be,
But I did scorn them all and answered them therefore:
'Go, go, go, seek some other where, importune me no more.'

How many weeping eyes I made to pine in woe,                    5
How many sighing hearts I have not skill to show,
But I the prouder grew and still this spake therefore:
'Go, go, go, seek some other where, importune me no more.'

Then spake fair Venus' son,* that brave victorious boy,
Saying: 'You dainty dame, for that you be so coy,              10
I will so pluck your plumes* as you shall say no more:
"Go, go, go, seek some other where, importune me no
    more." '

As soon as he had said, such change grew in my breast
That neither night nor day I could take any rest.
Wherefore I did repent that I had said before:                15
'Go, go, go, seek some other where, importune me no more.'

                                                    (Undated)

# ANNE CECIL DE VERE

## Four Epitaphs

*made by the Countess of Oxford after the
death of her young son, the Lord Bulbeck**

### I *

Had with mourning the gods left their wills undone
They had not so soon 'herited such a soul;
Or if the mouth Time did not glutton up* all,
Nor I, nor the world, were deprived of my son;
Whose breast Venus* with a face doleful and mild          5
Doth wash with golden tears, inveighing* the skies;
And when the water of the goddess's eyes
Makes almost alive the marble of my child.
  One bids her leave still her dolour* so extreme,
  Telling her it is not her young son Papheme;*          10
  To which she makes answer with a voice inflamed,
  (Feeling therewith her venom* to be more bitter)
  'As I was of Cupid,* even so of its mother,
  And a woman's last child is the most beloved.'

### 2 *

In doleful* ways I spend the wealth of my time:
Feeding on my heart that ever comes again.
Since the ordinance of the Destin's* hath been
To end of the seasons, of my years, the prime.*
With my son, my gold, my nightingale, and rose,          5
Is gone, for 'twas in him and no other where,
And well though mine eyes run down like fountains here,
The stone will not speak yet that doth it enclose.
  And Destins and gods you might rather have tane,*
  My twenty years than the two days of my son.          10
  And of this world what shall I hope, since I know
  That in his respect it can yield me but moss;
  Or what should I consume* any more in woe,
  When Destins, gods, and worlds are all in my loss.

3 *

The heavens, death, and life have conjured my ill,
For death has take away the breath of my son,
Th'heavens receive and consent that he has done,
And my life does keep me here against my will.
But if our life be caused with moisture and heat,                5
I care neither for the death, the life, nor skies;
For I'll sigh him warmth and wet him with my eyes
    (And thus I shall be thought a second Promet*).
    And as for life, let it do me all despite;
    For if it leave me, I shall go to my child;              10
And it* in the heavens, there is all my delight;
And if I live, my virtue is immortal,
So that the heavens, death and life, when they do all
Their force, by sorrowful virtue they are beguiled.

4 *

Idal* for Adon* never shed so many tears,
    Nor Thet' for Pelid,* nor Phoebus for Hyacinthus,*
    Nor for Atis, the mother of prophetesses,*
    As for the death of Bulbeck the gods have cares.
At the brute* of it, the Aphroditan queen*                    5
    Caused more silver to distil* from her eyes
    Than when the drops of her cheeks raised daisies;*
    And to die with him, mortal, she would have been.
        The Charits* for it break their perugs* of gold,
        The Muses* and the Nymphs* of caves, I behold.      10
All the gods under Olympus* are constraint
    On Laches, Clothon, and Atropos* to plain.*
    And yet Beauty, for it doth make no complaint,
    For it lived with him, and died with him again.


My son is gone and with it death end my sorrow;
But Death makes me answer: 'Madam, cease these moans,
My force is but on bodies of blood and bones;
And that of yours is no more now, but a shadow.'*


Amphion's wife* was turned to a rock.
How well I had been had I had such adventure,
For then I might, gain have been the sepulchre*
Of him that I bare in me, so long ago.

                                            (1584)

# ANNE DOWRICHE

## The French History

*That is, a lamentable discourse of three of the
chief, and most famous bloody broils\* that have
happened in France for the gospel of Jesus Christ\**

As walking on a day, the woods and forests nigh
In shrilling voice, and mournful tunes, methought I\* heard one
   cry;
Which sudden fear so dashed my blood and senses all,
That as one in a trance I stayed to see what would befall.
A thousand thoughts oppressed my fearful wavering brain,     5
In musing what amid the woods that fearful voice should mean,
I feared lest thieves had robbed and cast some man aside;\*
Because it was the common way where men did use to ride.
Among the savage beasts that in these woods remain,
I doubted lest some travller stood in danger to be slain.     10
But casting fear apart, I ran toward the place,
To see the wight\* that did lament, and wail his woeful case;
Alone, no peril nigh, within a bushy dale,
A stranger sat, I got aside to hear his doleful tale.
'O noble France,' quod he,\* 'that bor'st sometime the bell,\*     15
And for thy pleasure and thy wealth all nations did excel!
How art thou now of late with mischief so possessed,
That all the realms of Christendom thy falsehoods do detest?
Where is thy verdant\* hue, thy fresh and flowering fame?
What fell unlucky spot is this that so does stain thy name?     20
Where is thy mirth become? Where is thy smiling cheer?
Where is thy joyful peace that erst\* did make thee shine so clear?
Where are thy youthly troops, the nobles of thy land?
Where is thy faith without the which no realm can ever stand?
Where is the mutual love that prince and people had?     25
Where is the noble union that makes the country glad?
Where is the due regard that princes ought to have
From all the bands or tyranny their people for to save?
Where is thy pity gone, where is thy mercy fled,

That lion-like in every place such Christian blood is shed? 30
But these of late to thee, O France, have bid adieu;
That rigour reigns in mercy's seat, alas, it is too true.
For having no remorse to hear thy children's groan,
Like as a widow comfortless thou shalt be left alone.
For they that fear the Lord and have for him a care, 35
Have learned too late the costly wit thy treasons to beware.*
Therefore thy children have their native coasts* resigned,
With better hope in foreign lands more mercy for to find.
And that which is the worst, I see thou dost not weigh,
The spider's spite,* that long has wove the web of thy decay. 40
Therefore if thou will know the cause of all thy woe,
Then mark the judgements of the Lord, from which thou cannot
    go.
If Juda* now', saith he, 'should ask the causes why
Their land was like a wilderness that no man passed by;
He makes no long delay, but bids the prophet show, 45
This plague does always follow them that do despise his law.
For they that idols serve, and from the Lord do shrink,
They shall be fed with bitter gall and wormwood* water drink.
And why at sundry times was Egypt plagued so?
But for because he would not yield to let God's people go.* 50
Why was the Lord with Saul* so wrath and full of ire,
In sparing Agag and the beasts the people did desire?
For he had now accursed both Agag and his land,
Commanding Saul without remorse to kill them out of hand;
Because this Amalek* would not at all vouchsave 55
Within his land God's chosen flock a passage for to have,
But falsely did conspire to work their open shame;
To snare their feet, they lay in wait from Egypt* as they came.
And thou Jerusalem, what sin did file* thy fall,
When Titus and Vespasian did tumble down thy wall? 60
Why did the Lord depart from thee that was so brave,
And to thy foes made thee a prey, a jest, a servile slave?
Because amidst thy mirth thy God thou did'st forget,
And would'st not have his prophets live, but did'st them ill
    intreat.*
O France, therefore be wise, learn ere it be too late 65
By these examples to begin these bloody sins to hate.
For thou with Juda* land has done thy God great wrong,
To serve and set up other gods to run a-whoring long.
Thou has for wooden gods God's lively image spilled,

And with the streams of Christian blood the streets and canals
   filled.                                                                                      70
Thou hast with Egypt long God's word in prison pent,
And wilfully refused the light that he has sent.
The Moses* that begins this light for to unfold,
Thou seek'st to lap* him presently in chains and irons cold.
Thou does with Amalek with all thy wit assay                               75
To lie in wait that in thy land the truth may have no way.
And thou a cruel nurse to God's elect* has been,
To blemish thus the shining light that in thee has been seen.
And with Jerusalem God's prophets thou has slain,
That in thy Popish ignorance though mightest still remain.          80
If Juda shall be fed with wormwood mixed with gall,
If wilful Egypt plagued were that kept God's church in thrall,
If God no pity showed, and mercy none would have
Upon the land of Amalek, nor man nor beast to save,
And if the blinded pride that in Jerusalem dwelt                           85
Could not escape God's heavy wrath, but man and child it felt,
What shall become of thee, thou blind and bloody land?
How dost thou think for to escape God's just revenging hand?
But sith* I do not doubt that God will revenge our case,
And for his chosen, when he list,* provide a dwelling place;          90
I will no more lament in sad and mourning style,
But thank the Lord that set me safe within this pleasant isle.*
O happy England, thou from God above are blessed,
Which has the truth established with peace and perfect rest.
God give thee therewithal a good and thankful mind,                    95
That to thy loving God no way thou show thyself unkind;
But still thou may'st remain as thou has been of yore,*
A nurse to God's afflicted flock, that he may bless thee more.
But now I will depart, the Lord direct my way,
And send me in this pleasant isle some simple slender stay,           100
Till God grant me return, or otherwise provide.
But is not that an Englishman* that I have yonder spied?'
   'Well met, my friend, tell what thou are that mak'st this moan,
And why within these desert woods are thou thyself alone?'
   'I am a stranger wight, and France my native soil                    105
From which, of late, by luckless chance, and need, am forced to
   toil;
Such troubles and such wars of late have there befell,
That such as fear the Lord aright no surety have to dwell
Within that woeful land; so God me hither sent

To live with you in happy state, which he this land has lent.'      110
  'Oh happy then am I; my friend I thee desire
Come, go with me, for of these wars I greatly long to hear.
And if that thou will stay, as long as thou will crave,
My house as thine and all therein thou shall be sure to have.
Therefore, my friend, I pray, thy wit and tongue prepare,      115
The cause of all these bloody broils in verse for to declare;
And first of all describe the matter and the man,
The place, the time, the manner how this civil war began.'
  'O sir, but this request doth pierce my wounded heart,
Which gladly would forget again my woeful country's smart.      120
For who can well display the treasons and the guiles,
The bloody murders merciless, the snares and crafty wiles,
Which France has put in use these thirty years and more,
The like of which in Christendom was never seen before?
But sith it is your will to know the woeful state      125
Of Christ's afflicted church in France, which Antichrist* does
    hate,
Come, rest you here awhile, and mark what I shall tell,
Great wars and broils I must declare, God grant it may be well;
And first to pitch* the plot that you do so desire,
I will unfold the chiefest cause that kindled first this fire.      130
About the very year of Christ his incarnation
A thousand five hundred fifty-seven by just computation,
Henry wore the crown, the second of that name,
In whose unhappy reign began this fearful fiery flame.
For now in France began God's truth for to appear,      135
Whose joyful beams in Germany at this time shone full clear;
But as the Jews sometimes God's prophets did despise,
And as the scribes and Pharisees did set their whole device
To shade the shining light, which God to them had sent,*
So France in fury blindly set against God's truth is bent;      140
Which truth but lately sown, and scant appearing green,
They seek by force, by fire and sword, to root and rase it clean.
But though proud Pharaoh did God's chosen long oppress,*
Yet still amidst the fiery broils his people did increase.
So now amidst the flame God's word a passage found,      145
Which did increase his chosen flock by force of silver sound.*
Which sound in God's elect did work such sudden change
In all estates, that at the first in France it seemed strange.
God's mighty spirit did work, his mercy still was pressed,
That some of all estates were called their blindness to detest;      150

Though riches be a let,* and noble birth some stay,
That very few of these, says Christ,* do find the perfect way;
Yet God to bring to pass the work he did intend,
Did also raise some noble men the poorer to defend.
So now they fall at square,* now here began the strife,                    155
For Satan could not bear to see a new reformed life;
That prophecy* is true, for Christ did speak the word:
"I came not to give peace to mine, but strife, debate and sword;
The son against the sire, one friend against another,
The word shall brothers part, set the daughter 'gainst the
     mother."                                                              160
So fell it out in France, his word did now divide
His chosen from the rest of those that took the adverse side.
The land divided thus, two parts there fell at first,
God's people were in number least, the greater was the worst.
Now Satan was afraid, for now he strived sore                              165
To keep the King and chiefest states* in blindness as of yore.*
It pinched him to the quick to lose his kingdom so,
It grieved him to the heart that he should let his servants go.
He sits not idle now, he calls his wits in place,
Some cunning knack* for to contrive to help him in this case.             170
His wily wilful craft by long experience bred
Has taught him now an ancient feat* to crush the gospel's head.*
Now summons he his men and servants to appear:
"Now help me at this need," quoth he,* "my friends and fellows
     dear;
Now is the time to stir while matters yet be new,                          175
While blinded minds in doubting hang, not knowing what is true.
For if the word of God do once begin to shine,
Then farewell all, I shall fain my kingdom to resign;
But if you will agree and follow my advice,
We shall cut off this sowen word, as fast as it shall rise.                180
And first we must give out some vile and lewd report
Of such as do profess the truth, and such as do resort
Unto their sermons; so this way it will be best
To make the King and many more their dealings to detest.
And when as they shall meet in church to serve the Lord,                   185
We'll say they do defile themselves, to make them more abhorred.
And when in fields they join their joyful psalms to sing,
We must give out that they conspire which way to kill the King,
So to their filed* talk the King will give no heed,
But give us leave, and join with us against them to proceed.               190

And many that shall hear this smooth invented lie,
Will never seek the truth, but then condemn them by and by.
So shall we have our will, so shall we set a stay
For those that seek to know the truth, to stop them in their way.
And that we may the more their dealings quite deface,          195
I must devise to point you all your office and your place:
For some must captains be to lie in wait for blood,
And burn them in their temples all, to do your master good;
And such must always be abroad to range the coasts,
In every place to lie in wait, and meet them at their hosts;*    200
And some must stay at home to lie in prince's ear,
That of these men within his sight not one may dare appear;
If force will not prevail, if nobles take their part,
By flattery then some must attempt these nobles to subvert."
    This said it was agreed; the counsel cried, "Amen!"         205
And everyone to play his part did give his promise then.
O poor unhappy place, O France how art thou led,
Thou gleanst* the sap* of deadly food instead of lively bread.
The Mother Queen* as chief does promise to begin,
By treason joined with flattery to trap them in her gin;*       210
And he that was ordained to watch the prince's hall
Was bloody Lewes of Lorraine town,* that filthy cardinal;
And they that took in hand false rumours for to sow,
Were priests and friars, with device God's truth to overthrow;
The captains that were glad to take this cause in hand          215
The blinded Guises* were, which swore to lead this bloody band.
Now let us see the end, how these their parts do play,
And mark where all things fall not out as we have heard them
    say.

### The first outrage and horrible murder of the
### Godly, called the winning of
### Saint James, his street

Now at this very time,* when Philip King of Spain
Came to St Quentin, guarded with a great and mighty train,     220
The Constable of France to meet him made some haste,
Whose power was vanquished there, and he fell prisoner at the
    last.*
The faithful, which beheld great danger nigh at hand,
Which God did threaten now to fall on them, their prince and
    land,

With one consent they meet, to God they cry and pray,*                    225
Which is the only means for sin God's heavy wrath to stay.
But once above the rest, as in St James his street,
In Paris town, they did agree great numbers for to meet,
To pray unto the Lord to quench this flaming fire,
They might receive His sacraments, and eke His word to hear.              230
The spies* that lay in wait such vantage for to get,
In tumult armed the common sort their houses to beset,
Whose folly thus abused, which fury did incense,
With weapons ran as if these men had done some great offence.
The faithful closed thus, no way there was to fly,                        235
The rage and tumult was so great, they yielded all to die.
To God they did commend their bodies and their life,
And with their humble suits* afraid to 'swage* their raging strife.
But all could not prevail, their words could not be heard,
For fury to their just excuse did give but small regard.                  240
But God, that never fails his servants at their need,
By stretching out his helping hand, did stand them now in steed;*
For as to Peter* once in prison closely pent,*
To loose his locks and set him free, an angel there was sent;
So God now made a way, a passage strange to give,*                        245
By opening of a mighty door the weaker to relieve,
By which the fainter sort without all danger fled.
The greater sort were taken then, and straight to prison led.
Among which godly troop that did their bodies yield
Were women of great parentage, which were with shame reviled             250
(Of them whom fury fed) to prison as they went;
Yet for all this, these noble minds their deeds did not repent.
And that which was the worst, in prison where they were,
The thieves and bloody murderers did find more favour there,
For they that death deserved were taken from their clink,*               255
And in their cold and ugly pits which breathed a deadly stink
These men were thrust and bound, and kept with watch and
    ward,*
That all access of worldly joy from them might quite be barred.
Yet now because they had not room enough for all
In diverse wards alone to pen these captives thus in thrall,*            260
Great numbers they were fain* together for to place;
To comfort them God did devise to bring it so to pass.
The prisons now did ring with psalms and joyful songs,
They prayed God, when he thought best, to ease them of these
    wrongs.

When this was noised* abroad, and some were thither sent*        265
To know the cause, then this was found the sum of their intent:
At first when they did meet a lecture there was read
In vulgar tongue out of God's book,* whereby their souls were
     fed,
Then did the preacher show, and there he did recite
The use of that most sacred feast whereof St Paul did write       270
Unto the Corinths once; in which he showed plain
The use and abuse of the same, to comfort or to pain.*
When this was done, again they fell upon their knees
And for the King and commons* all they prayed with watery
     eyes:
That God would yet withhold his just revenging hand              275
And bless with perfect truth and peace, their king and eke their
     land.
Then did they all receive Communion bread and wine
To stay their faith in Christ his death, whereof this is a sign.
Now this was all the hurt which they did then procure
For which this raging tumult rose, and they these pains endure.   280
But mark the creeping craft of Satan in this case,
How he by false report does seek the truth for to deface.
His servants now he sends, and bids them ride in post,*
These new invented lies to spread abroad in every coast:
First how the Lutherans* (so Satan did them name),               285
Great wickedness did put in use in places where they came;
And how that in the night, when others were at sleep,
In darkness where no candles were, great numbers on a heap
Of men and women both together did resort
To match themselves, for to fulfil a stinking filthy sport;       290
And how these godly men all sitting in a round,
Upon the tables where they sat great dainties there were found,
As wine and belly cheer;* and each with other's wife
In these their privy* Bacchus* feasts did lead a filthy life;
And how among the rest to work their wicked will,                295
Their usage was (O shameless lie!) their infants for to kill.
These godly men (say they) that seem to shine so clear,
Now under show of godly life most filthy do appear.
The monks, as legates lewd of Pluto's bloody mind,*
Do sweat and some to blaze* abroad this stinking hellish wind,*   300
As men that were most fit to spread this lying fame,
Which in their lives as does appear do daily use the same.
But they in open places these matters so dilate,

That in the minds of blinded fools they raise a deadly hate
Against these silly* souls, which never meant this ill,                    305
That eke the common sort did long these godly men to kill.
And not the common sort are now deceived alone,
But this assails the noblemen, and strikes the prince's throne,
Which lie, no sooner came before the Prince's* face,
But stood in hope by Satan's means, to find assured grace,                310
Whose mind by light* belief in fury so was bent,
That to destroy these hurtless men, he plants his whole intent.
So now he gives in charge to have their dealings tried,
And chosen men he did appoint the same for to decide.
These men in office put, no time could idle spend,                        315
But hard against these silly sheep their wolfish wits do bend.
This poor afflicted flock that now in prison lay
In godly joy but worldly grief did pass the time away;
And they that were in faith more stronger than the rest,
To comfort those that were but weak, their will was ever
    pressed;*                                                             320
And those that were at large did trudge from place to place,
To ease the outward grief of such as saw this heavy case,
Declaring by the word that this came not by chance,
But God was he for some intent which led this woeful dance.
Perchance to show his will, perchance to try their faith,                 325
Perchance to plant his hidden truth by their most happy death,
Perchance to be a means their foes for to confound,
As once amidst the floods he struck proud Pharaoh* to the
    ground.
"Perchance amidst our mirth, our God we did forget,
And youthly bent to vain delights perchance our minds did set,            330
So God in mercy now to call us home again
And see ourselves, has thought it good to let us feel some pain.
Yet still amidst the flames let this be all our rest:
That all things done to God's elect are always for the best."*
Thus did they still remain, to God they did commend                       335
Themselves, their case, content to bear whatever God should
    send.
And now with solemn fasts and prayer put in ure,*
And eke by writing* they assay* some favour to procure.
The King they do request that Truth might try their deeds,
That Justice's sickle might divide the roses from the weeds;              340
That fickle flying tales from credit might be barred,
Till that by just and equal proof both parties have been heard;

And if it were his will that they might now dispute.
They doubted not by written word the Sorbonne's* to confute.
Yet this could not prevail, for all this good device,                              345
For some stood by that told the King their writings were all lies.
The godly grieved thus, as reason did them bind,
By other letters try to change the King's affected mind,
   In which they warn his Grace to look unto himself,
Not to prefer before his God this wicked worldly pelf;*                            350
And therewithal to view the state of that his land,
How all things prospered well which he did take in hand
So long as to the truth he bent a willing ear,*
And to the godly Christian flock a faithful heart did bear.
But since he broke his faith he gave the German* band,                            355
And to that great priest of Rome* again did give his hand,
How all things since have gone a clean contrary way,*
And nothing prospered well since he the truth did so betray.
"And now, O prince", quoth they, "except thou do repent,
Assure thyself to plague this sin the Lord is fully bent.*                         360
And he that now has lent to thee this happy reign,
Will for thy sin most surely turn thy pleasure into pain.
The Constable of France* a looking-glass may be
In whom the end of swelling pride your Grace may plainly see,
Who proudly swearing said, if he returned sound,                                  365
He would not cease till he had quashed Geneva* to the ground.
But God that sits above his folly did deride,
And at St Quentin did confound his purpose and his pride,
So he that lately swore against the Lord to fight
Was taken captive by the foe, his army put to flight.                             370
Of wicked wilful wits this is the woeful end,
When fancy's ruled by witless will, their strength will strive to
      bend
Against the Lord. But now, O King, we do not care,
For whatsoever God shall send we willing are to bear.
But yet of this be sure, the blood* that thou dost wring                          375
From us unjustly is the seed whereby the church does spring,
And though our bodies be consumed in the flame,
Yet of our ashes God will raise* that shall defend the same.
To shade the shining light no wit* can well prevail,
So vain to strive to stay the truth which God does now reveal."                   380
   Thus while the godly work their causes to defend,
The wicked imps of Satan lurk to bring them to their end.
But one above the rest their death did daily crave:

Munerius,* that bloody wretch, that false and perjured knave,
Who having now of late by falsehood cracked his fame,                385
Did hope by hate of God's elect again to win the same.
And having now attained the Prince's bill assigned,
In Paris town before the states* he shows the Prince's mind:
Which was, that presently (all business set aside),
The King would have the prisoners called, their dealings to be
    tried,                                                          390
And that they should proceed to judge, and eke believe,
According to the evidence Munerius then should give.
These letters being read, the Senate all agree
Not to receive* Munerius, nor anything that he
Should lay against the life of those that faithful were,           395
For that himself had falsed his faith, which lately did forswear.
And yet they did proclaim that they would not refuse
If any other would step forth the faithful to accuse.
So, willing to perform the King's intended mind,
Their cankered* malice plant the plot to have the day assigned     400
When these afflicted souls from prison to their doom,
Before the whelps of Pilate's brood,* to judgement now should
    come.
The day is come, and they that were before ordained
To show the glory of the Lord, could not now be constrained
By all their brave device the truth for to deny,                   405
But for the same amidst the flame they willing were to die.
The bloody sentence passed (which was the King's desire)
The valiant troop of godly men were drawn unto the fire,
And chained to their stakes all naked as they stood,
Unto the Lord their cry was heard from out amidst the wood,        410
But to the wicked troop which longed to see that day,
They knowing sure their causes good, this or the like did say:
"Now shall you have your will, now shall you do your worst,
Now shall ye have our guiltless blood, for which ye long did
    thirst.
We fear not of this death, we know that all must die,              415
Yea, happy are those silly souls who thus the Lord does try.
O welcome joyful day, O welcome happy pain;
A crown immortal with this flesh,* we shall receive again.
Now has the Lord here brought and placed us in this death,
Not for because he hates his truth, but for to try our faith.      420
The counsel of the Lord* has sent what we receive,
And you to us shall do no more than God shall give you leave.

And you that are our foes, beware the deadly sign,*
Which shows you none of God's elect, while thus ye do repine
Against his knowen truth, for which we undertake                    425
To spend our blood in his defence, and suffer for his sake.
The blood of Abel* cried for vengeance to the Lord,
Which fell on Cain and all his seed (whom men and earth
  abhorred),
From which the Lord defend both you, and eke our land;
O Lord, revenge not this our wrong, but stay thy furious hand,      430
And give them yet some space for to repent this thing,*
And for our death we do forgive both them and eke our king,
Whose life the Lord preserve in health and perfect peace,
And grant that under him the truth may have some joyful ease.
And though you have some power this flesh for to destroy,           435
Yet cannot us your rage divide from Christ's immortal joy.
And though our breakfast seem to flesh and blood some pain,
Yet shall we sup with Jesus Christ, and ease receive again.
Into thy blessed hands, O Lord, our souls receive,
For of this earth and earthly trash,* O Lord, we take our leave."   440
  Thus on the Lord they cried, which was their only trust,
Till that the flame had stayed their voice, and body burned to
  dust.
Now we that do remain our parts are yet to play,
But when, O Lord, our time shall come, grant us like happy day;
And when our trial draws,* no matter where nor when,               445
That God will give like constant faith, let us cry all amen.

[The conclusion of the first narrative sequence describes God's
punishment of the 'bloody persecutors' as they die confessing their
sins (447–510). The poem then turns to a further attempt by Henry
II to crush the Protestants (511–70) and begins with an account of
his speech to Senate.]

"The Lord that lendeth all and wields the golden sphere
Has sent us now a wished peace, devoid of foreign fear,
Which peace is aye confirmed by band of solemn vow,
And plighted* faith of solemn match, which none can
  disallow.
Yet, one thing there remains to perfect this my state,              575
That in religion one consent must banish all debate,
Which is the only cause that moves my pensive heart
In this your meeting for to join and bear a careful part.

This is therefore in few our crave* and eke request,
That every man do show his mind as he shall think it best."      580
    Here some that had before in words been very rife
Began to stay, and doubted* much the danger of their life.
Yet there were some which now a noble courage take;
Annas Burgeus* as the chief this doubtful silence break,
Who, lifting up his hands, in heart began to pray,              585
With thanks to God that he did live to see that happy day
Wherein the Lord had wrought such care within his Grace,
That he would bend his willing ear to judge so weighty case.
"The cause", saith he, "is Christ's which we have now in
    hand,
For which the Lord will surely bless both you and eke your
    land.                                                      590
This is the blessed ark* that came to Edom's hall,
For which the Lord has blessing sent on him, his house and
    all.
This is the dusty book which good Hilkiah* found,
Which read before the King did give a sweet and silver sound.
This is the angel which to Gideon* did appear,                 595
This is the dew upon the fleece, which set him void of fear.
This is the sword that made blind Balaam's ass* to speak.
This is the flame* the prophet forced his silence forth to
    break.
This is the lively spring,* which cools the thirsty heat,
This is the shining lantern,* which gives light unto our feet.  600
This is the flame* that earst* by night did show the way,
This is the blessed cloud that led God's chosen in the day.
This is Elgathe's* flake* that made his offering fume;*
And this the blast* which from the Lord great rebels did
    consume.
This is the mighty voice* that makes the mountains shake,      605
This makes the Liban* cedars stoop, and fearful hinds to
    quake.
And this the pleasant wine* to weak that comfort gives,
And this the wholesome milk* whereby the sucking infant
    lives.
Now as the Lord does bless the land that loves the same,
So for condemners of his truth, he still provides a shame.      610
For why came Ashur* up God's chosen to molest,
And led the King with commons all in Babel for to rest?
But for because they all their God did often grieve,

Which hated truth and were content their faith to idols give.
And if he do not spare a king, O King, take heed;                               615
If people all to thraldom go, this land, O lord, had need
To weigh the cursed cause of this their final fall;
Lest for the like, the like consume our King and commons all.
Now is the angel* come with open book in hand,
Which long ere this was sealed close from us and eke our
    land.                                                                        620
Now must the godly crave of this to eat their fill,
So God with plenty will not fail to love and feed them still.
Now see this angel which to us doth offer grace
Is Jesus Christ, which by his death our sins doth quite
    deface.*
If we by lively faith* of him can take good hold,                               625
Then void of fear before the Lord to come we may be bold.
It's he that shows the way the truth to entertain,
It's he that clears the blinded eyes,* it's he that parteth plain
The truth from Popish lies,* the sun from misty shades,
It's he that calls our straying steps from Satan's sinful trades.*              630
O well is he that can this book, this truth embrace,
O ill is he that shall refuse when Christ doth offer grace.
And though this book at first be sweet unto our taste,
Yet Satan's rages make the same seem bitter at the last.
And what though Satan rage, what though the end be gall?*                        635
Shall bitter blasts make us foresake our Christ, our life, and
    all?
No, God forbid, O King, that he should knock in vain,
Lest being gone we justly doubt when he will come again.
As yet, he stands without, and knocketh at thy door;
O King, receive that blessed guest, that he may bless thee
    more.                                                                        640
If that we let him in,* his promise is to stay,
But when from us he shall depart, O most unhappy day!
The supper* is prepared, the angels sent to call
The straying guests of this your land unto his sacred hall,
But if by fond excuse we shun his proffered grace,                              645
He shuts the door and will admit some others in our place.
The marriage of the Lamb,* that blessed Lamb, is nigh,
Which makes with all her Romish tricks that whore of Babel*
    fly.
Then happy is the man and blessed from the Lord,
That with the Lamb may have a place, and sit at sacred
    board.                                                                       650

If now we see the light that daunted* Saul* to ground,
If now we hear that sacred voice, that sweet and joyful sound,
Then let us now enquire, what voice it is that calls,
And let us yield unto the truth, that from our eyes the scales
Of darkness may depart. For vain it is to kick,                              655
And labour lost for wilful colt to strive against the prick.*
And if the hidden truth the Lord will now reveal,
To daunt the same (O noble King), your force shall not
    prevail.
What giant can withstand of Truth the piercing might?
What earthly force of shining sun at noon can quench the
    light?                                                                   660
If Truth do conquer kings, if Truth do conquer all,
Then leave to love these Popish lies, let whorish Babel fall.*
Grieve not that blessed spirit of life that seals the band
For which King David* did request, by which we understand
Our calling to be sure, our striving not in vain,                           665
By which we know we are ordained for Christ to suffer pain.
Now sith* we have the seal from fear that makes us free,
And shining light from Popish shades the Lord has made us
    see,
We may no longer then dissemble in this case,
But what we think must plainly show (O King) before your
    face.                                                                    670
We cannot (as you would) the certain truth deny,*
But that defend, though for the same we were condemned to
    die.
And whereas you do thirst to suck the guiltless blood
Of them whom you name Lutherans,* O King, we think not
    good
To strengthen that device which Satan did invent,                           675
Lest that with Cain* our bloody fact* too late we should
    repent.
For those whom you do hate and push with heavy hand,
In very truth are godly men, the best in all your land,
Whose faith you do not see, whose life you do not know;
Take heed lest you in them do seek the Lord to overthrow,                    680
Which feat by wanton* will if now your Grace assay,*
Be wise in time, lest that in this, you frame your own decay.
But this we think the best, that straightway out of hand
A lawful counsel may be called to have the matter scanned;*

Till which, let godly men whom envy cannot stain,                     685
In lieu of all their cursed wrong, in rest at home remain.
But if to this (O King), you stop your princely ear,
Lest God with blindness strike your heart,* your friends may
    justly fear,
For they that do not care aright to serve the Lord,
He leaves them to their filthy lusts to make them more
    abhorred.                                                          690
Remember Ahab's* fall, that sold himself to death;
Forget not those two wicked men* which long withstood the
    faith;
Corrupted men shall fade, the reprobates shall die;
God will not long maintain their reign that shall his truth
    deny;
Their madness shall be plain, their follies seen, and then            695
The godly shall deride the rage of sinful wicked men
Because (saith God) you stayed to come when I did call,*
I will be deaf when you lament, and laugh when you do fall.
Which plague the Lord withhold from you and eke your land;
The Lord preserve your noble Grace, and shield ye with his
    hand,                                                             700
That long in perfect peace your Grace may rule and reign,
That in your time God's knowen truth may once revive again.
And this is all we wish, and this the worst we crave,
That Christ will open once your heart, by faith your soul to
    save."
This said, he sat again. The King* in fiery heat,                    705
Scant able to forbear so long, spoke thus from out his seat:
"Indeed, and is it so? Well then, we know the worst,
To speak or think as we have heard we deemed no subject
    durst.*
But now with grief we see that this infectious seed
Has taken rooting in our court, whereof this is the seed.            710
But most, we marvel why the nobles of our land
So blinded are, that they will needs these matters take in
    hand;
We thought it most unlike that men so grave and wise
Should ever stoop to give consent unto so lewd* device.
But now we must correct our mind and former thought,                715
And give these new religious men the guerdon* they have
    sought,
And trust us, so we will, now that we know the crew,

We doubt not but the proudest shall this day and dealings
  rue.
Now sith we know the good the rest shall know our mind;
We doubt not for these bleeding wounds some healing salve
  to find.                                                                                720
Such tools we have in store to fell this rotting moot,*
That quickly shall pull up and raise the branches with the
  root.
This seed of Luther's sect* which now begins to spring,
Shall to the fields where it doth grow a woeful harvest bring.
It's time to look about, it's time to set some stay;*                         725
For if we sleep, we see there be that watch for our decay.
But they shall have their meed,* they shall not lose their
  hire,*
They shortly shall with sorrow feel the weight of prince's ire."
  Thus said, in raging wise, he turneth quite about,
And pausing stayed awhile, as one that seemed to doubt;              730
But yet, such rancour rose and boiled in his breast
That presently he gave in charge that there they should arrest
Annas Burgeus as the chief, and him to prison bring,
Who was, he thought, the only root by whom the rest did
  spring.

[Subsequently, Burgeus is tried as a heretic and sentenced to death,
at which point he makes a long speech in defence of his faith
(735–954).]

  Thus having said his mind, and ready to depart,                   955
The hangman takes and ties his hands and lays him on a cart,
In which he was conveyed unto a place fast* by,
Where chained to a stake it was ordained that he should die.
The streets of Paris town were kept with watch and ward,*
There went with him of armed men four hundred for his
  guard;                                                                              960
The ways on every side that led unto the place
Were stopped up, as if they had foreseen some doubtful case.
And where we plainly see these tyrants all afraid,
The godly man for all this broil was not a whit dismayed,
For when he was unbound, there was in him no fear,                   965
He put his clothing off himself with bold and constant cheer,
Where standing naked then and stripped unto his skin,
With cheerful voice he did at last this heavy speech begin:

"The cause why I am come (good people) to this death
Is not for murder, theft, or wrong: but for a lively faith."*          970
Which said, he held his peace, and kneeling on the ground
With sighs he prayed, till to the stake by hangman he was
    bound,
Where he did oft* repeat: "O Lord forsake not me,
Least by the frailness of my flesh I hap* to slide from thee.
O Lord receive my soul into thy blessed rest,                         975
Give me thy strength while I do live, O Lord, I thee
    request."*
Thus with a quiet mind and heart devoid of strife,
For Christ amidst the fiery flame, he yielded up his life.
    But what a joy is this to us that do remain,
That God does give to his elect* such strength to conquer
    pain.                                                             980
This is the godly end that blessed man did make,
Whom life and honour could not bend his Christ for to
    forsake;
He lived with good report, his death deserveth fame,
And he hath left unto his foes a lewd and filthy shame.
A rare and passing* sign no doubt the Lord did give             985
To see that noble constancy in him while he did live.
Whose constant death in France, and blood, did sow the seed
Whereby the church did much increase, and godly yet do feed.
He came of honest house, in learning spent his youth,
And being placed in high degree he sought to learn the truth,       990
Whereof when he had felt the sweet and pleasant taste
He joined himself unto the church, and sticks to them at last.
Well, he is gone before, and we that are behind
Lord grant to us in Jesus Christ like faith and constant mind.
                        Amen

*The judgement of the Lord which fell upon
King Henry the second after he had caused
Burgeus to be imprisoned, Anno 1559. Dilated\*
by the examples of Ahab, Amaziah, and
Zedechiah, wicked kings, which used the like
cruelty against the Word.\**

The Lord on Eli's sons* and sins this sentence gave:              995
They that do love and honour me, great honour still shall
    have,
But they that do despise my word, my law, and will,

They shall be sure of every man to be abhorred still.
Which sentence of the Lord for ever shall be true,
As by examples we may see of such as do ensue.                    1000
For when as Ahab* was in fond and foolish rage
To Ramoth Gilead stoutly bent unjustly wars to wage,
A prophet from the Lord did tell him very plain,
That if this war he took in hand, King Ahab should be slain.
But to the prison straight this prophet then was led;             1005
The King gave charge that he should be with bread and water
      fed,
Till he returned safe from Gilead home again.
But what befell? It came to pass the King indeed was slain.
So Amaziah* (which by idols did offend)
Unto the prophet would not yield his willing ear to bend,         1010
But did with bitter scoffs and scorns reprove the word,
For which he was by Jehu spoiled* and taken by the sword.
So Zedekiah* proud from sin would not return,
But rebel-like the word of God he did with fire burn;
And Jeremy by him was oft in prison pent,*                        1015
Because he said the King and all to Babel should be sent.
But let us see his end: the King of Babel came
Who took him captive with his men and put them all to
      shame.
And he that was content God's prophet to disgrace
Was forced to see the murder of his sons before his face;         1020
His eyes that would not see God's truth and shining light,
The King of Babel put them out as they deserved of right.
So Henry King of France, which all his force did bend
Against the truth, did from the Lord receive a fearful end.
For now amidst the ruff* of all their mirth and joy,              1025
When every man devised how the godly to destroy,
The time appointed came, for marriage of the King,
Which to the court and courtiers did great mirth and pleasure
      bring.
And for the greater pomp of all this princely train,
A solemn joust the youthly King by crier did proclaim;            1030
In which he meant to show his manhood and his might,
And being horsed with limber* spear in armour shining
      bright,
He chose amongst the rest (the challenge now begun)
Montgomery,* captain of his guard, against him for to run,
Which he did oft refuse, and wisely did withstand,                1035

Ill that the King the fatal spear put in his captain's hand.
Where charging with their spears, and forcing might and
    main,*
A splinter pierced the Prince's eye and ran unto his brain.
The King, with sudden wound and bleeding much dismayed,
Within the next adjoining house to bed he was conveyed,          1040
Where plunged with grievous pain, his conscience did lament
The wrong which he had done to those whom he to prison
    sent.
"I greatly fear," said he, "lest I have done some ill
Against Burgeus and the rest, whose blood I sought to spill."
But Elymas* the witch does spend his cursed wind                 1045
From such remorse to keep in thrall the King's afflicted mind.
"It is," said he, "thy foe that doth assault thy faith,
In which take heed that thou remain still constant to thy
    death."
This heavy hap* befell (as many men have told)
Near to the place wherein as then Burgeus was in hold;           1050
And many did observe that he did kill the King
Which was commanded to the jail Burgeus for to bring.
The King did often brag those eyes of his should see
Burgeus burned; but lo, the Lord did alter that decree,
For ere Burgeus was unto the fire led,                           1055
Montgomery had those eyes of his thrust clean out of his
    head.*
Now here we plainly see the life and heavy end
Of them which persecute the truth, which God does often
    send;
And let us warning take by this most fearful fate,
For to return and loath our sin, before it be too late.          1060
                    Amen

[Despite these attempts to crush the Protestants, however, some
noblemen, including Gaspard de Coligny, the Admiral of France,
and Prince Henry of Navarre adopt the cause, thereby arousing
Satan's anger. Consequently the Devil* offers some advice to the
Queen Mother* and the other noble Catholics (1061–84). The
following speech is given by Satan.]

"There is a subtle vein that feeds this cankered* sore,          1085
For now the deeper it is lanced it riseth still the more.
We see that fire and sword cannot at all prevail;

We see that all our bloody broils their courage cannot quail;
We see how noble men their forces daily bend
To counter-cross our planted plots, this cause for to defend.          1090
Two civil wars* are past, the third is now in hand,
We see how stoutly they are bent our forces to withstand.
Therefore we must devise to play some other part,
Or else in vain we take in hand these princes* to subvart.*
Now lend your listening ears and mark what I shall say,          1095
A secret thing I have bethought which here I will bewray:*
You must make show, as though you loved to live at ease,
As weary of these broils, you must entreat to have a peace.
The King, as chiefest man, this play must first begin
By loving letters, words, and cheer at first to bring them in          1100
And look what they mislike, the King must rase* it out,
And yield to all things they request to put them out of doubt.
The King must show such face to them above the rest,
As though he did unfeignedly of all men love them best;
The worst of all their band the King must entertain          1105
With such good will, that no mistrust in any may remain.
And he must make them know, as though of late he felt
Some prick in conscience for the cause against the which he
     dealt,
And that he will forgive all quarrels that are past,
In hope that this their new goodwill with love may ever last,          1110
And he must make complaint, as though he did of late
Mislike the dealings of the Guise,* and such as they do hate,
And then the Guises must awhile from court retire,
For thus you shall entrap them all, and have your full desire.
The King must yield to all that they request or crave,          1115
And he must grant for to confirm the thing that they would
     have.
The Mother Queen in this must also play her part,
That no suspect of treason may remain within their heart
And here you must give out, as though you would employ
Their service in some foreign wars, which doth your state
     annoy,          1120
As if you would not trust the weight of such affairs
To any man, but them alone, whose faith and watchful cares
You long have tried; and so you may your plot prepare
By these and suchlike feigned things, to trap them in your
     snare.
If this prevail not, then I stand in fearful doubt          1125

What practice next to put in ure* to have them rooted out.
Now therefore say your mind, if thus it be not best
To cut them off, that so again we all may live in rest."
    The counsel did agree this was the only way,
And every man did give his word this sentence to obey,                1130
And that they would devise such things to put in ure
As best might fit this cursed plot, and make the same most
    sure;
Which Satan hearing, rose and thanked them with his heart,
That they to him so willing were, and so they did depart.

[The King and his counsel follow Satan's advice and deceive, first,
the Admiral of France, and, second, Henry of Navarre, who is
betrothed to the King's sister. Nevertheless, when the marriage is
celebrated in Paris the Protestant Queen of Navarre is murdered
with a pair of 'gloves perfumed' with poison and, five days later,
the Admiral is wounded by a would-be assassin (1135–1392).]

    But here the prologue ends, and here begins the play,*
For bloody minds resolved quite to use no more delay.
The Mother Queen appears now first upon the stage,                    1395
Where like a devilish sorceress with words demure and sage
The King she calls aside, with other trusty mates
Into a close and secret place, with whom she now debates
The great desire she had to quit them all from care,
In planting long a bloody plot, which now she must declare.          1400
"O happy light," quoth she,* "O thrice most happy day,
Which thus has thrust into our hands our long desired prey.
We have them all in hold, we have the chiefest fast,
And those* for whom we waited long we have them all at
    last.
Why should we longer stay? What can we further crave?                1405
What, are not all things come to pass which we do long to
    have?
Does not our mightiest foe lie wounded in his bed,
Not able now to help himself, which others long have led?
The captains captive are, the King of Navarre sure,
The Prince of Condé with the rest that mischief did procure,         1410
Are close within our walls, we have them in a trap,
Good fortune (lo), has brought them all, and laid them in our
    lap
By force or flight to save their lives, it is too late,

If we (to cut off future fear and cause of all debate)
Do take the proffered time, which time is only now,                        1415
And wisdom matched with policy our dealings does allow,
We need not fear the spot of any cruel fame,
So long as we may feel some ease or profit by the same.
For wisdom does allow the prince to play the fox,
And lion-like to rage, but hates the plainness of an ox.                   1420
What though ye do forswear? What though ye break your
    faith?
What though ye promise life, and yet repay it with their
    death?
Is this so great a fault? Nay, nay, no fault at all,
For this we learn we ought to do, if such occasions fall.
Our masters* do persuade a king to cog* and lie,                           1425
And never keep his faith, whereas his danger grows thereby.
Cut off therefore the head of this infectious sore,
So may you well assure yourselves this bile will rise no more;
The captains being slain, the soldiers will be faint,
So shall we quickly on the rest perform our whole intent.                  1430
Pluck up therefore your spirits, and play your manly parts,
Let neither fear nor faith prevail to daunt your warlike hearts.
What shame is this that I (a woman by my kind)*
Need thus to speak, or pass you men in valour of the mind?
For here I do protest, if I had been a man,                                1435
I had myself before this time this murder long began
Why do you doubting stand, and wherefore do you stay?
If that you love your peace, or life, procure no more delay.
We have them in our hands, within our castle gates,
Within the walls of Paris town, the masters and their mates,               1440
This is the only time this matter to dispatch;
But being fled, these birds are not so easy for to catch.
The town of Paris will most gladly give consent,
And threescore thousand fighting men provide for this intent,
So shall we quickly see the end of all our strife,                         1445
And in a moment shall dispatch these rebels of their life.
But if we stand in fear and let them scape our hand,
They will procure in time to come great trouble in our land.
For if the Admiral his strength receive again,
Can any doubt but that he will be mindful of his pain?                     1450
It is a simple* thing for princes to believe
That new goodwill an ancient hate from galled* hearts can
    drive.

Therefore if we permit these rebels to retire,
We soon shall see by wars again our country set on fire.
This is a woman's mind, and thus I think it best,                    1455
Now let us likewise hear I pray the sentence of the rest."
   This counsel of them all was liked passing* well,
And in respect of present state, all others did excel.
Some doubting, mused long which were the better way:
The King of Navarre and the Prince of Condé for to slay,            1460
Or else to save their lives in hope they would recant,
Because the proof of perfect years* they both as yet did want.
But here they did prevail (as God, no doubt, would have)
Who thought it best in this assault these princely youths to
   save,
Because they were in hope, that when those imps* should see         1465
Their mates tormented thus, they would most willingly agree
To bow where they would bind, to go where they would
   call,*
And to forswear their former faith would make no doubt at
   all.
But all the rest remain condemned for to die,
Which cruel verdict must be put in practice presently;              1470
The night that should ensue then next without delay,
Beginning ere the same were spent long time before the day;
The Duke of Guise was thought the fittest of the train
To take in hand this bloody plot to have the godly slain.
Concluding thus, they go each one unto his place,                   1475
The godly doubting nothing less than this so heavy case.
   Here is the first part played, and here I do lament
My slender skill wants fitted phrase the sequel to depaint.*
The Duke in office put begins for to prepare,
So that in troops the armed men ran bustling here and there         1480
With noise and threatening words, as though some tumult
   were
Preparing now in every street, which made the wisest fear
What would ensue. At length, the Admiral did hear
This tumult, and not knowing how the truth for to enquire,
He sent unto the King to know the full intent,                      1485
Why in the night, in riot-wise, these armed people went
Thus raging in the streets, and where* it were his will?
If so, he would not fear, but rest in hope of safety still.
   The King returned word, and willed him not to fear,
For this was done by his advice, yet not in everywhere,             1490

But in some certain ways these armed men were set,
The foolish rage of lewd* attempts by this in hope to let.*
   O lewd and filthy lie! Unseemly for a king!
What Turk or devil* could devise a more unworthy thing.
For when the Duke of Guise had all in order set,                    1495
And nothing rested which might seem their purpose for to let,
He Marcell* calls in haste, and wills him have a care
That all the masters of the streets ere midnight did repair
Unto the council hall, where they should hear at large
Great matters from the King himself of strange and special
   charge.                                                          1500
The message being done, they all without delay
Assembled were, to know the thing the Guises had to say.
Where Provost Carron* rose with stomach* stout and bold,
And guarded with a Guisan troop, this bloody message told:
"My friends," quoth he, "give ear, and mark what I shall say:      1505
The King's intent is presently this night, without delay,
Those rebels to destroy, which now these latter years
Bore arms against his Grace, which, though they be his peers,
Yet will he quite pull up and root the lawless race
Of them that long have sought by force his dealings to
   disgrace.                                                        1510
And what a happy time, I pray, my mates is this,
When fast within our city walls the captain closed is
That fiercely brewed the broil of this our doubtful* strife,
And many times has put us all in danger of our life.
Their trust by treason trained,* is cause of this deceit;          1515
O happy she* that wrought the mould of this so cunning feat.
Their friends will prove their foes, sweet pleasures will have
   pain;
And being here they are not like to see their homes again.
Their chambers prisons are, their beds shall be their grave,
And ere the day appear we must a glorious conquest have.           1520
Be strong therefore my friends, make sharp the fatal knife;
For of these rebels ere the day, not one shall scape with life.
Their leader and their guide lies wounded in his bed,
And therefore as the chiefest foe, we'll first have off his head.
And when we have dispatched the rebels we have here,               1525
We'll likewise ransack all the land of like that shall appear.
This is the King's intent, this is his Grace's mind,
To do this feat, let him in us a willing courage find;
And for a token when this murder shall begin,

The warlike trumpet shall not sound, nor banner shall be
    seen,                                                       1530
But tocsin* shall be heard this bloody news to bring,
For then begin, when as you hear this palace bell to ring.
The badge which you shall bear by which you shall be
    known,
Shall be a linen cloth of white, made fast about the brawn*
Of left-side arm; and eke a cross upon your cap,      1535
Of white likewise; and these keep fast whatever chance may
    hap.*
And this is all, my friends, that I have now to say,
Come follow me, and let's begin, and use no more delay."
    This while the Duke of Guise did show his whole intent
Unto the captains of the guard, and bade them give consent    1540
With courage to perform so great and famous* act,
Which service as the case did stand, they might not long
    protract.
Now shortly after this, the Duke with many more,
Accompanied with the Chevalier* and armed men great store,
Came posting* to the gate which Cossin* took to keep,    1545
Woe worth* the time when they did trust the wolf to guard
    the sheep.*
The Admiral knew well the tumult of this rout;
Yet this, nor anything, could make his valiant heart to doubt,
For though he had but few, scarce ten within the place,
Yet nothing could at all prevail to make him doubt his case.    1550
    For oft he would repeat the King's assured love,
Approved by so many signs as you have heard above:
"What though the Commons rise? What though the tumult
    rage?
When they shall see the prince's guard, their malice will
    assuage.
I know the King will not by treason false* his faith,    1555
Though for the same there might ensue the hazard of his
    death,
The oath that he has sworn so oft, to keep the peace,
No Christian conscience can assent at all for to release.
His mother gave her faith, his brothers swore likewise,
The public records of the land do witness this device.    1560
What band* may surer be? What more may you desire?
What can we further wish? And yet if more you do require,
The Queen of England is a witness of the same,

The Prince of Orange, and the States that from the Germans
    came;*
This royal match likewise my heart doth well assure        1565
That such a seal of perfect love for ever will endure;
Which marriage lately made with counsel grave and good,
The King will not permit to be so soon defiled with blood.
For what would strangers say if such things should befall?
But such things, Lord, be far from us, and Lord preserve us
    all.        1570
What would the future age of imps as yet unborn,
What would all nations think, if we by trust should be
    forlorn?*
The stout and constant mind, and honour of the King,
Will never give consent, I know, to do so lewd a thing."
    Thus whilst amongst the rest the case he did debate,     1575
His trusty keeper, Cossin, came and knocked at his gate,
Who was no sooner come within the outward door,
But that there came in after him of armed men great store,
Then after went the lords, the nobles, and the rest,
For to dispatch this noble man, whom they did most detest.    1580
And those whom Cossin found within to lie or stand
He slew them with a partisan* which he had in his hand.
Which woeful news when as the Admiral perceived,
"Woe worth the time," quoth he, "that I by trust have been
    deceived.
Well, now the time is come, I may no longer doubt,      1585
Come lend your help my friends (I pray) from bed to lift me
    out.
To Christ my only hope my soul I do betake,
And in this place from off my couch this life I will forsake."
Then standing on his feet his night-gown on his back,
"Shift for yourselves, my friends," quoth he, "that you go not
    to wrack.       1590
And have no care for me, for I am well content
This life to yield unto the Lord, which he to me has lent;
It grieves me not to die, God's will is always best,
From future fears I know with Christ my soul shall be in rest.
This plot is not prepared alone to murder me,      1595
But for the rasing* of that truth, which they are loath to see;
The godly for to spoil which have received the word,
These tyrants seek with cruel hate by falsehood and by sword,
Which word unto my power I always did defend,

The malice of which godly course hath brought me to my
    end, 1600
Which does rejoice my heart and soul exceedingly,
That for his truth the Lord has thought me worthy for to die,
For though our sins do cause these troubles in our land,
Yet shall these tyrants not escape the Lord's revenging hand.
And though our God do seem from us to hide his face, 1605
And arms our foes with cruel death his people to disgrace,
Yet if we be content, his mercy will retire.*
Have mercy Lord upon thy church, O Christ, I thee desire.
And you, O traitors* vile that laid this trothless train,*
Against the Lord have lifted up your wicked hearts in vain, 1610
For you are puffed up with hope that is not sure;
For these our pains, you shall receive the pains that shall
    endure.*
And you that dare to lift your hands against the Lord,
Before your death most justly shall of all men be abhorred.
Though yet you do not feel the sentence that is due 1615
To this your bloody traitor's act, yet know that you shall rue
Your breach of plighted faith, your deep dissembling heart;
There is a God will judge us all, that will revenge our smart.
The pain that we receive doth breed eternal joy,
But for the wrong that you have done, the Lord will you
    destroy. 1620
O Lord, confirm my faith, which now must here be tried,
Reach me thy hand (O Christ) that I from thee may never
    slide;
My fearful flesh is weak, my heart and will is pressed,
Forsake me not my God, but now receive me to thy rest;
Let not this irksome shade, this dark and doleful night 1625
Keep from my heart in this assault thy sweet and pleasant
    light.
For though the worldly sun mine eye shall see no more,
Thy blessed Son let me enjoy whom I by faith adore,
And whereas I despair no more to see the day,
Instead of that, thy loving face show me (my God) I pray. 1630
Lo then, a blessed chance, and happy change for me,
That from this vale of wretched life* with Christ in joy shall
    be.
Now let these traitors come, the fear of death is past,
And fainting flesh that did rebel has yielded at the last.
Now does my soul rejoice, my heart most gladly say, 1635

Thou Son of God, my Saviour, come, my Christ now come
   thy way;
For here again to thee my soul I do commend,
And to thy poor afflicted church, O Lord, thy mercy send,
So shall they be at rest, so shall they praise thy name;
Let not these tyrants longer, Lord, thy servants put to shame,    1640
Lest they do proudly brag, and say within their heart:
'Where is the God whom they do serve, that now should take
   their part?'
Come quickly Lord, therefore, and make no more delay
To end these fierce and bloody broils; Amen, Amen, I say."
   By this came up the stairs ere ended were his words,    1645
One Benvise and two other mates* with targets* and with
   swords.
The chamber broken up, this Benvise swearing came
With sword drawn, to the Admiral, and asking for his name:
"Art thou the Admiral?" The man, not much appalled,
With quiet mind, gave answer thus: "Indeed, I am so called."    1650
Then seeing Benvise bend his naked sword to slay,
"My friend", quoth he, "that bloody blade I pray thee for to
   stay,
And have respect unto my age and weak estate
To which by treason wrought by trust I have been drawn of
   late."
But beastly Benvise would to this no answer give,    1655
But swearing, to this noble man his pointed sword let drive
And thrust him to the heart; but yet not fully dead,
With force he laid a mighty blow and struck him on the head;
With that came Attin* in with pistol in his hand
And shot him in the wounded breast, yet did he stoutly stand;    1660
Till Benvise came again with third repeated wound,
And slashed him on the thigh, which done, he fell unto the
   ground,
Where he gave up the ghost. The bloody Guise, that stayed
This while within the lower court, with lifted voice now said,
"Ho, Benvise, hast thou done?" Who straightway did reply,    1665
"Yes sir, this happy deed is done, and that most perfectly."
Then said the Duke of Guise, "Come, throw him down to me,
That where it be the same, or not, we here may quickly see."
For now our chevalier will think it but a lie,
Except at window thrown out he see him with his eye.    1670
Then Benvise with his mates to put them out of doubt,

Took up this bloody corse, and so from window cast him out.
Where from his wounded head sprung out so fresh a flood,
That vizard-like* his face was all imbrued* with gory blood
Whereby they could not well at first discern his face:                    1675
Till that the Duke of Guise himself first kneeling in the place
Had with his napkin wiped the clotted blood away,
And searching viewed every part, he rose without delay,
And crying to his crew, devoid of fear and shame:
"It's he (my friends) I know him well, trust me, it is the
    same!"                                                               1680
The Duke, descending then from out the stately gates,
With bloody heart and cursed mouth he cried unto his mates,
"O happy luck, that we so good beginnings have,
Lo, Fortune frames her willing hand to give that we do crave.
And sith it pleased the Fates at first such hap to send,                 1685
It gives me cause of future hope to see some happy end.
Come on, my valiant hearts, so place your warlike bands,
That marching forward to the rest, not one may scape our
    hands.
This is the King's decree, this hath he given out,
We do no more than he commands, to put you out of doubt;                 1690
Let pity take no place till rebels all be rid,
Thus saith the King, fear not therefore to do what he does
    bid.
Let nothing now prevail to daunt your hardy mind;
No, though with tears they pity crave, let them no mercy find.
Have no remorse unto the young, nor yet the old;                         1695
Without regard to anyone to kill them all be bold.
Now sanctify your swords, and bathe them in the blood
Of these religious rebels which do mean the King no good.
So shall we quickly find a path to perfect peace;
So shall we see assured means at length to live at ease:                 1700
For if we can recount the troubles that are past,
Then happy time wherein we may dispatch them all at last."
    Which said, he bad in haste the tocsin* for to ring,
Which sounding bell appointed was the fatal news to bring
When as this raging rout this murder should begin,                       1705
Which they performed, as though they had no men, but
    monsters been;
And therewithal devise a larum* for to raise,
Pretending with some solemn lie the people for to please.
So now the trumpets sound this lie and shameful thing:

That certain traitors were in arms about to kill the King.            1710
Here, one among the rest from Rome that lately came,
(Desirous by some valiant act perhaps to get a name)
Cut off the bleeding head (imbrued with reeking blood)
Of that most worthy Admiral, in hope to do some good,
And sent it straight to Rome, as Lorraine had required,              1715
A present welcome to the Pope, which he had long desired.*
His hands cut off by some, by some his secret parts,
Declares what hate to shining light lies hid in blinded hearts.
His hacked and mangled corpse by space of certain days
Was dragged by rascals all along the streets and filthy ways.        1720
At length this rustic* rage, as fury thought it meet,
At common gallows of the town did hang him by the feet.
Thus came this noble man to this unworthy death,
Thus do the Papists learn to break the vow of plighted faith.

> *The Admiral being slain, they likewise*
> *murdered most cruelly, not only all such*
> *friends, physicians, preachers, and all others*
> *that were found hidden in the Admiral's*
> *lodging, but also as many as were suspected to*
> *be of that religion within the town or*
> *anywhere else, were lamentably put to the*
> *sword, as here following we may plainly see.*

These Furies frying* thus, yet thus were not content,               1725
But in the house from place to place, like greedy hounds they
    went,
To search the chambers all and corners of receipt,*
That from the wolf the sheep might save his throat by no
    deceit;
And such as sleeping were found naked in their bed,
Or gone to hide or save themselves, they first cut off their
    head                                                             1730
And after fiercely pierced with wounds both great and deep;
Which being done like cruel curs they throw them on a heap.
Among which woeful troop two noble youths there were
And pages of most worthy birth which likewise died there;
With these, among the rest, a man of noble fame,                     1735
The County Rouchfoucault* was forced at length to taste the
    same,
Whom for his pleasant wit the King did seem to love,
Yet in this fury nothing might the King to mercy move,

But now in haste must be to death untimely sent,
To yield again unto the Lord the life that he had lent.                    1740
So him at first De Nance* commanded was to kill;
But he most stoutly did refuse this guiltless blood to spill.
"Shall I," said he, "consent to do this fearful thing,
To shed this blood, because I am commanded by the King?
No, God forbid, I know I have a soul to save;                              1745
So bloody spot, to save my life my name shall never have.
I know there is a day,* a day that saints desire;
When of our deeds the King above a reckoning will require.
Obey the King;* that's true, in things that honest be;
When I obey in wicked hests,* woe worth the time to me.                    1750
For Joab* did not well King David to obey,
When wickedly the King him bade Uriah for to slay;
Those elders did offend which showed themselves too prone,
Those wicked letters to obey, poor Naboth* for to stone;
And cursed Doeg* which obeyed a wicked will,                               1755
Shall cursed stand for that he did the Lord's anointed kill.
A murder to be done the King does now request,
My God commands the contrary, now which to choose were
    best?
The King does threaten death, and God does threaten hell,
If for the King I should forsake my God, should I do well?                 1760
What others see, O King, I cannot well divine,
To kill the uncondemned man it is no charge of mine;
To slay my deadly foe except there were some cause
I would not yield, much less my friend against our sacred
    laws.
What envy doth report, O King, I cannot say,                               1765
But this my friend a faithful man to me hath been alway;
Therefore, I pray your Grace, your rigour to assuage,
Or bid some other whom you list to execute your rage.
In matters that be good if that you list to use
My service, you shall see that I no peril will refuse;                     1770
Therefore, I pray your Grace this answer for to take,
Which unto Saul* his soldiers once were not afraid to make.
De Nance to kill his friend no wight shall ever see,
Though for refusal he were sure beheaded for to be.
Take heed, O noble King, what sprite* you follow now,                      1775
Let no man force you do the thing that God does disallow.
While good King David* was by whoredom brought asleep,
He did the thing which being waked did force his heart to
    weep;

While Saul* in malice was against good David bent,
He ran to that which afterwards with tears he did lament;    1780
And whilst that Jezebel great mischief did intend
Against poor Naboth,* she at last came to a fearful end.
Look well therefore, O King, before you leap too far,
Lest in the end this testy* scab do breed a lasting scar.
Well I can say no more, but God preserve your Grace,    1785
And grant your soul when breath is gone, with him a resting-
    place."
    But this could not prevail this noble man to save,
For bloody Doeg did attend* his office for to have,
For which, an Auernois,* a man of cused* fame,
Made offer there before the King that he would do the same.    1790
The King was well content this office for to give
To him, so that this noble man of life he would bereave.
We see how Satan does by glory mixed with gain
Work to procure this worthy wight the sooner to be slain.

[The death of another nobleman, Theligny,* follows (1795–
1824).]

    Thus came this noble imp* untimely to his grave,    1825
For that he to a Papist's oath* too great affiance* gave;
And thus fell many more of nobles here and there,
Whose names and valiant acts were now too long for to
    declare;
Thus did those lawless bands go raging up and down
From house to house, they sought to spoil the wealthiest of
    the town;    1830
So they that beggars were when first this stir began
At last, with rich and flowing wealth, the chiefest credit wan.
This while the Duke of Guise these words repeated still,
With crying voice, "Kill, kill the knaves, this is the Prince's
    will!"
And lest the soldiers should wax faint with bloody toil,    1835
"Now rid them all, my friends," quoth he, "and you shall
    have the spoil."
Thus did they all a day from morning unto night
With bloody swords run up and down, no doubt a heavy
    sight;

They spared none they knew, no sex could pity find,
The rueful cry of tender babes could not assuage their mind;        1840
In great triumphing joy of this their warlike feat,
The bodies slain from windows high they throw into the
    street,
So that there was no way, no lane or passage by,
Where murdered men you might not see in heaps together lie.

[The Protestant King of Navarre and Prince of Condé are saved
from the general murder by being taken within the palace walls,
but their retinues are slain, including Monsieur de Pilles,* who
makes a final speech accusing the King of treachery and concluding
with the prediction of the King's death (1844–1924).]

This rout in Paris' streets which posted* up and down        1925
Four hundred houses sacked have within that wicked town.
The King therewith directs his letters out in post,*
To cities all his message flies, in haste to every coast,
That they, as Paris had, with murder should oppress
As many in the towns as did the Gospel there profess,        1930
Which lewd and bloody charge a wonder is to see,
How glad and willing to obey most towns and cities be.
But one among the rest, a place of ancient fame,
Did lion-like behave herself, as Lyons was her name,
For though in other towns by murder many fell,        1935
Yet Lyons for her cruel heart all others did excel.
Where then, unhappy then, a Lion as the chief
One Mandelot* was governor, a black and bloody thief,
Who having once received these letters from the King,
With greedy mind he sets about this vile unworthy thing,        1940
Who caused out of hand his crier to proclaim
That all within the town which did the Gospel then maintain
Should presently resort unto a certain place
Where Mandelot would have them all appear before his face.
This message being done, the godly do obey        1945
And to the place appointed them they came without delay,
Where Mandelot they found with visage pale and sad,
Who nothing said, but bids them all to prison to be had.
The godly trapped thus, and thus to thraldom sent,
As sheep unto the slaughter* they to prison meekly went,        1950
Where lying in the clink their feet and hands were bound,

And by the cruel gaolers were laid prostrate on the ground.
Then Mandelot commands the hangman for to call,
Whom he enjoins* to enter in with axe to kill them all;
But this so fearful fact the hangman* did refuse,                    1955
And bade him for so wicked act some fitter man to choose:
"For I will not defile my hands with guiltless blood,
Nor give consent," said he, "to do the thing that is not good.
On such as are condemned by justice and by law,
I only am in public place my deadly blade to draw."                 1960
    The man repelled thus, invents another way;
He wills the soldiers of the town these prisoners for to slay,
But they likewise replied, that they would not didstain*
The glory of their martial feats with fame* that they had slain
Poor, simple, naked men bound prostrate at their feet;              1965
"It is a service, sir," say they, "for soldiers far unmeet;
And therefore if you have this murder thus decreed,
Choose out some other men that list perform so hard a deed.
Yet if in rebel sort their banners were displayed,
To put them all unto the sword we would not be afraid.             1970
But now sith that we know no fault that they have done,
Let them, for us, proceed herein that have the same begun."
    Again refused thus, the man with fury bent*
For all the butchers of the town he straight his message sent;
To whom in savage sort his mind he did unfold,                     1975
And had them go and kill them all whom he had laid in hold.
These beastly butchers then no conscience made at all,
But with their bloody butchering knives like tigers they do fall
Upon these silly souls, in murder fiercely bent;*
Not like to men, but rather as some Furies had been sent           1980
From hell to stop the course of God's afflicted word,
So quickly did these hellhounds put these people to the sword.
Here some that prostrate were and did for mercy cry
And other some unto the Lord that lift their voices high,
They killed not, but did their hands cut off at first,             1985
And after chopped in savage sort with blood to quench their
    thirst;
Such shrieks and wailing cries from prisons did rebound
That every corner of the town might hear their woeful sound.
The mournful mothers wept whom nature did compel
To see these hounds before their face their loving babes to
    quell;                                                          1990

The tender infant does for help to father cry,
The woeful father cannot help his child before he die;
The husband to his wife, the friend to friend does call,
With heavy sighs lamenting this their most unhappy fall;
And they that strongest are, to weak do comfort give,                 1995
That so they may by sugred* words their fainting hearts
  relieve.
Of these captived souls such was the piteous plight,
That very Papists did lament to see this cruel sight;
And some that loved the Pope these dealings did detest,
Who for their credit did not think this rigour to be best;            2000
And many women of the town devoid of crime
With horror of this sudden feat, had child before their time,
For from the common gaol in sight of shining sun
The smoking blood, from street to street, with grief was seen
  to run.
But one amongst the rest, an old and aged man,                        2005
Called Francis Collute,* for his faith a lasting credit wan;*
To whom with bloody axe when butchers did resort,
Upon his sons with tears he fell and did them thus exhort:
"You know," quoth he, "my sons, what pain and tender care
Your loving father from your youth hath had for to prepare           2010
Your hearts to know the Lord, his truth to entertain,
Which far surmounteth fading wealth and hope of worldly
  gain.
Now is our harvest in, now must our fruit appear,
Now will the Lord require accompt* how we have lived here;
The final axe is laid to root of falling tree,                       2015
And how we have the truth embraced, the world forthwith
  must see.
Be strong, therefore, my sons, refuse not proffered death,
Which from the Lord is sent to be a trial of our faith.
But how should we be strong, when flesh does daily fall?
O Lord, increase our faith that we may come when thou dost
  call.                                                               2020
And from the Lord I know this butchering axe is sent,
Who Satan's sword hath loosed now no doubt for some
  intent;
This is no new device which Satan puts in ure,
For they that will embrace the truth of this shall still be sure,
For unto Truth belongs both fire, sword and rack,                    2025

And naked Truth hath always tied a whip unto her back.*
The ages that are past do yet declare the same,
Whose constant death for Christ, depaints* the glory of their
    name;
For as the silly sheep between the lion's jaws,
And like the meek and willing dove in goshawk's greedy
    paws,*                                                              2030
So is the present state of Christ's afflicted flock,
Who are content with Christ to lay their head unto the block.
Fear not therefore to taste this cup* of joyful pain,
That with the Lord in lasting joy we all may meet again;
Let nothing force your faith from Christ to go astray,                 2035
For I, your father, as your guide, will lead you first the way.
Our house hath held us all, one Christ hath been our joy,
This sweet and noble union let Satan not destroy,
And let us join in one this death for to embrace,
So joined with Christ we shall be sure with him to have a
    place.                                                              2040
I was not he that gave your use of lively breath,
I am not he that sets the time and order of your death;
It is the Lord alone, which will restore again
A better life, if for his law by death we suffer pain;
Come, let us gladly give our throats unto the knife,                   2045
And for our Christ let us rejoice to leave this wretched life.
And say you all with me, O Lord from these our bands*
Receive, we pray, our sinful souls into thy blessed hands,
And lend us, Lord, thy grace and mercy to the end;
Thy blessed help to come to thee, O Lord, of mercy send."             2050
    And this repeating oft, the butchers with their blade
Their bodies then with deadly wounds a bloody present*
    made;
Then joining on the ground, they clasped all in one
Where grovelling lay in folded arms the father with the son,
Which sudden heavy chance such woeful sight did give,                  2055
That just remorse of causeless death a flinty heart would
    grieve.
Thus hath this blessed man received a happy place;
The Lord grant us that be behind like portion of his grace.
                           Amen


[The next section of the poem describes the slaughter of the

Protestants in Angiers and describes the heroic farewell speech of the Protestant martyr Masson de Rivers* (2059–2164).]

*The judgement of the Lord against this bloody and perjured King of France, Charles the 9. Dilated\* by the sentence of God in the law against murder; by examples both out of the Scriptures, and other authors, concerning the horrible end that hath fallen upon wilful murderers; and lastly, the bloody death of this blood-sucking King himself.*

Now let us see the end of this perjured King,                              2165
And let us weigh in future time what fearful fruit did spring
From falsed faith. And first I briefly will repeat
The sentence of the mighty God 'gainst murder and deceit;
Then shall we plainly see how that in every land
The Lord according to his law with just revenging hand            2170
The bloody tyrants strikes, with all their faithless crew,
As by examples we may see of such as shall ensue.
Whoso saith God shall shed the blood of man in vain,
Shall with the shedding of his blood requite* the same again;
And he that by deceit his neighbour shall betray,                       2175
Or shall with guile presumptuously his brother seek to slay,
He shall not scape, although he to the altar fly,
But drawn forth he justly shall without all pity die.*
Such cursed bloody men God's plague does follow still,
For wicked King Abimelech,* who was content to kill                2180
His seventy brothers all the kingdom for to have,
From just revenge he could not long his cursed carcass save,
For from a woman's hand a millstone down was sent
From off a wall, which with the weight his brain pan all to-
    rent,*
And after by his page was thrust unto the heart                          2185
With sword, lest that a woman's stroke his glory should
    subvert.
As Tryphon* did entrap with face of friendly cheer
Good Jonathan, to whom he did a faithful friend appear,
So did he quickly feel the weight of falsed word,
Who shortly was by Simon slain, and justly put to sword.         2190
I read also of one, Aristobolus* by name,
Who has for murder left behind a black and bloody fame,

For first he did consent with famine for to pine
His mother, for because she would the kingdom not resign,
And also was content by death to make away                          2195
Antigonus his brother dear, which was his own decay,
For when the deed was done, he felt a present grief
In conscience for so cruel act, which then without relief
Did daily so torment his sore afflicted heart
That fresh remorse did often give new cause of greater smart;       2200
At length from grisly corse* his blood by piecemeal came,
For brother's blood from earth did call* his blood to quit the
    same,
And thus in fearful wise he yielded up his breath,
So was his fierce and wicked life repaid with worthy death.
Our Charles like unto this from God's revenging hand                2205
By bloody death repays the blood he shed within his land;
From ears, from nose, from mouth, from heart that was so
    stout,
From every part his blood was seen, where blood might issue
    out.
The man that would not yield when men did mercy crave,
For mercy cries unto the Lord, but mercy none can have;             2210
For he that will not help the poor when they doth call,
Shall call himself when he hath need, and not be heard at all;
The heart that was so proud, now feels the bitter pain,
Whereas he jested when he saw his faithful subjects slain;
The ears that would not hear the poor afflicted cry,                2215
But greedily to suck their blood would credit every lie,
With blood are stopped up that they shall hear no more,
Such heavy plagues for wicked men the Lord hath still in
    store;
The mouth that would not speak to do his brother good,
Instead of words doth vomit out the clots of filthy blood;          2220
The nose that did detest of truth the pleasant smell,
From filthy heart doth willingly the stinking blood expel.
So that we plainly see, that blood for blood does crave,
And he shall not escape that seeks his brother's blood to have.
Then cursed be the mouth and man* that did persuade                 2225
This wretched King that he was in a good and godly trade,
In that he did by guile the godly so allure,
And afterwards by treason did their wished death procure.
"Much like," said he, "you be to Lewes*, which heretofore
Said in the Latin that he knew one sentence and no more,            2230

Which was: "That he which truth in words will always bring,
And not dissemble, knoweth not the skill to be a King."
Nay, this was rather like the red and cruel reign
Of Mithridates,* who did cause of Romans to be slain
A hundred fifty thousand once by message that was sent, 2235
When outwardly there did appear nothing but friendship
  meant.
The King of Arragon,* like mate of cursed crew,
By like deceit in Sicill* once eight thousand Frenchmen slew.
To Philip* once, it was his ruin and his death
In that he often broke his oath and vow of plighted faith. 2240
Then happy is the man that timely can beware
Of Popish treason, which does seem great favour for to bear.
Now have you heard at large the chief of bruited broils
That lately for the truth hath been in France, my native soil.
The Lord grant England peace and mercy from above, 2245
That from the truth no trouble may their fixed heart remove;
With wished life and health, Lord, long preserve and keep
That noble queen, Elizabeth, chief pastor of thy sheep,*
And that she may find out and hunt with perfect hate
The Popish hearts of feigned friends before it be too late; 2250
And that in woeful France the troubles that we see,
To England for to shun the like, may now a warning be;
And where our wound is seen as yet so fresh to bleed,
Lord grant to England that they may in time take better heed.
   Now sith you do perceive of France the woeful case, 2255
Good sir, I pray you, give me leave to seek some other place,
I fear that I have stayed and charged* you too long,
In warping* forth these bloody broils in rude and rustic song.'
  'Not so, good friend, but if with me thou wilt remain,
I shall not think it any charge* nor count it any pain 2260
To hear and keep thee still: but if thou wilt depart,
For thy discourse take this reward, and thanks from friendly
  heart.
And so, my friend, farewell. Lord shield thee from annoy,
And grant us all that we may meet with Christ in perfect joy.'
            Amen

    *Lord Jesus Christ, the praise be thine,*
    *For blessing of this work of mine.*
                Anna Dowriche

## *Verity Portrayed by the French Pilgrim* *

From seat supernal* of celestial Jove*
   Descended TRUTH, devoid of worldly weed,*
And with the brightness of her beams she strove
   'Gainst Satan, Sin, and Adam's fleshly seed;
   Reproving wrongs, bewailing worldlings' need,      5
Who think they swim in wealth (blinded by guile),
Yet wanting TRUTH, are wretched, poor and vile.

The World reproved, in rage attempts her wrack,
   Satan assists, malicious men devise
Torments for TRUTH, bind scourges at her back,      10
   Exclaim against her with blasphemous cries,
   Condemning her, exalting earthly lies,
Yet no despair or pain can cause her cease,
She wounded, springs, bedecked with crown of Peace.

(1589)

# MARY SIDNEY

## [To Queen Elizabeth]*

Even now that care which on thy crown attends
And with thy happy greatness daily grows
Tells me, thrice-sacred Queen, my muse offends,
And of respect to thee the line out goes.*
One instant will or willing can she lose                    5
I say not reading, but receiving rhymes,
On whom in chief dependeth to dispose*
What Europe acts in these most active times?

Yet dare I so, as humbleness may dare,
Cherish some hope they shall acceptance find;             10
Now weighing less thy state, lighter thy care,
But knowing more thy grace, abler thy mind.
What heavenly powers thee highest throne assigned,
Assigned thee goodness suiting that degree,
And by thy strength thy burthen so designed,             15
To others toil is exercise to thee.

Cares though still great, cannot be greatest still.
Business must ebb, though leisure never flow;
Then these the posts* of duty and goodwill
Shall press* to offer what their senders owe,             20
Which once in two, now in one subject go,*
The poorer left, the richer reft* away,
Who better might (O might, ah word of woe*)
Have given for me what I for him defray.

How can I name whom sighing signs extend,                 25
And not unstop my tears' eternal spring?
But he did warp, I weaved this web* to end;
The stuff* not ours, our work no curious* thing,
Wherein yet well we thought the Psalmist King*
How English denizened,* though Hebrew born,               30
Would to thy music undispleased sing,
Oft having worse, without repining* worn;

And I the cloth in both our names present,
A livery robe to be bestowed by thee;
Small parcel* of the undischarged* rent,                          35
From which no pains nor payments can us free.
And yet enough to cause our neighbours see
We will our best, though scanted* in our will;
And those nigh fields where sown they favours be
Unwealthy do, not else unworthy till.*                            40

For in our work what bring we but thine own?
What English is, by many names is thine,
There humble laurels* in thy shadows grown
To garland others would themselves repine.
Thy breast the cabinet, thy seat* the shrine,                     45
Where muses hang their vowed memories;
Where wit, where art, where all that is divine
Conceived best, and best defended lies.

Which if men did not (as they do) confess,
And wronging worlds would otherwise consent.                      50
Yet here who minds* so meet* a patroness
For authors' state or writings' argument?
A King should only to a Queen be sent;
God's loved choice unto his chosen love;
Devotion to devotion's president;*                                55
What all applaud, to her whom none reprove.

And who sees ought, but sees how justly square*
His haughty ditties* to thy glorious days?
How well beseeming thee his triumphs* are?
His hope, his zeal, his prayer, plaint, and praise,               60
Needless thy person to their height to raise;
Less need to bend them down to thy degree;
These holy garments* each good soul assays,*
Some sorting all, all sort* to none but thee.

For even thy rule is painted* in his reign,                       65
Both clear in right; both nigh by wrong oppressed;*
And each at length (man crossing God in vain)
Possessed of place, and each in peace possessed.
Proud Philistines* did interrupt his rest,

The foes of heaven no less have been thy foes;                 70
He with great conquest, thou with greater blessed;
Thou sure to win, and he secure to lose.

Thus hand in hand with him thy glories walk;
But who can trace them where alone they go?
Of thee who hemispheres on honour talk,                        75
And lands and seas thy trophies jointly show.
The very winds did on thy party blow,
And rocks in arms thy foemen eft* defy.
But soft, my muse, thy pitch* is earthly love;*
Forbear this heaven where only eagles fly.                     80

Kings on a Queen enforced their states to lay,*
Mainlands for empire waiting on an isle;
Men drawn by worth a woman to obey;
One moving all, herself unmoved the while;
Truth's restitution,* vanity exile,                            85
Wealth sprung of want, war held without annoy,
Let subject be of some inspired style,
Till then the object of her subjects' joy.

Thy* utmost can but offer to her sight
Her handmaids' task, which most her will endears;              90
And pray unto thy pains life from that light
Which lively light some, court and kingdom cheers,
What wish she may (far past her living peers
And rival still to Juda's faithful king*)
In more than he and more triumphant years,                     95
Sing what God doth, and do what men may sing.

                                            (c. 1599)


## To the Angel Spirit of the Most
## Excellent Sir Philip Sidney*

To thee, pure sprite, to thee alone's addressed
    This coupled work, by double interest thine:
    First raised by thy blessed hand, and what is mine
Inspired by thee, thy secret power impressed.
    So dared my Muse with thine itself combine,               5
    As mortal stuff* with that which is divine:
Thy lightning beams give lustre to the rest

That heaven's King may deign his own transformed
    In substance,* no, but superficial tire*
    By thee put on: to praise, not to aspire        10
To those high tones, so in themselves adorned,
    Which angels sing in their celestial choir;
    And all of tongues with soul and voice admire
These sacred hymns by kingly prophet formed.

Oh, had that soul, which Honour brought to rest,     15
    Too soon not left and reft* the world of all
    What man could show (which we Perfection call),
This half-maimed piece had sorted with the best.
    Deep wounds enlarged, long festered in their gall,
    Fresh-bleeding smart: not eye but heart tears fall:    20
Ah, memory, what needs this new arrest?

Yet here behold (oh wert thou to behold!)
    This finished now thy matchless Muse begun –
    The rest but pieced, as left by thee undone.
Pardon, O blessed soul, presumption too, too bold:    25
    If love and zeal such error ill become,
    'Tis zealous love, love which hath never done,
Nor can enough in world of words unfold.

And sith* it hath no further scope to go,
    Nor other purpose but to honour thee,        30
    Thee in thy works where all the graces be
(As little streams with all their all do flow
    To their great sea, due tribute's grateful fee)
    So press my thoughts, my burthened thoughts, in me
To pay the debt of infinites I owe        35

To thy great worth: exceeding Nature's store,
    Wonder of men, sole-born Perfection's kind,
    Phoenix* thou wert; so rare thy fairest mind
Heavenly-adorned, Earth justly might adore,
    Where truthful praise in highest glory shined:    40
    For there alone was praise to truth confined,
And where but there to live for evermore?

Oh! when to this accompt, this cast-up sum,
    This reckoning* made, this audit of my woe,
    I call my thoughts, whence so strange passions* flow,    45

How works my heart, my senses stricken dumb,
    That would thee more than ever heart could show!
    And all too short: who knew thee best doth know
There lives no wit that may thy praise become.

Truth I invoke (who scorn elsewhere to move,          50
    Or here in aught my blood should partialise),
    Truth, sacred Truth, thee sole to solemnise
Those precious rites well known best minds approve;
    And who but doth hath Wisdom's open eyes
    (Not owly blind the fairest light still flies)        55
Confirm no less? At least 'tis sealed above,*

Where thou art fixed among thy fellow lights:*
    My day put out, my life in darkness cast,
    Thy angel's soul with highest angels placed
There blessed sings, enjoying heaven-delights,       60
    Thy Maker's praise; as far from earthly taste
    As here thy works, so worthily embraced
By all of worth, where never Envy bites.

As goodly buildings to some glorious end,
    Cut off by Fate before the Graces had          65
    Each wondrous part in all their beauties clad
(Yet so much done as art could not amend):
    So thy rare works (to which no wit can add)
    In all men's eyes which are not blindly mad
Beyond compare above all praise extend.          70

Immortal monuments of thy fair fame
    (Though not complete, nor in the reach of thought),
    How on that passing piece Time would have wrought
Had heaven so spared the life of life to frame
    The rest? But ah! such loss hath this world aught    75
    Can equal it? or which like grievance brought?
Yet there will live thy ever-praised name,

To which these dearest offerings of my heart
    (Dissolved to ink, while pen's impressions move
    The bleeding veins of never-dying love)        80
I render here: these wounding lines of smart,
    Sad characters indeed of simple love
    (Not art nor skill which abler wits do prove)
Of my full soul receive the meanest part.

Receive these hymns, these obsequies receive.　　　　　85
　　If any mark of thy sweet sprite appear
　　Well are they born, no title else shall bear.
I can no more. Dear soul, I take my leave:
　　Sorrow still strives, would mount thy highest sphere
　　Presuming so just cause might meet thee there.　　　90
Oh happy change, could I so take my leave!

　　　　　　　　　　　　　　By the sister of that
　　　　　　　　　　　　　　incomparable Sidney
　　　　　　　　　　　　　　　(c. 1599)

## A Dialogue Between Two Shepherds, Thenot and Piers, in Praise of Astraea*

THENOT　I sing divine Astraea's praise,
　　O Muses!* Help my wits to raise
　　And heave my verses higher.
PIERS　Thou needst the truth but plainly* tell,
　　Which much I doubt thou canst not well,　　　　　5
　　Thou art so oft a liar.

THENOT　If in my song no more I show
　　Than heav'n, and earth, and sea do know,
　　Then truly I have spoken.
PIERS　Sufficeth not no more to name,　　　　　　　10
　　But being no less, the like, the same,
　　Else laws of truth be broken.

THENOT　Then say, she is so good, so fair,
　　With all the earth she may compare,
　　Not Momus'* self denying.　　　　　　　　　　15
PIERS　Compare may think where likeness holds,
　　Nought like to her the earth enfolds –
　　I looked to find you lying.

THENOT　Astraea sees with wisdom's sight,
　　Astraea works by virtue's might,　　　　　　　20
　　And jointly both do stay in her.
PIERS　Nay, take from them her hand, her mind;
　　The one is lame, the other* blind.
　　Shall still your lying stain her?

THENOT   Soon as Astraea shows her face,         25
      Straight every ill avoids the place,
        And every good aboundeth.
PIERS   Nay, long before her face doth show,
      The last doth come, the first doth go.
        How loud this lie resoundeth!         30

THENOT   Astraea is our chiefest joy,
      Our chiefest guard against annoy,
        Our chiefest wealth, our treasure.
PIERS   Where chiefest are, three others be,
      To us none else but only she.         35
        When wilt thou speak in measure?*

THENOT   Astraea may be justly said
      A field in flow'ry robe arrayed,
        In season freshly springing.
PIERS   That spring endures but shortest time,         40
      This never leaves Astraea's clime.*
        Thou liest, instead of singing.

THENOT   As heavenly light that guides the day,
      Right so doth thine each lovely ray
        That from Astraea flyeth.         45
PIERS   Nay, darkness oft that light enclouds,
      Astraea's beams no darkness shrouds.
        How loudly Thenot lieth!

THENOT   Astraea rightly term I may
      A manly palm, a maiden bay,*         50
        Her verdure* never dying.
PIERS   Palm oft is crooked, bay is low,
      She still upright, still high doth grow.
        Good Thenot leave thy lying.

THENOT   Then Piers, of friendship, tell me why         55
      My meaning true, my words should lie,
        And strive in vain to raise her?
PIERS   Words from conceit* do only rise,
      Above conceit her honour flies;
        But silence,* nought can praise her.         60

(1599)

# The Tragedy of Antonie*

## I*

ANTONIUS*

Since cruel heaven's against me obstinate;
Since all mishaps of the round engine* do
Conspire my harm; since men, since powers divine,
Air, earth, and sea, are all injurious;
And that my queen herself, in whom I lived,                    5
The idol of my heart, doth me pursue:
It's meet* I die. For her have I forgone
My country, Caesar unto war provoked
(For just revenge of sister's wrong, my wife,*
Who moved my queen – ah me! – to jealousy),                   10
For love of her, in her allurements caught,
Abandoned life. I honour have despised,
Disdained my friends, and of the stately Rome
Despoiled the empire of her best attire,
Contemned that power that made me so much feared;             15
A slave become unto her feeble face.
O cruel traitress, woman most unkind,
Thou dost, forsworn, my love and life betray,
And giv'st me up to rageful enemy,
Which soon (o fool!) will plague thy perjury.                 20
    Yielded Pelusium* on this country's shore,
Yielded thou hast my ships and men of war,
That nought remains (so destitute am I)
But these same arms which on my back I wear.
Thou should'st have had them too, and me unarmed              25
Yielded to Caesar naked of defence,
Which while I bear let Caesar never think
Triumph of me shall his proud chariot grace,
Nor think with me his glory to adorn,
On me alive to use his victory.                               30
    Thou only Cleopatra triumph hast,
Thou only hast my freedom servile made,
Thou only hast me vanquished; not by force
(For forced I cannot be) but by sweet baits*
Of thy eyes' graces, which did gain so fast                   35
Upon my liberty, that nought remained.
None else henceforth, but thou my dearest queen,
Shall glory in commanding Antonie.

Have Caesar fortune, and the gods his friends
To him have love, and fatal sisters* given                    40
The sceptre of the earth; he never shall
Subject my life to his obedience.
But when that death, my glad refuge, shall have
Bounded the course of my unsteadfast life,
And frozen corpse under a marble cold                         45
Within tomb's bosom, widow of my soul;
Then at his will let him it subject make,
Then what he will let Caesar do with me,
Make me limb after limb be rent, make me,
My burial take in sides of Thracian wolf.*                    50
    Poor Antonie! Alas what was the day,
The days of loss, that gained thee thy love
(Wretch Antonie), since Megaera* pale
With snaky hairs enchained thy misery?
The fire thee burnt was never Cupid's fire*                   55
(For Cupid bears not such a mortal brand),
It was some Fury's torch, Orestes'* torch,
Which sometimes burnt his mother-murdering soul
(When wandering mad, rage boiling in his blood,
He fled his fault which followed as he fled),                 60
Kindled within his bones by shadow pale
Of mother slain returned from Stygian* lake.
    Antony, poor Antony! Since that day
Thy old good hap did far from thee retire,
Thy virtue dead, thy glory made alive                         65
So oft by martial deeds is gone in smoke.
Since then the bays,* so well thy forehead knew,
To Venus' myrtles* yielded have their place;
Trumpets to pipes; field tents to courtly bowers;
Lances and pikes to dances and to feasts.                     70
Since then, o wretch, instead of bloody wars
Thou should'st have made upon the Parthian kings
For Roman honour filed* by Crassus'* foil,*
Thou threw'st thy cuirass* off, and fearful helm,
With coward-courage unto Egypt's queen                        75
In haste to run, about her neck to hang,
Languishing in her arms, thy idol make:
In sum, given up to Cleopatra's eyes.
Thou breakest at length from thence, as one encharmed
Breaks from th'enchanter that him strongly held.              80

For thy first reason (spoiling of their force,
The poisoned cups of thy fair sorceress)
Recured* thy spirit; and then, on every side
Thou mad'st again the earth with soldiers swarm!
All Asia hid; Euphrates'* banks do tremble                    85
To see at once so many Romans there;
Breath horror, rage, and, with a threatening eye,
In mighty squadrons cross his swelling streams.
Nought seen but horse and fiery sparkling arms;
Nought heard but hideous noise of muttering troops.          90
The Parth, the Mede,* abandoning their goods
Hide them for fear in hills of Hyrcanie:*
Redoubting thee. Then willing to besiege
The great Phraate,* head of Media,
Thou camped'st at her walls with vain assault,               95
Thy engines* fit (mishap!) not thither brought.
    So long thou stay'st, so long thou dost thee rest,
So long thy love, with such things nourished,
Reframes, reforms itself, and stealingly
Retakes his force and rebecomes more great.                  100
For of thy queen, the looks, the grace, the words,
Sweetness, allurements, amorous delights,
Entered again thy soul; and day and night,
In watch, in sleep, her image followed thee;
Not dreaming but of her, repenting still                     105
That thou for war had'st such a goddess left.
    That thou car'st no more for Parth, nor Parthian bow,
Sallies, assaults, encounters, shocks, alarms,
For ditches, ramparts, wards, entrenched grounds:
Thy only care is sight of Nilus'* streams,                   110
Sight of that face whose guileful semblant doth
(Wandering in thee) infect thy tainted heart.
Her absence thee besots; each hour, each hour
Of stay, to thee impatient seems an age.
Enough of conquest, praise thou deem'st enough,              115
If soon enough the bristled* fields thou see
Of fruitful Egypt and the stranger flood,
Thy queen's fair eyes', another Pharos',* lights.
    Returned low, dishonoured, despised,
In wanton love a woman thee misleads,                        120
Sunk in foul sink. Meanwhile respecting nought
Thy wife Octavia and her tender babes,

Of whom, the long contempt against thee whets
The sword of Caesar, now thy lord become.
   Lost thy great empire, all those goodly towns     125
Reverenced thy name, as rebels now thee leave,
Rise against thee, and to the ensigns flock
Of conquering Caesar, who enwalls thee round,
Caged in thy hold, scarce master of thyself;
Late master of so many nations.     130
   Yet, yet, which is of grief extremest grief?
Which is yet of mischief highest mischief?
It's Cleopatra alas! Alas, it's she;
It's she augments the torment of thy pain,
Betrays thy love, thy life alas betrays,     135
Caesar to please, whose grace she seeks to gain;*
With thought her crown to save and fortune make,
Only thy foe, which common ought have been.
   If I her always loved, and the first flame
Of her heart-killing love shall burn me last,     140
Justly complain I she disloyal is;
Not constant is, even as I constant am;
To comfort my mishap, despising me
No more than when the heavens favoured me.
   But ah, by nature women wavering are;     145
Each moment changing and rechanging minds;
Unwise who, blind in them, thinks loyalty
Ever to find in beauty's company.*

2 *

CLEOPATRA

That I have thee betrayed, dear Antonie,
My life, my soul, my sun? I, had such thought?
That I have thee betrayed my lord, my king?
That I would break my vowed-faith to thee?
Leave thee? Deceive thee? Yield thee to the rage     5
Of mighty foe? I ever had that heart?
Rather sharp lightning 'lighten* on my head;
Rather may I to deepest mischief fall;
Rather the opened earth devour me;
Rather fierce tigers feed them on my flesh;     10
Rather, o rather let our Nilus send,
To swallow me quick, some weeping crocodile.
   And did'st thou then suppose my royal heart

Had hatched, thee to ensnare, a faithless love?
And changing mind, as Fortune changed cheer,                    15
I would weak thee, to win the stronger, lose?
O wretch! O caitiff! O too cruel hap!*
And did not I sufficient loss sustain
Losing my realm, losing my liberty,
My tender offspring, and the joyful light                        20
Of beamy sun, and yet, yet losing more;
Thee Antony, my care, if I lose not,
What yet remained? Thy love, alas! Thy love,
More dear than sceptre, children, freedom, light.
    So ready I to row in Charon's barge*                         25
Shall lose the joy of dying in thy love,
So the sole comfort of my misery,
To have one tomb with thee is me bereft
So I in shady plains shall 'plain* alone,
Not (as I hoped) companion of thy moan.                          30
O height of grief.

3*

CLEOPATRA
O Goddess, thou whom Cyprus doth adore,
Venus of Paphos,* bent to work us harm
For old Iulus' brood, if thou take care
Of Caesar, why of us tak'st thou no care?
Antonie did descend, as well as he,                               5
From thine own son by long enchained line;
And might have ruled, by one and self same fate
True Trojan blood, the stately Roman state.
    Antonie, poor Antonie, my dear soul,
Now but a block,* the booty of a tomb,                            10
Thy life, thy heat is lost, thy colour gone,
And hideous paleness on thy face hath seized.
Thy eyes, two suns, the lodging place of love,
Which yet for tents to warlike Mars did serve,
Locked up in lids (as fair day's cheerful light,                 15
Which darkness flies) do winking hide in night.
    Antonie by our true loves I thee beseech –
And by our hearts' sweet sparks have set on fire
Our holy marriage, and the tender ruth*
Of our dear babes, knot of our amity* –                          20
My doleful voice thy ear let entertain,

And take me with thee to the hellish plain,
Thy wife, thy friend. Hear Antonie, O hear
My sobbing sighs, if here thou be, or there.
   Lived thus long, the winged race of years    25
Ended I have as destiny decreed,
Flourished and reigned, and taken just revenge
Of him who me both hated and despised.*
Happy, alas too happy – if of Rome
Only the fleet had hither never come.    30
And now of me an image great shall go
Under the earth to bury there my woe.
What say I? Where am I? O Cleopatra,
Poor Cleopatra, grief thy reason reaves.
No, no, most happy in this hapless case,    35
To die with thee, and dying thee embrace;
My body joined with thine, my mouth with thine,
My mouth, whose moisture-burning sighs have dried
To be in one self tomb, and one self chest,
And wrapped with thee in one self sheet to rest.    40
   The sharpest torment in my heart I feel,
Is that I stay from thee, my heart, this while;
Die will I straight now, now straight will I die,
And straight with thee a wandering shade will be,
Under the cypress trees thou haunt'st alone,    45
Where brooks of hell do falling seem to moan.*
But yet I stay, and yet thee overlive,
That ere I die due rites I may thee give.
   A thousand sobs I from my breast will tear,
With thousand plaints* thy funerals adorn;    50
My hair shall serve for thy oblations;
My boiling tears for thy effusions;
Mine eyes thy fire, for out of them the flame
(Which burnt thy heart on me enamoured) came.
   Weep my companions, weep, and from your eyes    55
Rain down on him of tears a brinish* stream.
Mine can no more, consumed by the coals
Which from my breast, as from a furnace, rise.
Martyr your breasts with multiplied blows,
With violent hands tear off your hanging hair,    60
Outrage your face. Alas, why should we seek
(Since now we die) our beauties more to keep?
   I spent in tears, not able more to spend,

But kiss him now, what rests me more to do?
Then let me kiss you, you fair eyes, my light,          65
Front seat of honour, face most fierce, most faire!
O neck, O arms, O hands, O breast where death
(O mischief) comes to choke up vital breath.
A thousand kisses, thousand, thousand more
Let you my mouth for honour's farewell give,          70
That in this office weak my limbs may grow,
Fainting on you, and forth my soul may flow.

(1595)


## The Psalms*

### PSALM 45*

My heart indites* an argument of worth,
    The praise of him that doth the sceptre sway:
My tongue the pen to paint his praises forth,
    Shall write as swift as swiftest writer may.
    Then to the king these are the words I say:          5
Fairer art thou than sons of mortal race:
    Because high God hath blessed thee for aye,
Thy lips, as springs, do flow with speaking grace.

Thy honour's sword gird* to this mighty side,
    O thou that dost all things in might excel:          10
With glory prosper, on with triumph ride,
    Since justice, truth, and meekness with thee dwell.
    So that right hand of thine shall teaching tell
Such things to thee, as well may terror bring,
    And terror such, as never erst* befell          15
To mortal mind at sight of mortal king.

Sharp are thy shafts to cleave their hearts in twain
    Whose heads do cast* thy conquests to withstand,
Good cause to make the meaner people fain*
    With willing hearts to undergo thy hand.          20
    Thy throne O God, doth never-falling stand:
Thy sceptre ensign* of thy kingly might,
    To righteousness is linked with such a band,
That righteous hand still holds thy sceptre right.

Justice in love, in hate thou holdest wrong,* 25
  This makes that God, who so doth hate and love:
Glad-making oil, that oil on thee hath flong,*
  Which thee exalts thine equals far above.
  The fragrant riches of Sabean* grove
Myrrh, aloes, cassia,* all thy robes do smell: 30
  When thou from ivory palace dost remove
Thy breathing odours all thy train excel.

Daughters of kings among thy courtly band,
  By honouring thee of thee do honour hold:
On thy right side thy dearest Queen doth stand 35
  Richly arrayed in cloth of Ophir* gold.
  O daughter hear what now to thee is told:
Mark what thou hear'st, and what thou mark'st obey
  Forget to keep in memory enrold*
The house, and folk, where first thou sawst the day. 40

So in the king, thy king, a dear delight
  Thy beauty shall both breed, and bred, maintain:
For only he on thee hath lordly right,
  Him only thou with awe must entertain.
  Then unto thee both Tyrus* shall be fain* 45
Presents present, and richest nations moe,*
  With humble suit thy royal grace to gain,
To thee shall do such homage as they owe.

This Queen that can a king her father call,
  Doth only she in upper garment shine? 50
Nay underclothes, and what she weareth all,
  Gold is the stuff, the fashion art divine;
  Brought to the king in robe embroidered fine,
Her maids of honour shall on her attend*
  With such, to whom more favour shall assign 55
In nearer place their happy days to spend.

Brought shall they be with mirth and marriage joy
  And enter so the palace of the king:
Then let no grief thy mind, O Queen, annoy,
  Nor parents left thy sad remembrance sting. 60
  Instead of parents, children thou shalt bring
Of partadg'd* earth the kings and lords to be;
  Myself* thy name in lasting verse will sing.
The world shall make no end of thanks to thee.

## PSALM 50*

The mighty God, the ever-living lord,
    All nations from earth's uttermost confines
Summoneth by his pursuivant,* his word,
    And out of beauty's beauty, Zion shines.
God comes, he comes with ear and tongue restored,        5
    His guard huge storms, hot flames his ushers go;
And called, their appearance to record,
    Heav'n hasteth from above, earth from below.

He sits his people's judge and thus commands:
    'Gather me hither that beloved line,        10
Whom solemn sacrifices, holy bands,*
    Did in eternal league with me combine
Then when the heav'ns subsigned* with their hands,
    That God in justice eminently reigns,
Controlling so, as nothing countermands        15
    What once decreed, his sacred doom contains.

You then, my folk, to me your God attend;
    Hark, Israel, and hear thy people's blame:
Nor want of sacrifice doth me offend,
    Nor do I miss thy altar's daily flame;        20
To me thy stall no fatted bull shall send.
    Should I exact one he-goat from thy fold,
I that as far as hills, woods, fields extend,
    All birds and beasts in known possession hold?

Suppose me hungry; yet to beg thy meat        25
    I would not tell thee that I hungry were;
Myself may take: what needs me then entreat,
    Since earth is mine and all that earth doth bear?
But do I long the brawny flesh* to eat
    Of that dull beast that serves the ploughman's need?    30
Or do I thirst, to quench my thirsty heat,
    In what the throats of bearded cattle* bleed?

Oh no: bring God of praise a sacrifice,
    Thy vowed debts unto the highest pay;
Invoke my name, to me erect thy cries,        35
    Thy praying plaints, when sorrow stops thy way.
I will undo the knot that anguish ties,
    And thou at peace shalt glorify my name'.
Mildly the good, God schooleth in this wise,
    But this sharp check doth to the godless frame:    40

'How fits it thee my statutes to report,
    And of my covenant in thy talk to prate,*
Hating to live in right-reformed sort,
    And leaving in neglect what I relate?*
See'st thou a thief? thou grow'st of his consort;*     45
    Dost with adult'rers to adult'ry go?
Thy mouth is slander's ever-open port,
    And from thy tongue doth nought but treason flow.

Nay, ev'n thy brother thy rebukes disgrace,
    And thou in spite defam'st thy mother's son;     50
And for I wink* a while, thy thoughts embrace:*
    "God is like me, and doth as I have done."
But lo, thou see'st I march another pace
    And come with truth thy falsehood to disclose;
Thy sin, revived, upbraids thy blushing face,     55
    Which thou long dead in silence didst suppose.

Oh lay up this in marking* memory,
    You that are wont God's judgements to forget:
In vain to others for release you fly
    If once on you I griping fingers set.     60
And know the rest: my dearest worship I
    In sweet perfume of offered praise do place;
And who directs his goings orderly,
    By my conduct shall see God's saving grace.'

### PSALM 52*

Tyrant, why swell'st* thou thus
    Of mischief vaunting,*
Since help from God to us
    Is never wanting?*

Lewd* lies thy tongue contrives,     5
    Loud lies it soundeth;
Sharper than sharpest knives
    With lies it woundeth.

Falsehood thy wit approves,
    All truth rejected;     10
Thy will all vices loves,
    Virtue neglected.

Not words from cursed thee
   But gulfs* are poured;
Gulfs wherein daily be                          15
   Good men devoured.

Think'st thou to bear it so?
   God shall displace thee;
God shall thee overthrow,
   Crush thee, deface thee.              20

The just shall fearing see
   These fearful chances,
And laughing shoot at thee
   With scornful glances.

Lo, lo, the wretched wight*                      25
   Who God disdaining,
His mischief made his might,
   His guard* his gaining.

I as an olive tree*
   Still green shall flourish;            30
God's house the soil shall be
   My roots to nourish.

My trust on his true love
   Truly attending,
Shall never thence remove,                       35
   Never see ending.

Thee will I honour still,
   Lord, for this justice;
There fix my hopes I will
   Where thy saints' trust is.            40

Thy saints trust in thy name,
   Therein they joy them;
Protected by the same,
   Nought can annoy them.

### PSALM 53*

'There is no God,' the fool doth say,
   If not in word, in thought and will:
This fancy* rotten deeds bewray,*
   And studies fixed on loathsome ill.
   Not one doth good: from heav'nly hill,    5

Jehova's eye one wiser mind
Could not discern, that held the way
To understand, and God to find.

They all have stray'd, are cankered* all:
    Not one I say, not one doth good.               10
But senselessness,* what should I call
    Such carriage* of this cursed brood?
    My people are their bread, their food,
Upon my name they scorn to cry:
Whom vain* affright doth yet appal,               15
Where no just ground of fear doth lie.

But on their bones shall wreaked be
    All thy invader's force and guile,
In vile* confusion cast by thee,
    For God himself shall make them vile.         20
    Ah! why delays that happy while
When Zion shall our saver bring?
The Lord his folk will one day free:
Then Jacob's house* shall dance and sing.

### PSALM 58*

And call ye this to utter what is just,
    You* that of justice hold the sov'reign throne?
And call ye this to yield, O sons of dust,
    To wronged brethren every man his own?
Oh no: it is your long* malicious will          5
    Now to the world to make by practice known,
With whose oppression you the balance* fill,
    Just to yourselves, indifferent* else to none.

But what could they, who ev'n in birth declined
    From truth and right to lies and injuries?*       10
To show the venom of their cankered mind
    The adder's image scarcely can suffice;
Nay scarce the aspic* may with them contend,
    On whom the charmer all in vain applies
His skilfull'st spells, aye missing of his end,       15
    While she self-deaf* and unaffected lies.

Lord crack their teeth, Lord crush these lions' jaws,
    So let them sink as water in the sand;
When deadly bow their aiming fury draws,

Shiver the shaft ere past the shooter's hand.                    20
So make them melt as the dishoused* snail,
   Or as the embryo, whose vital band*
Breaks ere it holds, and formless eyes do fail
   To see the sun, though brought to lightful land.

O let their brood, a brood of springing thorns,*          25
   Be by untimely* rooting overthrown
Ere bushes waxed, they push with pricking thorns,
   As fruits yet green are oft by tempest blown.
The good with gladness this revenge shall see
   And bathe his feet in blood of wicked one,          30
While all shall say: 'The just rewarded be;
   There is a God that carves to each his own'.*

PSALM 59*

Save me from such as me assail;
   Let not my foes,
O God, against my life prevail;
   Save me from those
Who make a trade of cursed wrong               5
And, bred in blood, for blood do long.

Of these one sort do seek by slight
   My overthrow;
The stronger part with open might
   Against me go;                                    10
And yet, thou God, my witness be,
From all offence my soul is free.

But what if I from fault am free?
   Yet they are bent
To band* and stand against poor me,               15
   Poor innocent.
Rise, God, and see how these things go,
And rescue me from instant woe.

Rise, God of armies, mighty God
   Of Israel;                                        20
Look on them all who spread abroad
   On earth do dwell,
And let thy hand no longer spare
Such as of wicked malice are.

When golden sun in west doth set,                    25
  Returned again
As hounds that howl their food to get,
  They run amain*
The city through from street to street,
With hungry maw* some prey to meet.                  30

Night elder grown,* their fittest day,
  They babbling prate,
How my lost life extinguish may
  Their deadly hate.
They prate and babble void of fear,                  35
For, 'Tush,' say they, 'who now can hear?'

Ev'n thou canst hear, and hearing, scorn
  All that they say;
For them (if not by thee upborne)
  What props do stay?*                         40
Then will I, as they wait for me,
O God my fortress, wait on thee.

Thou ever me with thy free grace
  Prevented hast;*
With thee my prayer shall take place                 45
  Ere from me past,
And I shall see who me do hate,
Beyond my wish, in woeful state.

For fear my people it forget,
  Slay not outright,                           50
But scatter them and so them set
  In open sight,
That by thy might they may be known
Disgraced, debased, and overthrown.

No witness of their wickedness                        55
  I need produce
But their own lips, fit to express
  Each vile abuse:
In cursing proud, proud when they lie,
O let them dear such pride abuy.*                     60

At length in rage consume them so
  That naught remain;
Let them all, being quite forego,*
  And make it plain

That God, who Jacob's rule upholds,    65
Rules all all-bearing earth enfolds.

Now thus they fare: when sun doth set,
  Returned again
As hounds that howl their food to get,
  They run amain    70
The city through from street to street,
With hungry maws some prey to meet.

Abroad they range and hunt apace
  Now that, now this,
As famine trails a hungry trace;*    75
  And though they miss,
Yet will they not to kennel hie,
But all the night at bay* will lie.

But I will of thy goodness sing,
  And of thy might,    80
When early sun again shall bring
  His cheerful light;
For thou, my refuge, and my fort,
In all distress dost me support.

My strength doth of thy strength depend;    85
  To thee I sing:*
Thou art my fort, me to defend;
  My God, my King,
To thee I owe, and thy free grace,
That free I rest in fearless place.    90

### PSALM 63 *

O God, the God where all my forces lie
  How do I hunt for thee with early haste!
How is for thee my spirit thirsty dry!
  How gasps my soul for thy refreshing taste!
  Witness this waterless, this weary waste:    5
Whence, O that I again transfer'd might be,
Thy glorious might in sacred place to see.

Then on thy praise would I my lips employ,
  With whose kind mercies nothing may contend;
No, not this life itself, whose care and joy    10
  In praying voice, and lifted hands should end.
  This to my soul should such a banquet send,

That, sweetly fed, my mouth should sing thy name
In gladdest notes contented mirth could frame.

And lo, ev'n here I mind thee in my bed,                    15
    And interrupt my sleeps with nightly thought,
How thou hast been the target of* my head,
    How thy wings' shadow hath my safety wrought.
    And, though my body from thy view be brought,
Yet fixed on thee my loving soul remains,                   20
Whose right right hand from falling, me retains.

But such* as seek my life to ruinate,
    Them shall the earth in deepest gulf* receive.
First murdering blade shall end their living date,*
    And then their flesh to teeth of foxes leave;          25
    As for the king, the king shall then conceive
High joy in God, and that God adore,
When lying mouths shall, stopped, lie no more.

PSALM 72*

Teach the king's son, who king himself shall be,
    Thy judgments Lord, thy justice make him learn:
To rule thy realm as justice shall decree,
    And poor men's right in judgment to discern.
        Then fearless peace,                                5
        With rich increase
    The mountain's proud shall fill:
        And justice shall
        Make plenty fall
    On ev'ry humble hill.                                   10

Make him the weak support, th'oppressed relieve,*
    Supply the poor, the quarrel-pickers quail:
So ageless ages shall thee reverence give,
    Till eyes of heav'n, the sun and moon, shall fail,
        And thou again                                      15
        Shalt blessings rain,
    Which down shall mildly flow,
        As showers thrown
        On meads* new mown
    Whereby they freshly grow.                              20

During his rule the just shall ay* be green,
    And peaceful plenty join with plenteous peace:

While of sad night the many-formed queen*
  Decreas'd, shall grow, and grown again, decrease.
            From sea to sea                                    25
            He shall survey
        All kingdoms as his own:
            And from the trace*
            Of Physon's race*
        As far as land is known.                               30

The desert-dwellers at his beck shall bend:
  His foes them suppliant at his feet shall fling:
The kings of Tharsis* homage-gifts shall send;
  So Seba, Saba,* ev'ry island king.
            Nay all, ev'n all                                  35
            Shall prostrate fall,
        That crowns and sceptres wear:
            And all that stand
            At their command,
        That crowns and sceptres bear.                         40

For he shall hear the poor when they complain,
  And lend them help, who helpless are oppressed:
His mercy shall the needy sort sustain;
  His force shall free their lives that live distressed.
            From hidden sleight,*                              45
            From open might,
        He shall their souls redeem:
            His tender eyes
            Shall highly prize,
        And dear their blood esteem.                           50

So shall he long, so shall he happy live;
  Health shall abound, and wealth shall never want:
They gold to him, Arabia gold, shall give,
  Which scantness dear, and dearness maketh scant.*
            They still shall pray                              55
            That still he may
        So live, and flourish so:
            Without his praise
            No nights, no days,
        Shall passport* have to go.                            60

Look how the woods, where interlaced* trees
  Spread friendly arms each other to embrace,

Join at the head, though distant at the knees,
　　Waving with wind, and lording on the place:
　　　　So woods of corn                                    65
　　　　By mountains born
　　　Shall on their shoulders wave:
　　　　And men shall pass
　　　　The numbrous* grass,
　　Such store each town shall have.                        70

Look how the sun, so shall his name remain;
　　As that in light, so this in glory one:
All glories that, at this all lights shall stain:*
　　Nor that shall fail, nor this be overthrown.
　　　　The dwellers all                                     75
　　　　Of earthly ball*
　　　In him shall hold them blest:
　　　　As one that is
　　　　Of perfect bliss
　　A pattern to the rest.                                  80

O God, who art, from whom all beings be;
　　Eternal Lord, whom Jacob's stock* adore,
And wondrous works are done by only thee,
　　Blessed be thou, most blessed evermore.
　　　　And let thy name,                                    85
　　　　Thy glorious fame,
　　　No end of blessing know:
　　　　Let all this round*
　　　　Thy honour sound,
　　So Lord, O* be it so.                                   90

### PSALM 73*

It is most true* that God to Israel
　　(I mean to men of undefiled hearts)
　　Is only good, and nought but good imparts.
Most true, I see, albe* almost I fell
　　From right conceit* into a crooked mind,              5
　　And from this truth with straying steps declined.*
For lo, my boiling breast did chafe and swell
　　When first I saw the wicked proudly stand,
　　Prevailing still in all they took in hand,
And sure no sickness dwelleth where they dwell;         10
　　Nay, so they guarded are with health and might,
　　It seems of them death dares not claim his right.

They seem as privileged from others' pain:
   The scouring plagues which on their neighbours fall
   Torment not them, nay touch them not at all.         15
Therefore with pride, as with a gorgeous chain,
   Their swelling necks encompassed they bear,
   All clothed in wrong, as if a robe it were;
So fat become, that fatness doth constrain
   Their eyes to swell; and if they think on aught,*     20
   Their thought they have, yea have beyond their thought.
They wanton* grow, and, in malicious vein,
   Talking of wrong, pronounce as from the skies,
   So high a pitch* their proud presumption flies.

Nay, heav'n itself, high heav'n escapes not free     25
   From their base mouths; and in their common talk
   Their tongues no less than all the earth do walk.
Wherefore ev'n godly men, when so they see
   Their horn of plenty* freshly flowing still,
   Leaning to them, bend from their better will;     30
And thus they* reasons frame: 'How can it be
   That God doth understand? that he doth know,
   Who sits in heav'n, how earthly matters go?'
See here the godless crew, while godly we
   Unhappy pine,* all happiness possess:     35
   Their riches more, our wealth still growing less.

Nay, ev'n within myself, myself did say:
   In vain my heart I purge, my hands in vain
   In cleanness washed, I keep from filthy stain,
Since thus afflictions scourge me every day,     40
   Since never a day from early east is sent
   But brings my pain, my check,* my chastisement.
And shall I then these thoughts in words bewray?*
   O let me, Lord, give never such offence
   To children thine that rest in thy defence.     45
So then I turned my thoughts another way,
   Sounding, if I this secret's depth might find;
   But cumbrous clouds my inward sight did blind.

Until at length nigh* weary of the chase,
   Unto thy house I did my steps direct:     50
   There, lo, I learned what end these* did expect,

And what but that in high but slipp'ry place
   Thou didst them set; whence, when they least of all
   To fall did fear, they fell with headlong fall.
For how are they in less than moment's space        55
   With ruin overthrown? with frightful fear
   Consumed so clean,* as if they never were,
Right as* a dream, which waking doth deface?
   So, Lord, most vain thou dost their fancies make,
   When thou dost them from careless sleep awake.    60

Then for what purpose was it? to what end
   For me to fume* with malcontented heart,
   Tormenting so in me each inward part?
I was a fool (I can it not defend)
   So quite deprived of understanding might,     65
   That as a beast I bare me in thy sight.
But as I was, yet did I still attend,
   Still follow thee, by whose upholding hand,
   When most I slide, yet still upright I stand.
Then guide me still, then still upon me spend    70
   The treasures of thy sure advice, until
   Thou take me hence into thy glory's hill.

O what is he will teach me climb the skies?*
   With thee, thee good, thee goodness to remain?
   No good on earth doth my desires detain.     75
Often my mind and oft my body tries
   Their weak defects; but thou, my God, thou art
   My endless lot* and fortress of my heart.
The faithless fugitives who thee despise
   Shall perish all, they all shall be undone    80
   Who leaving thee to whorish idols run.
But as for me, nought better in my eyes
   Than cleave to God, my hopes in him to place,
   To sing his works while breath shall give me space.

### PSALM 79*

The land of long by thee possessed,
The heathen, Lord, have now oppressed:
Thy temple holily* maintained
Till now, is now prophanely stained.
Jerusalem quite spoil'd and burned,     5
   Hath suffered sack

And utter wrack,
To stony heaps her buildings turned.

The lifeless carcasses of those,
That liv'd thy servants, serve the crows:                    10
The flock so dearly lov'd of thee
To ravening beasts' dear food they be;
Their blood doth stream in every street*
          As water spilled:
          Their bodies killed                              15
With sepulchure can nowhere meet.

To them that hold the neighbour places*
We are but objects of disgraces:
On ev'ry coast who dwell about us,
In ev'ry kind deride and flout* us.                        20
Ah, Lord! when shall thy wrath be ended?
          Shall still thine ire,
          As quenchless fire,
In deadly ardour be extended?

O kindle there thy fury's flame,                           25
Where lives no notice of thy name:
There let thy heavy anger fall,
Where no devotions on thee call.
For thence, they be who Jacob* eat,
          Who thus have razed,*                            30
          Have thus defaced,
Thus desert laid his ancient seat.

Lord rid us from our sinful cumbers,*
Count not of them the passed numbers:
But let thy pity soon prevent us,*                         35
For hard extremes have nearly spent us.
Free us, O God, our freedom-giver;
          Our misery
          With help supply:
And for thy glory us deliver.                              40

Deliver us, and for thy name
With mercy clothe our sinful shame:
Ah! why should this their* byword be,
Where is your God? where now is he?
Make them, and us on them behold,                          45

That not despised,
But dearly prized,
Thy wreakful* hand our blood doth hold.

Where grace, and glory thee enthroneth,
Admit the groans the prisoner groaneth:                    50
The poor condem'd, for death reserved,
Let be by thee in life preserved.
And for our neighbours, Lord, remember
     Th'opprobrious shame
     They lent thy name                      55
With sev'n-fold gain* to them thou render.

So we thy servants, we thy sheep,
Whom thy looks guide, thy pastures keep:
Till death define our living days,
Will never cease to sound thy praise.                      60
Nay, when we leave to see the sun,
     The after-goers
     We will make knowers
From age to age what thou hast done.

### PSALM 82*

Where poor men plead at princes' bar*
(Who gods, as God's vice regents,* are),
The God of gods hath his tribunal pight,*
  Adjudging right
Both to the judge and judged wight:*                       5

'How long will ye just doom neglect?
How long,' saith he, 'bad men respect?
You should his own* unto the helpless give,
  The poor relieve,
Ease him with right, whom wrong doth grieve.               10

You should the fatherless defend,
You should unto the weak extend
Your hand to loose* and quiet* his estate,
  Through lewd men's hate
Entangled now in deep debate.*                             15

This should you do; but what do ye?
You nothing know, you nothing see;
No light, no law; fie, fie, the very ground
  Becomes unsound,

So right, wrong, all your faults confound.*                    20

Indeed to you the style* I gave
Of gods and sons of God, to have;
But err not, Princes, you as men must die;
   You that sit high
Must fall, and low, as other lie'.                    25

Since men are such, O God, arise,
Thyself most strong, most just, most wise;
Of all the earth king, judge, disposer be,
   Since to decree
Of all the earth belongs to thee.                    30

### PSALM 88*

My God, my Lord, my help, my health:
   To thee my cry
   Doth restless fly,
  Both when of sun the day
  The treasures doth display,                    5
And Night locks up his golden wealth.

Admit to presence* what I crave:
   O bow thine ear
   My cry to hear,
  Whose soul with ills and woes                    10
  So flows, so overflows,
That now my life draws nigh* the grave.

With them that fall into the pit
   I stand esteemed,
   Quite forceless deemed,                    15
  As one who, free from strife
  And stir of mortal life,
Among the dead at rest doth sit;

Right like unto the murdered* sort
   Who in the grave                    20
   Their biding have
  Whom now thou dost no more
  Remember as before,
Quite, quite cut off from thy support.

Thrown down into the grave of graves                    25
   In darkness deep

Thou dost me keep,
Where lightning of thy wrath
Upon me lighted hath,
All overwhelmed with all thy waves.                          30

Who did know me, whom I did know,
Removed by thee
Are gone from me.
Are gone? that is the best:
They all me so detest                                        35
That now abroad I blush to go.

My wasted eye doth melt away,*
Fleeting amain*
In streams of pain
While I my prayers send,                                     40
While I my hands extend,
To thee, my God, and fail no day.

Alas, my Lord, will then be time,
When men are dead,
Thy truth to spread?                                         45
Shall they, whom Death hath slain,
To praise thee live again,
And from their lowly lodgings* climb?

Shall buried mouths thy mercies tell?
Dust and decay                                               50
Thy truth display?
And shall thy works of mark*
Shine in the dreadful dark?
Thy justice where oblivions dwell?

Good reason then, I cry to thee                              55
And, ere the light,
Salute thy sight,
My plaint to thee direct.
Lord why dost thou reject
My soul, and hide thy face from me?                          60

Ay me, alas, I faint, I die,
So still, so still
Thou dost me fill
(And hast from youngest years)
With terrifying fears                                        65
That I, in trance, amazed* do lie.

All over me thy furies passed;
   Thy fears my mind
    Do fettering bind,
  Flowing about me so               70
  As flocking waters flow:
No day can overrun their haste.

Who erst to me were near and dear
   Far now – O far –
    Disjoined are.                    75
  And when I would them see
  Who my acquaintance be,
As darkness they to me appear.

### PSALM 93*

Cloth'd in state and girt* with might,
  Monarch-like Jehova reigns,
He who earth's foundation pight,
  Pight at first, and yet sustains;
  He whose stable throne disdains       5
Motion's shock, and age's flight:
  He who endless one remains,
One, the same, in changeless plight.*

Rivers, yea, though rivers roar,
  Roaring though sea-billows* rise      10
Vex the deep, and break the shore:*
  Stronger art thou, Lord of skies.
  Firm and true thy promise lies
Now and still, as heretofore:
  Holy worship never dies           15
In thy house where we adore.

### PSALM 105*

Jehova's praise, Jehova's holy fame
  O show O sound, his acts to all relate:
To him your songs, your psalms unto him frame;
  Make your discourse his wonders celebrate.
Boast ye God-searchers in his sacred name     5
  And your contracted hearts with joy dilate:
To him, his ark,* his face, let be intended
Your due inquest* with service never ended.

Record, I say, in special memory
   The miracles he wrought, the laws he gave,     10
His servants you, O Abraham's progeny
   You Jacob's sons,* whom he doth chosen save.
We first and most on him our God rely
   All be* no bounds his jurisdiction have:
And he eternally that treaty mindeth,     15
Which him to us, untermed* ages bindeth:

A treaty first with Abraham begun,
   After again, by oath, to Isaac bound,
Lastly to Isaac's God-beholding son*
   Confirm'd, and made inviolably sound.     20
I give in fee* (for so the grant did run),
   Thee and thine heirs the Canaanian ground:
And that when few they were, few, unregarded,
Yea strangers too, where he their lot awarded.

They strangers were, and roam'd from land to land,     25
   From realm to realm: though seatless,* yet secure;
And so remote from wrong of meaner hand
   That kings for them did sharp rebuke endure.
Touch not I charge you, my anointed band,
   Nor to my Prophets least offence procure.*     30
Then he for famine spake: scarce had he spoken,
When famine came, the staff of bread was broken.

But he for them to Egypt had foresent*
   The slave-sold Joseph kindly to prepare:
Whose feet if fretting irons did indent,     35
   His soul was clog'd* with steely bolts of care;
Till fame abroad of his divining went,
   And heav'nly saws* such wisdom did declare
That him a message from the king addressed
Of bondage rid, of freedom repossessed.     40

No sooner freed, the monarch in his hands
   Without control both house and state doth lay;
He rulers rules, commanders he commands;
   Wills and all do: prescribes and all obey.
While thus in terms of highest grace he stands,     45
   Loe, Israel to Egypt takes his way,
And Jacob's line from holy Sem descended,
To sojourn comes where Cham* his tents extended.

Who now but they, in strength and number flow?
　　Rais'd by their God their haters far above?                    50
For, chang'd by him, their entertainers grow
　　With guile to hate, who erst with truth did love.
But he with sacred Moses wills to go
　　Aaron his choice, those mischiefs to remove:
By whose great works their sender's glory blazed,              55
Made Cham's whole land with frightful signs amazed.

Darkness from day the wonted sun doth chase
　　(For both he bids and neither dares rebel),
Late watery Nilus looks with bloody face:
　　How fishes die, what should I stand to tell?                 60
Or how of noisome* frogs the earth-bred race
　　Croak where their princes sleep, not only dwell?
How lice and vermin heav'nly voice attending
Do swarming fall, what quarter not offending?

No rainy cloud but break in stony hail:                        65
　　For cheerful lights dismayful lightnings shine:
Not shine alone, their fiery strokes assail
　　Each taller plant: worst fares the fig and vine,
Nor, call'd, to come, do caterpillars fail
　　With locusts more than counting can define:                 70
By these the grass, the grace of fields is wasted,
The fruits consum'd, by owners yet untasted.

Their eldest-born, that country's hopeful spring,
　　Prime of their youth, his plague doth lastly wound;
Then rich with spoil,* he out his flock doth bring;           75
　　In all their tribes not one a weakling found.
Egypt once wished now fears their tarrying,
　　And gladly sees them on their journey bound;
Whom God in heat a shading cloud provideth,
In dark with lamp of flamy pillar guideth.                     80

Brought from his store, at suit of Israel
　　Quails in whole bevies* each remove pursue;
Himself from skies, their hunger to repel,
　　Candies* the grass with sweet, congealed dew.
He wounds the rock, the rock doth, wounded, well:*            85
　　Welling affords new streams to channels new,
All for God's mindful will cannot be driven
From sacred word once to his Abraham given.

So then in joyful plight, his loved bands
   His chosen troops with triumph on he trains:*     90
Till full possession of the neighbour lands,
   With painless harvest of their thankless pains,
He safely leaves in their victorious hands,
   Where nought for them to do henceforth remains,
But only to observe and see fulfilled,     95
What he (to whom be praise) hath said and willed.

### PSALM 130*

From depth of grief
   Where drowned I lie,
Lord, for relief
   To thee I cry:
My earnest, vehement, crying, praying,     5
Grant quick, attentive, hearing, weighing,*

O Lord, if thou
   Offences mark,
Who shall not bow
   To bear the cark?*     10
But with thy justice mercy dwelleth,
Whereby thy worship more excelleth.

On thee my soul,
   On thee (O Lord)
Dependeth whole;     15
   And on thy word,
Though sore with blot of sin defaced,
Yet surest hope hath firmly placed.

Who longest watch,
   Who soonest rise,
Can nothing match     20
   The early eyes,
The greedy eyes my soul erecteth
While God's true promise it expecteth.

Then Israel     25
   On God attend:
Attend him well
   Who, still thy friend,
In kindness hath thee dear esteemed
And often, often erst redeemed.     30

Now, as before,
  Unchanged he
Will thee restore
  Thy state will free,
All wickedness from Jacob* driving,                     35
Forgetting follies, faults forgiving.

## PSALM 134*

You that Jehovah's servants are,
Whose careful watch,* whose watchful care,
  Within his house are spent,
  Say thus with one assent:
Jehovah's name be praised.                                5
  Then let your hands be raised
    To holiest place,
      Where holiest grace
        Doth aye
          Remain;                                        10
        And say
          Again
Jehovah's name be praised.
Say last unto the company
  Who tarrying make                                      15
  Their leave to take:
All blessings you accompany
From him in plenty showered,
  Whom Zion holds embowered,*
    Who heav'n and earth of nought hath raised.          20

## PSALM 139*

O Lord in me there lieth nought
  But to thy search revealed lies:
    For when I sit
    Thou markest it,
  No less thou notest when I rise;                       5
Yea, closest closet* of my thought
  Hath open windows to thine eyes.

Thou walkest with me when I walk,
  When to my bed for rest I go,
    I find thee there                                    10
    And everywhere;
  Not youngest thought in me doth grow,

No not one word I cast* to talk,
  But yet unuttered thou dost know.

If forth I march, thou go'st before,            15
  If back I turn, thou com'st behind;
    So forth nor back
    Thy guard I lack,
  Nay on me too thy hand I find.
Well I thy wisdom may adore,              20
  But never reach with earthy mind.

To shun thy notice, leave thine eye,
  O whither might I take my way?
    To starry sphere?
    Thy throne is there.              25
To dead men's undelightsome stay?*
There is thy walk, and there to lie
  Unknown, in vain I should assay.*

O sun, whom light nor flight can match,
  Suppose thy lightful flightful wings         30
    Thou lend to me,
    And I could flee
As far as thee the ev'ning brings;
Ev'n led to west he* would me catch,
  Nor should I lurk with western things.*     35

Do thou thy best, O secret night,
  In sable* veil to cover me,
    Thy sable veil
    Shall vainly fail;
  With day unmasked my night shall be,     40
For night is day, and darkness light,
  O father of all lights, to thee.

Each inmost piece in me is thine:
  While yet I in my mother dwelt,*
    All that me clad              45
    From thee I had.
Thou in my frame hast strangely* dealt:
Needs in my praise thy works must shine,
  So inly them my thoughts have felt.

Thou, how my back was beam-wise laid,     50
  And raft'ring of my ribs,* dost know;

Know'st every point
    Of bone and joint,
  How to this whole these parts did grow,
In brave* embroid'ry fair arrayed,                          55
    Though wrought in shop both dark and low.*

Nay fashionless, ere form I took,
    Thy all and more beholding eye
        My shapeless shape
        Could not escape:                                    60
    All these time framed successively
Ere one had being, in the book
    Of thy foresight enrolled did lie.

My God, how I these studies prize,
    That do thy hidden workings show!                        65
        Whose sum is such,
        No sum so much,
    Nay summed as sand they sumless grow.
I lie to sleep, from sleep I rise,
    Yet still in thought with thee I go.                     70

My God, if thou but one wouldst kill,
    Then straight would leave my further chase
        This cursed brood*
        Inured to blood,
    Whose graceless taunts at thy disgrace                   75
Have aimed oft, and hating still
    Would with proud lies thy truth outface.

Hate not I them, who thee do hate?
    Thine, Lord, I will the censure be.
        Detest I not                                         80
        The cankered knot*
    Whom I against thee banded see?
O Lord, thou know'st in highest rate
    I hate them all as foes to me.

Search me, my God, and prove my heart,                       85
    Examine me, and try my thought;
        And mark in me
        If aught there be
    That hath with cause their anger wrought.
If not (as not) my life's each part,                         90
    Lord safely guide from danger brought.

## PSALM 148*

Inhabitants of heavenly land
 As loving subjects praise your king:
You that among them highest stand,
 In highest notes 'Jehovah' sing;
 Sing angels all, on care-full wing     5
  You that his heralds fly;
 And you whom he doth soldiers* bring
  In field his force to try.

O praise him, Sun, the sea of light,
 O praise him, Moon, the light of sea;    10
You pretty Stars, in robe of night
 As spangles* twinkling, do as they.
 Thou sphere,* within whose bosom play
  The rest that earth emball;*
 You waters banked with starry bay:    15
  O praise, O praise him all.

All these, I say, advance that name
 That doth eternal being show:
Who bidding, into form and frame
 (Not being yet) they all did grow;     20
 All formed, framed, founded so,
  Till ages' utmost* date
 They place retain, they order know,
  They keep their first estate.

When Heaven hath praised, praise Earth anew:   25
 You dragons first (her deepest guests);
Then soundless deeps, and what in you
 Residing low or moves, or rests;
 You flames, affrighting mortal breasts;
  You stones* that clouds do cast;     30
 You feathery snows from Winter's nests;
  You vapours, Sun's appast;*

You boisterous winds, whose breath fulfils
 What in his word his will sets down;
Ambitious mountains, courteous hills;     35
 You trees that hills and mountains crown
 (Both you that, proud of native gown,
  Stand fresh and tall to see,

And you that have your more renown
    By what you bear, than be);               40

You beasts in woods untamed that range;
    You that with men familiar go;
You that your place by creeping change,
    Or airy streams with feathers row;
    You stately kings; you subjects low;        45
        You lords and judges all;
    You others whose distinctions show
        How sex or age may fall:

All these, I say, advance that name
    More high than skies, more low than ground.    50
And since, advanced by the same,
    You Jacob's sons* stand chiefly bound,
    You Jacob's sons be chief to sound
        Your God, Jehovah's, praise:
    So fits them well on whom is found        55
        Such bliss he on you lays.

### PSALM 150*

O laud* the Lord, the God of hosts commend,
    Exalt his pow'r, advance his holiness:
    With all your might lift his almightiness:
Your greatest praise upon his greatness spend.

Make trumpet's noise in shrillest notes ascend:    5
    Make lute and lyre his loved fame express:
    Him let the pipe, him let the tabret* bless,
Him organ's breath, that winds or waters lend.

Let ringing timbrels* so his honour sound,
    Let sounding cymbals so his glory ring,        10
That in their tunes such melody be found,
    As fits the pomp of most triumphant king.
Conclude: by all that air, or life enfold,
Let high Jehova highly be extold.

                                (1593–1600)

# AEMILIA LANYER

## Salve Deus Rex Judaeorum*

TO THE QUEEN'S MOST
EXCELLENT MAJESTY*

Renowned Empress, and great Britain's Queen,
Most gracious mother of succeeding kings;
Vouchsafe to view that which is seldom seen,
A woman's writing of divinest things:
  Read it, fair Queen, though it defective be,     5
  Your excellence can grace both it and me.

For you have rifled Nature of her store,
And all the goddesses have dispossessed
Of those rich gifts which they enjoyed before,
But now great Queen, in you they all do rest.     10
  If now they strived for the golden ball,
  Paris* would give it you before them all.

From Juno you have state and dignities,
From warlike Pallas, wisdom, fortitude,
And from fair Venus all her excellencies,     15
With their best parts your highness is indued:*
  How much are we to honour those that springs
  From such rare beauty, in the blood of kings?

The Muses* do attend upon your throne,
With all the artists at your beck and call;     20
The sylvan gods and satyrs every one,
Before your fair triumphant chariot fall:
  And shining Cynthia* with her nymphs attend
  To honour you, whose honour hath no end.

From your bright sphere of greatness where you sit,     25
Reflecting light to all those glorious stars
That wait upon your throne; to Virtue yet
Vouchsafe that splendour which my meanness bars:
  Be like fair Phoebe,* who doth love to grace
  The darkest night with her most beauteous face.     30

Apollo's* beams do comfort every creature,
And shines upon the meanest things that be;
Since in estate* and virtue none is greater,
I humbly wish that yours may light on me:
   That so these rude unpolished lines of mine,     35
   Graced by you, may seem the more divine.

Look in this mirror* of a worthy mind,
Where some of your fair virtues will appear;
Though all it is impossible to find,
Unless my glass* were crystal, or more clear:     40
   Which is dim steel,* yet full of spotless truth,
   And for one look from your fair eyes it su'th.*

Here may your sacred majesty behold
That mighty Monarch* both of heaven and earth,
He that all nations of the world controlled,     45
Yet took our flesh in base and meanest birth:
   Whose days were spent in poverty and sorrow,
   And yet all kings their wealth of him do borrow.

For he is crown and crowner of all kings,
The hopeful haven of the meaner sort,*     50
It's he that all our joyful tidings brings
Of happy reign within his royal court:
   It's he that in extremity can give
   Comfort to them that have no time to live.

And since my wealth within his region stands,     55
And that his cross my chiefest comfort is,
Yea, in his kingdom only rests my lands,
Of honour there I hope I shall not miss:
   Though I on earth do live unfortunate,
   Yet there I may attain a better state.     60

In the meantime, accept most gracious Queen
This holy work Virtue presents to you,
In poor apparel, shaming to be seen,
Or once t'appear in your judicial view:
   But that fair Virtue, though in mean attire,     65
   All princes of the world do most desire.

And sith* all royal virtues are in you,
The natural, the moral, and divine,
I hope how plain soever, being true,
You will accept even of the meanest line                    70
    Fair Virtue yields, by whose rare gifts you are
    So highly graced, t'exceed the fairest fair.

Behold, great Queen, fair Eve's apology,*
Which I have writ in honour of your sex,
And do refer unto your majesty,                             75
To judge if it agree not with the text:*
    And if it do, why are poor women blamed,
    Or by more faulty men so much defamed?

And this great lady* I have here attired,
In all her richest ornaments of honour,                     80
That you, fair Queen, of all the world admired,
May take the more delight to look upon her:
    For she must entertain you to this feast,*
    To which your highness is the welcom'st guest.

For here I have prepared my paschal lamb,*                  85
The figure of that living sacrifice;
Who dying, all the infernal powers o'ercame,
That we with him t'eternity might rise:
    This precious Passover* feed upon, O Queen,
    Let your fair virtues in my glass be seen.              90

And she* that is the pattern of all beauty,
The very model of your majesty,
Whose rarest parts enforceth love and duty,
The perfect pattern of all piety:
    O let my book by her fair eyes be blest,                95
    In whose pure thoughts all innocency rests.

Then shall I think my glass a glorious sky,
When two such glittering suns at once appear;
The one replete with sovereign majesty,
Both shining brighter than the clearest clear:              100
    And both reflecting comfort to my spirits,
    To find their grace so much above my merits.

Whose untuned voice the doleful notes doth sing
Of sad affliction in an humble strain;
Much like unto a bird that wants a wing,                    105

And cannot fly, but warbles forth her pain:
   Or he that barred from the sun's bright light,
   Wanting day's comfort, doth commend the night.

So I that live closed up in Sorrow's cell,
Since great Eliza's* favour blest my youth;        110
And in the confines of all cares do dwell,
Whose grieved eyes no pleasure ever vieweth:
   But in Christ's sufferings, such sweet taste they have,
   As makes me praise pale Sorrow and the grave.

And this great Lady* whom I love and honour,    115
And from my very tender years have known,
This holy habit still to take upon her,
Still to remain the same; and still her own:
   And what our fortunes do enforce us to,
   She of devotion and mere zeal doth do.        120

Which makes me think our heavy burden light,
When such a one as she will help to bear it;
Treading the paths that make our way go right,
What garment is so fair but she may wear it?
   Especially for her that entertains        125
   A glorious queen* in whom all worth remains.

Whose power may raise my sad dejected Muse,
From this low mansion of a troubled mind;
Whose princely favour may such grace infuse,
That I may spread her virtues in like kind:    130
   But in this trial of my slender skill,
   I wanted knowledge to perform my will.

For even as they that do behold the stars,
Not with the eye of learning but of sight,
To find their motions, want of knowledge bars    135
Although they see them in their brightest light:
   So although I see the glory of her state,
   It's she that must instruct and elevate.

My weak distempered brain and feeble spirits,
Which all unlearned have adventured this,    140
To write of Christ, and of his sacred merits,
Desiring that this book her hands may kiss:
   And though I be unworthy of that grace,
   Yet, let her blessed thoughts this book embrace.

And pardon me (fair Queen) though I presume,                    145
To do that which so many better can;
Not that I learning to myself assume,
Or that I would compare with any man:
    But as they are scholars, and by art do write,
    So Nature yields my soul a sad* delight.                    150

And since all arts at first from Nature came,
That goodly creature, mother of perfection,
Whom Jove's* almighty hand at first did frame,
Taking both her and hers* in his protection:
    Why should not she now grace my barren Muse            155
    And in a woman all defects excuse?

So, peerless Princess, humbly I desire,
That your great wisdom would vouchsafe t'omit
All faults, and pardon if my spirits retire,
Leaving to aim at what they cannot hit:                          160
    To write your worth, which no pen can express,
    Were but t'eclipse your fame and make it less.*

['To the Lady Elizabeth's Grace']

### TO ALL VERTUOUS LADIES IN GENERAL

Each blessed lady that in virtue spends
Your precious time to beautify your souls,
Come wait on her whom winged Fame attends
And in her hand the book where she enrols
Those high deserts that majesty commends:                         5
    Let this fair Queen* not unattended be,
    When in my glass she deigns herself to see.

Put on your wedding garments every one,
The Bridegroom* stays to entertain you all;
Let Virtue be your guide, for she alone                          10
Can lead you right, that you can never fall,
And make no stay for fear he should be gone:
    But fill your lamps with oil of burning zeal,*
    That to your faith he may his truth reveal.

Let all your robes be purple, scarlet, white,                    15
Those perfect colours purest Virtue* wore,

Come decked with lilies,* that did so delight
To be preferred in beauty, far before
Wise Solomon* in all his glory dight:*
    Whose royal robes did no such pleasure yield,       20
    As did the beauteous lily of the field.

Adorn your temples with fair Daphne's* crown,
The never-changing laurel, always green;
Let constant hope all worldly pleasures drown,
In wise Minerva's* paths be always seen,       25
Or with bright Cynthia,* though fair Venus* frown:
    With Aesop* cross the posts of every door,
    Where Sin would riot, making Virtue poor.

And let the Muses your companions be,
Those sacred sisters that on Pallas* wait,       30
Whose virtues with the purest minds agree,
Whose godly labours do avoid the bait
Of worldly pleasures, living always free
    From sword, from violence, and from ill report,
    To these nine worthies all fair minds resort.       35

Anoint your hair with Aaron's precious oil,*
And bring your palms of vict'ry in your hands,
To overcome all thoughts that would defile
The earthly circuit of your souls' fair lands;
Let no dim shadows your clear eyes beguile:       40
    Sweet odours, myrrh, gum, aloes, frankincense,*
    Present that King* who died for your offence.

Behold, bright Titan's* shining chariot stays,
All decked with flowers of the freshest hue,
Attended on by Age, Hours, Nights and Days,*       45
Which alters not your beauty, but gives you
Much more, and crowns you with eternal praise:
    This golden chariot wherein you must ride,
    Let simple* doves and subtle* serpents guide.

Come swifter than the motion of the sun,       50
To be transfigured with our loving Lord,
Lest glory end what grace in you begun,
Of heav'nly riches make your greatest hoard,
In Christ all honour, wealth and beauty's won:

By whose perfections you appear more fair                    55
Than Phoebus,* if he seven times brighter were.

God's holy angels will direct your doves,
And bring your serpents to the fields of rest,
Where he* doth stay that purchased all your loves
In bloody torments, when he died oppressed,                  60
There shall you find him in those pleasant groves
    Of sweet Elizium,* by the well of life,
    Whose crystal springs do purge from worldly strife.

Thus may you fly from dull and sensual* earth,
Whereof at first your bodies formed were,                    65
That new regen'rate in a second birth,*
Your blessed souls may live without all fear,
Being immortal, subject to no death:
    But in the eye of heaven so highly placed,
    That others by your virtues may be graced.*     70

Where worthy ladies I will leave you all,
Desiring you to grace this little book;
Yet some of you methinks I hear to call
Me by my name, and bid me better look,
Lest, unawares, I in an error fall:                          75
    In general terms to place you with the rest,
    Whom Fame commends to be the very best.

'Tis true, I must confess (O noble Fame)
There are a number honoured by thee,
Of which some few thou didst recite by name,                 80
And willed my Muse they should remembered be;
Wishing some would their glorious trophies frame,
    Which if I should presume to undertake,
    My tired hand for very fear would quake.

Only by name I will bid some of those,                       85
That in true Honour's seat have long been placed,
Yea, even such as thou hast chiefly chose,
By whom my muse may be the better graced;
Therefore, unwilling longer time to lose,
    I will invite some ladies that I know,           90
    But chiefly those as thou hast graced so.

['To the Lady Arabella']

TO THE LADY SUSAN,* COUNTESS DOWAGER
OF KENT, AND DAUGHTER TO THE DUCHESS
OF SUFFOLK

Come you that were the mistress of my youth,
The noble guide of my ungoverned days;
Come you that have delighted in God's truth,
Help now your handmaid to sound forth his praise:
   You that are pleased in his pure excellency,     5
   Vouchsafe to grace this holy feast,* and me.

And as your rare perfections showed the glass*
Wherein I saw each wrinkle of a fault;
You the sun's virtue, I that fair green grass,
That flourished fresh by your clear virtues taught:     10
   For you possessed those gifts that grace the mind,
   Restraining youth, whom Error oft doth blind.

In you these noble virtues did I note,
First, love and fear of God, of prince, of laws,
Rare patience with a mind so far remote     15
From worldly pleasures, free from giving cause
   Of least suspect to the most envious eye,
   That in fair Virtue's storehouse sought to pry.

Whose faith did undertake in infancy,
All dang'rous travels by devouring seas     20
To fly to Christ from vain idolatry,
Not seeking there this worthless world to please,
   By your most famous mother* so directed,
   That noble duchess, who lived unsubjected.

From Rome's ridiculous prier* and tyranny,     25
That mighty monarchs kept in awful fear;
Leaving here her lands, her state, dignity;
Nay more, vouchsafed disguised weeds* to wear:
   When with Christ Jesus she did mean to go,
   From sweet delights to taste part of his woe.     30

Come you that ever since have followed her,
In these sweet paths of fair Humility;
Condemning Pride pure Virtue to prefer,
Not yielding to base Imbecility,
   Nor to those weak enticements of the world,     35
   That have so many thousand souls ensnarled.

Receive your love* whom you have sought so far,
Which here presents himself within your view;
Behold this bright and all-directing star,
Light of your soul, that doth all grace renew:                    40
    And in his humble paths since you do tread,
    Take this fair bridegroom in your soul's pure bed.

And since no former gain hath made me write,
Nor my desertless* service could have won,
Only your noble virtues do incite                                 45
My pen, they are the ground I write upon;
    Nor any future profit is expected,
    Then how can these poor lines go unrespected?

### THE AUTHOR'S DREAM TO THE LADY MARY, THE COUNTESS DOWAGER OF PEMBROKE*

Methought I passed through th'Edalyan* groves
And asked the Graces,* if they could direct
Me to a lady whom Minerva chose,
To live with her in height of all respect.

Yet looking back into my thoughts again,                          5
The eye of reason did behold her there
Fast tied unto them in a golden chain,
They stood, but she* was set in Honour's chair.

And nine fair virgins* sat upon the ground,
With harps and viols in their lily hands;                         10
Whose harmony had all my senses drowned,
But that before mine eyes an object stands,

Whose beauty shined like Titan's clearest rays;
She blew a brazen* trumpet, which did sound
Through all the world that worthy lady's praise,                  15
And by eternal Fame I saw her crowned.

Yet studying if I were awake or no,
God Morphy* came and took me by the hand,
And willed me not from Slumber's bower to go,
Till I the sum of all did understand.                             20

When presently the welkin* that before
Looked bright and clear, me thought was overcast,
And dusky clouds with boisterous winds great store
Foretold of violent storms which could not last.

And gazing up into the troubled sky,                               25
Methought a chariot did from thence descend,
Where one did sit replete with majesty,
Drawn by four fiery dragons, which did bend

Their course where this most noble lady sate,
Whom all these virgins with due reverence                          30
Did entertain, according to that state
Which did belong unto her excellence.

When bright Bellona,* so they did her call,
Whom these fair nymphs so humbly did receive,
A manly maid which was both fair and tall,                         35
Her borrowed chariot by a spring did leave.

With spear, and shield, and cuirass on her breast,
And on her head a helmet wondrous bright,
With myrtle, bays and olive branches dressed,
Wherein methought I took no small delight.                         40

To see how all the Graces sought grace here,
And in what meek yet princely sort she came;
How this most noble lady did embrace her,
And all humours unto hers did frame.

Now fair Dictina* by the break of day,                             45
With all her damsels round about her came,
Ranging the woods to hunt, yet made a stay,
When harkening to the pleasing sound of Fame;

Her ivory bow and silver shafts she gave
Unto the fairest nymph of all her train;                           50
And wondering who it was that in so grave,
Yet gallant fashion did her beauty stain:

She decked herself with all the borrowed light
That Phoebus would afford from his fair face,
And made her virgins to appear so bright,                          55
That all the hills and vales received grace.

Then pressing where this beauteous troop did stand,
They all received her most willingly,
And unto her the lady gave her hand,
That she should keep with them continually.                        60

Aurora* rising from her rosy bed,
First blushed, then wept to see fair Phoebe* graced,
And unto Lady May* these words she said
'Come, let us go, we will not be outfaced.'

'I will unto Apollo's waggoner,                               65
A[nd] bid him bring his master presently,
That his bright beams may all her beauty mar,
Gracing us with the lustre of his eye.

'Come, come, sweet May, and fill their laps with flowers,
And I will give a greater light than she;                    70
So all these ladies' favours shall be ours,
None shall be more esteemed than we shall be.'

Thus did Aurora dim fair Phoebus' light,
And was received in bright Cynthia's place,
While Flora all with fragrant flowers dight,                 75
Pressed to show the beauties of her face.

Though these, methought, were very pleasing sights,
Yet now these worthies did agree to go,
Unto a place full of all rare delights,
A place that yet Minerva did not know.                       80

That sacred spring where Art and Nature strived
Which should remain as sov'reign of the place;
Whose ancient quarrel being new revived,
Added fresh beauty, gave far greater grace.

To which as umpires now these ladies go,                     85
Judging with pleasure their delightful case;
Whose ravished senses made them quickly know,
'Twould be offensive either to displace.

And therefore willed they should forever dwell,
In perfect unity by this matchless spring:                   90
Since 'twas impossible either should excel,
Or her fair fellow in subjection bring.

But here in equal sov'reignty to live,
Equal in state, equal in dignity,
That unto others they might comfort give,                    95
Rejoicing all with their sweet unity.

And now methought I long to hear her name,
Whom wise Minerva honoured so much,

She whom I saw was crowned by noble Fame,
Whom Envy sought to sting, yet could not touch.                    100

Methought the meagre elf did seek by ways
To come unto her, but it would not be;
Her venom purified by virtuous rays,
She pined and starved like an anatomy.*

While beauteous Pallas* with this lady fair,                       105
Attended by these nymphs of noble fame,
Beheld those woods, those groves, those bowers rare,
By which Pergusa,* for so hight* the name

Of that fair spring, his dwelling place and ground,
And through those fields with sundry* flowers clad,               110
Of sev'ral colours, to adorn the ground,
And please the senses ev'n of the most sad.

He trailed along the woods in wanton* wise,
With sweet delight to entertain them all;
Inviting them to sit and to devise                                115
On holy hymns; at last to mind they call

Those rare sweet songs which Israel's king* did frame
Unto the father of eternity;
Before his holy wisdom took the name
Of great Messiah, lord of unity.                                  120

Those holy sonnets they did all agree,
With this most lovely lady here to sing;
That by her noble breast's sweet harmony,
Their music might in ears of angels ring.

While saints like swans about this silver brook                   125
Should hallelujah sing continually,
Writing her praises in the eternal book
Of endless honour, true fame's memory.

Thus I in sleep the heavenliest music hard,*
That ever earthly ears did entertain;                             130
And durst not wake, for fear to be debarred
Of what my senses sought still to retain.

Yet sleeping, prayed dull Slumber to unfold
Her noble name, who was of all admired;
When presently in drowsy terms he told                            135

Not only that, but more than I desired.

'This nymph,' quoth he, 'great Pembroke hight by name,
Sister to valiant Sidney,* whose clear light
Gives light to all that tread true paths of Fame,
Who in the globe of heav'n doth shine so bright;          140

That being dead, his fame doth him survive,
Still living in the hearts of worthy men;
Pale death is dead, but he remains alive,
Whose dying wounds restored him life again.

And this fair earthly goddess which you see,              145
Bellona* and her virgins do attend;
In virtuous studies of divinity,
Her precious time continually doth spend.

So that a sister well she may be deemed,
To him that lived and died so nobly;                      150
And far before him is to be esteemed*
For virtue, wisdom, learning, dignity.

Whose beauteous soul hath gained a double life,
Both here on earth and in the heav'ns above,
Till dissolution end all worldly strife                   155
Her blessed spirit remains, of holy love,

Directing all by her immortal light,
In this huge sea of sorrows, griefs and fears;
With contemplation of God's powerful might
She fills the eyes, the hearts, the tongues, the ears     160

Of after-coming ages, which shall read
Her love, her zeal, her faith and piety;
The fair impression of whose worthy deed,
Seals her pure soul unto the Deity.

That both in heav'n and earth it may remain,              165
Crowned with her maker's glory and his love;'
And this did Father Slumber tell with pain,
Whose dullness scarce could suffer him to move.

When I awaking left him and his bower,
Much grieved that I could no longer stay;                 170
Senseless was sleep, not to admit me power,
As I had spent the night, to spend the day.

Then had god Morphy showed the end of all,
And what my heart desired, mine eyes had seen;
For as I waked methought I heard one call                    175
For that bright chariot lent by Jove's fair queen.*

But thou, base cunning thief,* that robs our spirits
Of half that span of life which years doth give;
And yet no praise unto thyself it merits,
To make a seeming death in those that live.                  180

Yea, wickedly thou dost consent to death,
Within thy restful bed to rob our souls;
In Slumber's bower thou steal'st away our breath
Yet none there is that thy base stealths controls.

If poor and sickly creatures would embrace thee,            185
Or they to whom thou giv'st a taste of pleasure,
Thou fliest as if Actaeon's* hounds did chase thee
Or that to stay with them thou hadst no leisure.

But though thou hast deprived me of delight,
By stealing from me ere I was aware;                         190
I know I shall enjoy the selfsame sight,
Thou hast no power my waking spirits to bar.

For to this lady now I will repair,
Presenting her the fruits of idle hours;
Though many books she writes that are more rare,            195
Yet there is honey in the meanest flowers:

Which is both wholesome and delights the taste:
Though sugar be more finer, higher prized,
Yet is the painful* bee no whit disgraced,
Nor her fair wax or honey more despised.                     200

And though that learned damsel and the rest
Have in a higher style her trophy framed;
Yet these unlearned lines being my best,
Of her great wisdom can no whit be blamed.

And therefore, first I here present my dream,               205
And next, invite her honour to my feast,*
For my clear reason sees her by that stream
Where her rare virtues daily are increased.

So craving pardon for this bold attempt,
I here present my mirror to her view,                         210
Whose noble virtues cannot be exempt,
My glass* being steel* declares them to be true.

And madam, if you will vouchsafe that grace,
To grace those flowers that springs from virtue's ground;
Though your fair mind on worthier works is placed,           215
On works that are more deep, and more profound;

Yet is it no disparagement to you
To see your Saviour in a shepherd's weed,*
Unworthily presented in your view,
Whose worthiness will grace each line you read.              220

Receive him here by my unworthy hand,
And read his paths of fair humility;
Who though our sins in number pass the sand,
They all are purged by his divinity.

['To the Lady Lucy, Countess of Bedford'; 'To the Lady Margaret,
Countess Dowager of Cumberland'; 'To the Lady Katherine,
Countess of Suffolk']

### TO THE LADY ANNE,* COUNTESS OF DORSET

To you I dedicate this work of grace,
This frame of glory which I have erected,
For your fair mind I hold the fittest place,
Where Virtue should be settled and protected;
If highest thoughts true Honour do embrace                    5
And holy Wisdom is of them respected,
   Then in this mirror let your fair eyes look
   To view your virtues in this blessed book.

Blest by our Saviour's merits, not my skill,
Which I acknowledge to be very small;                        10
Yet if the least part of his blessed will
I have performed, I count I have done all.
One spark of grace sufficient is to fill
Our lamps with oil, ready when he doth call
   To enter with the Bridegroom* to the feast          15
   Where he that is the greatest may be least.

Greatness is no sure frame to build upon,
No worldly treasure can assure that place;

God makes both even, the cottage with the throne,
All worldly honours there are counted base;                    20
Those he holds dear, and reckons as his own,
Whose virtuous deeds by his especial grace
    Have gained his love, his kingdom and his crown,
    Whom in the book of life he hath set down.

Titles of honour which the world bestows,                    25
To none but to the virtuous doth belong,
As beauteous bowers where true worth should repose,
And where his dwellings should be built most strong;
But when they are bestowed upon her foes,
Poor Virtue's friends endure the greatest wrong;                    30
    For they must suffer all indignity,
    Until in heav'n they better graced be.

What difference was there when the world began?
Was it not Virtue that distinguished all?
All sprang but from one woman and one man,                    35
Then how doth gentry come to rise and fall?
Or who is he that very rightly can
Distinguish of his birth, or tell at all,
    In what mean state his ancestors have been,
    Before some one of worth did honour win?                    40

Whose successors, although they bear his name,
Possessing not the riches of his mind,
How do we know they spring out of the same
True stock of honour, being not of that kind?
It is fair Virtue gets immortal fame,                    45
'Tis that doth all love and duty bind;
    If he that much enjoys, doth little good,
    We may suppose he comes not of that blood.*

Nor is he fit for honour, or command,
If base affections overrules his mind;                    50
Or that self-will doth carry such a hand
As worldly pleasures have the power to blind,
So as he cannot see, nor understand
How to discharge that place* to him assigned.
    God's stewards must for all the poor provide                    55
    If in God's house they purpose* to abide.

To you, as to God's steward I do write,
In whom the seeds of virtue have been sown
By your most worthy mother, in whose right
All her fair parts you challenge as your own;                    60
If you, sweet lady, will appear as bright
As ever creature did that time hath known,
  Then wear this diadem* I present to thee,
  Which I have framed for her eternity.

You are the heir apparent* of this crown                         65
Of goodness, bounty, grace, love, piety,
By birth it's yours; then keep it as your own,
Defend it from all base indignity;
The right your mother hath to it, is known
Best unto you, who reaped such fruit thereby:                    70
  This monument of her fair worth retain
  In your pure mind, and keep it from all stain.

And as your ancestors at first possessed
Their honours for their honourable deeds,
Let their fair virtues never be transgressed;                    75
Bind up the broken, stop the wounds that bleeds,
Succour the poor, comfort the comfortless,
Cherish fair plants, suppress unwholesome weeds;
  Although base pelf* do chance to come in place,
  Yet let true worth receive your greatest grace.                80

So shall you show from whence you are descended,
And leave to all posterities your fame;
So will your virtues always be commended,
And everyone will reverence your name;
So this poor work of mine shall be defended                      85
From any scandal that the world can frame;
  And you a glorious actor will appear,
  Lovely to all, but unto God most dear.

I know right well these are but needless lines,
To you, that are so perfect in your part,                        90
Whose birth and education both combines;
Nay, more than both, a pure and goodly heart,
So well instructed to such fair designs
By your dear mother, that there needs no art;
  Your ripe discretion in your tender years,                     95
  By all your actions to the world appears.

I do but set a candle in the sun,
And add one drop of water to the sea,
Virtue and Beauty both together run,
When you were born, within your breast to stay;            100
Their quarrel ceased, which long before begun,
They live in peace, and all do them obey:
    In you, fair madam, are they richly placed,
    Where all their worth by eternity is graced.

You goddess-like unto the world appear,                    105
Enriched with more than fortune can bestow,
Goodness and grace, which you do hold more dear
Than worldly wealth, which melts away like snow;
Your pleasure is the word of God to hear,
That his most holy precepts you may know:                  110
    Your greatest honour, fair and virtuous deeds,
    Which from the love and fear of God proceeds.

Therefore to you (good madam) I present
His lovely love, more worth than purest gold,
Who for your sake his precious blood hath spent,           115
His death and passion here you may behold,
And view this lamb,* that to the world was sent,
Whom your fair soul may in her arms enfold:
    Loving his love, that did endure such pain
    That you in heaven a worthy place might gain.          120

For well you know this world is but a stage,
Where all do play their parts,* and must be gone;
Here's no respect of persons, youth, nor age,
Death seizes all, he never spareth one;
None can prevent or stay that tyrant's rage,               125
But Jesus Christ the Just; by him alone
    He was o'ercome; he open set the door
    To eternal life, ne'er seen, nor known before.

He is the stone the builders did refuse,
Which you, sweet lady, are to build upon;                  130
He is the rock that holy church did choose,
Among which number you must needs be one;
Fair shepherdess,* 'tis you that he will use
To feed his flock, that trust in him alone;
    All worldly blessings he vouchsafes to you,            135
    That to the poor you may return his due.

And if deserts a lady's love may gain,
Then tell me, who has more deserved than he?
Therefore in recompense of all his pain,
Bestow your pains to read, and pardon me,     140
If out of wants, or weakness of my brain,
I have not done this work sufficiently;
    Yet lodge him in the closet of your heart,
    Whose worth is more than can be showed by art.

['To the Virtuous Reader']

### SALVE DEUS REX JUDAEORUM

Since Cynthia* is ascended to that rest
Of endless joy and true eternity,
That glorious place that cannot be expressed
By any wight clad in mortality,
In her almighty love so highly blest,     5
And crowned with everlasting sov'reignty;
    Where saints and angels do attend her throne,
    And she gives glory unto God alone.

To thee, great Countess,* now I will apply
My pen, to write thy never-dying fame;     10
That when to heav'n thy blessed soul shall fly,
These lines on earth record thy reverand name:
And to this task I mean my Muse* to tie,
Though wanting skill I shall but purchase blame:
    Pardon (dear lady) want of woman's wit     15
    To pen thy praise, when few can equal it.

And pardon (madam) though I do not write
Those praiseful lines of that delightful place,*
As you commanded me in that fair night,
When shining Phoebe gave so great a grace,     20
Presenting Paradise to your sweet sight,
Unfolding all the beauty of her face
    With pleasant groves, hills, walks, and stately trees,
    Which pleasures with retired minds agrees.

Whose eagle's eyes behold the glorious sun     25
Of th'all-creating providence, reflecting
His blessed beams on all by him begun;
Increasing, strengthening, guiding and directing
All worldly creatures their due course to run,

Unto his powerful pleasure all subjecting;                    30
   And thou (dear lady) by his special grace,
   In these his creatures dost behold his face.

Whose all-reviving beauty yields such joys
To thy sad soul, plunged in waves of woe,
That worldly pleasures seem to thee as toys,                    35
Only thou seek'st eternity to know,
Respecting not the infinite annoys*
That Satan to thy well-stayed* mind can show;
   Ne can he quench in thee the spirit of grace,
   Nor draw thee from beholding heaven's bright face.    40

Thy mind so perfect by thy maker framed,
No vain delights can harbour in thy heart;
With his sweet love, thou art so much inflamed
As of the world thou seem'st to have no part;
So, love him still, thou need'st not be ashamed,               45
'Tis he that made thee what thou wert and art,
   'Tis he that dries all tears from orphans' eyes,
   And hears from heaven the woeful widows' cries.

'Tis he that doth behold thy inward cares,
And will regard the sorrows of thy soul;                        50
'Tis he that guides thy feet from Satan's snares,
And in his wisdom doth thy ways control:
He through afflictions, still thy mind prepares,
And all thy glorious trials will enroll,*
   That when dark days of terror shall appear              55
   Thou as the sun shall shine, or much more clear.

The heavens* shall perish as a garment old,
Or as a vesture* by the maker changed,
And shall depart, as when a scroll is rolled;
Yet thou from him shall never be estranged,                     60
When he shall come in glory, that was sold
For all our sins; we happily are changed,
   Who for our faults put on his righteousness,
   Although full oft his laws we do transgress.

Long may'st thou joy in this almighty love,                     65
Long may thy soul be pleasing in his sight,
Long may'st thou have true comforts from above,
Long may'st thou set on him thy whole delight,

And patiently endure when he doth prove,
Knowing that he will surely do thee right:                    70
   Thy patience, faith, long suffering, and thy love,
   He will reward with comforts from above.

With majesty and honour is he clad,
And decked with light, as with a garment fair;
He joys the meek, and makes the mighty sad,                   75
Pulls down the proud, and doth the humble rear*
Who sees this bridegroom* never can be sad,
None lives that can his wondrous works declare:
   Yea, look how far the east is from the west,
   So far he sets our sins that have transgressed.           80

He rides upon the wings of all the winds,
And spreads the heavens with his all-powerful hand;
Oh! Who can loose when the Almighty binds?
Or in his angry presence dares to stand?
He searcheth out the secrets of all minds;                    85
All those that fear him shall possess the land:
   He is exceeding glorious to behold,
   Ancient of times, so fair and yet so old.

He of the watery clouds his chariot frames,
And makes his blessed angels powerful spirits,               90
His ministers are fearful fiery flames,
Rewarding all according to their merits;
The righteous for an heritage he claims,
And registers the wrongs of humble spirits:
   Hills melt like wax in presence of the Lord,             95
   So do all sinners, in his sight abhorred.

He in the waters lays his chamber beams,
And clouds of darkness compass him about,
Consuming fire shall go before in streams,
And burn up all his en'mies round about:                     100
Yet on these judgements worldlings never dreams,
Nor of these dangers never stand in doubt:
   While he shall rest within his holy hill,
   That lives and dies according to his will.

But woe to them that double-hearted be,                      105
Who with their tongues the righteous souls do slay;
Bending their bows to shoot at all they see,

With upright hearts their Maker to obey;
And secretly do let their arrows flee
To wound true-hearted people any way:                    110
    The Lord will root them out that speak proud things,
    Deceitful tongues are but false Slander's wings.

Froward* are the ungodly from their birth,
No sooner born, but they do go astray;
The Lord will root them out from off the earth,         115
And give them to their enemies for a pray,*
As venomous as the serpent's is their breath,
With poisoned lies to hurt in what they may
    The innocent: who as a dove shall fly
    Unto the Lord, that he his cause may try.              120

The righteous Lord doth righteousness allow,
His countenance will behold the thing that's just;
Unto the mean* he makes the mighty bow,
And raiseth up the poor out of the dust:
Yet makes no count to us, nor when, nor how,            125
But pours his grace on all, that put their trust
    In him, that never will their hopes betray,
    Nor lets them perish that for mercy pray.

He shall within his tabernacle* dwell,
Whose life is uncorrupt before the Lord,                130
Who no untruths of innocents doth tell,
Nor wrongs his neighbour, nor in deed, nor word,
Nor in his pride with malice seems to swell,
Nor whets* his tongue more sharper than a sword
    To wound the reputation of the just;                   135
    Nor seeks to lay their glory in the dust.

That great Jehovah,* king of heav'n and earth,
Will rain down fire and brimstone from above,
Upon the wicked monsters in their berth,*
That storm and rage at those whom he doth love:        140
Snares, storms, and tempests he will rain, and dearth,*
Because he will himself almighty prove:
    And this shall be their portion they shall drink,
    That thinks the Lord is blind when he doth wink.

Pardon (good madam)* though I have digressed            145
From what I do intend to write of thee,

To set his glory forth whom thou lov'st best,
Whose wondrous works no mortal eye can see;
His special care on those whom he hath blest,
From wicked worldlings, how he sets them free:      150
   And how such people he doth overthrow
   In all their ways, that they his power may know.

The meditation of this monarch's love,
Draws thee from caring what this world can yield;
Of joys and griefs both equal thou dost prove,      155
They have no force to force thee from the field:
Thy constant faith, like to the turtle dove*
Continues combat, and will never yield
   To base affliction, or proud pomp's desire,
   That sets the weakest minds so much on fire.      160

Thou from the court to the country art retired,
Leaving the world, before the world leaves thee:
That great enchantress of weak minds admired,
Whose all-bewitching charms so pleasing be
To worldly wantons;* and too much desired      165
Of those that care not for eternity:
   But yield themselves as preys to Lust and Sin,
   Losing their hopes of heav'n, hell pains to win.

But thou, the wonder of our wanton age,
Leav'st all delights to serve a heav'nly king:      170
Who is more wise? Or who can be more sage
Than she that doth affection subject bring?
Not forcing for the world, or Satan's rage,
But shrouding under the Almighty's wing;
   Spending her years, months, days, minutes, hours,      175
   In doing service to the heav'nly powers.

Thou fair example, live without compare,
With Honour's triumphs seated in thy breast;
Pale Envy never can thy name impair,
When in thy heart thou harbour'st such a guest:      180
Malice must live for ever in despair;
There's no revenge where Virtue still doth rest;
   All hearts must needs do homage unto thee,
   In whom all eyes such rare perfection see.

That outward beauty* which the world commends,                    185
Is not the subject I will write upon,
Whose date expired, that tyrant Time soon ends;
Those gaudy colours soon are spent and gone:
But those fair Virtues which on thee attends
Are always fresh, they never are but one:                    190
    They make thy beauty fairer to behold
    Than was that queen's* for whom proud Troy was sold.

As for those matchless colours red and white,
Or perfect features in a fading face,
Or due proportion pleasing to the sight;                    195
All these do draw but dangers and disgrace:
A mind enriched with virtue shines more bright,
Adds everlasting beauty, gives true grace,
    Frames an immortal goddess on the earth,
    Who though she dies, yet Fame gives her new birth.                    200

That pride of nature which adorns the fair,
Like blazing comets to allure all eyes,
Is but the thread, that weaves their web of care,
Who glories most, where most their danger lies;
For greatest perils do attend the fair,                    205
When men do seek, attempt, plot and devise,
    How they may overthrow the chastest dame,
    Whose beauty is the white* whereat they aim.

'Twas beauty bred in Troy the ten year's strife,
And carried Helen* from her lawful lord;                    210
'Twas beauty made chaste Lucrece* lose her life,
For which proud Tarquin's fact was so abhorred;
Beauty the cause Antonius* wronged his wife,
Which could not be decided but by sword,
    Great Cleopatra's* beauty and defects                    215
    Did work Octavia's* wrongs, and his neglects.

What fruit did yield that fair forbidden tree,*
But blood, dishonour, infamy, and shame?
Poor blinded* queen, could'st thou no better see,
But entertain disgrace, instead of fame?                    220
Do these designs with majesty agree?
To stain thy blood, and blot thy royal name.
    That heart that gave consent unto this ill,
    Did give consent that thou thyself should'st kill.

Fair Rosamund,* the wonder of her time,                    225
Had been much fairer had she not been fair;
Beauty betrayed her thoughts aloft to climb,
To build strong castles in uncertain air,
Where th'infection of a wanton crime
Did work her fall; first poison, then despair,             230
    With double death did kill her perjured soul,
    When heavenly justice did her sin control.

Holy Matilda* in a hapless hour
Was born to sorrow and to discontent,
Beauty the cause that turned her sweet to sour,            235
While Chastity sought Folly to prevent.
Lustful King John refused, did use his power,
By fire and sword, to compass his content:
    But friend's disgrace, nor father's banishment,
    Nor death itself could purchase her consent.          240

Here beauty in the height of all perfection,
Crowned this fair creature's everlasting fame,
Whose noble mind did scorn the base subjection
Of fears or favours, to impair her name:
By heavenly grace she had such true direction,             245
To die with honour, not to live in shame,
    And drink that poison with a cheerful heart,
    That could all heavenly grace to her impart.

This grace, great lady,* doth possess thy soul,
And make thee pleasing in thy Maker's sight;              250
This grace doth all imperfect thoughts control,*
Directing thee to serve thy God aright;
Still reckoning him the husband of thy soul,
Which is most precious in his glorious sight:
    Because the world's delights she doth deny           255
    For him who for her sake vouchsafed to die.

And dying made her dowager* of all,
Nay more, co-heir of that eternal bliss
That angels lost, and we, by Adam's fall;
Mere cast-aways, raised by a Judas-kiss,*                  260
Christ's bloody sweat, the vinegar and gall,
The spear, sponge, nails, his buffeting with fists,
    His bitter passion, agony and death,
    Did gain us heaven, when he did lose his breath.

These high deserts* invites my lowly muse                    265
To write of him,* and pardon crave of thee,
For time so spent I need make no excuse,
Knowing it doth with thy fair mind agree
So well, as thou no labour will refuse,
That to thy holy love may pleasing be:                       270
    His death and passion I desire to write,
    And thee to read, the blessed soul's delight.

[Lines 273–744: Lanyer makes the conventional statement of how
unworthy she is to write the poem and calls upon God 't'illuminate
my spirit' (321); she then proceeds with the story of how Christ
was betrayed, charged by the Jewish priests and finally taken
before Pontius Pilate.]

Now Pontius Pilate* is to judge the cause                    745
Of faultless Jesus who before him stands,
Who neither hath offended prince nor laws,
Although he now be brought in woeful bands:
O noble governor, make thou yet a pause,
Do not in innocent blood imbrue thy hands,                   750
    But hear the words of thy most worthy wife*
    Who sends to thee to beg her Saviour's life.

'Let barb'rous cruelty far depart from thee,
And in true justice take affliction's part,
Open thine eyes, that thou the truth may'st see,            755
Do not the thing that goes against thy heart,
Condemn not him that must thy Saviour be,
But view his holy life, his good desert,
    Let not us women glory in men's fall,
    Who had power given to over-rule us all.                  760

Till now your indiscretion sets us free,
And makes our former fault much less appear,
Our mother Eve* who tasted of the tree,
Giving to Adam what she held most dear,
Was simply* good and had no power to see,                    765
The after-coming harm did not appear:
    The subtle serpent that our sex betrayed,
    Before our fall so sure a plot had laid.

That undiscerning ignorance perceived
No guile, or craft that was by him* intended,                    770
For had she known of what we were bereaved,
To his request she had not condescended.
But she (poor soul) by cunning was deceived,
No hurt therein her harmless heart intended,
 For she alleged God's word, which he denies,              775
 That they should die, but even as gods, be wise.*

But surely Adam cannot be excused,
Her fault, though great, yet he was most to blame,*
What weakness offered, strength might have refused,
Being lord of all, the greater was his shame;                    780
Although the serpent's craft had her abused,
God's holy word ought all his actions frame,
 For he was lord and king of all the earth,
 Before poor Eve had either life or breath.*

Who being framed by God's eternal hand                           785
The perfectest man that ever breathed on earth,
And from God's mouth received that strait* command,
The breath whereof he knew was present death;
Yea, having power to rule both sea and land,
Yet with one apple won to lose that breath                       790
 Which God had breathed in his beauteous face,
 Bringing us all in danger and disgrace.

And then to lay the fault on Patience back,
That we (poor women) must endure it all;
We know right well he did discretion lack,                       795
Being not persuaded thereunto at all,
If Eve did err it was for knowledge sake,
The fruit being fair persuaded him to fall,
 No subtle serpent's falsehood did betray him,
 If he would eat it, who had power to stay him?              800

Not Eve, whose fault was only too much love,
Which made her give this present to her dear,
That what she tasted he likewise might prove,*
Whereby his knowledge might become more clear,
He never sought her weakness to reprove,                         805
With those sharp words which he of God did hear;
 Yet men will boast of knowledge, which he took
 From Eve's fair hand, as from a learned book.

If any evil did in her remain,
Being made of him,* he was the ground of all;                810
If one of many worlds could lay a stain
Upon our sex, and work so great a fall
To wretched man, by Satan's subtle train,*
What will so foul a fault amongst you all?
   Her weakness did the serpent's words obey,          815
   But you in malice God's dear son betray.

Whom, if unjustly you condemn to die,
Her sin was small to what you do commit,
All mortal sins that do for vengeance cry
Are not to be compared unto it;                              820
If many worlds would altogether try
By all their sins the wrath of God to get,
   This sin of yours surmounts them all as far
   As doth the sun another little star.

Then let us have our liberty again,                          825
And challenge* to yourselves no sovereignty;
You came not in the world without our pain,
Make that a bar against your cruelty;
Your fault being greater why should you disdain
Our being, your equals, free from tyranny?                   830
   If one weak woman simply did offend,
   This sin of yours hath no excuse, nor end.'

To which (poor souls) we never gave consent,
Witness thy wife (O Pilate), speaks for all,
Who did but dream and yet a message sent,                    835
That thou should'st have nothing to do at all
With that just man, which if thy heart relent,
Why will thou be a reprobate with Saul?*
   To seek the death of him that is so good,
   For thy soul's health to shed his dearest blood.      840

Yea, so thou may'st these sinful people please
Thou art content against all truth and right,
To seal this act, that may procure thine ease,
With blood, and wrong, with tyranny and might;
The multitude thou seekest to appease,                       845
By base dejection* of this heavenly light,
   Demanding which of these that thou should'st loose,
   Whether the thief, or Christ King of the Jews.

Base Barabbas* the thief they all desire,
And thou more base than he, perform'st their will;                    850
Yet when thy thoughts back to themselves retire,
Thou art unwilling to commit this ill,
Oh, that thou could'st unto such grace aspire,
That thy polluted lips might never kill
    That honour which right judgement ever graceth,       855
    To purchase shame, which all true worth defaceth.

Art thou a judge, and asketh what to do
With one in whom no fault there can be found?
The death of Christ wilt thou consent unto,
Finding no cause, no reason, nor no ground?                           860
Shall he be scourged and crucified too?
And must his miseries by thy means abound?
    Yet not ashamed to ask what he hath done
    When thine own conscience seeks this sin to shun.

Three times thou ask'st, 'What evil hath he done?'                    865
And say'st thou find'st in him no cause of death,
Yet wilt thou chasten God's beloved son,
Although to thee no word of ill he say'th,
For Wrath must end what Malice hath begun,
And thou must yield to stop his guiltless breath;                     870
    This rude tumultuous rout doth press so sore,
    That thou condemnest him thou shouldst adore.

Yet Pilate, this can yield thee no content,
To exercise thine own authority,
But unto Herod* he must needs be sent                                 875
To reconcile thyself by tyranny;
Was this the greatest good in justice meant,
When thou perceiv'st no fault in him to be?
    If thou must make thy peace by virtue's fall,
    Much better 'twere not to be friends at all.                     880

Yet neither thy stern brow nor his great place*
Can draw an answer from the Holy One,
His false accusers, nor his great disgrace,
Nor Herod's scoffs, to him they are all one,
He neither cares nor fears his own ill case,                          885
Though being despised and mocked of everyone:
    King Herod's gladness gives him little ease,
    Neither his anger seeks he to appease.

Yet, this is strange, that base impiety
Should yield those robes of honour* which were due,       890
Pure white to show his great integrity
His innocency that all the world might view,
Perfection's height in lowest penury,
Such glorious poverty as they never knew,
   Purple and scarlet well might him beseem,          895
   Whose precious blood must all the world redeem.

And that imperial crown of thorns* he wore,
Was much more precious than the diadem
Of any king that ever lived before,
Or since his time, their honour's but a dream           900
To his eternal glory, being so poor,
To make a purchase of that heavenly realm,
   Where God with all his angels lives in peace,
   No griefs, no sorrows, but all joys increase.

Those royal robes, which they in scorn did give,        905
To make him odious to the common sort,
Yield light of grace to those whose souls shall live
Within the harbour of this heavenly port,
Much do they joy, and much more do they grieve,
His death, their life, should make his foes such sport, 910
   With sharpest thorns to prick his blessed face,
   Our joyful sorrow, and his greater grace.

Three fears at once possessed Pilate's heart:
The first, Christ's innocency which so plain appears,
The next, that he which now must feel this smart        915
Is God's dear son, for anything he hears,
But that which proved the deepest wounding dart
Is people's threat'nings which he so much fears,
   That he to Caesar could not be a friend,
   Unless he sent sweet Jesus to his end.               920

Now Pilate thou art proved a painted wall,
A golden sepulchre with rotten bones,
From right to wrong, from equity to fall,
If none upbraid thee, yet the very stones
Will rise against thee, and in question call            925
His blood, his tears, his sight, his bitter groans,
   All these will witness at the latter day,
   When water cannot wash thy sin away.*

Can'st thou be innocent, that gainst all right
Will yield to what thy conscience does withstand?  930
Being a man of knowledge, power and might,
To let the wicked carry such a hand,
Before thy face to blindfold Heaven's bright light,
And thou to yield to what they did demand?
    Washing thy hands, thy conscience cannot clear,  935
    But to all worlds this stain must needs appear.

For, lo, the guilty does accuse the just,
And faulty judge condemns the innocent;
And wilful Jews to exercise their lust
With whips and taunts against their lord are bent;  940
He, basely used, blasphemed, scorned, and cursed,
Our heavenly king to death for us they sent,
    Reproaches, slanders, spittings in his face,
    Spite doing all her worst in his disgrace.

And now this long expected hour* draws near,  945
When blessed saints and angels do condole;
His holy march, soft pace, and heavy cheer,
In humble sort to yield his glorious soul,
By his deserts the foulest sins to clear,
And in the eternal book of heaven to enroll  950
    A satisfaction till the general doom,*
    Of all sins past, and all that are to come.

They that had seen this pitiful procession,
From Pilate's palace to Mount Calvary,
Might think he answered for some great transgression,  955
Being in such odious sort condemned to die,
He plainly showed that his own profession
Was virtue, patience, grace, love, piety,
    And how by suffering he could conquer more
    Than all the kings that ever lived before.  960

First went the crier with open mouth proclaiming
The heavy sentence of iniquity,
The hangman next, by his base office claiming
His right in hell, where sinners never die,
Carrying the nails, the people still blaspheming  965
Their maker, using all impiety,
    The thieves attending him on either side,
    The sergeants watching, while the women cried.

Thrice happy women* that obtained such grace
From him whose worth the world could not contain,          970
Immediately to turn about his face,
As not remembering his great grief and pain,
To comfort you, whose tears poured forth apace
On Flora's* banks like showers of April's rain,
 Your cries enforced mercy, grace and love              975
  From him, whom greatest princes could not move.

To speak one word, nor once to lift his eyes
Unto proud Pilate, no nor Herod, king,
By all the questions that they could devise,
Could make him answer to no manner of thing;              980
Yet these poor women by their piteous cries
Did move their lord, their lover and their king,
 To take compassion, turn about and speak,
  To them whose hearts were ready now to break.

Most blessed daughters of Jerusalem,                      985
Who found such favour in your saviour's sight,
To turn his face when you did pity him,
Your tearful eyes beheld his eyes more bright,
Your faith and love unto such grace did climb,
To have reflection from this heavenly light:             990
 Your eagle's eyes* did gaze against this sun,
  Your hearts did think, he dead, the world were done.

When spiteful men with torments did oppress,
The afflicted body of this innocent dove,
Poor women seeing how much they did transgress,          995
By tears, by sighs, by cries, entreat, nay prove
What may be done among the thickest press,
They labour still these tyrants' hearts to move,
 In pity and compassion to forbear,
  Their whipping, spurning, tearing of his hair.      1000

But all in vain, their malice hath no end,
Their hearts more hard than flint, or marble stone,
Now to his grief, his greatness they attend,
When he (God knows) had rather be alone;
They are his guard, yet seek all means t'offend,         1005
Well may he grieve, well may he sigh and groan,
 Under the burden of a heavy cross,
  He faintly goes to make their gain, his loss.

His woeful mother* waiting on her son,
All comfortless in depth of sorrow drowned,                1010
Her griefs extreme, although but new begun,
To see his bleeding body oft she swooned;
How could she choose but think herself undone,
He dying, with whose glory she was crowned?
   None ever lost so great a loss as she,           1015
   Being son, and father of eternity.

Her tears did wash away his precious blood,
That sinners might not tread it under feet,
To worship him, and that it did her good,
Upon her knees, although in open street,                   1020
Knowing he was the Jesse flower and bud,*
That must be gathered when it smelled most sweet:
   Her son, her husband, father, saviour, king,
   Whose death killed Death and took away his sting.

Most blessed Virgin,* in whose faultless fruit             1025
All nations of the earth must needs rejoyce,
No creature having sense though ne'er so brute
But joys and trembles when they hear his voice;
His wisdom strikes the wisest persons mute,
Fair chosen vessel, happy in his choice,                   1030
   Dear mother of our Lord, whose reverand name
   All people blessed call and spread thy fame.

For the Almighty magnified thee
And looked down upon thy mean estate;
Thy lowly mind and unstained chastity                      1035
Did plead for love at great Jehovah's gate,
Who sending swift-winged Gabriel unto thee,
His holy will and pleasure to relate;
   To thee, most beauteous queen of womankind,
   The angel did unfold his maker's mind.                   1040

He thus began, 'Hail Mary full of grace,
Thou freely art beloved of the Lord,
He is with thee, behold thy happy case.'
What endless comfort did these words afford
To thee, that saw'st an angel in the place                 1045
Proclaim thy virtue's worth and, to record
   Thee blessed among women, that thy praise
   Should last so many worlds beyond thy days.

Lo, this high message to thy troubled spirit,
He doth deliver in the plainest sense,                          1050
Says, thou should'st bear a son that shall inherit
His father David's throne, free from offence,
Calls him, that holy thing, by whose pure merit
We must be saved, tells what he is, of whence,
    His worth, his greatness, what his name must be,      1055
    Who should be called the Son of the Most High.

He cheers thy troubled soul, bids thee not fear,
When thy pure thoughts could hardly apprehend
This salutation, when he did appear;
Nor could'st thou judge whereto those words did tend,   1060
His pure aspect did move thy modest cheer*
To muse, yet joy that God vouchsafed to send
    His glorious angel, who did thee assure
    To bear a child, although a virgin pure.

Nay more, thy son should rule and reign forever,         1065
Yea, of his kingdom there should be no end,
Over the house of Jacob,* heaven's great giver,
Would give him power, and to that end did send
His faithful servant Gabriel to deliver
To thy chaste ears no word that might offend,            1070
    But that this blessed infant born of thee,
    Thy son, the only Son of God should be.

When on the knees of thy submissive heart
Thou humbly did'st demand, how should that be?
Thy virgin thoughts did think, none could impart        1075
This great good hap, and blessing unto thee,
Far from desire of any man thou art,
Knowing not one, thou art from all men free;
    When he, to answer this thy chaste desire,
    Gives thee more cause to wonder and admire.          1080

That thou a blessed virgin should'st remain,
Yea, that the Holy Ghost should come on thee,
A maiden mother, subject to no pain,
For highest power should overshadow thee;
Could thy fair eyes from tears of joy refrain,           1085
When God looked down upon thy poor degree?
    Making thee servant, mother, wife and nurse
    To heaven's bright king, that freed us from the curse.*

Thus being crowned with glory from above,
Grace and perfection resting in thy breast, 1090
Thy humble answer doth approve* thy love,
And all these sayings in thy heart do rest:
Thy child a lamb,* and thou a turtle dove,*
Above all other women highly blest,
　　To find such favour in his glorious sight, 1095
　　In whom thy heart and soul do most delight.

What wonder in the world more strange could seem,
Than that a virgin could conceive and bear
Within her womb a son, that should redeem
All nations on the earth, and should repair 1100
Our old decays, who in such high esteem,
Should prize all mortals, living in his fear,
　　As not to shun death, poverty and shame,
　　To save their souls, and spread his glorious name.

And partly to fulfil his father's pleasure, 1105
Whose powerful hand allows it not for strange,
If he vouchsafe the riches of his treasure,
Pure righteousness to take such ill exchange;
On all iniquity to make a seizure,
Giving his snow-white weed for ours in change, 1110
　　Our mortal garment in a scarlet dye,*
　　Too base a robe for immortality.

Most happy news that ever yet was brought,
When poverty and riches met together,
The wealth of heaven, in our frail clothing wrought 1115
Salvation by his happy coming hither,
Mighty Messiah, who so dearly bought
Us slaves to sin, far lighter than a feather,
　　Tossed to and fro with every wicked wind,
　　The world, the flesh, or devil gives to blind. 1120

Who on his shoulders our black sins does bear,
To that most blessed, yet accursed, cross,
Where fastening them, he rids us of our fear,
Yea, for our gain he is content with loss,
Our ragged clothing scorns he not to wear, 1125
Though foul, rent, torn, disgraceful, rough and gross,
　　Spun by that monster Sin and weaved by Shame,
　　Which grace itself, disgraced with impure blame.

How can'st thou choose (fair Virgin) then but mourn,
When this sweet offspring of thy body dies,                    1130
When thy fair eyes, behold his body torn,
Thy people's fury, hears the women's cries,
His holy name prophaned, he made a scorn,
Abused with all their hateful, slanderous lies,
    Bleeding and fainting in such wondrous sort,        1135
    As scarce his feeble limbs can him support.

[Lines 1137–1288 describe Christ's crucifixion and conclude with
the discovery of his empty tomb.]

For he is rise* from death t'eternal life,
And now those precious ointments he desires                    1290
Are brought unto him by his faithful wife,
The holy Church, who in those rich attires,
Of patience, love, long suffering, void of strife,
Humbly presents those ointments he requires:
    The oils of mercy, charity and faith,               1295
    She only gives that which no other hath.

These precious balms do heal his grievious wounds,
And water of compunction washeth clean
The sores of sins, which in our souls abounds,
So fair it heals, no scar is ever seen,                        1300
Yet all the glory unto Christ* redounds,
His precious blood is that which must redeem;
    Those well may make us lovely in his sight,
    But cannot save without his powerful might.

This is that bridegroom that appears so fair,                  1305
So sweet, so lovely in his spouse's sight,
That unto snow we may his face compare,
His cheeks like scarlet, and his eyes so bright
As purest doves that in the rivers are
Washed with milk, to give the more delight,                    1310
    His head is likened to the finest gold,
    His curled locks so beauteous to behold,

Black as a raven in her blackest hue,
His lips like scarlet threads, yet much more sweet
Than is the sweetest honey dropping dew,                       1315
Or honeycombs where all the bees do meet,

Yea, he is constant and his words are true;
His cheeks are beds of spice, flowers sweet,
   His lips like lillies, dropping down pure myrrh,
   Whose love, before all worlds we do prefer.        1320

Ah! Give me leave (good Lady)* now to leave
This task of beauty which I took in hand,
I cannot wade so deep, I may deceive
Myself before I can attain the land;
Therefore (good Madam), in your heart I leave      1325
His perfect picture, where it still shall stand,
   Deeply engraved in that holy shrine,
   Environed with love and thoughts divine.

There may you see him as a God in glory,
And as a man in miserable case,             1330
There may you read his true and perfect story,
His bleeding body there you may embrace,
And kiss his dying cheeks with tears of sorrow,
With joyful grief, you may entreat for grace,
   And all your prayers, and your alms-deeds,*    1335
   May bring to stop his cruel wounds that bleeds.

Oft times hath he made trial of your love,
And in your faith hath took no small delight,
By crosses* and afflictions he doth prove,
Yet still your heart remaineth firm and right,     1340
Your love so strong as nothing can remove,
Your thoughts being placed on him both day and night,
   Your constant soul doth lodge between her* breasts,
   This sweet of sweets in which all glory rests.

Sometimes h'appears to thee in shepherd's weed,   1345
And so presents himself before thine eyes,
A good old man that goes his flock to feed,
Thy colour changes, and thy heart does rise,
Thou call'st, he comes, thou find'st 'tis he indeed,
Thy soul conceives that he is truly wise,       1350
   Nay more, desires that he may be the book,
   Whereon thine eyes continually may look.

Sometime imprisoned, naked, poor and bare,
Full of diseases, impotent and lame,
Blind, deaf and dumb, he comes unto his fair,    1355

To see if yet she will remain the same;
Nay, sick and wounded, now thou do'st prepare
To cherish him in thy dear lover's name,
   Yea, thou bestow'st all pains, all cost, all care,
   That may relieve him, and his health repair.        1360

These works of mercy are so sweet, so dear,
To him that is the lord of life and love,
That all thy prayers he vouchsafes to hear,
And sends his holy spirit from above;
Thy eyes are opened, and thou see'st so clear,        1365
No worldly thing can thy fair mind remove;
   Thy faith, thy prayers, and his special grace
   Doth open heaven, where thou behold'st his face.

These are those keys Saint Peter* did possess,
Which with a spiritual power* are given to thee,        1370
To heal the souls of those that do transgress,
By thy fair virtues; which if once they see,
Unto the like they do their minds address,
Such as thou art, such they desire to be;
   If they be blind, thou giv'st to them their sight,        1375
   If deaf or lame, they hear and go upright.

Yea, if possessed with any evil spirits,
Such power thy fair examples have obtained,
To cast them out, applying Christ's pure merits,
By which they are bound, and of all hurt restrained,        1380
If strangely taken,* wanting sense or wits,
Thy faith applied unto their souls so pained,
   Healeth all griefs, and makes them grow so strong,
   As no defects can hang upon them long.

Thou being thus rich, no riches do'st respect,        1385
Nor do'st thou care for any outward show,
The proud that do fair Virtue's rules neglect,
Desiring place,* thou sittest them below,
All wealth and honour thou do'st quite reject,
If thou perceiv'st that once it proves a foe,        1390
   To virtue, learning and the powers divine,
   Thou may'st convert, but never will incline

To foul disorder or licentiousness,
But in thy modest veil do'st sweetly cover

The stains of other sins, to make themselves,*                    1395
That by this means thou may'st in time recover
Those weak lost sheep* that did so long transgress,
Presenting them unto thy dearest lover;
  That when he brings them back unto his fold,
  In their conversion then he may behold                          1400

Thy beauty shining brighter than the sun,
Thine honour more than ever monarch gained,
Thy wealth exceeding his that kingdoms won,
Thy love unto his spouse, thy faith unfeigned,
Thy constancy in what thou hast begun,                            1405
Till thou his heavenly kingdom have obtained,
  Respecting worldly wealth to be but dross,*
  Which, if abused, doth prove the owner's loss.

Great Cleopatra's* love to Anthony,*
Can no way be compared unto thine;                                1410
She left her love in his extremity,
When greatest need should cause her to combine
Her force with his, to get the victory;
Her love was earthly, and thy love divine,
  Her love was only to support her pride,                         1415
  Humility thy love and thee doth guide.

That glorious part of death which last she played,
T'appease the ghost of her deceased love,
Had never needed, if she could have stayed,
When his extremes made trial, and did prove                       1420
Her leaden* love unconstant and afraid:
Their wicked wars the wrath of God might move
  To take revenge for chaste Octavia's wrongs,*
  Because she enjoys what unto her belongs.

No Cleopatra, though thou wert as fair                            1425
As any creature in Antonius' eyes,
Yea, though thou wert as rich, as wise, as rare,
As any pen could write, or wit devise,
Yet with this lady* canst thou not compare,
Whose inward virtues all thy worth denies,                        1430
  Yet thou a black Egyptian do'st appear,
  Thou false, she true, and to her love more dear.

She sacrificeth to her dearest love,
With flowers of faith and garlands of good deeds,
She flies not from him when afflictions prove,          1435
She bears his cross, and stops his wounds that bleeds;
She loves and lives chaste as the turtle dove,
She attends upon him and his flock she feeds,
    Yea, for one touch of death which thou did'st try,
    A thousand deaths she every day doth die.          1440

Her virtuous life exceeds thy worthy death,
Yea, she hath richer ornaments of state,
Shining more glorious than in dying breath
Thou didst, when either pride or cruel fate
Did work thee to prevent a double death,                1445
To stay the malice, scorn and cruel hate
    Of Rome,* that joyed to see thy pride pulled down,
    Whose beauty wrought the hazard of her crown.

Good Madam, though your modesty be such,
Not to acknowledge what we know and find,              1450
And that you think these praises overmuch,
Which do express the beauty of your mind,
Yet pardon me, although I give a touch
Unto their eyes,* that else would be so blind,
    As not to see thy store, and their own wants,          1455
    From whose fair seeds of virtue spring these plants.

And know, when first into this world I came,
This charge was giv'n me by the eternal powers,
Th'everlasting trophy of thy fame
To build and deck it with the sweetest flowers          1460
That virtue yields; then Madam, do not blame
Me when I show the world but what is yours,
    And deck you with that crown which is your due,
    That of Heav'n's beauty Earth may take a view.

Though famous women elder times have known,*          1465
Whose glorious actions did appear so bright,
That powerful men by them were overthrown,
And all their armies overcome in fight;
The Scythian women* by their power alone,
Put King Darius unto shameful flight,                   1470
    All Asia yielded to their conq'ring hand,
    Great Alexander could not their power withstand.

Whose worth, though writ in lines of blood and fire,
Is not to be compared unto thine;
Their power was small to overcome desire,                    1475
Or to direct their ways by Virtue's line:
Were they alive they would thy life admire,
And unto thee their honours would resign,
　　For thou a greater conquest do'st obtain,
　　Than they who have so many thousands slain.              1480

Wise Deborah* that judged Israel,
Nor valiant Judith,* cannot equal thee;
Unto the first God did his will reveal,
And gave her power to set his people free,
Yea, Judith had the power likewise to queal*                1485
Proud Holofernes, that the just might see
　　What small defence vain pride and greatness hath
　　Against the weapons of God's word and faith.

But thou far greater war do'st still maintain
Against that many-headed monster Sin,                        1490
Whose mortal sting hath many thousand slain,
And every day fresh combats do'st begin,
Yet cannot all his venom lay one stain
Upon thy soul, thou do'st the conquest win,
　　Though all the world he daily doth devour,               1495
　　Yet over thee he never could get power.

For that one worthy deed by Deb'rah done,
Thou hast performed many in thy time;
For that one conquest that fair Judith won,
By which she did the steps of honour climb,                  1500
Thou hast the conquest of all conquests won,
When to thy conscience hell can lay no crime,
　　For that one head that Judith bare away,
　　Thou tak'st from Sin a hundred heads each day.

Though virtuous Hester* fasted three days space,            1505
And spent her time in prayers all that while,
That by God's power she might obtain such grace,
That she and hers might not become a spoil
To wicked Haman, in whose crabbed face
Was seen the map of malice, envy, guile;                     1510
　　Her glorious garments though she put apart,
　　So to present a pure and single heart

To God, in sack-cloth, ashes, and with tears,
Yet must fair Hester needs give place to thee,
Who hath continued days, weeks, months and years          1515
In God's true service, yet thy heart being free
From doubt of death, or any other fears:
Fasting from sin, thou pray'st thine eyes may see
 Him that hath full possession of thine heart,
 From whose sweet love thy soul can never part.          1520

His love, not fear, makes thee to fast and pray,
No kinsman's counsel needs thee to advise;
The sack-cloth thou do'st wear both night and day,
Is worldly troubles, which thy rest denies,
The ashes are the vanities that play          1525
Over thy head and steal before thine eyes,
 Which thou shak'st off when mourning time is past
 That royal robes thou may'st put on at last.

Joachim's wife,* that fair and constant dame,
Who rather chose a cruel death to die,          1530
Than yield to those two elders, void of shame,
When both at once her chastity did try,
Whose innocency bore away the blame,
Until the Almighty Lord had heard her cry,
 And raised the spirit of a child* to speak,          1535
 Making the powerful judged of the weak.

Although her virtue do deserve to be
Writ by that hand that never purchased blame,
In Holy Writ,* where all the world may see
Her perfect life, and ever-honoured name;          1540
Yet was she not to be compared to thee,
Whose many virtues do increase thy fame,
 For she opposed against old doting lust,
 Who with life's danger she did fear to trust.

But your chaste breast, guarded with strength of mind,          1545
Hates the embracements of unchaste desires;
You, loving God, live in your self confined
From unpure love, your purest thoughts retires,
Your perfect sight could never be so blind
To entertain the old or young desires          1550
 Of idle lovers, which the world presents,
 Whose base abuses worthy minds prevents.

Even as the constant laurel,* always green,
No parching heat of summer can deface,
Nor pinching winter ever yet was seen,                          1555
Whose nipping frosts could wither or disgrace;
So you (dear lady) still remain as queen,
Subduing all affections that are base,
    Unalterable by the change of times,
    Not following, but lamenting other's crimes.                1560

No fear of death, or dread of open shame,
Hinders your perfect heart to give consent;
Nor loathsome Age, whom Time could never tame
From ill designs, whereto their youth was bent;
But love of God, care to preserve your fame,                    1565
And spend that precious time that God hath sent
    In all good exercises of the mind,
    Whereto your noble nature is inclined.

That Ethiopian queen* did gain great fame,
Who from the southern world did come to see                     1570
Great Soloman, the glory of whose name
Had spread itself o'er all the earth, to be
So great, that all the princes hither came
To be spectators of his royalty:
    And this fair Queen of Sheba came from far,                 1575
    To reverence this new-appearing star.

From th'utmost part of all the earth she came
To hear the wisdom of this worthy king,
To try if wonder did agree with fame,
And many fair rich presents did she bring;                      1580
Yea, many strange hard questions did she frame,
All which were answered by this famous king;
    Nothing was hid that in her heart did rest,
    And all to prove this king so highly blessed.

Her majesty with majesty did meet,                              1585
Wisdom to wisdom yielded true content,
One beauty did another beauty greet,
Bounty to bounty never could repent;
Here all distaste is trodden under feet
No loss of time where time was so well spent                    1590
    In virtuous exercises of the mind,
    In which this queen did much contentment find.

Spirits affect* where they do sympathise,
Wisdom desires wisdom to embrace,
Virtue covets her like and doth devise                          1595
How she her friends might entertain with grace,
Beauty sometime is pleased to feed her eyes
With viewing beauty in another's face;
    Both good and bad in this point do agree,
    That each desireth with his like to be.                      1600

And this desire did work a strange effect,
To draw a queen forth of her native land
Not yielding to the niceness and respect
Of woman-kind;* she passed both sea and land,
All fear of dangers she did quite neglect,                       1605
Only to see, to hear, and understand,
    That beauty, wisdom, majesty and glory,
    That in her heart impressed his perfect story.

Yet this fair map of majesty and might,
Was but a figure of thy dearest love,*                           1610
Born to express that true and heavenly light,
That doth all other joys imperfect prove;
If this fair earthly star did shine so bright,
What doth that glorious son* that is above?
    Who wears the imperial crown of heaven and earth,   1615
    And made all Christians blessed in his birth.

If that small spark could yield so great a fire
As to inflame the hearts of many kings,
To come to see, to hear, and to admire,
His wisdom, tending but to worldly things,                       1620
Then much more reason have we to desire,
That heavenly wisdom which salvation brings,
    The son of righteousness, that gives true joys,
    When all they sought for were but earthly toys.

No travels ought th'affected soul to shun,                       1625
That this fair heavenly light desires to see,
This king of kings to whom we all should run,
To view his glory and his majesty,
He, without whom we all had been undone,
He, that from sin and death hath set us free,                    1630
    And overcome Satan, the world, and sin,
    That by his merits we those joys might win.

Prepared by him, whose everlasting throne
Is placed in heaven, above the starry skies,
Where he that sate was like the jasper stone,                     1635
Who rightly knows him shall be truly wise,
A rainbow round about his glorious throne,
Nay more, those winged beasts so full of eyes,*
    That never cease to glorify his name,
    Who was, and will be, and is now the same.                    1640

This is that great almighty Lord that made
Both heaven and earth, and lives for evermore,
By him the world's foundation first was laid,
He framed the things that never were before,
The Sea within his bounds by him is stayed,                      1645
He judgeth all alike, both rich and poor,
    All might, all majesty, all love, all law,
    Remains in him that keeps all worlds in awe.

From his eternal throne the lightning came,
Thunderings and voices did from thence proceed,                  1650
And all the creatures glorified his name,
In heaven, in earth and seas, they all agreed,
When lo, that spotless Lamb so void of blame,
That for us died, whose sins did make him bleed,
    That true physician that so many heals,                       1655
    Opened the Book and did undo the seals.

He only worthy to undo the Book
Of our charged souls full of iniquity,
Where with the eyes of mercy he doth look
Upon our weakness and infirmity;                                 1660
This is that cornerstone* that was forsook,
Who leaves it, trusts but to uncertainty,
    This is God's son, in whom he is well-pleased,*
    His dear beloved, that his wrath appeased.

He that had power to open all the seals                          1665
And summon up our sins of blood and wrong,
He unto whom the righteous souls appeals,
That have been martyred and do think it long,
To whom in mercy he his will reveals,
That they should rest a little in their wrong,                   1670
    Until their fellow servants should be killed,
    Even as they were, and that they were fulfilled.

Pure-thoughted Lady,* blessed be thy choice
Of this almighty, everlasting king;
In thee his saints and angels do rejoice,                        1675
And to their heavenly Lord do daily sing
Thy perfect praises in their loudest voice,
And all their harps and golden viols* bring
    Full of sweet odors, even thy holy prayers
    Unto that spotless lamb that all repairs.            1680

Of whom that heathen queen obtained such grace,
By honouring but the shadow of his love,
That great judicial day* to have a place,
Condemning those that do unfaithful prove,
Among the hapless, happy is her case                             1685
That her dear Saviour spake for her behove,*
    And that her memorable act should be
    Writ by the hand of true eternity.

Yet this rare phoenix* of that worn-out age,
This great majestic queen comes short of thee,                   1690
Who to an earthly prince did then engage
Her heart's desires, her love, her liberty,
Acting her glorious part upon a stage
Of weakness, frailty, and infirmity,
    Giving all honour to a creature,* due                1695
    To her Creator, whom she never knew.

But lo, a greater thou hast sought and found,
Than Soloman in all his royalty,
And unto him thy faith most firmly bound
To serve and honour him continually,                             1700
That glorious God, whose terror doth confound,
All sinful workers of iniquity;
    Him hast thou truely served all thy life,
    And for his love, lived with the world at strife.

To this great Lord thou only art affected,*                      1705
Yet came he not in pomp or royalty,
But in an humble habit, base, dejected,
A King, a God, clad in mortality,
He hath thy love, thou art by him directed,
His perfect path was fair humility;                              1710
    Who being monarch of heaven, earth and seas,
    Endured all wrongs, yet no man did displease.

Then how much more art thou to be commended,
That seek'st thy love in lowly shepherd's weeds?
A seeming tradesman's son, of none attended,          1715
Save of a few in poverty and need,
Poor fishermen* that on his love attended,
His love that makes so many thousands bleed,
    Thus did he come to try our faiths the more,
    Possessing worlds, yet seeming extreme poor.          1720

The pilgrim's travels and the shepherd's cares,
He took upon him to enlarge our souls,
What pride hath lost humility repairs,
For by his glorious death he us enrols
In deep characters,* writ with blood and tears,          1725
Upon those blessed, everlasting scrolls,
    His hands, his feet, his body and his face,
    Whence freely flowed the rivers of his grace.*

Sweet holy rivers,* pure celestial springs,
Proceeding from the fountain of our life;          1730
Swift sugred currents that salvation brings,
Clear crystal streams, purging all sin and strife,
Fair floods, where souls do bathe their snow-white wings,
Before they fly to true eternal life:
    Sweet nectar and ambrosia, food of saints,          1735
    Which, whoso tasteth, never after faints.

This honey-dropping dew of holy love,
Sweet milk wherewith we weaklings are restored,
Who drinks thereof, a world can never move,
All earthly pleasures are of them abhorred,          1740
This love made martyrs many deaths to prove,
To taste his sweetness whom they so adored;
    Sweetness that makes our flesh a burden to us,
    Knowing it serves but only to undo us.

His sweetness sweet'ned all the sour of death,          1745
To faithful Stephen,* his appointed saint,
Who by the river stones did lose his breath,
When pains nor terrors could not make him faint:
So was this blessed martyr turned to earth,
To glorify his soul by death's attaint,*          1750
    This holy saint was humbled and cast down,
    To win in heaven an everlasting crown.

Whose face replete with majesty and sweetness,
Did as an angel unto them appear,
That sate in counsel hearing his discreteness,*          1755
Seeing no change, or any sign of fear,
But with a constant brow did there confess,
Christ's high deserts, which were to him so dear,
    Yea, when these tyrant's storms did most oppress,
    Christ did appear to make his grief the less.          1760

For, being filled with the Holy Ghost,
Up unto heaven he looked with steadfast eyes,
Where God appeared with his heavenly host
In glory to this saint before he dies;
Although he could no earthly pleasures boast,          1765
At God's right hand sweet Jesus he espies;
    Bids them behold Heaven's open, he doth see
    The son of man at God's right hand to be.

Whose sweetness sweet'ned that short sour of life,
Making all bitterness delight his taste,          1770
Yielding sweet quietness in bitter strife,
And most contentment when he died disgraced;
Heaping up joys where sorrows were most rife,
Such sweetness could not choose but be embraced,
    The food of souls, the spirit's only treasure,          1775
    The paradise of our celestial pleasure.

This Lamb of God, who died and was alive,
Presenting us the life of bread eternal,
His bruised body powerful to revive
Our sinking souls, out of the pit infernal;          1780
For by this blessed food he did contrive
A work of grace, by this his gift external,
    With heavenly manna, food of his elected,
    To feed their souls, of whom he is respected.

This wheat of heaven, the blessed angels' bread,          1785
Wherewith he feeds his dear adopted heirs,
Sweet food of life that doth revive the dead
And from the living takes away all cares;
To taste this sweet Saint Laurence* did not dread,
The broiling gridiron cooled with holy tears,          1790
    Yielding his naked body to the fire,
    To taste this sweetness, such was his desire.

Nay, what sweetness did th'Apostles taste,
Condemned by counsel when they did return,
Rejoicing that for him they died disgraced,                    1795
Whose sweetness made their hearts and souls so burn
With holy zeal and love most pure and chaste;
From him they sought from whom they might not turn,
    Whose love made Andrew* go most joyfully,
    Unto the cross on which he meant to die.                   1800

The princes of th'Apostles* were so filled
With the delicious sweetness of his grace,
That willingly they yielded to be killed,
Receiving deaths that were most vile and base
For his name sake, that all might be fulfilled,                1805
They did with great joy all torments did embrace,
    The ugliest face that Death could ever yield,
    Could never fear these champions from the field.

They still continued in their glorious fight,
Against the enemies of flesh and blood,                        1810
And in God's law did set their whole delight,
Suppressing evil and erecting good,
Not sparing kings in what they did not right,
Their noble acts they sealed with dearest blood,
    One chose the gallows,* that unseemly death,               1815
    The other by the sword* did lose his breath.

His head did pay the dearest rate of sin,
Yielding it joyfully up unto the sword,
To be cut off as he had never been,
For speaking truth according to God's word,                    1820
Telling King Herod of incestuous sin
That hateful crime of God and man abhorred,
    His brother's wife, that proud licentious dame,
    Cut off his head to take away his shame.

Lo Madam, here you take a view of those                        1825
Whose worthy steps you do desire to tread,
Decked in those colours which our Saviour chose,
The purest colours both of white and red,*
Their freshest beauties would I fain disclose,
By which our Saviour most was honoured,                        1830
    But my weak muse desireth now to rest,
    Folding up all the beauties in your breast.

Whose excellence hath raised my spirits to write
Of what my thoughts could hardly apprehend,
Your rarest virtues did my soul delight,                          1835
Great Lady of my heart, I must commend
You that appear so fair in all men's sight,
On your deserts my muses do attend,
    You are the arctic star* that guides my hand,
    All what I am, I rest at your command.                    1840
                                   (1610)

## The Description of Cooke-Ham*

Farewell (sweet Cooke-Ham) where I first obtained
Grace from that Grace where perfect grace* remained,
And where the Muses gave their full consent,
I should have power the virtuous to content;
Where princely palace willed me to indite*                        5
The sacred story of the soul's delight.*
Farewell (sweet place) where virtue then did rest,
And all delights did harbour in her breast,
Never shall my sad eyes again behold
Those pleasures which my thoughts did then unfold,                10
Yet you (great Lady)* mistress of that place,
From whose desires did spring this work of grace,*
Vouchsafe to think upon those pleasures past,
As fleeting worldly joys that could not last,
Or as dim shadows of celestial pleasures,                         15
Which are desired above all earthly treasures.
Oh how (methought) against you thither came
Each part did seem some new delight to frame!
The house received all ornaments to grace* it,
And would endure no foulness to deface it.                        20
The walks put on their summer liveries,
And all things else did hold like similes:*
The trees, with leaves, with fruits, with flowers, clad,
Embraced each other seeming to be glad,
Turning themselves to beauteous canopies                          25
To shade the bright sun from your brighter eyes;
The crystal streams with silver spangles graced,
While by the glorious sun they were embraced;
The little birds in chirping notes did sing,
To entertain both you and that sweet spring;                      30

And Philomela* with her sundry lays,
Both you and that delightful place did praise.
Oh how methought each plant, each flower, each tree,
Set forth their beauties then to welcome thee!
The very hills right humbly did descend,                    35
When you to tread upon them did intend.
And as you set your feet they still did rise,
Glad that they could receive so rich a prize.
The gentle winds did take delight to be
Among those woods that were so graced by thee,              40
And in sad* murmur uttered pleasing sound,
That pleasure in that place might more abound;
The swelling banks delivered all their pride,
When such a phoenix* once they had espied.
Each arbour, bank, each seat, each stately tree,            45
Thought themselves honoured in supporting thee.
The pretty birds would oft come to attend thee,
Yet fly away for fear they should offend thee;
The little creatures in the burrow by,
Would come abroad to sport them in your eye,               50
Yet fearful of the bow in your fair hand
Would run away when you did make a stand.*
Now let me come unto that stately tree,
Wherein such goodly prospects you did see,
That oak* that did in height his fellows pass,             55
As much as lofty trees, low-growing grass,
Much like a comely cedar,* straight and tall,
Whose beauteous stature far exceeded all;
How often did you visit this fair tree,
Which seeming joyful in receiving thee,                     60
Would like a palm* tree spread his arms abroad,
Desirous that you there should make abode,
Whose fair green leaves much like a comely veil,
Defended Phoebus* when he would assail,
Whose pleasing boughs did yield a cool fresh air,          65
Joying his happiness when you were there;
Where being seated you might plainly see
Hills, vales and woods, as if on bended knee
They had appeared, your honour to salute,
Or to prefer* some strange, unlooked-for suit;*            70
All interlaced with brooks and crystal springs,
A prospect fit to please the eyes of kings,

And thirteen shires* appear all in your sight,
Europe could not afford much more delight.
What was there then but gave you all content,      75
While you the time in meditation* spent,
Of their creator's power, which there you saw,
In all his creatures held a perfect law,
And in their beauties did you plain descry
His beauty, wisdom, grace, love, majesty.      80
In these sweet woods how often did you walk,
With Christ and his apostles* there to talk,
Placing his holy writ in some fair tree,
To meditate what you therein did see;
With Moses* you did mount his holy hill,      85
To know his pleasure and perform his will;
With lovely David* you did often sing,
His holy hymns to heaven's eternal king.
And in sweet music did your soul delight,
To sound his praises, morning, noon and night.      90
With blessed Joseph* you did often feed
Your pined* brethren when they stood in need;
And that sweet lady* sprung from Clifford's race,
Of noble Bedford's blood, fair stem of grace,
To honourable Dorset now espoused,      95
In whose fair breast true virtue then was housed,
Oh what delight did my weak spirits find,
In those pure parts of her well-framed mind;
And yet it grieves me that I cannot be
Near unto her whose virtues did agree      100
With those fair ornaments of outward beauty,
Which did enforce from all both love and duty.
Unconstant Fortune, thou art most to blame,
Who casts us down into so low a frame,
Where our great friends we cannot daily see,      105
So great a difference is there in degree.
Many are placed in those orbs of state,*
Parters* in honour, so ordained by Fate,
Nearer in show, yet farther off in love,
In which the lowest, always are above.      110
But whither am I carried in conceit?*
My wit too weak to conster* of the great.
Why not? Although we are but born of earth,
We may behold the heavens, despising death,

And loving heaven that is so far above                        115
May in the end vouchsafe us entire love.
Therefore, sweet Memory, do thou retain
Those pleasures past which will not turn again:
Remember beauteous Dorset's former sports,*
So far from being touched by ill reports,                     120
Wherein myself did always bear a part,
While reverend love presented my true heart;
Those recreations let me bear in mind,
Which her sweet youth and noble thoughts did find,
Whereof deprived, I evermore must grieve,                     125
Hating blind Fortune, careless to relieve.
And you sweet Cooke-Ham, whom these ladies leave,
I now must tell the grief you did conceive
At their departure, when they went away,
How everything retained a sad dismay;                         130
Nay, long before, when once an inkling came,
Methought each thing did unto sorrow frame,
The trees that were so glorious in our view,
Forsook both flowers and fruit, when once they knew
Of your depart, their very leaves did wither,                 135
Changing their colours as they grew together.
But when they saw this had no power to stay you,
They often wept, though speechless, could not pray you,*
Letting their tears in your fair bosoms fall,
As if they said, 'Why will you leave us all?'                 140
This being vain,* they cast their leaves away,
Hoping that pity would have made you stay;
Their frozen tops like Age's hoary hairs,
Shows their disasters, languishing in fears,
A swarthy rivelled rine* all over spread                      145
Their dying bodies, half-live, half-dead.
But your occasions* called you so away,
That nothing there had power to make you stay;
Yet did I see a noble grateful, mind,
Requiting each according to their kind,                       150
Forgetting not to turn and take your leave,
Of these sad creatures, powerless to receive
Your favour, when with grief you did depart,
Placing their former pleasures in your heart;
Giving great charge to noble Memory,                          155
There to preserve their love continually;

But specially the love of that fair tree,
That first and last you did vouchsafe to see,
In which it pleased you oft to take the air,
With noble Dorset,* then a virgin fair,                         160
Where many a learned book was read and scanned;
To this fair tree, taking me by the hand,
You did repeat the pleasures which had passed,
Seeming to grieve they could no longer last;
And with a chaste, yet loving kiss took leave,                  165
Of which sweet kiss I did it soon bereave,*
Scorning a senseless* creature should possess
So rare a favour, so great happiness.
No other kiss it could receive from me,
For fear to give back what it took of thee;                     170
So I, ungrateful creature, did deceive it,
Of that which you vouchsafed* in love to leave it.
And though it oft had given me much content,
Yet this great wrong I never could repent,
But of the happiest made it most forlorn,                       175
To show that nothing's free from Fortune's scorn,
While all the rest with this most beauteous tree,
Made their sad consort,* Sorrow's harmony.
The flowers that on the banks and walks did grow,
Crept in the ground, the grass did weep for woe.               180
The winds and waters seemed to chide together,
Because you went away, they knew not whither,
And those sweet brooks that ran so fair and clear,
With grief and trouble wrinkled did appear.
Those pretty birds that wonted* were to sing,                   185
Now neither sing, nor chirp, nor use their wing,
But with their tender feet on some bare spray,
Warble forth sorrow and their own dismay.
Fair Philomela* leaves her mournful ditty,
Drowned in dead sleep, yet can procure no pity,                190
Each arbour, bank, each seat, each stately tree,
Looks bare and desolate for want of thee,
Turning green tresses into frosty grey,
While in cold grief they whither all away.
The sun grew weak, his beams no comfort gave,                   195
While all green things did make the earth their grave;
Each briar, each bramble, when you went away,
Caught fast your clothes, thinking to make you stay;

Delightful Echo* wonted to reply
To our last words, did now for sorrow die;                      200
The house cast off each garment that might grace it,
Putting on dust and cobwebs to deface it.
All desolation then there did appear,
When you were going whom they held so dear.
This last farewell to Cooke-Ham here I give,                    205
When I am dead thy name in this might live,
Wherein I have performed her* noble hest,
Whose virtues lodge in my unworthy breast,
And ever shall, so long as life remains,
Tying my heart to her by those rich chains.                     210

(1609–10)

# RACHEL SPEGHT

### A Mouzell for Melastomus*

I f reason had but curbed thy witless will
O r fear of God restrained thy raving quill,
S uch venom foul thou wouldst have blushed to spew,
E xcept that grace have bidden thee adieu:
P rowess disdains to wrestle with the weak,                    5
H eathenish affected, care not what they speak.

S educer of the vulgar sort of men,
W as Satan crept into thy filthy pen,
E nflaming thee with such infernal smoke,
T hat (if thou hadst thy will) should women choke?    10
N efarious fiends thy sense herein deluded,
A nd from thee all humanity excluded.
M onster of men, worthy of no other name,
   For that thou didst essay our sex to shame.

(1617)

### Mortality's Memorandum, with a dream prefixed, imaginary in manner, real in matter

*Live to die, for die thou must,*
*Die to live, amongst the just.*

THE DREAM

When splendent Sol,* which riseth in the East,
Returning thence took harbour in the West;
When Phoebus* laid her head in Titan's* lap,
And creatures sensitive made haste to rest;
When sky which earst looked like to azure blue,    5
Left colour bright and put on sable hue.

Then did Morpheus* close my drowsy eyes
And stood as porter at my senses' door;

Diurnal cares excluding from my mind,
Including rest (the salve for labours sore).                    10
Night's greatest part in quiet sleep I spent,
But nothing in this world is permanent.

For ere Aurora* spread her glittering beams
Or did with robes of light herself invest,*
My mental quiet Sleep did interdict                    15
By entertaining a nocturnal guest,
A *Dream* which did my mind and sense possess
With more than I by pen can well express.

At the appointment of supernal* power,
By instrumental means, me thought I came                    20
Into a place most pleasant to the eye,
Which for the beauty some did Cosmus name,
Where stranger-like on everything I gazed,
But wanting wisdom was as one amazed.

Upon a sudden, as I gazing stood,                    25
Thought came to me and asked me of my state,
Inquiring what I was, and what I would,
And why I seemed as one disconsolate.
To whose demand I thus again replied,
'I, as a stranger in this place abide.                    30

'The haven of my voyage is remote,
I have not yet attained my journey's end;
Yet know I not, nor can I give a guess,
How short a time I in this place shall spend.
For that high power, which sent me to this place,                    35
Doth only know the period of my race.

'The reason of my sadness at this time
Is 'cause I feel myself not very well;
Unto you I shall much obliged be,
If for my grief a remedy you'll tell.'                    40
Quoth she, 'If you your malady will show,
My best advice I'll willingly bestow.'

'My grief,' quoth I, 'is called Ignorance,
Which makes me differ little from a brute;
For animals are led by nature's lore,                    45
Their seeming science* is but custom's fruit;
When they are hurt they have a sense of pain,
But want the sense to cure themselves again.

'And ever since this grief did me oppress
Instinct of nature is my chiefest guide;                           50
I feel disease, yet know not what I ail,
I find a sore, but can no salve provide;
I hungry am, yet cannot seek for food,
Because I know not what is bad or good.

'And sometimes when I seek the golden mean*          55
My weakness makes me fail of mine intent,
That suddenly I fall into extremes;
Nor can I see a mischief to prevent,
But feel the pain when I the peril find
Because my malady doth make me blind.                     60

'What is without the compass of my brain
My sickness makes me say it cannot be,
What I conceive* not, cannot come to pass,
Because for it I can no reason see.
I measure all men's feet by mine own shoe,              65
And count all well which I appoint* or do.

'The pestilent effects of my disease
Exceed report their number is so great;
The evils, which through it I do incur,
Are more than I am able to repeat.                             70
Wherefore, good Thought, I sue to thee again,
To tell me how my cure I may obtain.'

Quoth she, 'I wish I could prescribe your help;
Your state I pity much and do bewail,
But for my part, though I am much employed,        75
Yet in my judgement I do often fail.
And therefore I'll commend unto your trial,
Experience, of whom take no denial.

'For she can best direct you what is meet
To work your cure and satisfy your mind.'               80
I thanked her for her love and took my leave,
Demanding where I might Experience find.
She told me if I did abroad enquire
'Twas likely Age could answer my desire.

I sought, I found; she asked me what I would. 85
Quoth I, 'Your best direction I implore,
For I am troubled with an irksome grief,'
Which when I named, quoth she, 'Declare no more,
For I can tell as much as you can say,
And for your cure I'll help you what I may. 90

'The only medicine for your malady
By which, and nothing else, your help is wrought,
Is knowledge, of the which there is two sorts:
The one is good, the other bad and nought;
The former sort by labour is attained, 95
The latter may without much toil be gained.

'But 'tis the good which must effect your cure.'
I prayed her then that she would further show
Where I might have it. 'That I will,' quoth she,
'In Erudition's garden it doth grow, 100
And in compassion of your woeful case
Industry shall conduct you to the place.'

Dissuasion hearing her assign my help
(And seeing that consent I did detect),
Did many remoraes* to me propose, 105
As dullness and my memory's defect,
The difficulty of attaining lore,
My time, and sex, and many others more.

Which when I heard my mind was much perplexed
And, as a horse new-come into the field 110
Who with a harquebuz* at first does start,
So did this shot make me recoil and yield.
But of my fear when some did notice take,
In my behalf they this reply did make.

First quoth Desire, 'Dissuasion, hold thy peace! 115
These oppositions come not from above.'
Quoth Truth, 'They cannot spring from reason's root
And therefore now thou shall no victor prove.'
'No,' quoth Industry, 'be assured this:
Her friends shall make thee of thy purpose miss. 120

'For with my sickle I will cut away
All obstacles that in her way can grow,
And by the issue of her own attempt
I'll make thee *labor omnia vincet** know.'

Quoth Truth, 'And since her sex thou do'st object          125
Thy folly I by reason will detect.

'Both man and woman of three parts consist,
Which Paul* doth body, soul and spirit call;
And from the soul three faculties arise,
The mind, the will, the power; then wherefore shall          130
A woman have her intellect in vain,
Or not endeavour knowledge to attain?

'The talent* God does give must be employed,
His own, with vantage, he must have again;
All parts* and faculties were made for use;          135
The God of knowledge* nothing gave in vain.
'Twas Mary's choice* our Saviour did approve,
Because that she the better part did love.

'Cleobulina* and Demophila*
With Telesilla,* as historians tell          140
(Whose fame doth live, though they have long been dead),
Did all of them in poetry excel.
A Roman matron that Cornelia* hight
An eloquent and learned style did write.

'Hypatia* in astronomy had skill;          145
Aspatia* was in rhet'ric so expert
As that Duke Pericles of her did learn;
Areta* did devote herself to art,
And by consent (which shows she was no fool),
She did succeed her father in his school.          150

'And many others here I could produce
Who were in science counted excellent;
But these examples, which I have rehearsed
To show thy error, are sufficient.'
Thus having said, she turned her speech to me,          155
That in my purpose I might constant be.

'My friend,' quoth she, 'regard not vulgar talk;
For dunghill cocks at precious stones will spurn,
And swine-like natures prize not crystal streams,
Contemned* mire and mud will serve their turn.          160
Good purpose seldom oppositions want;
But constant minds Dissuasion cannot daunt.

'Shall every blast disturb the sailor's peace?
Or boughs and bushes travellers affright?
True valour does not start at every noise,                    165
Small combats must instruct for greater fight,
Disdain to be with every dart dismayed;
'Tis childish to be suddenly afraid.

'If thou didst know the pleasure of the place
Where knowledge grows, and where thou mayst it gain,     170
Or rather knew the virtue of the plant,
Thou would'st not grudge at any cost or pain
Thou can'st bestow to purchase* for thy cure
This plant, by which of help thou shall be sure.

'Let not Dissuasion alter thy intent,                         175
'Tis sin to nip good motions in the head;
Take courage and be constant in thy course,
Though irksome be the path which thou must tread.
Sick folks drink bitter medicines to be well,
And to enjoy the nut men crack the shell.'                    180

When Truth had ended what she meant to say
Desire did move me to obey her will,
Whereto consenting I did soon proceed
Her counsel and my purpose to fulfil;
And by the help of Industry, my friend,                       185
I quickly did attain my journey's end.

Where being come, Instruction's pleasant air
Refreshed my senses which were almost dead;
And fragrant flowers of sage and fruitful plants
Did send sweet savours* up into my head;                      190
And taste of science, appetite did move
To augment theory of things above.

There did the harmony of those sweet birds
(Which higher soar with contemplation's wings
Than barely with a superficial view                           195
Denote the value of created things),
Yield such delight as made me to implore
That I might reap this pleasure more and more.

And as I walked, wandering with Desire
To gather that for which I thither came                       200
(Which by the help of Industry I found),

I met my old acquaintance, Truth by name,
Whom I requested briefly to declare
The virtue of that plant I found so rare.

Quoth she, 'By it God's image* man does bear,                205
Without it he is but a human shape,
Worse than the Devil, for he knoweth much.
Without it who can any ill escape?
By virtue of it evils are withstood;
The mind without it is not counted good.'*                   210

Who wanteth knowledge is a scripture fool;
Against the ignorant the prophets pray;
And Hosea* threatens judgement unto those
Whom want of knowledge made to run astray.
Without it thou no practice good can'st show                 215
More than by hap,* as blind men hit a crow.*

'True knowledge is the window of the soul
Through which her objects she does speculate;*
It is the mother of faith, hope, and love;
Without it who can virtue estimate?                          220
By it, in grace thou shall desire to grow;
'Tis life eternal God and Christ to know.*

'Great Alexander* made so great account
Of knowledge that he oftentimes would say,
That he to Aristotle was more bound                          225
For knowledge, upon which Death could not prey,
Than to his father, Philip, for his life,
Which was uncertain, irksome, full of strife.'

This true report put edge unto Desire,
Who did incite me to increase my store,                      230
And told me was a lawful avarice
To covet knowledge daily more and more.
This counsel I did willingly obey,
Till some occurrence called me away.*

And made me rest content with that I had,                    235
Which was but little, as effect does show;
And quenched hope for gaining any more,
For I my time must other-ways bestow.
I therefore to that place returned again
From whence I came, and where I must remain.                 240

But by the way I saw a full-fed beast,*
Which roared like some monster or a devil,
And on Eve's sex he foamed filthy froth,
As if that he had had the falling evil;*
To whom I went to free them from mishaps                245
And with a Mouzel* sought to bind his chaps.*

But, as it seems, my mood outrun my might,
Which when a self-conceited creature* saw,
She passed her censure on my weak exploit,
And gave the beast a harder bone to gnaw.               250
Haman* she hangs; 'tis past he cannot shun it,
For Ester* in the pretertense* has done it.

And yet her enterprise had some defect,
The monster surely was not hanged quite;
For as the child of Prudence* did conceive,            255
His throat not stopped, he still had power to bite.
She therefore gave to Cerberus a sop,*
Which is of force his beastly breath to stop.

But yet if he do swallow down that bit,
She otherwise has bound him to the peace;               260
And like an artist* takes away the cause
That the effect by consequence may cease.
This frantic dog, whose rage did women wrong,
Hath Constance* wormed to make him hold his tongue.

Thus leaving them I passed on my way;                   265
But ere that I had little further gone
I saw a fierce, insatiable foe,
Depopulating countries, sparing none;
Without respect of age, sex, or degree,
It did devour and could not daunted be.                 270

Some feared this foe, some loved it as a friend;
For though none could the force of it withstand,
Yet some by it were sent to Tophet's flames,*
But others led to heavenly Canaan land.*
On some it seized with a gentle power,                  275
And others furiously it did devour.

The name of this impartial foe was Death,
Whose rigour whilst I furiously did view,
Upon a sudden, ere I was aware,

With piercing dart my mother dear it slew;                           280
Which when I saw it made me so to weep
That tears and sobs did rouse me from my sleep.

But when I waked, I found my dream was true;
For Death had ta'ne* my mother's breath away,
Though of her life it could not her bereave                          285
Since she in glory lives with Christ for aye;
Which makes me glad and thankful for her bliss,
Though still bewail her absence, whom I miss.

A sudden sorrow pierceth to the quick,
Speedy encounters, fortitude doth try,                               290
Unarmed men receive the deepest wound,
Expected perils time doth lenify.*
Her sudden loss has cut my feeble heart
So deep, that daily I endure the smart.

The root is killed, how can the boughs but fade?                     295
But since that death this cruel deed has done,
I'll blaze* the nature of this mortal foe,
And show how it to tyrannise begun.
The sequel then with judgement view aright
The profit may and will the pains requite.                           300

*Esto Memor Mortis**

## Mortality's Memorandum

When Elohim* had given time beginning,
In the beginning God began to make
The heavens and earth* with all that they contain,
Which were created for his glory's sake;*
And to be Lord of part of work o'er-past,                            5
He Adam made, and Eve of him, at last.

In Eden garden God did place them both,
To whom command of all the trees he gave,
The fruit of one tree only to forbear,
On pain of death (his own he did but crave),                         10
And Satan thinking this their good too great,
Suggests the woman, she the man, they eat.

Thus eating both, they both did jointly sin;*
And Elohim dishonoured by their act

Does ratify what he had earst decreed,                          15
That death* must be the wages of their fact;*
Thus on them and their offspring henceforth seized
Mortality, because they God displeased.

In Adam all men die;* not one that's free
From that condition we from him derive;                         20
By sin death entered, and began to reign.
But yet in Christ* shall all be made alive,
Who did triumph o'er sin, o'er death, and hell,
That all his chosen may in glory dwell.

Considering then Jehovah's* just decree,                        25
That man shall surely taste of death through sin,
I much lament, whenas I meet in mind,
The dying state securely men live in,
Excluding from their memories that day
When they from hence by death must pass away.                   30

The Scripture mentioneth, three kinds of death:
The first whereof is called death in sin,*
Whenas the body lives and soul is dead;
This sort of death did other deaths begin.
The widows whom Saint Paul* does specify                        35
Their life in pleasure caused their souls to die.

The unregenerated sinful man,
That seems to live but is in spirit dead,
Lives to the world and daily dies to God,
Preposterously his course of life is led;                       40
He lives and dies and cannot die and live;
The children's bread to whelps, God will not give.*

The second kind of death is death to sin,*
Whereby the faithful and regenerate man
Does daily mortify his ill desires,                             45
That sin does neither reign in him nor can.
Thus dying in this life, in death he lives,
And after death to him God glory gives.

The third and last of these is death by sin,
Which as a root, two branches forth does send:                  50
The former bough, whereof is corporal death,
The latter death eternal without end.
Which end, without end, God does destinate
To be the stipend of the reprobate.

This is that death which sacred Scripture calls               55
The second death or separation
Of soul and body from the love of God,
The sinner's lot, just condemnation,
Which cannot be to them that are in Christ,*
Whose life is hid with him in God the highest.*              60

A corporal death is common unto all,
To young and old, to godly and unjust;
The Prince that sways the sceptre of a realm
Must with his subjects turn by death to dust.
This is the period of all Adam's line,                        65
Which epilogue of life I thus define.

When soul and body by one spirit knit
Unloosed are and dust returns to earth,*
The spirit unto God that gave it man,
By which he lives in womb before his birth;                   70
The body void of soul bereft of breath,
Is that condition called corporal death.

This is that death which leads the soul to life,
This is that friend which frees us from our pain,
This is the portal of true Paradise                           75
Through which we pass eternal life to gain,
This is the leader unto joy or woe,
This is the door through which all men must go.

Death was at first inflicted as a curse,
But woman's seed has broke the serpent's head;*              80
His bitter death for us has gained life,
His agony has freed his own from dread.
Death is that guest the godly wish to see,
For when it comes their troubles ended be.

All things do work together for the best                      85
To those that love and are beloved of God;*
If all things, then must also sin and death,
Sickness and sorrows, world's own scourging rod;
For in despite of flesh, the world, and Devil,
God to his children brings good out of evil.                  90

First we by death are freed from present woe,
And such God's spirit hath pronounced blessed
As in the Lord depart this irksome life,
For from their labours they for ever rest.*
'Tis death conducts us to this land of peace; 95
Then welcome death, which does all sorrow cease.

If man were fettered in a loathsome gaol,
Without one spark of hope to come from thence
Till prison walls were level with the ground,
He would be glad to see their fall commence. 100
Thy body's ruin then rejoice to see,
That out of gaol thy soul may loosed be.

What worse bocardo* for the soul of man
Than is the body, which with filth is fraught;
Witness the sinks* thereof, through which do pass 105
The excrements, appointed for the draught;*
Evacuations, loathsome in their smell,
Egested* filth, unfit for tongue to tell.

'From out of prison bring my soul, O Lord',*
Was David's earnest and sincere desire; 110
Elijah* in the anguish of his heart
Did death instead of irksome life require.
*Vile, Live* and *Evil*, have the self-same letters:
He *lives* but *vile* whom *evil* holds in fetters.

The heathens make report that Argis* 115
To yield requital for the toil and pain,
Which Biton and Cleobis* for her took,
Desired the goddess Juno* they might gain
The greatest good she could to man bequeath,
Which granted was, and paid with sudden death. 120

The Thracians* sadly sorrow and lament
Whenas their children first behold the light,
But with great exultation they rejoice
What time their friends do bid the world good night.
When David's child was sick he would not eat, 125
But being dead he rose and called for meat.*

By death we secondly delivered are
From future sorrows and calamities;
The godly perish and are ta'ne away
From ill to come, as Esay* testifies. 130

And thus God cut off Jeroboam's son,*
Because he saw some good in him begun.

We thirdly are, by death, exempt from sin
And freed from bondage of enthralled woe;
'Tis true that life's the blessing of the Lord,                      135
But yet by it sin doth increase and grow;
And sin is but the offspring of the Devil,
Then blessed is he, whom death frees from this evil.

To some the Lord in mercy granteth space
For true repentance of committed sin                                 140
And reformation of those evil ways,
Which through corruption they have walked in;
And other some, who sin as earst before,
He takes away, that they may sin no more.

Death corporal in fine* is as a door,                                145
Through which our souls do pass without delay
Into those joys which cannot be conceived;
This truth is proved plain, where Christ does say,
'Today thou shalt be with me', to that thief
Which at last gasp did beg his soul's relief.*                       150

What is this world if balanced with heaven?
Earth's glory fades, but heavenly joys endure;
This life is full of sickness, want and woe,
But life through Christ hath no disease to cure;
In heaven there is no malady or pain,                                155
But melody, true comfort to maintain.

There saints are crowned with matchless majesty,
Invested with eternal robes of glory;
There sun does shine and suffers no eclipse;
Earth's chiefest joys are vain and transitory,                       160
Inconstant, fading, fickle, and unsure,
But heaven's pleasures permanent endure.

There is no penury or choking care
For present time or the succeeding morrow;
But there are riches without toil attained,                          165
Mirth without mourning, solace without sorrow,
Peace without peril, plenty without want,
Where without asking God does all things grant.

The eye of man has never yet beheld,
Nor has his ear attended once to hear,                          170
Nor yet his heart conceived or understood,
The joys prepared and purchased for the dear
And chosen children of our heavenly Father,*
Who does his sheep into one sheep-fold gather.

And as our souls possess true happiness,                        175
So shall our mortal bodies vile and base
Be raised immortal by the power of Christ,*
And with our souls enjoy a glorious place
That reunited they may join in one
To sing the praises of the cornerstone.*                        180

The day of death, says Solomon* the wise
(Which paradox the godly approbate),
Is better than the day that one is born,
For death conducts us to a blissful state.
'Tis Lazar's friend, though it seem Dives' foe;*               185
But life inducts us to a world of woe.

The mariner, which does assay to pass
The raging seas into some foreign land,
Desires much to have his voyage ended
And to arrive upon the solid land.                              190
All creatures with desire do seek for rest,
After they have with labour been oppressed.

The pilgrim which a journey undertakes,
Feeding his fancy with exotic sights,
Deems not his way much irksome to his foot,                     195
Because his pain is mixed with delights.
For 'tis his joy to think upon that day
When he shall see the period of his way.

Men are as sailors in this irksome life,
Who at the haven always cast their eye;                         200
As pilgrims wandering in an uncouth land;
Then who is he, that will not wish to die?
And he whom God by death does soonest call,
Is in my mind the happiest wight* of all.

When Simeon had embraced in his arms                            205
His Lord, whom he had waited long to see,
He of his Saviour instantly desired

A *nunc dimittis*,\* that he might be free
From bitter bondage of unpleasant life,
Where flesh and spirit always are at strife.                    210

By their contraries things may best be seen:
Jet makes the ivory most white appear,
'Tis darkness which does manifest the light,
And sickness makes us value health most dear.
Life's misery does best make known the gain                    215
And freedom which by death we do obtain.

Consider then the evils of this life,
Whose pleasures are as honey mixed with gall,
Or banks of flowers which cover lurking snakes,
Snares to entrap, and blocks whereat some fall.                    220
What wise man, then, of them will reckoning make,
Or wish to live for fading pleasure's sake?

It were some motive to induce delight
In living long, if life would certain last,
But infancy and childhood scarce are seen                    225
Before that both of them are overpast.
Juventus\* suddenly does fly away,
Adolescency makes but little stay.

Virility does not continue long,
Old age is short and hastens to an end;                    230
Our longest life and pleasure is but brief;
Thus tedious griefs on every age attend,
Which like to sable clouds eclipse our sun
And makes our glass of life with sorrow run.

Consider man in his abridged time,                    235
What pricking\* peril he therein doth bear:
Youth is encumbered with untimely harms,
Continual care does middle age outwear;
Old age is testy, subject unto grief,
Diseases steal upon it as a thief.                    240

The body is in danger (every part),
Of hurt, disease, and loss of sense and limb;
Auditus\* unto deafness subject is,
Visus\* of blindness, or of being dim,
Gustus\* of savours, bitter, tart, and sour,                    245
Olfactus\* unto loathsome stinks each hour.

Tactus* is subject to benumbedness,
Our goods to spoil by thieves or sudden fire,
Good name is liable to false reports,
Invective, obtrectations,* fruits of ire;                           250
Our kindred and acquaintance subject are
To like mishap, which falleth to our share.

Our soul in danger is of vice and error;
Our body subject to imprisonment,
To hurt by beasts, as horses and the like,                          255
Or else to spoil by creatures virulent
Which with their stings do give untimely wound,
Or else to squats* and bruises on the ground.

Those dews which Sol attracteth from the earth,
Prove most pernicious when they do descend;                         260
To number all the evils of this life
May have beginning, but can find no end.
For new enormities, new plagues procure;
'Tis just to scourge, where love cannot allure.

What course or trade of life is free from grief?                    265
Or what condition void of all annoy?*
To live in office* trouble is our lot,
To live at home is uncouth without joy,
To work in field is toilsome, full of pain,
At sea are fears, in traffic* little gain.                          270

In journey jeopardy does us attend,
In marriage grief and care oppress the mind,
The single life is solitary, vain;*
The rich can little joy in riches find,
For having much, his care must watch his wealth                     275
From secret pilfring and from open stealth.

If poverty be our appointed lot
Our grief is great, relief and comfort small,
We must endure oppression, suffer wrong;
The weak in wrestling goeth to the wall,                            280
If we be bit we cannot bite again,
If rich men strike, we must their blow sustain.

If we be eminent in place of note,
Then stand we as a mark* for envy's dart,
Conjecture censures our defect of worth,                            285

Enquiry does anatomise* each part;
And if our reputation be but small,
Contempt and scorn does us and ours befall.

The infant from the womb into the world
Comes crying, by the which it does presage 290
The pains and perils it must undergo
In childhood, manhood, and decreped age;
He that most knows this life, least does it love;
Except affection may affection move.*

Man's life on earth is like a ship at sea, 295
Tossed on the waves of troubles, to and fro,
Assailed by pirates, crossed by blustering winds,
Where rocks of ruin menace overthrow,
Where storms molest, and hunger pincheth sore,
Where death does lurk at every cabin door. 300

Yet some afflictions in this irksome life
God does in mercy to his children send,
Thereby to wean them from the love of that
Which is but noisome* and will soon have end,
That so their liking may be set above,* 305
Upon those pleasures which shall never move.

Which made the chosen vessel of the Lord,
That he might be with Christ, desire to die;*
And Job* to wish his days were at an end
Because his life was nought but misery. 310
The godly man is tired with his breath,
And finds no rest till he be free by death.

What then is life that it should be desired?
Or what advantage by it does man win?
Is not this world a net to snare the soul? 315
Do not long livers multiply their sin?
Is not this life a map of misery,
The quite contrary of tranquillity?

For though the seeming pleasures of this life
Do cause us love it, yet the pains may move 320
Us to contemplate the bait which hides the hook;
And rather loath than either like or love,
A path of ice where footing is unsure,
Or bitter pills though gilded to allure.

But some (who live as Dives* did) may say                      325
That life is sweet and comfort does afford,
That there are few whom sickness does arrest
But wish most earnestly to be restored.
That Hezekiah* wept when he heard tell
That God would have him bid the world farewell.                330

As also David* to the Lord did say;
'Let my soul live, that it may praise thee still,'
And Christ did pray, his cup from him might pass,
If so it were his holy Father's will;*
But Hezekiah wept because that yet,                            335
He had no issue on his throne to sit.

And David's wish from reason did proceed,
For he was then perplexed with his foe,
Who would with exultation have affirmed
That God in wrath had wrought his overthrow.                   340
And of Christ's prayer, this was the reason why:
Because he was a cursed death* to die.

When godly men do dread the sight of death
Their fearfulness is but of nature's* error,
The spirit's ready but the flesh is weak;*                     345
Assisting grace will mitigate their terror.
Yet some men's fear does issue from mistrust
That they shall never shine among the just.

The conscience of whose life in sin misled,*
At sight of death does make them trembling stand,              350
And like Belshazzar* change their wonted* looks,
Because that their destruction is at hand;
For when that God o'er them gives death full power,
Grave takes their bodies, hell their souls devour.

They know that sin deserves eternal death,                     355
And therefore fear when they depart from hence,
And that their lamp of life is quite extinct,
Their pleasures shall conclude and pains commence;
The worm of conscience gnaws so in their breast,
As makes their terror not to be expressed.                     360

And when (too late) with Balaam* they desire
(When they perceive their latter end draw nigh),
That they the righteous may assimilate*

In their departure, and like them may die.
But holy life is that portendeth bliss;                                365
He that lives well can never die amiss.

That man which lives a sanctified life,
Yet does not die with outward peace and rest
Through conflicts had with Satan and his lusts,
Judge not amiss of him, whom God has blessed,                          370
In leading by the gate of hell to joy,
Where he shall be exempt from all annoy.*

For sometimes 'tis the lot of wicked men,
Which in impiety their lives have led,
To outward view to leave their world in peace,                         375
Without so much as struggling on their bed.
The death of Nabal,* who so noteth well,
Shall find that many pass like stones to hell.

Death is the messenger of weal* and woe;
Like Joseph,* which foretold of dignity                                380
That Pharaoh on his butler would bestow,
But to the baker fatal misery
He did predict should suddenly ensue;
Which, as he said, did quickly fall out true.

Unto the faithful death does tidings bring                             385
Of life, of favour,* and eternal rest,
How they from out the prison of this world,
In which with griefs they have been sore oppressed,
Shall be received through Christ's eternal love
To live forever with their God above.                                  390

For though that death considered in itself
Be fearful, and does many terrors bring,
Yet unto them there is no cause of dread,
For by Christ's death grim Mors* has lost its sting,
That as a toothless snake no hurt can do,                              395
No more can death procure the godly woe.

The sting of death the Scripture says is sin;*
Christ's powerful death has took death's power away,
That by the merit of his conquering word,*
To death and Hell we may with boldness say,                            400
'Death, where's thy sting? Hell, where's thy victory?'*
In Christ we live, maugre* thy tyranny!

The godly only comfort find in death,
They view the end and not regard the way,
And with the eye of faith they see that God                    405
Intends more good to them than earth can pay;
And though to die they dare not supplicate,
Yet for their dissolution* they do wait.

So that if death arrest them unawares,
Yet can it not them unprepared find;                           410
And if with respite they depart this world,
Their well-led life does consolate their mind,
And makes them welcome death with joy of heart;
'Tis happy news that they from life must part.

But, to the wicked death brings word of death,                 415
For why to them it has not lost its sting,
It is but the exordium* of their woes,
And as a gaoler does from prison bring
Their guilty souls, to suffer for their sin
Those pains which end not, though they do begin.               420

Within them terror does affright their minds,
Above them they the face of justice see,
Beneath them horror does affront their sight,
About them ugly devils ready be
With watchful eyes, most willing without grudge,               425
To execute the pleasure of the judge.

Death takes them as it finds them, and forthwith
It does present them, as it does them take,
Unto the Lord, who censures* their deserts*
As they are found, when they appearance make;                  430
And as they are adjudged, so they must
Forever undergo their sentence just.

Mortality is God's exact decree,
Which as the deluge of his kindled ire,
Has overwhelmed with a dying life                              435
Decaying man, whose state does still require,
And pregnantly* induce, to think on death,
Ere it obstruct the passage of his breath.

Three motives moving man to meditate
On death, ere death, I briefly will declare:                   440
First the necessity that men must die,

By which they are forewarned to prepare
Against that time when they must go from hence;
This strict oportet* will with none dispense.*

Those daily objects man does speculate*                445
Present unto his thought that he must die;
For all things in this world declare and show,
That man is subject to mortality;
Those vegetives,* which bud and spring out most,
Does Hiems* kill and cut away with frost.              450

The elements must be dissolved with heat,*
The Macrocosmus it must pass away,*
And man the Microcosmus needs must die;
Both young and old must go to Golgotha.*
Fair buildings level with the ground must lie,         455
And strongest cities come to nullity.

The Medes and Persians did their laws confirm
So strongly that they could not altered be,*
And this appointment,* all men once must die,*
Is as infallible as their decree.                      460
We needs must die to pay what God does lend;*
Life had beginning, and must have an end.

From earth man came, to dust he must return,
This is the descant* of death's fatal ditty;
All men are mortal, therefore must they die,           465
And Paul sayth, 'Here is no abiding city';*
Man's days consume like wax against the sun,
And as a weaver's shuttle, swiftly run.*

That thing, which may be, may be doubted of,
And as a thing uncertain pass neglected;               470
But things that must be, greater heed require,
And of necessity must be expected.
Then think on death, ere death, for truth does show
That death must come, but when we may not know.

The second motive, moving thought of death             475
Is the impartiality of it,
Respecting neither persons, age, nor sex;
By bribes sinister* it does none acquit;
Friends nor entreaties can no whit prevail;
Where death arrests, it will admit no bail.            480

What is become of Absolom* the fair?
David* the victor? Solomon* the wise?
Crassus* the worldly rich? Dives* the wretch?
Samson* the strong that was bereft of eyes?
From these, and more than these, with whetted knife    485
Death has cut off the silver thread of life.*

It is hereditary unto all:
Lazarus dead, Dives must also die,*
Pass from his down-bed* to his bed of dust
And until doomsday in earth's bowels lie.    490
Death scatters that, which life had carking* got,
And casts on youthful years old age's lot.

Like Jehu's shaft, it spares not Joram's heart,*
But makes kings subject to its aweless* power;
David* must yield to tread the beaten path    495
When death with open mouth means to devour;
And having changed corps* to dust, who then
Can well distinguish kings from other men?

The greatest monarch of earth's monarchy,
Whom God with worldly honours highly blessed,    500
Death's beesome* from this life has swept away;
Their story's epilogue is *Mortuus est.**
For death to all men dissolution brings,
Yea, the catastrophe it is of kings.

Great Alexander* conquered many lands,    505
And savage creatures he bereft of breath;
But in the records of his famous acts,
It is not writ that he did conquer death.
The stoutest soldier fitted for the field,
Maugre his might, to death his life must yield.    510

Methuselah,* one of the longest livers,
Could not escape the piercing dart of death,
But when the sand out of his glass was run
Mors stopped the passage of his vital breath.
Death from the stately throne to grave dejects;*    515
No more the prince than peasant it respects.

It does dissolve the knot by friendship knit,
From David it takes Jonathan away;*
And children of their parents it bereaves,

Parents their children must not have for aye;                    520
Without respect of any or remorse,
It works the husband's and his wife's divorce.

'Tis so impartial that it spareth none,
But does surprise the rich as well as poor;
It was not Tully's* learned eloquence                            525
That could persuade death to pass by his door;
Nor is it wealth or prowess that can tame
Death's vigour, for it sends men whence they came.*

The third and last is the uncertainty
Of death's approach, as when or at what time                     530
It will arrest us, whether in old age,
Or our virility and youthful prime;
The which must cause continual thought of death,
That unawares it may not stop our breath.

Time turns the heavens in a certain course,                      535
The stork and crane appointed seasons know,*
The stars their constant motions do observe,
Tides have their times to ebb and overflow.
Man's fickle state does only rest unsure
Of certain course and season to endure.                          540

The tenant thinks upon that date of time
Which will his lease of house or land expire;
But of the end or *punctum** of this life,
Whereof we have no lease, who does enquire?
We in this life are tenants but at will,                         545
God only knows the time we must fulfil.

The preter* time which is already past
Was ours, but never will be so again;
The future time perhaps shall not be ours,
To make account thereof is therefore vain;                       550
The instant time which present we enjoy
Is only ours to manage and employ.

I make no doubt but many men would mourn
If they exactly knew their final day
Should be within a year of present time,                         555
Yet now with mirth they pass their time away,
When as perhaps they shall not live one hour,
Nay, in a moment, death may them devour.

Some tender infants in their cradle die,
Like blooming blossoms blown from off the tree;                    560
David's young son* must die, it is decreed
That length of days he shall not live to see.
Thus greedy death plucks buds from off the tree,
When fruits mature grow and ungathered be.

There is no man on earth that can foretell                          565
Where death, or in what place, will us select;
Abroad, at home, in city, or the field,
It is uncertain that we may expect,
Death's coming always, and in every place,
To make complete the current of our race.                           570

The manner of death's coming, how 'twill be,
God has concealed to make us vigilant;
Some die by sickness, others by mishap,
Some die with surfeit,* other some with want,
Some die by fire, some perish by the sword,                         575
Some drowned in water swim unto the Lord.

Pope Adrian* was stifled with a gnat,
Old Anacreen* strangled with a grape,
A little hair did choke great Fabius,*
Saphira* could not sudden death escape.                             580
Into this life we all but one way came,
But diverse ways we go out of the same.

If God from peril did us not protect,
Our daily food might stop our vital breath,
The things we neither doubt, nor fear, may prove                    585
The instruments of an untimely death,
And in a moment work our lives' decay
When we least think upon our ending day.

'Tis God omniscient which does only know
The time of life that man on earth must live,                       590
At his appointment Moses* must go die,
Who bounds and limit unto time does give:
Man happen may to ask, 'Where, when, and how?'
Death will surprise, but God says, 'Thus, here, now.'

Of life's decay man information hath,                               595
From certain monitors, which usher death:
The first whereof proclaims th'uncertainty

Of time determined for man's use of breath;
The second does discover misery;
The third, inevitable certainty.                                    600

The first of these is sudden casualty,
Which does suggest that death may doubtful be;
The second, sickness, which with irksome groans
Declares that death may grievous be to thee;
Thirdly, old age this rule does verify,                            605
Young men may fail, but aged men must die.

It therefore is most requisite for those
That wish to be upright in judgement found,
Not by their works, but for their saviour's meed,*
To think they always hear the last trump* sound,                  610
That they their souls in readiness may make;
For when death comes 'twill no excuses take.

Jehovah by his *utinam** does show*
His great desire that men should have respect
To understand and think upon their end,                           615
Which want of wisdom causeth them neglect;
For surely where the Lord does knowledge give,
Men live and learn to die, and die to live.

To entertain a legate from a king
In costly manner many will prepare;                               620
Yet death that comes from him that's King of Kings,
Welcome to bid there are but few that care;
But as the tree* does fall, so shall it lie,
And men must rise to judgement as they die.

That thing which at all seasons may be done,                      625
Whenever done is not done out of season;
A daily expectation of that guest,
Which anytime may come, proceeds from reason;
Jerusalem* her latter end forgot,
And therefore desolation was her lot.                             630

Invading Mors without remorse devours,
And if we be not armed ere it assault,
We shall be foiled ere we can be armed;
If we be taken tardy* 'tis our fault,
For since 'tis certain Mors will surely strike,                   635
We must expect death's poison pointed pike.

That unawares we may not be surprised,
But ready to receive that fatal blow,
Which cannot be resisted when it comes,
No more than force of floods which overflow,          640
Premeditation is the best defence
Against this foe, which will with none dispense.*

For from continual thought of Death's assault
Do sundry special benefits arise,
Careless security it first prevents                    645
Wherewith our ghostly foe does blind our eyes,
And by the which he makes us quite forget
That there's a centre in our circle set.

By thought of Death (in second place) we gain
Acquaintance with our foe, afore our fight;            650
Expected dangers lose their greatest force,
Paul's* dying daily put false fear to flight;
Those faces, which at first have ugly hue,
Grow into liking through their often view.

Thirdly, by thought of death, ere life decay,          655
We shall condemn this world and hold it vain,*
Into the which we nothing brought at first,
Nor from it can we carry ought again;*
As also know whilst on this sea we float,
We are but strangers from our home remote.             660

The dove,* which Noah sent from forth the ark,
Could find no rest till she returned again;
Nor can the faithful, till they go to Christ,
True rest and quiet without grief obtain;
Heaven is the haven of the faithful wight,             665
Christ's love the object of their soul's delight.

The soul of David* panted after God,
And thirsted oft his presence to obtain;
The father of the faithful lived in tents,
And stranger-like in Canaan did remain,*               670
That he might nowhere seek his abode
But in the city of the living God.

Fourthly, premeditation of our death
Does cause us crucify our sinful lust
And by the spirit mortify the flesh,*                  675

That soul may live when body turned to dust,
And makes us know that costly robes and meat
Do deck and nourish food for worms to eat.

Fifthly, the thought of our decease by death
Does move us seriously to weigh in mind                    680
How that our first material* was on earth,
That life is short, inconstant as the wind,*
Like mist and dew which sun does drive away,
Or swift as eagles darting to their prey.*

Man is in sacred writ compared to grass,                   685
Which flourishing today sends forth its flower,
Withering* at night is cast into the fire;
Of short persistence like an April shower.
For whoso now perceives the sun to shine,
His life is done before that it decline.                   690

Our days consume and pass away like smoke,*
Like bavin's* blaze, soon kindled, soon extinct;
Or like a ship* which swiftly slides the sea,
Uncertain, fickle, irksome, and succinct.
Recite I all the fading types I can,                       695
Yet none so momentary as is man.

Unto a shadow Job* does life compare,
Which when the body moves does vanish quite,
To vanity and likewise to a dream,
Whereof we have a hundred in one night;                    700
David's* resembling life unto a span,
Does show the short continuance of man.

If happiness consist in length of days,
An oak more happy than a man appears,
So does the elephant, and sturdy stag,                     705
Which commonly do live two hundred years;
But mortal man, as Moses* does unfold,
If he live four score years is counted old.

When Xerxes* with ten hundred thousand men
Attempted war, his eyes did shower forth tears;            710
To think not one of those whom he employed
Should be alive within one hundred years.
For Adam's heirs engaged do remain
To pay what he received and lost again.

The day wherein we first behold the light 715
Begins our death, for life does daily fade;
Our day of death begins our happy life,
We are in danger till our debt is paid;
Life is but lent, we owe it to the Lord,
When 'tis demanded, it must be restored. 720

A false imagination of long life
Made Dives* sing a requiem to his soul,
Enlarge his barns, disport* and make good cheer,
Till just Jehovah did his thoughts control,
Who calls him fool and quells his fond delight, 725
By threatening judgement to befall that night.

Sixthly, the thought of death's most sure approach
Does move contrition for our preter sin,
And works restraint of present ill desires,
Inspiring constant purpose to begin 730
A faithful life by God's assisting grace,
That to his glory we may run our race.

Lastly, premeditation of our death
Induces us to commendable care,
For settling and disposing our estate 735
To those whom we intend shall have a share,
That when we are departed from this life,
Our goods may prove no coals to kindle strife.

When Hezekiah, Judah's king, was sick
And at the entry of death's door did lie, 740
The prophet Esay* came to him and said,
'Put thou thy house in order, thou must die';
Which paradigma plainly does engrave,
That 'tis a duty God himself does crave.

Neglect of which disturbs us about end, 745
When we should be exempt from worldly care,
When doubt of who shall reap what we have sown
Distracts our thoughts and does our peace impair,
Withdrawing our affection from above,
Where we and nowhere else should fix our love. 750

Unto that place prepared for God's elect
Afore the world, the Lord conduct us still,
And grant that we the measure of our days

To his good pleasure may on earth fulfil,
That when we to our period do attain,                    755
We may with Christ in glory ever reign.

Amen

Lord Jesus come quickly.

(1621)

# MARY WROTH

## Pamphilia to Amphilanthus

### SONNET 1 (P 1)

When night's black mantle could most darkness prove,*
  And sleep, death's image, did my senses hire*
  From knowledge of myself, then thoughts did move
  Swifter than those, most swiftness need require.*
In sleep, a chariot drawn by winged desire          5
  I saw, where sat bright Venus, Queen of Love,*
  And at her feet her son, still adding fire
  To burning hearts, which she did hold above;
But one heart* flaming more than all the rest
  The goddess held, and put it to my breast.         10
  'Dear son, now shoot,'* said she, 'Thus must we win.'
He her obeyed, and martyred* my poor heart.
  I, waking, hoped as dreams it would depart;
  Yet since, O me, a lover I have been.

### SONNET 2 (P 2)

Dear eyes, how well, indeed, you do adorn
  That blessed sphere which gazing souls hold dear,
  The loved place of sought for triumphs, near
  The court* of glory, where love's force was born.
How may they term you April's sweetest morn,      5
  When pleasing looks from those bright lights appear,
  A sun-shine day; from clouds and mists still clear,
  Kind nursing fires for wishes yet unborn!
Two stars* of heaven, sent down to grace the earth,
  Placed in that throne which gives all joys their birth,    10
  Shining and burning, pleasing yet their charms,
Which, wounding, even in hurts are deemed delights,
  So pleasant is their force, so great their mights
  As, happy, they can triumph in their harms.

### SONNET 3 (P 3)

Yet is there hope. Then, Love, but play thy part,
    Remember well thyself, and think on me;
    Shine* in those eyes which conquered have my heart,
    And see if mine be slack to answer thee.
Lodge in that breast, and pity moving see          5
    For flames which in mine* burn in truest smart,
    Exiling thoughts that touch inconstancy,
    Or those which waste not in the constant art.
Watch but my sleep, if I take any rest
    For thought of you, my spirit so distressed          10
    As, pale and famished, I for mercy cry.
Will you your servant leave? Think but on this:
    Who wears love's crown* must not do so amiss,
    But seek their good, who on thy force do lie.*

### SONNET 4 (P 4)

Forbear, dark night, my joys now bud again,
    Lately grown dead, while cold aspects did chill
    The root at heart, and my chief hope quite kill,
    And thunders struck me in my pleasure's wane.*
Then I, alas, with bitter sobs and pain          5
    Privately groaned my fortune's present ill;
    All light of comfort dimmed, woes in prides fill,*
    With strange increase of grief I grieved in vain.
And most, as when a memory to good
    Molested me, which still as witness stood          10
    Of these best days in former times I knew,
Late gone, as wonders past, like the great Snow,*
    Melted and wasted, with what change must know:
    Now back the life comes where as once it grew.

### SONNET 5 (P 5)

Can pleasing sight misfortune ever bring?
    Can firm desire a painful torment try?
    Can winning eyes prove to the heart a sting?
    Or can sweet lips in treason hidden lie?
The sun, most pleasing, blinds the strongest eye          5
    If too much looked on, breaking the sight's string;*
    Desires still crossed must unto mischief hie,
    And as despair a luckless chance may fling.
Eyes, having won, rejecting proves a sting,
    Killing the bud before the tree doth spring;         10

Sweet lips, not loving, do as poison prove.
Desire, sight, eyes, lips, seek, see, prove and find,
    You love may win, but curses if unkind:
    Then show you harms dislike, and joy in love.*

### SONNET 6 (P 6)

O strive not still to heap disdain on me,
    Nor pleasure take, your cruelty to show
    On hapless me, on whom all sorrows flow,
    And biding make, as given and lost by thee.
Alas, ev'n grief is grown to pity me;                          5
    Scorn cries out 'gainst itself such ill to show,
    And would give place for joy's delights to flow;
    Yet wretched I all tortures bear from thee.
Long have I suffered, and esteemed it dear,
    Since such thy will,* yet grew my pain more near.          10
    Wish you my end? Say so, you shall it have,
For all the depth of my heart-held despair
    Is that for you I feel not death for care;
    But now I'll seek it, since you will not save.

### SONG I (P 7)

'The spring now come at last
    To trees, fields, to flowers
And meadows makes to taste
    His pride, while sad showers
Which from mine eyes do flow,                                  5
    Makes known with cruel pains
    Cold winter yet remains,
No sign of spring we know.

'The sun which to the earth
    Gives heat, light and pleasure,                            10
Joys in spring, hateth dearth,
    Plenty makes his treasure.
His heat to me is cold,
    His light all darkness is,
    Since I am barred of bliss                                 15
I heat nor light behold.'

A shepherdess* thus said,
    Who was with grief oppressed,
For truest love betrayed

Barred her from quiet rest;                            20
And weeping, thus said she:
  'My end approacheth near,
  Now willow* must I wear,
My fortune so will be.

'With branches of this tree                            25
  I'll dress my hapless head,
Which shall my witness be
  My hopes in love are dead;
My clothes embroidered all
  Shall be with garlands round,                 30
  Some scattered, others bound,
Some tied, some like to fall.

The bark* my book shall be,
  Where daily I will write
This tale of hapless me,                               35
  True slave to fortune's spite;
The root shall be my bed,
  Where nightly I will lie
  Wailing inconstancy,
Since all true love is dead.                           40

'And these lines I will leave,
  If some such lover come
Who may them right conceive,
  And place them on my tomb:
She who still constant* loved,                         45
  Now dead with cruel care,
  Killed with unkind despair
And change, her end here proved.'

### SONNET 7 (P 8)

Love, leave to urge, thou know'st thou hast the hand;*
  'Tis cowardice to strive where none resist;
  Pray thee leave off, I yield unto thy band;
  Do not thus still in thine own power persist.*
Behold, I yield; let forces be dismissed;             5
  I am thy subject, conquered, bound to stand;
  Never thy foe, but did thy claim assist,
  Seeking thy due of those who did withstand.
But now, it seems, thou would'st I should thee love.
  I do confess, 'twas thy will made me choose,     10

And thy fair shows made me a lover prove,
When I my freedom did for pain refuse.
Yet this, Sir God,* your boyship I despise;
Your charms I obey, but love not want of eyes.*

### SONNET 8 (P 9)

Led by the pow'r of grief, to wailings brought
  By false conceit* of change fall'n on my part,
  I seek for some small ease by lines which, bought,
  Increase the pain; grief is not cured by art.
Ah! how unkindness moves within the heart      5
  Which still is true and free from changing thought;
  What unknown woe it breeds, what endless smart,
  With ceaseless tears which causelessly are wrought.
It makes me now to shun all shining light,
  And seek for blackest clouds me light to give,      10
  Which to all others only darkness drive;*
  They on me shine, for sun disdains my sight.*
Yet though I dark do live, I triumph may:
Unkindness nor this wrong shall love allay.

### SONNET 9 (P 10)

Be you all pleased? Your pleasures grieve not me.
  Do you delight? I envy not your joy.
  Have you content? Contentment with you be.
  Hope you for bliss? Hope still, and still enjoy.
Let sad misfortune hapless me destroy,      5
  Leave crosses* to rule me, and still rule free,
  While all delights their contraries employ
  To keep good back, and I but torments see.
Joys are bereaved, harms do only tarry,
  Despair takes place, disdain has got the hand;      10
  Yet firm love holds my senses in such band
  As, since despised, I with sorrow marry.*
Then if with grief I now must coupled be,
Sorrow I'll wed:* despair thus governs me.

### SONNET 10 (P 11)

The weary traveller* who, tired, sought
  In places distant far, yet found no end
  Of pain or labour, nor his state to mend,
  At last with joy is to his home back brought,
Finds not more ease, though he with joy be fraught,*      5

When past is fear, content like souls ascend,
Then I, on whom new pleasures do descend,
Which now as high as first born bliss is wrought.
He, tired with his pains, I with my mind;
    He all content receives by ease of limbs,                    10
    I, greatest happiness that I do find
    Belief for faith, while hope in pleasure swims.
Truth saith, 'twas wrong conceit bred my despite,
Which, once acknowledged, brings my heart's delight.

### SONNET 11 (P 12)

You endless torments that my rest oppress,
    How long will you delight in my sad pain?
    Will never love your favour more express?
    Shall I still live, and ever feel disdain?
Alas, now stay, and let my grief obtain                              5
    Some end; feed not my heart with sharp distress;
    Let me once see my cruel fortunes gain
    At least release, and long felt woes redress.
Let not the blame of cruelty disgrace
    The honoured title of your godhead, Love;                      10
    Give not just cause for me to say, a place
    Is found for rage alone on me to move.
O quickly end, and do not long debate
My needful aid, lest help do come too late.

### SONNET 12 (P 13)

Cloyed with the torments of a tedious night,
    I wish for day; which come, I hope for joy;
    When cross* I find new tortures to destroy
    My woe-killed heart, first hurt by mischief's might;
Then cry for night, and once more day takes flight.*                 5
    And brightness gone, what Rest* should here enjoy
    Usurped is: Hate will her force employ;
    Night cannot Grief entomb, though black as spite.
My thoughts are sad, her face as sad does seem;
    My pains are long, her hours tedious are;                       10
    My grief is great, and endless is my care;
    Her face, her force, and all of woes esteem.
Then welcome Night, and farewell flatt'ring Day,
Which all hopes breed, and yet our joys delay.

## SONG 2 (P 14)

All night I weep, all day I cry, ay me,
I still do wish, though yet deny, ay me,
I sigh, I mourn, I say that still
I only am the store for ill, ay me.

In coldest hopes I freeze, yet burn,* ay me,          5
From flames I strive to fly, yet turn, ay me,
From grief I haste, but sorrows hie,
And on my heart all woes do lie, ay me.

From contraries I seek to run, ay me,
But contraries I cannot shun; ay me,                  10
For they delight their force to try,
And to despair my thoughts do tie, ay me.

Whither, alas, then shall I go, ay me,
When as despair all hopes outgo? ay me,
If to the forest, Cupid hies,                         15
And my poor soul to his laws ties, ay me.

To the Court?* O no, he cries, ay me,
There no true love you shall espy, ay me,
Leave that place to falsest lovers,
Your true love all truth discovers, ay me.            20

Then quiet rest, and no more prove, ay me,
All places are alike to love; ay me,
And constant be in this begun,
Yet say, till life with love be done, ay me.

## SONNET 13 (P 15)

Dear, famish not what you yourself gave food,
    Destroy not what your glory is to save,*
    Kill not that soul to which you spirit gave:
    In pity, not disdain, your triumph stood.
An easy thing it is to shed the blood                 5
    Of one who, at your will, yields to the grave,
    But more you may true worth* by mercy crave
    When you preserve, not spoil but nourish good.
Your sight is all the food I do desire;
    Then sacrifice me not in hidden fire,             10
    Or stop the breath which did your praises move.

Think but how easy 'tis a sight to give,
   Nay, ev'n desert, since by it I do live;
   I but chameleon-like* would live, and love.

### SONNET 14 (P 16)

Am I thus conquered? Have I lost the powers
   That to withstand, which joys to ruin me?
   Must I be still, while it my strength devours,
   And captive leads me prisoner, bound, unfree?
Love first shall leave men's fancies to them free,     5
   Desire shall quench love's flames, Spring hate sweet showers,
   Love shall lose all his darts, have sight, and see
   His shame and wishings hinder happy hours.
Why should we not Love's purblind* charms resist?
   Must we be servile, doing what he list?*     10
   No, seek some host to harbour thee: I fly
Thy babish* tricks, and freedom do profess.
   But O, my hurt makes my lost heart confess:
   I love, and must; so, farewell liberty.*

### SONNET 15* (P 17)

Truly, poor Night, thou welcome art to me,
   I love thee better in this sad attire
   Than that which raiseth some men's fancies higher,
   Like painted outsides, which foul inward be.
I love thy grave and saddest looks to see,     5
   Which seems my soul and dying heart entire,
   Like to the ashes of some happy fire
   That flamed in joy, but quenched in misery.
I love thy count'nance, and thy sober pace
   Which evenly goes, and as of loving grace     10
   To us, and me amongst the rest oppressed,
Gives quiet peace to my poor self alone,
   And freely grants day leave, when thou art gone,
   To give clear light to see all ill redressed.

### SONNET 16* (P 18)

Sleep, fie, possess me not, nor do not fright
   Me with thy heavy, and thy deathlike might:
   For counterfeiting vilder* than death's sight,
   And such deluding more my thoughts do spite.

Thou suff'rest falsest shapes my soul t'affright,⠀⠀⠀⠀⠀5
⠀⠀Sometimes in likeness of a hopeful sprite,
⠀⠀And oft times like my love, as in despite,
⠀⠀Joying thou canst with malice kill delight,
When I (a poor fool made by thee) think joy
⠀⠀Does flow, when thy fond* shadows do destroy⠀⠀⠀10
⠀⠀My that while senseless self, left free to thee.
But now do well, let me for ever sleep,
⠀⠀And so for ever that dear image keep,
⠀⠀Or still wake, that my senses may be free.

### SONNET 17 (P 19)

Sweet shades,* why do you seek to give delight
⠀⠀To me, who deem delight in this vild* place
⠀⠀But torment, sorrow, and mine own disgrace
⠀⠀To taste of joy, or your vain pleasing sight?
Show them your pleasures who saw never night⠀⠀⠀5
⠀⠀Of grief, where joying's fawning, smiling face
⠀⠀Appears as day, where grief found never space
⠀⠀Yet for a sigh, a groan, or envy's spite.
But O, on me a world of woes do lie,
⠀⠀Or else on me all harms strive to rely,⠀⠀⠀⠀⠀10
⠀⠀And to attend like servants bound to me.
Heat in desire, while frosts of care I prove,
⠀⠀Wanting my love, yet surfeit do with love,
⠀⠀Burn, and yet freeze: better in hell to be.*

### SONNET 18 (P 20)

Which should I better like of, day or night?*
⠀⠀Since all the day I live in bitter woe,
⠀⠀Enjoying light more clear, my wrongs to know,
⠀⠀And yet most sad, feeling in it all spite.
In night, when darkness does forbid all light⠀⠀⠀5
⠀⠀Yet see I grief apparent to the show,
⠀⠀Followed by jealousy, whose fond tricks flow,
⠀⠀And on unconstant waves of doubt alight.
I can behold rage cowardly to feed
⠀⠀Upon foul error, which these humours* breed,⠀⠀⠀10
⠀⠀Shame, doubt and fear, yet boldly will think ill.
All these in both I feel; then which is best,
⠀⠀Dark to joy by day, light in night oppressed?
⠀⠀Leave both, and end; these but each other spill.*

## SONG 3 (P 21)

Stay, my thoughts, do not aspire
   To vain hopes of high desire;
   See you not all means bereft
   To enjoy? No joy is left,
   Yet still methinks my thoughts do say,        5
   Some hopes do live amid dismay.

Hope, then once more, hope for joy,
   Bury fear which joys destroy;
   Thought hath yet some comfort giv'n,
   Which despair hath from us driv'n;        10
   Therefore dearly my thoughts cherish,
   Never let such thinking perish.

'Tis an idle thing to plain,*
   Odder far to die for pain;
   Think, and see how thoughts do rise,        15
   Winning where there no hope lies,
   Which alone is lovers' treasure,
   For by thoughts we love do measure.

Then, kind thought, my fancy guide,
   Let me never hapless slide;        20
   Still maintain thy force in me,
   Let me thinking still be free,
   Nor leave thy might until my death,
   But let me thinking yield up breath.

## SONNET 19* (P 22)

Come darkest night, becoming sorrow best,
   Light, leave thy light, fit for a lightsome soul:
   Darkness doth truly suit with me oppressed,
   Whom absence' power does from mirth control.
The very trees with hanging heads condole        5
   Sweet summer's parting, and, of leaves distressed
   In dying colours make a grief-full role,
   So much, alas, to sorrow are they pressed.
Thus of dead leaves her farewell carpet's made;
   Their fall, their branches, all their mournings prove,        10
   With leafless, naked bodies, whose hues vade*

From hopeful green, to wither in their love.
If trees and leaves, for absence, mourners be,
No marvel that I grieve, who like want see.

### SONNET 20* (P 23)

The sun which glads the earth at his bright sight,
  When in the morn he shows his golden face,
  And takes the place from tedious drowsy night,
  Making the world still happy in his grace,
Shows happiness remains not in one place,                5
  Nor may the heavens alone to us give light,
  But hide that cheerful face, though no long space,
  Yet long enough for trial of their might.
But never sun-set could be so obscure,
  No desert* ever had a shade so sad,                    10
  Nor could black darkness ever prove so bad
  As pains which absence makes me now endure.
The missing of the sun awhile makes night,
But absence of my joy sees never light.

### SONNET 21 (P 24)

When last I saw thee, I did not thee see,
  It was thine image, which in my thoughts lay
  So lively figured, as no time's delay
  Could suffer me in heart to parted be;
And sleep so favourable is to me,                        5
  As not to let thy loved remembrance stray,
  Lest that I, waking, might have cause to say,
  There was one minute found to forget thee.
Then since my faith is such, so kind my sleep
  That gladly thee presents into my thought,*            10
  And still true lover like thy face does keep,
  So as some pleasure shadow-like is wrought:
Pity my loving, nay, of conscience, give
Reward to me, in whom thy self does live.

### SONNET 22 (P 25)

Like to the Indians,* scorched with the sun,
  The sun which they do as their god adore,
  So am I used by Love, for, ever more
  I worship him, less favours have I won.
Better are they who thus to blackness* run,              5

And so can only whiteness' want deplore,
    Than I who pale and white am with grief's store,
    Nor can have hope, but to see hopes undone.*
Besides, their sacrifice received's* in sight
    Of their chose saint, mine hid as worthless rite.*          10
    Grant me to see where I my off'rings give,
Then let me wear the mark of Cupid's might
    In heart, as they in skin of Phoebus'* light,
    Not ceasing off'rings to Love while I live.

### SONNET 23 (P 26)

When everyone to pleasing pastime hies,*
    Some hunt,* some hawk, some play, while some delight
    In sweet discourse, and music shows joy's might;
    Yet I my thoughts do far above these prize.
The joy which I take is, that free from eyes*                    5
    I sit, and wonder at this day like night,
    So to dispose themselves, as void* of right,
    And leave true pleasure for poor vanities.
When others hunt, my thoughts I have in chase,*
    If hawk, my mind at wished end doth fly;                     10
    Discourse, I with my spirit talk, and cry
    While others music choose as greatest grace.
O God, say I, can these fond pleasures move,
Or music be but in sweet thoughts of love?

### SONNET 24 (P 27)

Once did I hear an aged father* say
    Unto his son, who with attention hears
    What age and wise experience ever clears
    From doubts of fear or reason to betray,
'My son,' said he, 'behold thy father grey;                      5
    I once had, as thou hast, fresh tender years,
    And like thee sported, destitute of fears;
    But my young faults made me too soon decay.
Love once I did, and like thee feared my love,
    Led by the hateful thread of jealousy:                       10
    Striving to keep, I lost my liberty,
    And gained my grief, which still my sorrows move.
In time shun this; to love is no offence,
But doubt in youth, in age breeds penitence.'

## SONG 4 (P 28)

Sweetest love return again,*
  Make not too long stay
Killing mirth and forcing pain,
  Sorrow leading way:
Let us not thus parted be,               5
Love and absence ne'er agree.

But since you must needs depart,
  And me hapless leave,
In your journey take my heart,
  Which will not deceive:               10
Yours it is, to you it flies,
Joying in those loved eyes.

So in part we shall not part,
  Though we absent be;
Time nor place nor greatest smart      15
  Shall my bands* make free:
Tied I am, yet think it gain;
In such knots I feel no pain.

But can I live, having lost
  Chiefest part of me?                20
Heart is fled, and sight is crossed:*
  These my fortunes be.
Yet dear heart go, soon return:
As good there, as here to burn.

## SONNET 25 (P 29)

Poor eyes be blind, the light behold no more,
  Since that is gone which is your dear delight,
  Ravished from you by greater pow'r and might,
  Making your loss a gain to others' store.*
O'erflow and drown, till sight to you restore    5
  That blessed star, and, as in hateful spite,
  Send forth your tears in floods,* to kill all sight
  And looks, that lost wherein you joyed before.
Bury these beams which in some kindled fires,
  And conquered have, their love-burnt hearts' desires  10
  Losing, and yet no gain by you esteemed;
Till that bright star do once again appear,
  Brighter than Mars* when he does shine most clear,
  See not; then by his might be you redeemed.

### SONNET 26 (P 30)

Dear, cherish this,* and with it my soul's will,*
  Nor for it ran away do it abuse:
  Alas, it left poor me, your breast to choose,
  As the blest shrine where it would harbour still.
Then favour show, and not unkindly kill
  The heart which fled to you, but do excuse
  That which for better, did the worse refuse,
  And pleased I'll be, though heartless my life spill.*
But if you will be kind, and just indeed,
  Send me your heart, which in mine's place shall feed          10
  On faithful love to your devotion bound;
There shall it see the sacrifices made
  Of pure and spotless love which shall not vade*
  While soul and body are together found.*

### SONNET 27 (P 31)

Fie, tedious Hope, why do you still rebel?
  Is it not yet enough you flattered me,*
  But cunningly you seek to use a spell
  How to betray; must these your trophies* be?
I looked from you far sweeter fruit to see,                      5
  But blasted were your blossoms when they fell,
  And those delights expected from hands free,
  Withered and dead, and what seemed bliss proves hell.
No town was won by a more plotted sleight
  Than I by you, who may my fortune write                       10
  In embers of that fire which ruined me:
Thus, Hope, your falsehood calls you to be tried.
  You're loath, I see, the trial to abide;
  Prove true at last, and gain your liberty.

### SONNET 28 (P 32)

Grief,* killing Grief, have not my torments been
  Already great and strong enough, but still
  Thou dost increase, nay glory in, my ill,
  And woes new past, afresh new woes begin?
Am I the only purchase thou canst win?                          5
  Was I ordained to give despair her fill,
  Or fittest I should mount misfortune's hill,
  Who in the plain of joy cannot live in?

If it be so, Grief come as welcome guest,
 Since I must suffer for another's rest;     10
 Yet this, good Grief, let me entreat of thee:
Use still thy force, but not from those I love
 Let me all pains and lasting torments prove;
 So I miss these, lay all thy weights on me.

## SONNET 29 (P 33)

Fly hence, O Joy, no longer here abide:
 Too great thy pleasures are for my despair
 To look on; losses now must prove my fare
 Who, not long since, on better fair relied.
But fool, how oft had I heav'n's changing* spied,   5
 Before of mine own fate I could have care,
 Yet now, past time I can too late beware,
 When nothing's left but sorrows faster tied.
While I enjoyed that sun whose sight did lend
 Me joy, I thought that day could have no end:   10
 But soon a night came clothed in absence dark,
Absence more sad, more bitter than is gall,
 Or death when on true lovers it does fall,
 Whose fires of love, disdain rests* poorer spark.

## SONNET 30 (P 34)

You blessed shades, which give me silent rest,
 Witness but this when death has closed mine eyes,
 And separated me from earthly ties,
 Being from hence to higher place addressed,
How oft in you I have lain here oppressed,    5
 And have my miseries in woeful cries
 Delivered forth, mounting up to the skies
 Yet helpless back returned to wound my breast,
Which wounds did but strive how to breed more harm
 To me, who can be cured by no one charm    10
 But that of love, which yet may me relieve;
If not, let death my former pains redeem,
 My trusty friends, my faith untouched esteem,
 And witness I could love, who so could grieve.*

## SONG 5 (P 35)

Time, only cause of my unrest,
By whom I hoped once to be blessed,
 How cruel art thou turned,

That first gav'st life unto my love,
And still a pleasure not to move                                  5
   Or change, though ever burned;

Have I thee slacked, or left undone
One loving rite, and so have won
   Thy rage or bitter changing,
That now no minutes I shall see                                   10
Wherein I may least happy be,
   Thy favours so estranging?

Blame thy self and not my folly,
Time gave time but to be holy;
   True love such ends best loveth.                     15
Unworthy love does seek for ends,
A worthy love but worth* pretends,
   Nor other thoughts it proveth.

Then stay thy swiftness, cruel Time,
And let me once more blessed climb                                20
   To joy, that I may praise thee:
Let me, pleasure sweetly tasting,
Joy in love, and faith not wasting,
   And on Fame's* wings I'll raise thee;

Never shall thy glory dying                                       25
Be until thine own untying,
   That Time no longer liveth;
'Tis a gain such time to lend,
Since so thy fame shall never end,
   But joy for what she giveth.                          30

### SONNET 31 (P 36)

After long trouble in a tedious way
   Of love's unrest, laid down to ease my pain,
   Hoping for rest, new torments I did gain,
   Possessing me, as if I ought t'obey,
When Fortune came, though blinded,* yet did stay,                 5
   And in her blessed arms did me enchain;
   I, cold with grief, thought no warmth to obtain,
   Or to dissolve that ice of joy's decay,
Till, 'Rise,' said she, 'Reward to thee does send
   By me, the servant of true lovers, joy;                 10
   Banish all clouds of doubt, all fears destroy,

And now on Fortune, and on Love depend.'
I her obeyed, and rising felt that love
Indeed was best, when I did least it move.*

### SONNET 32 (P 37)

How fast thou fliest, O Time, on Love's swift wings,*
    To hopes of joy, that flatters our desire,
    Which to a lover still contentment brings;
    Yet, when we should enjoy, thou does retire.
Thou stay'st thy pace, false Time, from our desire,            5
    When to our ill thou hast'st with eagle's wings,
    Slow only to make us see thy retire
    Was for despair and harm, which sorrow brings.
O slack thy pace, and milder pass to Love,
    Be like the bee,* whose wings she doth but use           10
    To bring home profit, master's good to prove,
    Laden and weary, yet again pursues.
So lade* thy self with honey of sweet joy,
And do not me, the hive of love, destroy.

### SONNET 33 (P 38)

How many eyes, poor Love, hast thou to guard
    Thee from thy most desired wish and end?
    Is it because some say thou'rt blind that, barred
    From sight, thou should'st no happiness attend?
Who blame thee so, small justice can pretend,                5
    Since 'twixt thee and the sun no question hard
    Can be, his sight but outward, thou canst bend
    The heart, and guide it freely; thus, unbarred*
Art thou, while we, both blind and bold, oft dare
    Accuse thee of the harms ourselves should find:*        10
    Who, led with folly and by rashness blind,
    Thy sacred pow'r do with a child's compare.
Yet Love, this boldness pardon: for admire
Thee sure we must, or be born without fire.

### SONNET 34 (P 39)

Take heed mine eyes, how you your looks do cast,
    Lest they betray my heart's most secret thought:
    Be true unto yourselves, for nothing's bought
    More dear than doubt, which brings a lover's fast.*
Catch you all watching eyes,* ere they be past,              5

Or take yours, fixed where your best love has sought
    The pride of your desires; let them be taught
    Their faults, for shame they could no truer last.
Then look, and look with joy, for conquest won
    Of those that searched your hurt in double kind;                    10
    So you kept safe, let them themselves look blind,
    Watch, gaze, and mark, till they to madness run;
While you, mind eyes, enjoy full sight of love,
Contented that such happinesses move.

### SONNET 35 (P 40)

False Hope, which feeds but to destroy, and spill
    What it first breeds;* unnatural to the birth
    Of thine own womb, conceiving but to kill,
    And plenty gives to make the greater dearth.*
So tyrants do who, falsely ruling earth,                               5
    Outwardly grace them, and with profit's fill
    Advance those who appointed are to death,
    To make their greater fall to please their will.*
Thus shadow* they their wicked vile intent,
    Colouring evil with a show* of good,                               10
    While in fair shows* their malice so is spent:
    Hope kills the heart, and tyrants shed the blood.
For Hope deluding brings us to the pride*
Of our desires, the farther down to slide.

### SONNET 36 (P 41)

How well, poor heart, thou witness,* canst I love,
    How oft my grief has made thee shed forth tears,
    Drops of thy dearest blood, and how oft fears
    Born, testimony of the pains I prove;*
What torments has thou suffered, while above                           5
    Joy thou tortured were with racks which longing bears;
    Pinched with desires which yet but wishing rears,
    Firm in my faith, in constancy to move.
Yet is it said, that sure love cannot be
    Where so small show of passion is descried;*                       10
    When thy chief pain is, that I must it hide
    From all save only one,* who should it see.
For know, more passion in my heart does move,
Than in a million that make show of love.

## SONG 6* (P 42)

You happy blessed eyes,
   Which in that ruling place
   Have force both to delight, and to disgrace,
Whose light allures and ties
   All hearts to your command:          5
   O, look on me, who do at mercy stand.

'Tis you that rule my life,
   'Tis you my comforts give,
   Then let not scorn to me my ending drive;
Nor let the frowns of strife          10
   Have might to hurt those lights
   Which while they shine they are true love's delights.

See but when night appears,
   And sun has lost his force,
   How his loss does all joy from us divorce;      15
And when he shines, and clears
   The heav'ns from clouds of night,
   How happy then is made our gazing sight.

But more than sun's fair light
   Your beams do seem to me,          20
   Whose sweetest looks do tie and yet make free;
Why should you then so spite
   Poor me, as to destroy
   The only pleasure that I taste of joy?

Shine then, O dearest lights,          25
   With favour and with love,
   And let no cause your cause of frownings move;
But as the soul's delights
   So bless my then-blest eyes,
   Which unto you their true affection ties.      30

Then shall the sun give place
   As to your greater might,
   Yielding that you do show more perfect light.
O then but grant this grace
   Unto your love-tied slave,          35
   To shine on me, who to you all faith gave.

And when you please to frown,
   Use your most killing eyes

On them who in untruth and falsehood lies,
But, dear, on me cast down                                    40
   Sweet looks, for true desire,
   That banish do all thoughts of feigned fire.

### SONNET 37 (P 43)

Night, welcome art thou to my mind distressed,
   Dark, heavy, sad, yet not more sad than I:
   Never could'st thou find fitter company
   For thine own humour* than I, thus oppressed.
If thou beest dark, my wrongs still unredressed          5
   Saw never light, nor smallest bliss can spy;
   If heavy, joy from me too fast does hie,*
   And care outgoes my hope of quiet rest.
Then now in friendship join with hapless me,
   Who am as sad and dark as thou canst be,              10
   Hating all pleasure or delight of life;
Silence, and Grief, with thee I best do love,
   And from you three* I know I cannot move;
   Then let us live companions without strife.

### SONNET 38 (P 44)

What pleasure can a banished* creature have
   In all the pastimes that invented are
   By wit or learning, absence making war
   Against all peace that may a biding* crave?
Can we delight but in a welcome grave                     5
   Where we may bury pains, and so be far
   From loathed company, who always jar
   Upon the string of mirth that pastime gave?
The knowing part of joy is deemed the heart;
   If that be gone, what joy can joy impart,              10
   When senseless is the feeler of our mirth?
No, I am banished, and no good shall find,
   But all my fortunes must with mischief bind,
   Who but for misery did gain a birth.

### SONNET 39 (P 45)

If I were giv'n to mirth, 'twould be more cross
   Thus to be robbed of my chiefest joy,
   But silently I bear my greatest loss;
   Who's used to sorrow, grief will not destroy.

Nor can I, as those pleasant wits,* enjoy                                   5
   My own framed words, which I account the dross
   Of purer thoughts, or reckon them as moss,*
   While they, wit sick, themselves to breath employ.
Alas, think I, your plenty shows your want,
   For where most feeling is, words are more scant.                   10
   Yet pardon me, live, and your pleasure take;
Grudge not if I, neglected, envy show;
   'Tis not to you that I dislike do owe,
   But, crossed* myself, wish some like me to make.*

### SONNET 40 (P 46)

It is not love which you poor fools* do deem,
   That does appear by fond and outward shows
   Of kissing, toying,* or by swearing's gloze:*
   O no, these are far off from Love's esteem.
Alas, they are not such that can redeem                                   5
   Love lost, or winning, keep those chosen blows;
   Though oft with face and looks Love overthrows,
   Yet so slight conquest does not him beseem.*
'Tis not a show of sighs or tears can prove
   Who loves indeed, which blasts of feigned love                     10
   Increase or die, as favours from them slide;
But in the soul true love in safety lies,
   Guarded by faith, which to desert* still hies;
   And yet kind looks do many blessings hide.

### SONNET 41* (P 47)

You blessed stars which does heaven's glory show,
   And at your brightness make our eyes admire:
   Yet envy not, though I on earth below
   Enjoy a sight which moves in me more fire.
I do confess such beauty breeds desire,                                   5
   You shine, and clearest light on us bestow,
   Yet does a sight on earth more warmth inspire
   Into my loving soul, his grace to know.
Clear, bright and shining as you are, is this
   Light of my joy, fixed steadfast, nor will move                    10
   His light from me, nor I change from his love,
   But still increase, as th'height of all my bliss.
His sight gives life unto my love-ruled eyes,
My love content, because in his, love lies.

## SONNET 42 (P 48)

If ever Love had force in human breast,
  If ever he could move in pensive heart,
  Or if that he such pow'r could but impart
  To breed those flames whose heat brings joy's unrest,
Then look on me: I am to these addressed,*          5
  I am the soul that feels the greatest smart,
  I am that heartless trunk* of heart's depart,
  And I that one by love and grief oppressed.
None ever felt the truth of Love's great miss
  Of eyes, till I deprived was of bliss;          10
  For had he* seen, he must have pity showed;
I should not have been made this stage* of woe,
  Where sad disasters have their open show:
  O no, more pity he had sure bestowed.

## SONG 7 (P 49)

Sorrow, I yield, and grieve that I did miss:*
Will not thy rage be satisfied with this?
  As sad a devil as thee,
  Made me unhappy be;
Wilt thou not yet consent to leave, but still          5
Strive how to show thy cursed, devil'sh skill?

I mourn, and dying am; what would you more?
My soul attends, to leave this cursed shore
  Where harms do only flow,
  Which teach me but to know          10
The saddest hours of my life's unrest,
And tired minutes with grief's hand oppressed.

Yet all this will not pacify thy spite:
No, nothing can bring ease but my last night.
  Then quickly let it be,          15
  While I unhappy see
That Time, so sparing to grant lovers bliss,
Will see, for time lost, there shall no grief miss.*

Nor let me ever cease from lasting grief,
But endless let it be, without relief,          20
  To win again of Love

The favour I did prove,
And with my end please him, since, dying, I
Have him offended, yet unwillingly.

### SONNET 43 (P 50)

O dearest eyes, the lights and guides of love,
    The joys of Cupid* who, himself born blind,
    To your bright shining does his triumphs bind,
    For in your seeing does his glory move.
How happy are those places where you prove        5
    Your heavn'ly beams, which makes the sun to find
    Envy and grudging, he so long hath shined,
    For your clear lights to match his beams above.
But now, alas, your sight is here forbid,
    And darkness must these poor lost rooms* possess,     10
    So be all blessed lights from henceforth hid,
    That this black deed of darkness have excess.
For why should heaven afford least light to those
Who for my misery such darkness chose?

### SONNET 44 (P 51)

How fast thou hast'st, O Spring,* with sweetest speed
    To catch thy waters which before are run,
    And of the greater rivers welcome won,
    Ere* these thy newborn streams these places feed.
Yet you do well, lest staying here might breed       5
    Dangerous floods, your sweetest banks t'o'er-run,
    And yet much better my distress to shun,
    Which makes my tears your swiftest course succeed;
But best you do when with so hasty flight
    You fly my ills, which now my self outgo,     10
    Whose broken heart can testify such woe
    That, so o'ercharged, my life blood wasteth quite.
Sweet Spring, then keep your way,* be never spent,
And my ill days, or griefs, asunder rent.

### SONNET 45* (P 52)

Good now, be still, and do not me torment
    With multitudes of questions, be at rest,
    And only let me quarrel with my breast,
    Which still lets in new storms my soul to rent.
Fie, will you still my mischiefs more augment?       5

You say I answer cross,* I that confessed
Long since; yet must I ever be oppressed
With your tongue torture which will ne'er be spent?
Well then, I see no way but this will fright
    That devil speech: alas, I am possessed,*        10
    And mad folks senseless are of wisdom's right;
The hellish spirit, Absence, doth arrest
    All my poor senses to his cruel might:
    Spare me then till I am myself, and blest.

### SONNET 46 (P 53)

Love, thou hast all, for now thou hast me made
    So thine, as if for thee I were ordained;
    Then take thy conquest, nor let me be pained
    More in thy sun, when I do seek thy shade.
No place for help have I left to invade,        5
    That showed a face where least ease might be gained;
    Yet found I pain increase, and but obtained*
    That this no way was to have love allayed,
When hot and thirsty, to a well I came,
    Trusting by that to quench part of my flame,        10
    But there I was by love afresh embraced;
Drink I could not, but in it I did see
    Myself a living glass* as well as she,
    For Love to see himself in, truly placed.

### SONNET 47 (P 54)

O stay, mine eyes, shed not these fruitless tears,
    Since hope is past to win you back again
    That treasure which, being lost, breeds all your pain;
    Cease from this poor betraying of your fears.
Think this too childish is, for where grief rears       5
    So high a pow'r for such a wretched gain,
    Sighs nor laments should thus be spent in vain:
    True sorrow never outward wailing bears.
Be ruled by me, keep all the rest in store,
    Till no room is that may contain one more,       10
    Then in that sea of tears drown hapless me,
And I'll provide such store of sighs, as part
    Shall be enough to break the strongest heart;
    This done, we shall from torments freed be.

### SONNET 48 (P 55)

How like a fire does love increase in me,
  The longer that it lasts, the stronger still,
  The greater, purer, brighter, and does fill
  No eye with wonder more; then hopes still be
Bred in my breast, when fires of love are free          5
  To use that part to their best pleasing will,*
  And now impossible it is to kill
  The heat so great, where Love his strength do see.
Mine eyes can scarce sustain the flames, my heart
  Does trust in them my passions to impart,          10
  And languishingly strive to show my love;
My breath not able is to breath least part
  Of that increasing fuel of my smart;
  Yet love I will, till I but ashes prove.*

                                        Pamphilia.*

### SONNET* (P 56)

Let grief as far be from your dearest breast
  As I do wish, or in my hands to ease;
  Then should it banished be, and sweetest rest
  Be placed to give content by love to please.
Let those disdains which on your heart do seize          5
  Doubly return to bring her* soul's unrest,
  Since true love will not that belov'd displease,
  Or let least smart to their minds be addressed;
But oftentimes mistakings be in love,
  Be they as far from false accusing right,          10
  And still truth govern with a constant might,
  So shall you only wished pleasures prove.
And as for me, she that shows you least scorn,
With all despite and hate, be her heart torn.

### SONG (P 57)

O me, the time is come to part,
  And with it my life-killing smart:
Fond hope leave me, my dear must go
  To meet more joy, and I more woe.

Where still of mirth enjoy thy fill,          5
  One is enough to suffer ill:
My heart so well to sorrow used
  Can better be by new griefs bruised.

Thou whom the heavens themselves like made
   Should never sit in mourning shade:              10
No, I alone must mourn and end,
   Who have a life in grief to spend.

My swiftest pace, to wailings bent,
   Shows joy had but a short time lent
To bide in me, where woes must dwell,          15
   And charm me with their cruel spell.

And yet when they their witchcrafts* try,
   They only make me wish to die:
But ere my faith in love they change,
   In horrid darkness will I range.             20

### SONG (P 58)

Say Venus how long have I loved, and served you here,
   Yet all my passions scorned or doubted, although clear?
Alas, think love deserveth love, and you have loved:
   Look on my pains, and see if you the like have proved.
Remember then you are the goddess of desire,        5
   And that your sacred pow'r hath touched and felt this fire.

Persuade these flames in me to cease, or them redress
   In me, poor me, who storms of love have in excess.
My restless nights may show for me, how much I love,
   My sighs unfeigned can witness what my heart does prove,   10
My saddest looks do show the grief my soul endures,
   Yet all these torments from your hands no help procures.

Command that wayward child* your son to grant your right,
   And that his bow and shafts he yield to your fair sight,
To you who have the eyes of joy, the heart of love,       15
   And then new hopes may spring, that I may pity move:
Let him not triumph that he can both hurt and save,
   And more, brag that to you yourself a wound he gave.

Rule him, or what shall I expect of good to see,
Since he that hurt you, he alas may murder* me?        20

### SONG (P 59)

I, that am of all most crossed,*
Having, and that had, have lost,
May with reason thus complain,
Since love breeds love, and love's pain.

That which I did most desire                    5
To allay my loving fire,
I may have, yet now must miss,
Since another ruler* is.

Would that I no ruler had,
Or the service not so bad,                       10
Then might I with bliss enjoy
That which now my hopes destroy.

And that wicked pleasure got,
Brings with it the sweetest lot:
I, that must not taste the best,                 15
Fed, must starve, and restless rest.

### SONG (P 60)

'Love as well can make abiding
  In a faithful shepherd's breast
As in princes', whose thoughts sliding
  Like swift rivers never rest.

Change, to their minds, is best feeding,         5
  To a shepherd all his care,
Who, when his love is exceeding,
  Thinks his faith his richest fare;

Beauty, but a slight inviting,
  Cannot stir his heart to change;              10
Constancy, his chief delighting,
  Strives to flee from fancies strange;

Fairness to him is no pleasure,
  If in other than his love;
Nor can esteem that a treasure                  15
  Which in her smiles does not move.'

This a shepherd once confessed,
  Who loved well but was not loved;
Though with scorn and grief oppressed,
  Could not yet to change be moved.             20

But himself he thus contented,
  While in love he was accursed:
This hard hap he not repented,
  Since best lovers speed* the worst.

## SONG (P 61)

Dearest, if I, by my deserving,
  May maintain in your thoughts my love,
    Let me it still enjoy
    Nor faith destroy,
But pity love where it does move.                        5

Let no other new love* invite you
  To leave me who so long have served,
    Nor let your pow'r decline,
    But purely shine
On me, who have all truth preserved;                    10

Or had you once found my heart straying,
  Then would I not accuse your change,
    But being constant still,*
    It needs must kill
One whose soul knows not how to range.                  15

Yet may you love's sweet smiles recover,
  Since all love is not yet quite lost,
    But tempt not love too long,
    Lest so great wrong
Make him think he is too much crossed.*                 20

## SONG (P 62)

Fairest and still truest eyes,
Can you the lights be, and the spies
    Of my desires?
Can you shine clear for love's delight,
And yet the breeders be of spite,                        5
    And jealous* fires?

Mark what looks you do behold,
Such as by jealousy are told
    They want your love;
See how they sparkle in distrust,                       10
Which by a heat of thoughts unjust
    In them do move.

Learn to guide your course by art,
Change your eyes into your heart,
    And patient be,                              15

Till fruitless jealousy gives leave
By safest absence to receive
    What you would see;

Then let Love his triumph have,
And suspicion such a grave                                   20
    As not to move,
While wished freedom brings that bliss,
That you enjoy what all joy is,
    Happy to love.

### SONNET I (SECOND SERIES)* (P 63)

In night yet may we see some kind of light,
    When as the moon does please to show her face
    And in the sun's room yields her light and grace,
    Which otherwise must suffer dullest night.
So are my fortunes, barred from true delight,               5
    Cold and uncertain, like to this strange place,
    Decreasing, changing in an instant space,
    And even at full of joy turned to despite.
Justly on Fortune* was bestowed the wheel,
    Whose favours fickle and unconstant reel,               10
    Drunk with delight of change and sudden pain;
Where pleasure has no settled place of stay,
    But turning still, for our best hopes decay,
    And this, alas, we lovers often gain.

### SONNET 2 (SECOND SERIES) (P 64)

Love like a juggler* comes to play his prize,*
    And all minds draw his wonders to admire,
    To see how cunningly he, wanting eyes,*
    Can yet deceive the best sight of desire.
The wanton child, how he can feign his fire                 5
    So prettily,* as none sees his disguise,
    How finely do his tricks, while we fools hire*
The badge and office* of his tyrannies!
For in the end, such juggling he doth make,
    As he our hearts instead of eyes does take;            10
    For men can only by their sleights abuse
The sight with nimble and delightful skill;
    But if he play, his gain is our lost will;*
    Yet childlike, we cannot his sports refuse.

### SONNET 3 (SECOND SERIES) (P 65)

Most blessed night, the happy time for love,
   The shade for lovers, and their love's delight,
   The reign of love for servants free from spite,
   The hopeful season for joy's sports to move:
Now hast thou made thy glory higher prove          5
   Than did the god* whose pleasant reed* did smite
   All Argus' eyes into a deathlike night,
   Till they were safe, that none could love reprove;
Now thou hast closed those eyes from prying sight,
   That nourish jealousy more than joys right,        10
   While vain suspicion fosters their mistrust,
Making sweet sleep to master all suspect,
   Which else their private fears would not neglect,
   But would embrace both blinded, and unjust.

### SONNET 4 (SECOND SERIES) (P 66)

Cruel suspicion, O! be now at rest,
   Let daily torments bring to thee some stay;
   Alas, make not my ill thy easeful prey,
   Nor give loose reigns to rage, when love's oppressed.
I am by care sufficiently distressed;          5
   No rack can stretch my heart more, nor a way
   Can I find out for least content to lay
   One happy foot of joy, one step that's blest.
But to my end thou fliest with greedy eye,
   Seeking to bring grief by base jealousy;        10
   O, in how strange a cage am I kept in!
No little sign of favour can I prove
   But must be weighed, and turned to wronging love,
   And with each humour must my state begin.

### SONNET 5 (SECOND SERIES) (P 67)

How many nights have I with pain endured,
   Which as so many ages I esteemed,
   Since my misfortune, yet no whit redeemed
   But rather faster tied, to grief assured?
How many hours have my sad thoughts endured     5
   Of killing pains? Yet is it not esteemed
   By cruel Love, who might have these redeemed,
   And all these years of hours to joy assured:
But, fond child,* had he had a care to save

As first to conquer, this my pleasure's grave                    10
Had not been now to testify my woe;
I might have been an image of delight,
As now a tomb for sad misfortune's spite,
Which Love unkindly for reward does show.

### SONNET 6 (SECOND SERIES)* (P 68)

My pain, still smothered in my grieved breast,
Seeks for some ease, yet cannot passage find
To be discharged of this unwelcome guest;
When most I strive, more fast his burdens bind.
Like to a ship on Goodwins* cast by wind,                         5
The more she strives, more deep in sand is pressed,
Till she be lost, so am I, in this kind,
Sunk, and devoured, and swallowed by unrest,
Lost, shipwrecked, spoiled, debarred of smallest hope,
Nothing of pleasure left; save thoughts have scope,               10
Which wander may. Go then, my thoughts, and cry
Hope's perished, Love tempest-beaten, Joy lost:
Killing Despair hath all these blessings crossed,
Yet Faith still cries, Love will not falsify.

### SONNET 7 (SECOND SERIES) (P 69)

An end, fond jealousy; alas, I know
Thy hiddenest and thy most secret art;
Thou canst no new invention frame, but part
I have already seen, and felt with woe.
All thy dissemblings which by feigned show                        5
Won my belief, while truth did rule my heart,
I with glad mind embraced, and deemed my smart
The spring of joy, whose streams with bliss should flow.
I thought excuses had been reasons true,
And that no falsehood could of thee ensue,                        10
So soon belief in honest minds is wrought;
But now I find thy flattery and skill,
Which idly made me to observe thy will:*
Thus is my learning by my bondage bought.

### SONNET 8 (SECOND SERIES) (P 70)

Poor Love in chains and fetters, like a thief,
I met led forth, as chaste Diana's* gain,
Vowing the untaught lad should no relief
From her receive, who gloried in fond pain.

She called him thief; with vows he did maintain                    5
   He never stole, but some sad slight* of grief
   Had giv'n to those who did his pow'r disdain.
   In which revenge, his honour, was the chief.*
She said he murdered, and therefore must die;
   He, that he caused but love, did harms deny.                    10
   But while she thus discoursing with him stood,
The nymphs untied him, and his chains took off,
   Thinking him safe; but he, loose, made a scoff,
   Smiling, and scorning them, flew to the wood.

### SONNET 9 (SECOND SERIES) (P 71)

Pray do not use these words, 'I must be gone'.
   Alas, do not foretell mine ills to come,
   Let not my care be to my joys a tomb,*
   But rather find my loss with loss alone.
Cause me not thus a more distressed one,                    5
   Not feeling bliss because of this sad doom
   Of present cross, for thinking will* o'ercome
   And lose all pleasure, since grief breedeth none.
Let the misfortune come at once to me,
   Nor suffer me with grief to punished be;                    10
   Let me be ignorant of mine own ill,
Than with the fore-knowledge quite to lose
   That which, with so much care and pains, love chose
   For his reward: but joy now, then mirth kill.

### SONNET 10 (SECOND SERIES) (P 72)

Folly* would needs make me a lover be,
   When I did little think of loving thought,
   Or ever to be tied, while she told me
   That none can live but to these bands* are brought.
I, ignorant, did grant, and so was bought,                    5
   And sold again to lovers' slavery;
   The duty to that vanity* once taught,
   Such band is, as we will not seek to free.
Yet when I well did understand his might,
   How he* inflamed, and forced one to affect,                    10
   I loved and smarted, counting it delight
   So still to waste, which Reason did reject.
When Love came blindfold, and did challenge me:
Indeed I loved, but, wanton boy, not he.*

## SONG* (P 73)

The spring* time of my first loving
  Finds yet no winter of removing,
Nor frosts to make my hopes decrease,
  But with the summer still increase.

The trees may teach us love's remaining,      5
  Who suffer change with little paining:
Though winter make their leaves decrease,
  Yet with the summer they increase.

As birds by silence show their mourning
  In cold, yet sing at spring's returning,      10
So may love, nipped awhile, decrease,
  But as the summer soon increase.

Those that do love but for a season,
  Do falsify both love and reason,*
For reason wills, if love decrease,      15
  It like the summer should increase.

Though love some times may be mistaken,
  The truth yet ought not to be shaken,
Or though the heat awhile decrease,
  It with the summer may increase.      20

And since the spring time of my loving
  Found never winter of removing,
Nor frosts to make my hopes decrease,
  Shall as the summer still increase.

## SONG (P 74)

Love, a child, is ever crying,
Please him, and he straight is flying,
Give him, he the more is craving,
Never satisfied with having.

His desires have no measure,      5
Endless folly is his treasure,
What he promiseth he breaketh,
Trust not one word that he speaketh.

He vows nothing but false matter,
And to cozen* you he'll flatter,      10
Let him gain the hand,* he'll leave you,
And still glory to deceive you.

He will triumph in your wailing,
And yet cause be of your failing:
These his virtues are, and slighter                                    15
Are his gifts, his favours lighter.

Feathers are as firm in staying,
Wolves no fiercer in their preying.
As a child then leave him crying,
Nor seek him, so giv'n to flying.                                      20

### SONG (P 75)

Being past the pains of love,
Freedom gladly seeks to move,
Says that love's delights were pretty,
But to dwell in them 'twere pity;

And yet truly says that love                                           5
Must of force in all hearts move,
But though his delights are pretty,
To dwell in them were a pity.

Let love slightly pass like love,
Never let it too deep move,                                            10
For though love's delights are pretty,
To dwell in them were great pity.

Love no pity hath of love,
Rather griefs than pleasures move,
So though his delights are pretty,                                     15
To dwell in them would be pity.

Those that like the smart of love,
In them let it freely move,
Else, though his delights are pretty,
Do not dwell in them, for pity.                                        20

### SONNET (P 76)

O pardon, Cupid,* I confess my fault:
    Then mercy grant me in so just a kind,
    For treason never lodged in my mind
    Against thy might, so much as in a thought.
And now my folly have I dearly bought,                                 5
    Nor could my soul least rest or quiet find

Since rashness did my thoughts to error bind,
  Which now thy fury, and my harm, hath wrought.
I curse that thought and hand which that first framed
  For which by thee I am most justly blamed;                    10
  But now that hand shall guided be aright,
And give a crown* unto thy endless praise,
  Which shall thy glory, and thy greatness raise
  More than these poor things could thy honour spite.

## A Crown of Sonnets Dedicated to Love*

### SONNET I (THIRD SERIES) (P 77)

In this strange labyrinth* how shall I turn?
  Ways are on all sides, while the way I miss:
  If to the right hand, there in love I burn;
  Let me go forward, therein danger is.
If to the left,* suspicion hinders bliss;                       5
  Let me turn back, shame cries I ought return,
  Nor faint, though crosses* with my fortunes kiss;
  Stand still is harder, although sure to mourn.
Thus let me take the right, or left hand way,
  Go forward, or stand still, or back retire:                   10
  I must these doubts endure without allay*
  Or help, but travail* find for my best hire.*
Yet that which most my troubled sense does move,
Is to leave all, and take the thread* of Love.

### SONNET 2 (THIRD SERIES) (P 78)

Is to leave all, and take the thread of Love,
  Which line straight leads unto the soul's* content,
  Where choice delights with pleasure's wings do move,
  And idle fancy* never room had lent.
When chaste thoughts guide us, then our minds are bent          5
  To take that good which ills from us remove:
  Light of true love brings fruit which none repent,
  But constant lovers* seek, and wish to prove.
Love is the shining star of blessing's light,
  The fervent fire of zeal, the root of peace,                  10
  The lasting lamp, fed with the oil of right,
  Image of faith, and womb for joy's increase.*
Love is true virtue, and his ends delight;
His flames are joys, his bands true lovers' might.

### SONNET 3 (THIRD SERIES)* (P 79)

His* flames are joys, his bands true lovers' might,
  No stain is there, but pure, as purest white,
  Where no cloud can appear to dim his light,
  Nor spot defile, but shame will soon requite.
Here are affections tried by Love's just might,     5
  As gold by fire, and black discerned by white,
  Error by truth, and darkness known by light,
  Where faith is valued for Love to requite.*
Please him, and serve him, glory in his might,
  And firm he'll be, as innocency white,     10
  Clear as th'air, warm as sun's beams, as day light,
  Just as truth, constant as fate, joyed to requite.
Then Love obey, strive to observe his might,
And be in his brave court a glorious light.

### SONNET 4 (THIRD SERIES) (P 80)

And be in his brave court a glorious light:
  Shine in the eyes of faith and constancy,
  Maintain the fires of love still burning bright,
  Not slightly sparkling, but light flaming be,
Never to slack till earth no stars can see,     5
  Till sun and moon do leave us to dark night,
  And second chaos* once again do free
  Us and the world from all division's spite.
Till then, affections, which his followers are,
  Govern our hearts, and prove his power's gain     10
  To taste this pleasing sting, seek with all care,
  For happy smarting is it, with small pain;
Such as, although it pierce your tender heart
And burn, yet burning you will love the smart.

### SONNET 5 (THIRD SERIES) (P 81)

And burn, yet burning you will love the smart,
  When you shall feel the weight of true desire,
  So pleasing, as you would not wish your part
  Of burden should be missing from that fire;
But faithful and unfeigned heat aspire,     5
  Which sin abolisheth, and does impart
  Salves to all fear, with virtues which inspire
  Souls with divine love, which shows his* chaste art,
And guide he is to joyings; open eyes

He hath to happiness, and best can learn                          10
  Us means how to deserve: this he descries,
  Who, blind, yet does our hiddenest thoughts discern.
Thus we may gain, since living in blest love,
He may our prophet* and our tutor prove.

### SONNET 6 (THIRD SERIES) (P 82)

He may our prophet and our tutor prove,*
  In whom alone we do this power find,
  To join two hearts as in one frame to move,
  Two bodies, but one soul to move the mind,*
Eyes, which must care to one dear object bind,                     5
  Ears to each other's speech, as if above
  All else they sweet and learned were; this kind
  Content of lovers witnesseth true love:
It does enrich the wits, and make you see
  That in yourself which you knew not before,                 10
  Forcing you to admire such gifts should be
  Hid from your knowledge, yet in you the store.
Millions of these adorn the throne of Love,
How blest be they then, who his favours prove.*

### SONNET 7 (THIRD SERIES) (P 83)

How blest be they then, who his favours prove,
  A life whereof the birth is just desire,
  Breeding sweet flame, which hearts invite to move
  In these loved eyes which kindle Cupid's fire,*
And nurse his longings with his thoughts entire,                   5
  Fixed on the heat of wishes formed by love;
  Yet whereas fire destroys, this does aspire,
  Increase, and foster all delights above.
Love will a painter* make you, such, as you
  Shall able be to draw your only dear                        10
  More lively, perfect, lasting and more true*
  Than rarest workman, and to you more near.
These be the least, then all must needs confess,
He that shuns love does love himself the less.

### SONNET 8 (THIRD SERIES) (P 84)

He that shuns love does love himself the less,
  And cursed he whose spirit not admires
  The worth* of love, where endless blessedness
  Reigns, and commands, maintained by heav'nly fires

Made of virtue, joined by truth, blown by desires,                    5
   Strengthened by worth, renewed by carefulness,
   Flaming in never-changing thoughts: briars
   Of jealousy shall here miss welcomeness,
Nor coldly pass in the pursuits of love,
   Like one long frozen in a sea of ice;                    10
   And yet but chastely* let your passions move,
   Nor thought from virtuous love your minds entice.
Never to other ends your fancies* place,
But where they may return with honour's grace.

### SONNET 9 (THIRD SERIES) (P 85)

But where they may return with honour's grace,
   Where Venus'* follies can no harbour win,
   But chased are, as worthless* of the face
   Or style of Love, who hath lascivious been.
Our hearts are subject to her son,* where sin                    5
   Never did dwell, or rest one minute's space;
   What faults he hath, in her did still begin,
   And from her breast he sucked his fleeting pace.
If lust be counted love,* 'tis falsely named
   By wickedness, a fairer gloss* to set                    10
   Upon that vice which else makes men ashamed
   In the own* phrase to warrant, but beget
This child for love,* who ought, like monster born,
Be from the Court of Love and Reason torn.

### SONNET 10 (THIRD SERIES) (P 86)

Be from the Court of Love and Reason* torn,
   For Love in Reason now does put his trust,
   Desert* and liking are together born
   Children of Love and Reason, parents just.
Reason adviser is, Love ruler must                    5
   Be of the state, which crown he long hath worn,
   Yet so, as neither will in least mistrust
   The government where no fear is born of scorn.
Then reverence both their mights thus made of one,
   But wantonness and all those errors shun,                    10
   Which wrongers be, impostures, and alone
   Maintainers of all follies ill begun:
Fruit of a sour,* and unwholesome ground,
Unprofitably pleasing, and unsound.

## SONNET 11 (THIRD SERIES) (P 87)

Unprofitably pleasing, and unsound,
    When heaven* gave liberty to frail dull earth
    To bring forth plenty that in ills abound,
    Which ripest yet do bring a certain dearth.*
A timeless and unseasonable birth,                 5
    Planted in ill, in worse time springing found,
    Which hemlock like* might feed a sick-wit's* mirth,
    Where unruled vapours* swim in endless round.
Then joy we not in what we ought to shun,
    Where shady pleasures show, but true born fires     10
    Are quite quenched out, or by poor ashes won
    Awhile to keep those cool and wan desires.
O no, let Love his glory have, and might
Be given to him, who triumphs in his right.

## SONNET 12 (THIRD SERIES) (P 88)

Be given to him, who triumphs in his right,
    Nor fading be, but like those blossoms fair
    Which fall for good, and lose their colours bright,
    Yet die not, but with fruit their loss repair.
So may love make you pale with loving care,          5
    When sweet enjoying shall restore that light
    More clear in beauty than we can compare,
    If not to Venus in her chosen night.
And who so give themselves in this dear kind,
    These happinesses shall attend them, still     10
    To be supplied with joys, enriched in mind,
    With treasures of content, and pleasure's fill.
Thus Love to be divine does here appear,
Free from all fogs, but shining fair and clear.

## SONNET 13 (THIRD SERIES) (P 89)

Free from all fogs, but shining fair and clear,
    Wise in all good, and innocent in ill,
    Where holy friendship is esteemed dear,
    With truth in love, and justice in our will.*
In Love these titles only have their fill*          5
    Of happy life maintainer, and the mere
    Defence of right, the punisher of skill
    And fraud; from whence directions do appear.
To thee then, Lord,* commander of all hearts,

Ruler of our affections, kind and just,                                    10
    Great King of Love, my soul from feigned* smarts
    Or thought of change I offer to your trust
This crown,* my self, and all that I have more,
Except my heart, which you bestowed before.

### SONNET 14 (THIRD SERIES) (P 90)

Except my heart, which you bestowed before,
    And for a sign of conquest gave away
    As worthless* to be kept in your choice store,*
    Yet one* more spotless with you does not stay.
The tribute which my heart does truly pay                                    5
    Is faith untouched, pure thoughts discharge the score*
    Of debts for me, where Constancy* bears sway,
    And rules as Lord, unharmed by envy's sore.
Yet other mischiefs fail not to attend,
    As enemies to you, my foes must be:                                     10
    Curst Jealousy* does all her forces bend
    To my undoing; thus my harms I see.
So though in love I fervently do burn,
In this strange labyrinth how shall I turn?*

### SONG 1 (SECOND SERIES)* (P 91)

Sweet, let me enjoy thy sight
    More clear, more bright than morning sun,
Which in spring time gives delight
    And by which summer's pride is won.
Present sight does pleasures move,                                           5
    Which in sad absence we must miss,
But when met again in love,
    Then twice redoubled is our bliss.

Yet this comfort absence gives,
    And only faithful loving tries,                                          10
That, though parted, love's force lives
    As just in heart as in our eyes.
But such comfort banish quite,
    Far sweeter is it, still to find
Favour in thy loved sight,                                                   15
    Which present smiles with joys combined.

Eyes of gladness, lips of love,
    And hearts from passions not to turn,

But in sweet affections move
   In flames of faith to live and burn.           20
Dearest, then this kindness give,
   And grant me life, which is your sight,
Wherein I more blessed live,
   Than graced with the sun's fair light.

### SONG 2 (SECOND SERIES) (P 92)

Sweet Silvia* in a shady wood,
   With her fair nymphs laid down,
Saw not far off where Cupid* stood,
   The monarch of Love's crown,*
All naked, playing with his wings,           5
   Within a myrtle* tree,
Which sight a sudden laughter brings,
   His godhead so to see.

And fondly they began to jest,
   With scoffing and delight,           10
Not knowing he did breed unrest,
   And that his will's* his right.
When he perceiving of their scorn,
   Grew in such desp'rate rage,
Who, but for honour first was born,          15
   Could not his rage assuage,

Till shooting of his murd'ring dart,*
   Which not long 'lighting* was,
Knowing the next way to the heart,
   Did through a poor nymph pass.          20
This shot, the others made to bow,
   Besides all those to blame,
Who scorners be, or not allow
   Of pow'rful Cupid's name.

Take heed then, nor do idly smile,          25
   Nor Love's commands despise,
For soon will he your strength beguile,
   Although he want his eyes.*

### SONG 3 (SECOND SERIES) (P 93)

Come, merry Spring, delight us,
For Winter long did spite us,
In pleasure still persever,

Thy beauties ending never:
  Spring, and grow
  Lasting so,
With joys increasing ever.

Let cold from hence be banished,
Till hopes from me be vanished,
But bless thy dainties, growing                    10
  In fullness freely flowing:
  For the Spring
All mirth is now bestowing.

Philomel* in this arbour
Makes now her loving harbour,                       15
Yet of her state complaining,
Her notes in mildness straining,
  Which, though sweet,
  Yet do meet
Her former luckless paining.                        20

### SONG 4 (SECOND SERIES) (P 94)

Lovers, learn to speak but truth,
  Swear not, and your oaths forgo,
Give your age a constant youth,
  Vow no more than what you'll do.

Think it sacrilege to break                          5
  What you promise shall in love,
And in tears what you do speak,
  Forget not, when the ends you prove.

Do not think it glory is
  To entice and then deceive,                10
Your chief honours lie in this:
  By worth* what won is, not to leave.

'Tis not for your fame to try
  What we, weak, not oft refuse,
In our bounty our faults lie,                        15
  When you to do a fault will* choose.

Fie, leave this, a greater gain
  'Tis to keep when you have won,
Than what purchased is with pain,
  Soon after in all scorn to shun.          20

For if worthless to be prized,
    Why at first will you it move,
And if worthy, why despised?
    You cannot swear, and lie, and love.

Love, alas, you cannot like,               25
    'Tis but for a fashion moved,
None can choose and then dislike,
    Unless it be by falsehood proved.

But your choice is, and your love,
    How most number to deceive,           30
As if honour's claim did move
    Like Popish law,* none safe to leave.

Fly this folly, and return
    Unto truth in love, and try,
None but martyrs* happy burn,          35
    More shameful ends they have that lie.

### SONNET 1 (FOURTH SERIES)* (P 95)

My heart is lost, what can I now expect:
    An ev'ning fair, after a drowsy day?
    Alas, fond fancy,* this is not the way
    To cure a mourning* heart, or salve neglect.
They who should help, do me and help reject,     5
    Embracing loose desires and wanton play,
    While wanton base delights do bear the sway,
    And impudency reigns without respect.
O Cupid, let your mother* know her shame,
    'Tis time for her to leave this youthful flame     10
    Which does dishonour her, is age's blame,
    And takes away the greatness of thy name.
Thou God of love, she only Queen of lust,
Yet strives by weak'ning thee, to be unjust.

### SONNET 2 (FOURTH SERIES) (P 96)

Late in the forest I did Cupid* see
    Cold, wet and crying; he had lost his way,
    And, being blind, was farther like to stray,
    Which sight a kind compassion bred in me.
I kindly took and dried him, while that he,     5

Poor child, complained he starved was with stay,*
And pined for want of his accustomed prey,
For none in that wild place his host would be.
I glad was of his finding, thinking sure
This service should my freedom still procure,                    10
And in my arms I took him then unharmed,
Carrying him safe unto a myrtle* bower,
But in the way he made me feel his pow'r,
Burning my heart, who had him kindly warmed.

### SONNET 3 (FOURTH SERIES) (P 97)

Juno, still jealous of her husband Jove,*
Descended from above, on earth to try
Whether she there could find his chosen love,
Which made him from the heavens so often fly.
Close by the place where I for shade did lie                      5
She chasing came, but when she saw me move,
'Have you not seen this way,' said she, 'to hie*
One, in whom virtue never ground did prove,
He, in whom love does breed to stir more hate,
Courting a wanton nymph for his delight?                          10
His name is Jupiter, my lord by fate,
Who for her leaves me, heav'n, his throne and light.'
'I saw him not,' said I, 'although here are
Many, in whose hearts love hath made like war.'

### SONNET 4 (FOURTH SERIES) (P 98)

When I beheld the image* of my dear,
With greedy looks mine eyes would that way bend,
Fear and Desire did inwardly contend,
Fear to be marked, Desire to draw still near;
And in my soul a Spirit would appear,                             5
Which boldness warranted, and did pretend
To be my Genius,* yet I durst not lend
My eyes in trust, where others seemed so clear.
Then did I search from whence this danger 'rose,
If such unworthiness in me did rest                               10
As my starved eyes must not with sight be blest,
When Jealousy her poison did disclose.
Yet in my heart, unseen of jealous eye,
The truer image shall in triumph lie.*

### SONNET 5 (FOURTH SERIES) (P 99)

Like to huge clouds of smoke which well may hide
  The face of fairest day, though for a while,
  So wrong may shadow me,* till truth do smile,
  And Justice, sun-like, hath those vapours tied.
O doting Time, canst thou for shame let slide     5
  So many minutes, while ills do beguile
  Thy age and worth, and falsehoods thus defile
  Thy ancient good, where now but crosses* bide?
Look but once up, and leave thy toiling pace,
  And on my miseries thy dim eye place;     10
  Go not so fast, but give my care some end,
Turn not thy glass, alas, unto my ill,
  Since thou with sand it canst not so far fill,
  But to each one my sorrows will extend.

### SONNET 6 (FOURTH SERIES) (P 100)

O! that no day would ever more appear,
  But cloudy night to govern this sad place,
  Nor light from heav'n these hapless rooms to grace,
  Since that light's shadowed which my love holds dear.
Let thickest mists in envy master here,     5
  And sun-born day for malice show no face,
  Disdaining light, where Cupid and the race
  Of lovers are despised, and shame shines clear.
Let me be dark, since barred of my chief light,
  And wounding Jealousy commands by might,     10
  But stage play like* disguised pleasures give:
To me it seems, as ancient fictions make
  The stars all fashions and all shapes partake,
  While in my thoughts true form of love shall live.

### SONNET 7 (FOURTH SERIES) (P 101)

No time, no room,* no thought or writing* can
  Give rest or quiet to my loving heart.
  Or can my memory or fancy scan
  The measure* of my still renewing smart.
Yet would I not, dear Love, thou shouldst depart,     5
  But let my passions, as they first began,
  Rule, wound and please: it is thy choicest art*
  To give disquiet which seems ease to man.
When all alone, I think upon thy pain,

How thou dost travail* our best selves to gain:          10
Then hourly thy lessons I do learn,
Think on thy glory, which shall still ascend
Until the world come to a final end,
And then shall we thy lasting pow'r discern.*

### SONNET 8 (FOURTH SERIES) (P 102)

How glow-worm-like the sun does now appear:
Cold beams do from his glorious face descend,
Which shows his days and force draw to an end,
Or that to leave taking his time* grows near.
This day his face did seem but pale, though clear;          5
The reason is, he to the north* must lend
His light, and warmth must to that climate bend,
Whose frozen parts could not love's heat hold dear.
Alas, if thou, bright sun, to part from hence
Grieve so, what must I, hapless, who from thence,          10
Where thou dost go, my blessing shall attend?
Thou shalt enjoy that sight* for which I die,
And in my heart thy fortunes do envy;
Yet grieve; I'll love thee, for this state may end.

### SONNET 9 (FOURTH SERIES) (P 103)

My muse, now happy, lay thyself to rest,
Sleep in the quiet of a faithful love,
Write* you no more, but let these fancies* move
Some other hearts; wake not to new unrest.
But if you study, be those thoughts addressed          5
To truth, which shall eternal goodness prove,
Enjoying of true joy, the most and best,
The endless gain which never will remove.
Leave the discourse of Venus and her son*
To young beginners, and their brains inspire          10
With stories of great love, and from that fire
Get heat to write the fortunes they have won.
And thus leave off;* what's past, shows you can love,
Now let your constancy* your honour prove.

                                                  (1621)

# DIANA PRIMROSE

## A Chain of Pearl*

*Dat ROSA mel apibus, qua fugit ARANEA virus.* *

### TO ALL NOBLE LADIES AND GENTLEWOMEN

To you, the honour of our noble sex,*
I send this chain with all my best respects,
Which if you please to wear for her* sweet sake,
For whom I did this slender poem make,
    You shall erect a trophy* to her name,        5
    And crown yourselves with never-fading fame.

### TO THE EXCELLENT LADY, THE COMPOSER OF THIS WORK

Shine forth, Diana,* dart thy golden rays*
On her* blest life and reign, whose noble praise
Deserves a quill* plucked from an angel's wing,
And none to write it but a crowned king.
She, she it was, that gave us golden days*        5
And did the English name to heaven raise;
    Blest be her name! Blest be her memory!
    That England crowned with such felicity.
And thou, the Prime-Rose* of the Muses nine,*
In whose sweet verse Eliza's fame doth shine        10
Like some resplendent star in frosty night,
Has made thy native* splendour far more bright;
Since all thy pearls are peerless-orient,*
And to thyself a precious ornament.
    This is my censure* of thy royal chain,*        15
    Which a far better censure well may claim.
            Dorothy Berry*

### THE INDUCTION*

As golden Phoebus* with his radiant face
Enthroned in his triumphant chair of state,
The twinkling stars and asterisms* doth chase

With his imperial sceptre, and doth hate
   All consorts in his starry monarchy                                    5
   As prejudicial to his sovereignty,
So great Eliza, England's brightest sun,
The world's renown and ever-lasting lamp,
Admits not here the least comparison,
Whose glories do the greatest princes damp,*                                       10
   That ever sceptre swayed or crown did wear,
   Within the verge* of either hemisphere.
Thou English goddess, empress of our sex,*
O thou whose name still reigns in all our hearts,
To whom are due our ever-vow'd respects,                                           15
How shall I blazon* thy most royal parts?*
   Which in all parts did so divinely shine,
   As they deserve Apollo's* quill, not mine.
Yet, since the gods accept the humble vows
Of mortals, deign, O thou star-crowned queen,                                      20
T'accept these ill-composed pearly rows,*
Wherein thy glory chiefly shall be seen;
   For by these lines so black and impolite,*
   Thy swan-like lustre* shall appear more white.
     Thy Imperial Majesty's eternal Votary,*
       DIANA

### THE FIRST PEARL
### RELIGION*

The goodliest Pearl in fair Eliza's Chain*
Is true religion,* which did chiefly gain*
A royal lustre to the rest, and tied
The hearts of all to her when Mary* died.
And though she found the realm infected much                                       5
With superstition and abuses, such
As, in all human judgement, could not be
Reformed without domestic mutiny,
And great hostility from Spain and France,*
Yet she, undaunted, bravely did advance                                            10
Christ's glorious ensign,* maugre* all the fears
Or dangers which appeared; and for ten years*
She swayed the sceptre with a lady's hand,
Not urging any Romist* in the land
By sharp edicts the temple to frequent,                                            15
Or to partake the holy sacrament.*

But factious* Romanists not thus content,
Their agents to their holy father* sent,
Desiring him, by solemn bull,* proclaim
Elizabeth an heretic,* and name                              20
Some other sovereign, which might erect
Their masking* mass, and hence forthwith eject
The evangelical profession,*
Which flourished under her protection.
The Pope to this petition condescends                        25
And soon his leaden* bull to England sends,
By which one Felton,* on the Bishop's Gate
Of London was affixed; but the state
For that high treason punished him with death,
That would dethrone his queen, Elizabeth.                    30
Yet was this ball of wild-fire* working still,
In many Romanists which had a will
The present state and government to change,
That they in all idolatry* might range.*
And hence it came that great Northumberland*                 35
Associate with Earl of Westmoreland,*
And many mo,* their banners did display
In open field, hoping to win the day.
Against these rebels, noble Sussex* went,
And soon their bloody purpose did prevent.                   40
Westmoreland fled, Northumberland did die
For that foul crime and deep disloyalty,
Having engaged thousands in that cause.
After which time the Queen made stricter laws*
Against the recusants,* and with lion's heart                45
She bang'd* the Pope and took the gospel's part.*
The Pope, perceiving that his bull was bated*
In such rude sort,* and all his hopes defeated,
Cries out to Spain for help, who takes occasion
Thereby t'attempt the conquest of this nation.*              50
But such sage counsellors Eliza had,
As, though both Spain and Rome were almost mad
For grief and anger, yet they still did fail,
And against England never could prevail.

### THE SECOND PEARL
### CHASTITY*

The next fair Pearl* that comes in order here
Is Chastity, wherein she had no peer

'Mongst all the noble princesses which then
In Europe were the royal anadem,*
And though for beauty she an angel was,                         5
And all our sex did therein far surpass,
Yet did her pure unspotted chastity
Her heavenly beauty rarely* beautify.
How many kings and princes did aspire
To win her love? In whom that vestal* fire              10
Still flaming, never would she condescend
To Hymen's rites,* though much she did commend
That brave French Monsieur* who did hope to carry
The golden fleece* and fair Eliza marry.
Yea, Spanish Philip,* husband to her sister,            15
Was her first suitor, and the first that missed her;
And though he promised that the Pope by bull
Should license it,* she held it but a gull,*
For how can Pope* with God's own law dispense?
Was it not time such Popes to cudgel hence?             20
Thus her impregnable virginity
Throughout the world her fame did dignify.
    And this may be a document to all,
The pearl of chastity not to let fall
Into the filthy dirt of foul desires,                   25
Which Satan kindles with his hell-bred fires;
For whether it be termed virginal
In virgins, or in wives styled conjugal,
Or vidual* in widows, God respects
All equally, and all alike affects.*                    30
    And here I may not silent overpass
That noble lady* of the court, which was
Solicited by Taxis,* that great Don,
Ambassador for Spain, when she* was gone,
Who to obtain his will gave her a chain                 35
Of most rare Orient pearl, hoping to gain
That worthy lady to his lust; but she,
That well-perceived his Spanish policy,
His fair chain kept, but his foul offer scorned,
That sought thereby her husband to have horned;*        40
Taxis repulsed sent to her for his chain,
But, as a trophy,* she it did retain.
    Which noble precedent may all excite
To keep this Pearl* which is so Orient bright.

### THE THIRD PEARL
### PRUDENCE*

How prudent was her government appeared
By her wise counsels, by the which she steered
In the most dangerous times that ever were,
Since king or queen did crown in England wear.
Her choice of famous counsellors did show            5
That she did all the rules of prudence know,
For though her wit and spirit were divine,
Counsels, she knew, were best where more combine,
That for experience and deep policy
Are well approved, whose fidelity                    10
Retains them in the bonds of loyal love,
And no great pensions* from their prince can move.*
Thus ruled she prudently with all her power,
With Argus-eyes* foreseeing every hour
All dangers immanent, lest any harms                 15
Should us befall by Spanish arts or arms.*
   This gift in her was much more eminent,
In that it is so rarely incident
To our weak sex;* and as a precious stone
Deep set in gold shines fairer, than alone,*         20
Or set in lead; so did all graces shine
In her most gloriously, because divine.
For kings are gods, and queens are goddesses
On earth, whose sacred virtues best expresses
Their true divinity; wherein, if we                  25
Them imitate, 'tis our felicity.
This Pearl of Prudence* then we all should prize
Most highly, for it doth indeed comprise
All moral virtues which are resident
In that blest soul, where this is president.*        30

### THE FOURTH PEARL
### TEMPERANCE*

The golden bridle of Bellerophon*
Is temperance, by which our passion
And appetite we conquer and subdue
To reason's regiment, else may we rue
Our yielding to men's siren-blandishments,           5
Which are attended with so foul events.*
   This Pearl* in her was so conspicuous,

As that the King,* her brother, still did use
To style her his sweet Sister Temperance,*
By which her much-admired self-governance                    10
Her passions still she checked, and still she made
The world astonished, that so undismayed
She did with equal tenor* still proceed
In one fair course, not shaken as a reed,
But built upon the rock of temperance;*                    15
Not dazed with fear, not mazed* with any chance,*
Not with vain hope, as with an empty spoon,
Fed,* or allured to cast beyond the moon,*
Not with rash anger too precipitate,
Not fond to love,* nor too, too prone to hate,           20
Not charmed with parasites, or siren-songs,*
Whose hearts are poisoned, though their sugred* tongues
Swear, vow and promise all fidelity,
When they are brewing deepest villainy.*
Not led to vain or too profuse expense,                    25
Pretending thereby state magnificence;
Not spending on these momentary pleasures
Her precious time, but deeming her best treasures
Her subjects' love,* which she so well preserved
By sweet and mild demeanour, as it served                 30
To guard her surer than an army royal,
So true their loves were to her, and so loyal.
O golden age! O blest and happy years!
O music sweeter than that of the spheres!*
When prince and people mutually agree                      35
In sacred concord and sweet symphony!

### THE FIFTH PEARL
### CLEMENCY*

Her royal clemency comes next in view,
The virtue which in her did most renew
The image of her maker,* who in that*
Exceeds himself, and doth commiserate
His very rebels,* lending them the light                    5
Of sun and moon and all those diamonds bright.*
So did Eliza cast her golden rays
Of clemency on those which many ways
Transgressed her laws, and sought to undermine
The church and state, and did with Spain combine.*         10

And though by rigour of the law she might,
Not wronging them, have taken all her right,
Yet her innate and princely clemency
Moved her to pardon their delinquency,
Which sought her gracious mercy and repented                15
Their misdemeanours and their crimes lamented.
So doth the kingly lion with his foe,
Which, once prostrate, he scorns to work his woe;
So did this virtue's sacred auri* flame
Immortalize our great Eliza's name.                         20

### THE SIXTH PEARL
### JUSTICE*

Her justice next appears which did support
Her crown and was her kingdom's strongest fort;
For should not laws be executed well,
And malefactors* curbed, a very hell
Of all confusion and disorder would                          5
Among all states ensue. Here to unfold
The exemplary penalties of those
Which to the realm were known and mortal foes,
And as some putrid members pared away,*
Lest their transcendent villainy should sway                10
Others to like disloyalty, would ask
A larger volume, and would be a task
Unfit for feminine hands,* which rather love
To write of pleasing subjects, than approve
The most deserved slaughtering of any,                      15
Which justly cannot argue tyranny.
For though the Pope hath lately sent from Rome
Strange books and pictures painting out the doom
Of his pretended martyrs,* as that they
Were baited in bears' skins, and made a prey                20
To wild beasts, and had their boots with boiling lead
Drawn on their legs, and horns nailed to their head,
Yet all our British world knows these are fables,
Children's phantasms,* dreams, and very bables*
For fools to play with, and right goblin-sprites,           25
Wherewith our nurses oft* their babes affrights.
His holiness these martyrdoms may add
To the Golden Legend,* for they are as mad
That first invented them, as he* that write

That brainless book, and yet some credit it;                    30
For cruelty and fond credulity
Are the main pillars of Rome's hierarchy.

### THE SEVENTH PEARL
### FORTITUDE*

This goodly Pearl is that rare fortitude
Wherewith this sacred princess was endued.*
Witness her brave, undaunted look when Parry*
Was fully bent she should by him miscarry;
The wretch confessed, that her great majesty                    5
With strange amazement did him terrify,
So heavenly, graceful, and so full of awe,
Was that majestic queen, which when some saw
They thought an angel did appear, she shone
So bright, as none else could her paragon.*                    10
But that which doth beyond all admiration
Illustrate her, and in her this whole nation,
Is that heroic march of hers, and speech
At Tilbury,* where she did all beseech
Bravely to fight for England, telling them                    15
That what their fortune was, should hers be then;
And that with full resolve she thither came,
Ready to win, or quite to lose the game.
Which words, delivered in most princely sort,*
Did animate the army, and report                    20
To all the world her magnanimity,
Whose haughty courage nought could terrify;
Well did she show great Henry* was her sire,
Whom Europe did for valour most admire
'Mongst all the warlike princes which were then                    25
Enthronized with regal diadem.*

### THE EIGHTH PEARL
### SCIENCE*

Among the virtues intellectual
The van* is led by that we science call,
A Pearl* more precious than the Egyptian queen
Quaffed* oft to Anthony;* of more esteem
Than Indian gold,* or more resplendent gems                    5
Which ravish* us with their translucent beams.
How many arts and sciences did deck*

This heroina?* Who still had at beck*
The Muses and the Graces,* when that she
Gave audience in state and majesty;                              10
Then did the goddess Eloquence inspire
Her royal breast; Apollo with his lyre*
Ne'er* made such music; on her sacred lips
Angels enthroned, most heavenly manna* sips.
Then might you see her nectar-flowing vein*                      15
Surround the hearers, in which sugred stream
She able was to drown a world of men,*
And drowned, with sweetness to revive again.
Alasco,* the ambassador Polonian*
Who perorated* like a mere Slavonian,*                           20
And in rude* rambling rhetoric did roll,*
She did with Attic* eloquence control.
Her speeches to our Academians*
Well showed she knew among Athenians*
How to deliver such well-tuned words,                            25
As with such places punctually accords.*
But with what oratory ravishments*
Did she imparadise her parliaments?*
Her last most princely speech doth verify
How highly she did England dignify,                              30
Her loyal commons how did she embrace,
And entertain with a most royal grace.*

### THE NINTH PEARL
### PATIENCE*

Now come we her rare Patience to display
Which, as with purest gold, did pave her way
To England's crown, for when her sister* ruled
She was with many great afflictions schooled;
Yet all the while her mot* was *Tanquam Ovis*,*                  5
Nor could her enemies prove ought amiss
In her, although they thirsted for her blood,
Reputing it, once shed, their sovereign good.
Sometime in prison this sweet saint was pent,*
Then hastily away she thence was sent                            10
To places more remote, and all her friends
Debarred access, and none but she attends
As ready were with poison, or with knife,
To sacrifice this sacred princess' life,

At bloody Bonner's* beck,* or Gardiner's* nod,                    15
Had they not been prevented by that God,
Who did Susanna* from the elders free,
And at the last, gave her, her liberty.
Thus by her patient bearing of the cross*
She reaped greatest gain from greatest loss,              20
For he that loseth his blest liberty
Hath found a very hell of misery;
By many crosses thus she got the crown,
To England's glory, and her great renown.

### THE TENTH PEARL
### BOUNTY*

As rose and lily challenge chiefest place
For milk-white lustre and for purple grace,*
So England's rose and lily had no peer
For princely bounty shining everywhere.
This made her fame with golden wings to fly              5
About the world, about the starry sky.
Witness France, Portugal, Virginia,
Germany, Scotland, Ireland, Belgia,*
Whose provinces and princes found her aid
On all occasions, which sore dismayed                    10
Spain's king* whose European monarchy
Could never thrive during her sovereignty;
So did she beat him with her distaff* so
By* sea and land she did him overthrow,
Yea, so that tyrant on his knees she brought,            15
That of brave England peace he* begged, and thought
Himself most happy, that by begging so
Preserved all Spain from beggery and woe.
  Here all amazed my Muse sets up her rest,
  Adoring her was so divinely blest.                      20

  *At nos horrifice cinefactam T'E propé Busto,*
  *Insatiabiliter deflebimus asternumqué.* *

                                              (1630)

# ALICE SUTCLIFFE

## Meditations of Man's Mortality or, a Way to True Blessedness

Written by Mrs Alice Sutcliffe, wife of
*John Sutcliffe*, Esquire Groom of His Majesty's
Most Honourable Privy Chamber

Romans 6
*The wages of sin is Death, but the gift of GOD
is eternal life, through JESUS CHRIST our Lord.*

AN ACROSTIC,*
UPON THE RENOWNED NAME OF THE
MOST VIRTUOUS PRINCESS, KATHERINE,
DUCHESS OF BUCKINGHAM*

Know you this princess, BUCKINGHAM's chaste duchess?
Ask aged Time with his worm-eaten crutches
To find amongst the numbers of his roll
Her parallel, of such a heavenly moul,*
Excelling so i'th beauties of the soul;                    5
Rich in all treasures that to virtue tend:
In faith, hope, charity, the blessed's end.
Nor is there aught that lives in woman kind:
Exceeding the rare prowess* of her mind.

Born of high blood, from RUTLAND's* family,        10
United to a duke of royal state;
Cursed be the time, more cursed his cruelty,
Killed him and 'reaved* this turtle* of her mate;
In peerless woe, we still lament that fate,
Nor shall his memory e'er out of date.*               15
Go on then gracious princess, graced by Fame,
Honour shall still attend your noble name,
And as your goodness has abounded, so
May heaven the greatest good on you bestow.

AN ACROSTIC,
UPON THE NAME OF THE RIGHT
HONOURABLE AND TRULY VIRTUOUS, LADY
SUSANNA, COUNTESS OF DENBEIGH*

See here a lady, blessed in her birth,
Unto whose greatness, goodness joined is still;
Susanna* ne're so famous was on earth
As is this lady, led by virtuous will.
Nothing so sweet to her as heavenly mirth,                    5
No music sounds like Hallelujah,
A happy soul, which those delights does fill.

Deign then to view these lines, where truly I
Express but truth, not using flattery,
No falseness within my mouth once lurks,                    10
But hates all those that use dissembling works,
Even as your goodness merits, so speak I.
I am your servant, bound until I die.
Give leave, then gracious Lady, for I find
Heaven has endowed you with a virtuous mind.                    15

AN ACROSTIC,
UPON THE NAME AND TITLES OF THE RIGHT
HONOURABLE AND MY EVER HONOURED
LORD, PHILIP, EARL OF PEMBROKE AND
MONTGOMERY,* LORD CHAMBERLAIN OF
HIS MAJESTY'S HOUSEHOLD

PEMBROKE's great peer, your princely favour I
Here humbly crave to guerdon* my weak pen.
If this does show my imbecility,
Like good patron, shroud it from bad men;
I, by your favours moved, do this present,                    5
Pray then, my Lord, accept my good intent.

Poor are my weak endeavours, yet if you
Encourage my Minerva's infant muse,*
My cherished thoughts by that may frame anew
Book of true thanks unto your Lordship's use;                    10
Right Noble then, view but the virtuous tract
Of this small volume, and if you shall find
Ought good expressed by our sex's* act,
Know honoured Lord, my stars are very kind.

MONTGOMERY, my coeliac* muse does mount                    15
On cherub's wing from this low orb to heaven;
Virtue is here expressed, vices account;
Nor is't a tale or fable that is given,
Truth never is ashamed to show its face,
Great man and good, but always loves the light.           20
O may it then find an accepted grace;
More cause a woman did the same endite,
Even then as Deborah's* sweet tuned song
Rung out her sacred peal in holy writ,
O so, I pray my heart, my pen, my tongue,                 25
Yea all my faculties may follow it.

> *Of our loss by Adam, and our gain by Christ;*
> *The first Adam was made a living soul, the*
> *second Adam a quickening spirit; For as in*
> *Adam we all die, so in Christ shall all be made*
> *alive. I Corinthians 15.**

God* by his wisdom and all-seeing power
Ordained man unto eternity;
Satan through malice turns that sweet to sour,
Man eating the forbidden fruit must die;
No remedy was left to 'scape this curse,                   5
The sore* still looked on became the worse.

He out of that delightsome place is thrown
To travel in the world, with woe distressed;
Through all his life a pilgrim he is known,
With cares and sorrows and with griefs oppressed;         10
The more he looks into his wretched state,
The more he rues his fact, but all too late.

Whereas he was created king of all
The creatures God on earth created had,
His glory bated is by this his fall,                      15
No creature now on earth remains so bad,
The senseless beast the sense of this has found,
And having man possessed, with death does wound.

The earth disdains to yield to him her strength,
But pricking thorns and brambles forth does send,        20
Till with his sweat and labour she at length,
Only for sustenance some food does lend;

Thus he that was a heavenly creature formed,
By disobedience to a wretch is turned.

Of all the trees that in the garden grew,                    25
He only was forbidden that alone,
His wife from that obedience soon him drew,
And taste thereof he did, although but one.
O wretched man! What has thou lost hereby?
Wicked woman, to cause thy husband die.                      30

'Tis not saying the serpent thee deceived
That can excuse the fault thou didst commit;
For of all joys thou hast thyself bereaved
And by thy conscience thou does stand convict;
Thy husband not alone the fault must rue,                    35
A punishment for sin to thee is due.

For as thou now conceives thy seed in sin,
So in great sorrow thou must bring it forth,*
The grave which thou by that same fruit didst win,
Thou now does find to be but little worth;                   40
Obedience to thy husband yield thou must,
And both must die, and turned be to dust.

The truth sometimes is used by the Devil,
When as he said, your eyes should open be;
And thus you should discern the good from evil,              45
When you the fruit had tasted of that tree.
But he told not your actions should be sin,
And death should be the good which you should win.

For now your strength to weakness turned is,
You know the good, but have no power to chose't;             50
Your eye is ope to see your own amiss*
And to behold the bliss you have refused;
You see your nakedness made vile by sin,
And now seek for a place to hide you in.

But O alas! your deeds discovered are,                       55
You naked lie to those all-seeing eyes,
He views your actions and does see you bare,
Bare of all goodness, vile deformities,
And in yourselves you have no power to mend,
For all your strength is sin, Satan does lend.               60

Now seizes on your sickness, griefs and fears,
When night and day with trouble will torment;
Your sweet delights are turned all to tears,
And now what you have done with woe repent;
Nothing but griefs, and fears, and sad annoys 65
You now possess, instead of endless joys.

You were immortal, but are mortal made;
You were created pure, but now are vile;
Your splendant glories turned all to shade,
Your innocence the devil has beguiled; 70
You were created children of the Lord,
But now are loathsome dung to be abhorred.

Which way can you recover this your loss?
What friend have you that will this great debt pay?
Can you gain pure gold from filthy dross? 75
Or have you power to call again that day?
No, you are in a labyrinth of woe,
And endless is the maze in which you go.

Yet courage, woman,* whose weak spirit's dead!
God in his love a help for thee has found, 80
Be sure thy seed shall bruise the serpent's head,*
Christ by his death shall Satan deadly wound;
The Lion of Judea* resist who can,
In him is blessed the whole offspring of man.

This promise in due time fulfilled has God, 85
Unto the comfort of each mortal wight;*
Christ pays our debt; he's beaten with that rod
That does belong unto our souls of right;
His Father's wrath was poured upon him,
Which does belong as due to us for sin. 90

He died upon the cross and conquered death,
That though we die, yet live again we must;
He buried was and risen is from earth,
And reigns with God in heaven amongst the just;
With him our souls and bodies raised have been, 95
And from death's thraldom now has set us free.

This causes Satan stir himself amain,*
To see if he can win what he has lost;
He strives to make our overthrow his gain,

He stormeth now that he by Christ is crossed;                    100
And to his aid he all his forces draws,
That he may cause us to obey his laws.

Whole armies of his Furies* forth he sends
In shapes transformed to delude our minds;
And unto them his greatest force he lends,                    105
To seize where fittest for his turn he finds;
He marks to what men are by nature given,
And unto that he turns his compass even.*

Satan's deceits are covered all with smiles,
That sin seems pleasing, which our souls destroys;                    110
With quaint allurements he man first beguiles,
With sweet delights he breeds man's sad annoys;
He imitates a poison rarely framed,
But once being taken, all the life blood's stained.

Old and crafty is our enemy grown,                    115
He knows all fish at one bait will not bite,
He'll try a thousand ways to gain his own,
He will not leave till he the mark hits right;
Some with drunkenness, murders, lust beside,
Others with idleness, excessive pride.                    120

Bacchus,* that drunken god from hell, comes forth,
And reeling here and there few scape his knocks;
Who shun his blows esteemed are of no worth,
One drunkard at another's weakness mocks;
What Isaiah* says, thereon they never think,                    125
Woe be to them! are strong to pour in drink.

God in his love formed all things for man's use,
That for his comfort they might daily be,
But they prove poison through man's vile abuse,
Sin changes all into deformity;                    130
Paul* for man's health, to drink wine does advise,
But through excess both soul and body dies.

Man, by this sin, more vile is than a beast,
For but sufficient they will never take,
Man's senses fail him, sins are still increased,                    135
He, tracing vices, doth all good forsake;
In drunkenness Lot* does to incest fall,
Noah* in his wine, his secrets shows to all.

Then lust and murder hands together take,
Like full-fed beasts they neigh at neighbour's wife,                140
Stolen bread is sweet, hid water their thirsts slake,*
They fall to murder through discord and strife;
For when man's reason fails to guide his will,
He into mischief runneth headlong still.

Most people take idleness for no sin,                              145
Thus in simplicity Satan deludes;
That precious time is lost that grace might win,
And want of action, many sins includes;
That mind which unto idleness gives way,
Does open lie to be the Devil's prey.                              150

When David* unto ease himself had given,
His eyes extravagantly look about,
Uriah's wife he spieth in the even,
He must, and did, enjoy her, without doubt;
Satan, by this his fall, more strength does gain,                  155
For David bids Uriah should be slain.

Thus, by one means or other, Satan snares
Man's soul in sin, and hoodwinked tills* him on;
His cup of gold is filled up with tears,
A bitter pittance to their sweets belong,                          160
Pride in itself does bear a poisoned breath,
No sin so small, but punished is with death.

That sin's thought least, that's spent in trimming fine
That carcass vile, on which the worms must prey,
They think not how their hungry soul does pine,                    165
They count not of their reckoning at last day;
But time of grace, once lost, is without call,
So headlong to destruction they do fall.

Pride, of all other, sembleth most the Devil;
'Twas pride threw Satan down from Heaven to Hell,*                 170
'Twas pride that author was of all man's evil,
'Twas pride made Eve* desire first to excel,
When Satan said, 'As gods you then shall be!'
Incontinent she tasted of that tree.

This leprous sin infected so the blood,                            175
That through her offspring it has wholly run,
Before the child can know the bad from good,

It straight is proud, Nature this hurt has done;
A female sin it counted was to be,
But now hermaphrodite\* proved is she.                    180

Like Judas,\* Satan with each mortal deals;
His hail\* is hate, his flattering kiss is death;
He everywhere, still watching, creeping steals
With armed troops to stifle his soul's breath;
His siren\* songs man's mortal death intends,            185
And he must die that thereto his ear lends.

As a physician with his patient still
Applies his potion as he finds it fit,
Giving to some more strong because their ill-
Disposed body oft requireth it,                          190
Even so does Satan with each creature deal,
But his is meant for death and not to heal.

Nature and Satan are sworn brothers\* still,
For neither of them moveth man to good;
By Nature we incline to all that's ill,                  195
Which runneth through our body with our blood,
And by our nature oft he us assails,
And through our weakness he oftimes prevails.

He, by our nature, sees to what we bend,
Whether to goodness or to mischiefs run;                 200
And if he find man aim at the best end,
Then strives he for to mar all he has done;
And by a pride of goodness makes him be
Towards his God like the proud Pharisee.\*

The blessings God to man does often give,                205
As beauty, health, riches, honours and fame,
That he in thankfulness for them shouldst live,
Still using them to glorify his name,
Satan transformeth all this into sin,
Through vile abuse or confidence therein.                210

This thing the scripture evidently shows,
By David's\* numbering of Israel,
Whereby he thought more trust for to repose
In his great army, this to sin befell,
And drawing on God's judgement for the same              215
A heavy plague he on his realm did gain.

There is a sin on which small count is made,
And that is disobedience; for which sin
Samuel* the prophet unto Saul once said,
From being king God had rejected him; 220
When as he Amalek all should have slain,
Satan moved him to let the best remain.

This sin so great in God's pure sight does seem,
As that the prophet plainly does him tell;
The Lord no better of it does esteem 225
Than of vile witchcraft which in Israel
The Lord commanded banished quite to be;
This, like to that, and to idolatry.

This only sin on all mankind did draw
God's heavy wrath, for this, we suffer still; 230
By Adam's breaking God's commanded law,
Sin with a poisoned dart our souls did kill,
For through the breach thereof there entered death,
For so 'twas sentenced by God's own breath.

O this same sin as an accusing one 235
On all occasions still is guilty sayth;
Fulfil God's law who did ne're yet was known
But Christ, who came for to appease God's wrath;
Then by his law we all convicted stand
And hourly may look for God's wrath at hand. 240

Deferring off repentance is a bait
So closely laid by that old enemy
That few do dive* the depth of his deceit,
But unprovided many men do die;
He bids them on the good thief their eyes cast 245
Who never did repent him till the last.

O fly deceitful, cruel enemy,
How deadly is thy hatred to us all,
Thou Ehud-like* hides that will cause us die,
And since thou fell'st, thou aim'st still at our fall; 250
In Paradise the tree death did us give,
But by the tree in Golgotha, we live.*

From a decline in goodness let each soul
With heedful care still study to beware,
Lest in the end for it he does condole, 255

Whenas his foot is fettered in the snare;
Who once his hand upon the plough does lay,
Must by no means look back another way.

Ease it is to plunge ourselves in sin,
But, O alas, hard to get forth again;                        260
If by our faults our souls be black within,
We then shall find all his delusions vain;
His voice of peace all peace does from us take;
Then shun that herb* whereunder lies the snake.

Man ought at all times have a careful eye,                   265
For many are the snares which Satan lays;
When least he thinks on to cause him die,
He hides the bait the which man's soul betrays;
Of ease and pleasures he will always tell,
But his smooth path the broad way is to hell.               270

Who on this panther's skin* does gazing stand,
Had need beware who lies in wait to catch;
Who holds a wolf by th'ears but with one hand,
Must with the other muzzle up his chaps;*
If better thou does get, leave not off so,                   275
But of all means to hurt, deprive thy foe.

That man, the which his enemy foil'd hath,
Must straight unarm him, lest he gather strength;
Benhadad's* servants after Ahab's wrath,
With feigned words did come to him at length                280
And from his kindness they advantage draw,
For he, that feared to die, now made a law.

By his example let us warned be,
God's prophet unto Ahab straight does come,
And said, 'Because from death thou didst him free,          285
Be sure thy life shall stand in his life's room.
Leave thou not Satan till thou see'st him dead,
And Jael-like kill Sisera* in the head.'

He aims not at thy slips, but overthrow;
Small hurts content him not, he life would spill;           290
With slight advantages he will not go,
When thou securest art, he waits to kill;
And Joab-like* of thy health he'll enquire,
But 'tis not life, but death he does desire.

Can this old serpent, this deceiving devil,                    295
Get in his head, then follow shall his tail;
If man but yield a little unto evil,
Sin will increase, though creeping like a snail.
And if unto a custom it does come,
He feels it not, his soul is now grown numb.                   300

All Satan's baits are glittering to the eye,
He leads man on, in a delightsome train,*
Till Death arrests them saying, 'Thou must die,'
And then he lets them see all was but vain;
Then in the ugliest form he shows them all,                    305
That into desperation man may fall.

Now, having such a strong and powerful foe,
What need has man with heedful care to watch?
Lest on a sudden he from hence do go,
For Death as well does lie in wait to catch;                   310
Who proves a welcome guest to a good man,
For unprovided, come he never can.

Death's ghastly looks to a good man seem sweet,
Who still prepared has for that his end,
As Esau,* Jacob did embracing meet,                            315
So does he Death, accounting him his friend;
If tears do fall, they are not shed through fears,
For joy he's come forceth from him those tears.

Can he expect Death enemy to be,
Who by his present* has his force allayed;                     320
He sent before good works, much charity,
Blessings of orphans, which for him have prayed;
His sighs and tears appeased have his King,
And this supposed foe glad news does bring.

Death is our guide unto eternal bliss,                         325
Portal of Heaven, by which we enter must,
The ladder reaching to true happiness,
Which bringeth man to live amongst the just;
By him we come God's glorious face to see,
From which by life deprived we still shall be.                 330

Our flesh a prison is unto our soul
Which does deprive it of that heavenly light;
With spiritual groans and sighs it does condole,

Till it attain unto that wished sight;
Death is the key unlocks our misery,        335
Looseth our bonds and gives us liberty.

Death's fangs are pared,* his bitter potions sweet,
His edge abated, all his hurt is done,
A godly man most kindly he does meet,
And of a foe he is a friend become;        340
His stroke is like the striking of a vein,
By which small smart sick men their health do gain.

Death is the ending of our days, not life,
For having closed these eyes we wake to live;
Death having finished once this mortal strife,        345
Our faith in Christ new life to us does give;
Our night is passed, our day-star does appear,
Our cloud is vanished and our morn shines clear.

Now ends all sorrows, now all griefs are done,
Sin takes his leave and weakness has his end;        350
And now behold our jubilee is come,
The harvest of our labours we attend;
Death's potion only bitter is in show,
The taste once passed no operation* so.

Man's glass* once run, his flower of life once dead,        355
That vapour vanished, and that span* once grasped,
His breath once failing, all his body's lead,
In senseless coldness all his parts are clasped;
He came from earth, earth house-room now him gives,
His spirit from God, with God forever lives.        360

The carnal, wicked, worldly-minded men,
Who in this life their whole content have placed,
Do tremble when Death mentioned is to them,
Because by him all joys from them are chased;
Their ease and pleasures changed quite will be,        365
All mirth is dashed by present misery

The sight of him unto their minds do bring
Remembrance of their sins they slightly passed,
The which with woe their souls do sorely sting,
For that they see the count called in at last;        370
Which sure on earth a hell may deemed be,
When without mercy man his sins does see.

Those men which only to delight are given,
At the approach of Death do fear and quake,
What earth afforded they accounted heaven,                    375
And now perforce they must those joys forsake;
God's blessings they most viley have abused,
And proffered time of grace they have refused.

And now those words which Abraham* did say
To Dives, when for water he did call,                          380
He finds too true whose smarts without allay,
His sorrows far more bitter are than gall;
His good things only were upon this earth,
But life and them are parted quite by death.

Terrors and fears must needs their souls affright,            385
When guilty conscience shows God's angry eye,
O how they tremble to approach that sight,
To whom their sin will out for vengeance cry;
He who on earth to grieve they did not fear,
Will give a sentence which their souls will tear.             390

O how man's sins that mild aspect do change,
He, which for man did bleed, does man condemn;
If by their sins from the right path they range,
Wanting their guide, dangers approacheth them;
The wolf once seizing, 'tis in vain to fly,                   395
Their shepherd hears not, bootless* 'tis to cry.

Alas, who would this world as ought esteem,
If truly he consider everything;
Those pleasures which to man most happy seem,
Do soonest fade and gone they leave a sting;                  400
Man upon earth no sure abiding hath,
Then fear betime,* before thou feel God's wrath.

Belshazzar* when he was carousing set
Amongst his princes in his royal throne,
A writing turns those fair delights to jet,                   405
A hand then showed makes bone encounter bone,
He fearful sits whilst thus it does endite,*
'Thou'rt weighed in balance and art found too light.'*

Man's life a scene and tragic cues succeed,
A comet always future harms foretell,                         410
The happiest life by death is made to bleed,

If unprepared he die, he goes to hell;
The gate is shut, and they must take their lot
For 'twill be answered: 'Lo, I know you not!'

Unto a thorny field and barren land,                              415
How fitly may man's life compared be,
What cares, what fears, what griefs, are still at hand,
And for one joy ten discontents we see;
We always walk as on a bridge of glass,
And oft it cracks as over it we pass.                             420

Still barren is this world of true content,
Fruitful enough in procreating woes,
Thorny afflictions towards us are bent,
But certain joys still backwards from us goes;
Who thinks to catch them does a shadow chase,                     425
And like Ixion* does a cloud embrace.

Then why should man thus waste his precious time,
And triflingly let slip his golden days?
O! Turn to God whilst thou art in thy prime,
And put not off repentance with delays,                           430
For when death comes it then will be too late,
By tears or vows for to prorogue* thy fate.

Boast not of youth, or honours, wealth or strength,
Who trusts to them upon a reed doth lean,
The which be sure deceive thee will at length,                    435
Then strive from these vain thoughts thy self to wean,
And fill thy lamp with oil whilst thou has space,
Lest afterwards too late thou call for grace.

Break off thy sins by true repentant tears,
And turn to God whilst it is called today,                        440
And rest assured he their prayers hears,
That unto him incessantly do pray;
For to encourage thee, he this did say:
'Who comes to me I will not cast away.'

Is not man's life compared unto a flower,                         445
And, O how soon alas, the same does fade and die;
Then let man live prepared (each day and hour),
Lest unawares the force of death he try;
And bear this saying always in thy mind,
As death thee leaves, so judgement will thee find.                450

And as the flower in the chiefest prime,
Does fade and die when sun his face does hide,
For 'tis not in the earth's vast slippery clime,
An ever-fading being to provide,
No more can strength, or skill prevail at all,                    455
To lengthen life when God by death does call.

And as the spring the water forth does put,
And by the earth drunk up no more is seen,
So when by death our thread of life is cut,
On earth we are as we had never been;                            460
Then whilst we live lets strive to purchase grace,
That after death in Heaven we may have place.

Alas! How many are the snares and baits,
Which Satan lays, our poor souls to betray,
Hyena-like* he murders by deceits,                               465
Through false delights to cause us miss our way;
His mermaids' songs are only sweet in sound,
Approach them not, lest death thy life does wound.

Therefore the safest way unto our bliss
Is meditation of our certain death,                              470
And though we tread the steps of carefulness,
And all our life in sorrow draw our breath,
The guerdon* of our pains our Christ will give,
In causing us eternally to live.

Thus, by a godly and an upright life,                            475
Man, of a deadly foe, may make a friend,
And by a wise provision stint that strife,
Which Satan laid to bring us to our end;
And though our flesh prove false, our God is just,
By death our soul gains heaven, our body, dust.                  480

Be ever vigilant in all thy ways,
And always live as in the sight of God,
Perform good actions, and use no delays,
Then fear not death, it brings with it no rod;
With care attend that sure uncertainty,                          485
And live as every hour thou shouldest die.

This watchful care wounds Satan in the head,
For he that thinks of death does shun all sin,
By thought of this man, to the world, proves dead,

He counts all dross, and only Christ would win;                    490
No earthly joys can cause him life to love,
His soul is fixed, and nothing can him move.

Thus each weak Christian may this tyrant foil,
For by Christ's death man armed is with strength,
Though in this combat he a while may toil,                    495
But faith in Christ gives victory at length;
And with a courage bold man now may cry,
'Death, where's thy sting? Grave, where's thy victory?'

What though we die, as die we surely must,
Yet by this death we now are gainers made;                    500
For when our bodies are consumed to dust,
We shall be raised from that eternal shade;
Our mortal bodies shall immortal be,
And with our souls enjoy eternity.

Our troubles in this life now changed are,                    505
From tokens of his wrath, unto his love;
For though a while upon the earth we share
Of griefs and troubles, yet when God above
Shall by death call us from the vale of sin,
We shall enjoy eternal bliss with him.                    510

Where all tears shall be wiped from our eyes,
All griefs and sorrows then shall ended be,
We shall be freed from all clamorous cries,
No discontents nor troubles shall we see,
But peace, and joys, and comforts shall be found,                    515
And always in our ears a heavenly sound.

Our senses shall partake all of this bliss,
Our eyes shall evermore behold our King,
Our hearing heavenly music shall possess,
Our tongues shall evermore his praises sing;                    520
Thus smell and taste, thus hands and ears and sight,
Shall evermore enjoy a full delight.

Unto this happiness and place of joy,
In thy good time, sweet saviour Christ, us bring,
Where being freed from sorrows and annoy,                    525
We evermore thy blessed praise may sing,
Where we shall never cease, but night and day
Sing praise and glory unto thee alway.

(1634)

# JANE AND ELIZABETH CAVENDISH

## *The Concealed Fancies* *

LUCENY

I wonder what's the cause about you go,*
Thus to profane my sacred priesthood* so,                    45
As to name me wantonly* fair,
Chaste that I am; and it shall be my care
Your stealing language further shall not creep
Into my sacred church,* where I will weep;
Praying that all may truly, honest* keep,                    50
For my ambitious store in votes* ascends
For my loved, dear and absent friends,*
That each upon their temples truly may
Wear several laurels, of each sweeter bay;*
At their return then happy shall I be                        55
In that blessed day, I once them more do see ...

TATTINEY

Bless me what spirit possesses you*                          65
To speak to me as if I were not true?
But I am just and will be just to grief
And now without my friends have no relief.


LUCENY

When I in sadness am and then do think,*
I'm lulled asleep in melancholy wink;*
Each chamber ceiling doth create true sad,
Yet tempered so as I am quiet, glad.
Then when I walk nuns' gallery round,                        5
My thoughts tell me I'm falling in a swound,*
And when that flowers fine I have,
Then sure I'm decked for my grave.
So if each one will have a fine-loved death,
Enter your self in sadness, sweeter earth;                   10

Then, when my quiet soul desires to walk,
The gardens do revive my tongue to talk.
So in white sheet of innocence I pray,*
Each one that wishes me to see,
For ghosts do love to have their own delights          15
When others think they have designs of frights;
So even as they, I wish no fear to none,
But on my friends, contemplate alone.

TATTINEY

My grief doth make me for to look*
As if life I had quietly forsook;                      20
Then for my fine delitive* tomb,
Is my seeled chamber and dark parlour room.
Then when my spirit in the gallery doth walk,
It will not speak, for sin to it is talk.
At night I rise from tomb to see                       25
My friends pure well, but sleeping that must be;
This is my truer soul of glad;
And ghost's contentment, now you see, is sad.

# (JANE CAVENDISH)*

## An Answer to my Lady Alice Egerton's Song*

I cannot send you back my heart
  For I have but my own,
And as that sentry* stands apart
  So watchman* is alone.

Now I do leave you for to spy         5
  Where I my camp will place,
And if your scouts* do bring allay*
  Maybe yourself will face.*

Then if you will challenge me the field
  And would me battle set,         10
I then as master of the field
  Perhaps may prove your net.*

(c. 1644)

## On the Death of My Dear Sister*

O God thy judgement unto sinful eye
Were great when I did see my sister die;
Her last look was to heaven,* from whence she came,
And, thither going, she was still the same;
No discomposure in her life or death,         5
She lived to pray, prayer was her last breath.
And when Death's heavy hand had closed her eyes,
Me thought the world gave up its ghost in cries,
What ere* relations' choice, or nature made,
Lost their best light, and being in that shade,         10
For none can give example like her life
To friendship, kindred, family or wife.
A greater saint the earth did never bear,
She lived to love, and her last thought was care:
Her new born child she asked for, which ne'er cried,         15

Fearing to know its end, she bowed and died.
And her last vale* to heaven appeared to all,
How much she knew her glory in the call.

(Undated)

# (ELIZABETH CAVENDISH)*

## On My Boy Henry*

Here lies a boy, the finest child from me,
Which makes my heart and soul sigh for to see,
Nor can I think of any thought, but grieve,
For joy or pleasure could me not relieve;
It* lived days as many as my years,                     5
No more, which caused my grieved tears;
Twenty and nine was the number,
And death hath parted us asunder;
But you are happy, sweetest, on high,*
I mourn not for thy birth, nor cry.*                    10

(1656)

## Spoken Upon Receiving a Cake
## of Perfume Made up in the Shape
## of a Heart*

My dear, I thank thee, in it* you hast so well
Showed me the place wherein thy love doth dwell:
'Tis in thy heart, there let it ever be,
But when you putt'st it forth to show it me;
I love thee, ever have, and still shall do,            5
To show it you and I are one, not two.

(Undated)

# ANNE BRADSTREET

## In Honour of that High and Mighty Princess Queen Elizabeth* of Happy Memory*

### THE PROEM*

Although, great Queen, thou now in silence lie
Yet thy loud herald Fame does to the sky
Thy wondrous worth proclaim in every clime,*
And so has vowed while there is world or time.
So great's thy glory and thine excellence,                          5
The sound thereof rapts* every human sense,
That men account it no impiety,
To say thou were a fleshly deity.
Thousands bring offerings (though out of date)*
Thy world of honours to accumulate;                                10
'Mongst hundred hecatombs* of roaring verse,
Mine bleating stands before thy royal hearse.
Thou never didst, nor canst thou now, disdain
T' accept the tribute of a loyal brain;
Thy clemency did erst* esteem as much                              15
The acclamations of the poor as rich,
Which makes me deem my rudeness is no wrong,
Though I resound thy praises 'mongst the throng.

### THE POEM

No Phoenix* pen, nor Spenser's* poetry,
No Speed's nor Camden's* learned history,                          20
Eliza's works, wars, praise, can e'er compact;*
The world's the theatre where she did act.
No memories nor volumes can contain
The 'leven Olympiads* of her happy reign,
Who was so good, so just, so learn'd, so wise,                     25
From all the kings* on earth she won the prize.
Nor say I more than duly is her due,

Millions will testify that this is true.
She has wiped off th' aspersion of her sex,*
That women wisdom lack to play the rex;*                    30
Spain's monarch, says not so, nor yet his host
She taught them better manners, to their cost;*
The Salic law, in force now had not been,
If France had ever hoped for such a queen;*
But can you, doctors,* now this point dispute,            35
She's argument enough to make you mute.
Since first the Sun did run his ne'er run race,
And earth had, once a year, a new old face,
Since time was time, and man unmanly man,*
Come show me such a Phoenix if you can.                    40
Was ever people better ruled than hers?
Was ever land more happy freed from stirs?*
Did ever wealth in England more abound?
Her victories in foreign coasts resound:
Ships more invincible than Spain's, her foe,             45
She wracked,* she sacked, she sunk his Armado;*
Her stately troops advanced to Lisbon's wall,
Don Anthony in's* right there to install;*
She frankly helped Frank's brave distressed king;*
The states* united now her fame do sing,                  50
She their protectrix* was, they well do know
Unto our dread virago,* what they owe;
Her nobles* sacrificed their noble blood,
Nor men nor coin she spared to do them good.
The rude untamed Irish she did quell,*                     55
Before her picture the proud Tyrone* fell.
Had ever prince such counsellors as she?
Herself Minerva* caused them so to be;
Such captains and such soldiers never seen,
As were the subjects of our Pallas* queen.                60
Her seamen through all straits the world did round;*
*Terra incognita** might know the sound;
Her Drake* came laden home with Spanish gold;
Her Essex* took Cadiz, their Herculean hold.*
But time would fail me, so my tongue would too,           65
To tell of half she did, or she could do.
Semiramis* to her is but obscure,
More infamy than fame she did procure;

She built her glory but on Babel's* walls,
World's wonder for a while, but yet it falls.                70
Fierce Tomris* (Cyrus' headsman) Scythians' queen,
Had put her harness off, had she but seen
Our Amazon in th' Camp of Tilbury,*
Judging all valour and all majesty
Within that princess to have residence,                     75
And prostrate yielded to her excellence.
Dido,* first foundress of proud Carthage walls
(Who living consummates her funerals),
A great Eliza, but compared with ours,
How vanisheth her glory, wealth, and powers.                80
Profuse, proud Cleopatra,* whose wrong name,
Instead of glory, proved her country's shame,
Of her what worth in stories to be seen,
But that she was a rich Egyptian queen.
Zenobya,* potent empress of the East,                       85
And of all these without compare the best,
Whom none but great Aurelius could quell;
Yet for our Queen is no fit parallel.
She was a Phoenix queen, so shall she be,
Her ashes not revived, more Phoenix she;*                   90
Her personal perfections, who would tell
Must dip his pen in th' Heleconian well,*
Which I may not,* my pride doth but aspire
To read what others write and so admire.
Now say, have women worth? or have they none?               95
Or had they some, but with our Queen is't gone?
Nay masculines, you have thus taxed* us long,
But she, though dead, will vindicate our wrong;
Let such* as say our sex is void of reason,
Know 'tis a slander now, but once was treason.              100
But happy England which had such a queen,
Yea happy, happy, had those days still been;
But happiness lies in a higher sphere,
Then wonder not Eliza moves not here.
Full fraught* with honour, riches and with days             105
She set, she set, like Titan* in his rays;
No more shall rise or set* so glorious sun
Until the heaven's great revolution;*

If then new things their old forms shall retain,
Eliza shall rule Albion* once again.                                110
(1650)

## The Vanity of All Worldly Things

As he said vanity, so vain say I,
Oh! vanity, O vain all under sky;
Where is the man can say, 'Lo, I have found
On brittle earth a consolation sound?'
What is't in honour to be set on high?                              5
No, they* like beasts and sons of men shall die,
And whilst they live, how oft doth turn their fate;*
He's now a captive that was king of late.
What is't in wealth great treasures to obtain?
No, that's but labour, anxious care, and pain.                      10
He heaps up riches, and he heaps up sorrow,
It's his today, but who's his heir tomorrow?
What then? Content in pleasures canst thou find?
More vain than all, that's but to grasp the wind.
The sensual senses for a time they please,                          15
Meanwhile the conscience rage, who shall appease?
What is't in beauty? No that's but a snare,
They're foul enough today, that once were fair.
What is't in flow'ring youth, or manly age?
The first is prone to vice, the last to rage.                       20
Where is it then, in wisdom, learning, arts?
Sure if on earth, it must be in those parts;
Yet these the wisest man of men* did find
But vanity, vexation of mind;
And he that knows the most doth still bemoan                        25
He knows not all that here is to be known.
What is it then? to do as stoics* tell,
Nor laugh, nor weep, let things go ill or well?
Such stoics are but stocks,* such teaching vain,
While man is man, he shall have ease or pain.                       30
If not in honour, beauty, age, nor treasure,
Nor yet in learning, wisdom, youth, nor pleasure,
Where shall I climb, sound,* seek, search, or find
That *summum bonum** which may stay* my mind?
There is a path no vulture's eye hath seen,                         35
Where lion fierce, nor lion's whelps have been,

Which leads unto that living crystal fount,*
Who drinks thereof, the world doth nought account.
The depth and sea have said 'tis not in me,
With pearl and gold it shall not valued be;          40
For sapphire, onyx, topaz who would change,
It's hid from eyes of men, they count it strange.
Death and destruction the fame hath heard,
But where and what it is, from heaven's declared;
It brings to honour which shall ne'er decay,      45
It stores with wealth which time can't wear away;
It yieldeth pleasures far beyond conceit,*
And truly beautifies without deceit.
Nor strength, nor wisdom, nor fresh youth shall fade,
Nor death shall see, but are immortal made.      50
This pearl of price, this tree of life, this spring,*
Who is possessed of shall reign a king,*
Nor change of state nor cares shall ever see,
But wear his* crown unto eternity.          55
This satiates the soul, this stays the mind,
And all the rest, but vanity we find.

                         (1650)

## The Author to Her Book*

Thou ill-formed offspring of my feeble brain,
Who after birth didst by my side remain,
Till snatched from thence by friends, less wise than true,
Who thee abroad, exposed to public view,
Made thee in rags, halting to th' press to trudge,     5
Where errors were not lessened (all may judge).
At thy return my blushing was not small,
My rambling brat (in print) should mother call,
I cast thee by as one unfit for light,
Thy visage was so irksome in my sight;       10
Yet being mine own, at length affection would
Thy blemishes amend, if so I could:
I washed thy face, but more defects I saw,
And rubbing off a spot still made a flaw.
I stretched thy joints to make thee even feet,*     15
Yet still thou run'st more hobbling than is meet;*
In better dress to trim thee was my mind,

But nought save homespun cloth i' th' house I find;
In this array 'mongst vulgars* may'st thou roam,
In critic's hands beware thou dost not come;                    20
And take thy way where yet thou art not known;
If for thy father asked, say thou hadst none;
And for thy mother, she alas is poor,
Which caused her thus to send thee out of door.

                                                    (1678)


## Before the Birth of One of Her Children*

All things within this fading world hath end,
Adversity doth still our joys attend;
No ties so strong, no friends so dear and sweet,
But with death's parting blow is sure to meet.
The sentence past is more irrevocable,                          5
A common thing, yet oh, inevitable.
How soon, my Dear, death may my steps attend,
How soon't may be thy lot to lose thy friend?
We both are ignorant, yet love bids me
These farewell lines to recommend to thee,                      10
That when that knot's untied that made us one,
I may seem thine, who in effect am none.
And if I see not half my days that's due,*
What nature would, God grant to yours and you;
The many faults that well you know I have                       15
Let be interred in my oblivious grave;
If any worth or virtue were in me,
Let that live freshly in thy memory,
And when thou feel'st no grief, as I no harms,
Yet love thy dead, who long lay in thine arms;                  20
And when thy loss shall be repaid with gains
Look to my little babes, my dear* remains.
And if thou love thyself, or loved'st me,
These O protect from step-dame's* injury.
And if chance to thine eyes shall bring this verse,             25
With some sad sighs honour my absent hearse;
And kiss this paper for thy love's dear sake,
Who with salt tears this last farewell did take.

                                                    (1678)

## A Letter to Her Husband, Absent Upon
## Public Employment*

My head, my heart, mine eyes, my life, nay, more,
My joy, my magazine* of earthly store,
If two be one, as surely thou and I,
How stayest thou there, whilst I at Ipswich* lie?
So many steps, head from the heart to sever,                    5
If but a neck, soon should we be together.
I, like the Earth this season, mourn in black,
My Sun is gone so far in's zodiac,*
Whom whilst I 'joyed, nor storms, nor frost I felt,
His warmth such frigid colds did cause to melt.                10
My chilled limbs now numbed lie forlorn;
Return, return, sweet Sol,* from Capricorn;*
In this dead time, alas, what can I more
Than view those fruits* which through thy heat I bore?
Which sweet contentment yield me for a space,                  15
True living pictures of their father's face;
O strange effect! now thou art southward* gone,
I weary grow the tedious day so long;
But when thou northward to me shalt return,
I wish my Sun may never set, but burn                          20
Within the Cancer* of my glowing breast,
The welcome house of him my dearest guest.
Wherever, ever stay, and go not thence,
Till nature's sad decree* shall call thee hence,
Flesh of thy flesh, bone of thy bone,*                         25
I here, thou there, yet both but one.

                                        (1678)


## On My Dear Grandchild Simon
## Bradstreet,* Who Died on 16 November,
## 1669, Being But a Month, and
## One Day Old

No sooner came, but gone, and fall'n asleep,
Acquaintance short, yet parting caused us weep;
Three flowers,* two scarcely blown, the last i' th' bud,
Cropt by th' Almighty's hand; yet* is He good.
With dreadful awe before Him let's be mute,                     5

Such was His will, but why, let's not dispute,
With humble hearts and mouths put in the dust,
Let's say He's merciful as well as just.
He will return and make up all our losses,
And smile again after our bitter crosses*                    10
Go pretty babe, go rest with sisters twain;
Among the blest in endless joys remain.

(1678)


### Here Follows Some Verses Upon the Burning of Our House, July 10th, 1666. Copied Out of a Loose Paper*

In silent night when rest I took
For sorrow near I did not look
I wakened was with thund'ring noise
And piteous shrieks of dreadful voice.
That fearful sound of 'Fire!' and 'Fire!'                    5
Let no man know is my desire.
I, starting up, the light did spy,
And to my God my heart did cry
To strengthen me in my distress
And not to leave me succourless.                             10
Then, coming out, beheld a space
The flame consume my dwelling place.
And when I could no longer look,
I blest His name* that gave and took,
That laid my goods now in the dust.                          15
Yea, so it was, and so 'twas just;
It was His own, it was not mine,
Far be it that I should repine;
He might of all justly bereft
But yet sufficient for us left.                              20
When by the ruins oft I past
My sorrowing eyes aside did cast,
And here and there the places spy
Where oft I sat and long did lie:
Here stood that trunk, and there that chest,                 25
There lay that store* I counted best.
My pleasant things in ashes lie,
And them behold no more shall I.

Under thy roof no guest shall sit,
Nor at thy table eat a bit.                                    30
No pleasant tale shall e'er be told,
Nor things recounted done of old.
No candle e'er shall shine in thee,
Nor bridegroom's voice e'er heard shall be.
In silence ever shall thou lie,                                35
Adieu, Adieu, all's vanity.*
Then straight I 'gin* my heart to chide
And did thy wealth on earth abide?
Didst fix thy hope on mold'ring* dust?
The arm of flesh didst make thy trust?                         40
Raise up thy thoughts above the sky,
That dunghill mists away may fly.
Thou hast an house on high erect,
Framed by that mighty Architect,*
With glory richly furnished,                                   45
Stands permanent though this be fled.
It's purchased and paid for* too
By Him who hath enough to do.
A price so vast as is unknown
Yet by His gift is made thine own;                             50
There's wealth enough, I need no more,
Farewell, my pelf,* farewell my store.
The world no longer let me love,
My hope and treasure lies above.

(Published 1867)

NOTES

---

## Isabella Whitney

*A Communication ... to London*

Immediately before this introductory poem Whitney explains the purpose of her text: 'The author (though loath to leave the city) upon her friends' procurement [prompting] is constrained to depart. Whereof she feigns as she would die and makes her will and testament as follows: with large legacies of such goods and riches which she most abundantly has left behind her, and therefore makes London sole executor to see her legacies performed.'

3   **rue**: regret. **smart**: pain, misfortune.

8   **mo**: more.

11   **ere wit**: before understanding; Whitney points out, in time-honoured fashion, how women always love those men who are least deserving.

15   **mell**: concern oneself with.

24   **payed were**: were paid, that is, did not offer credit for lodgings or clothes.

28   **ere**: before.

34   **latest**: last.

35–6   **deceive ... till**: that you do not cheat my beneficiaries out of what I bequeath them.

*The Manner of Her Will*

1–2   **I ... purse**: an ironic inversion of the traditional opening phrase of a will.

6   **eke**: also.

13   **both**: body and soul.

14   **aye**: ever.

15   **Whereas**: When.

27   **store**: plenty, an ironic comparison with Whitney's own lack of material possessions; see also at lines 30, 35, 43, 73, 111, 222 and 275 below.

28   **Paul's**: St Paul's Cathedral, which will lead the other churches.

31   **craveth cost**: needs expenditure.

32   **him**: London; some editors substitute 'them', which misreads the syntax.

37   **such ... observe**: in 1563 an act was passed which increased the number of fast days (when no meat could be eaten) from two to three; from Whitney's

comment it is clear that not everyone obeyed this statute. The streets where fish were sold are unnamed.

39   **fraught**: filled.

41   **Watling ... Canwick**: both streets (the latter also known as Candlewick) were renowned for their cloth merchants.

47   **mercers**: dealers in expensive materials.

49   **Cheap**: Cheapside.

52   **meet**: suitable.

54   **Full brave**: Very fine.

55   **purl**: thread used for embroidery.

57   **bongraces**: veils or shades worn at the front of women's hats.

60   **feat**: nicely.

61   **nets**: hairnets.

62   **Pawn**: the gallery of the Royal Exchange on Lombard Street, known for its cloth merchants.

63   **French ruffs, high purls, gorgets, and sleeves**: a round pleated collar which stood out from the neck; a stiffened pleated collar which stood up from the neck; wimples, linen coverings for the neck and bosom; sleeves were often made separately from the main body of the garment and were of finer, more easily laundered material.

64   **lawn**: a fine linen.

66   **knack**: trinket, trifle.

67   **Stocks**: a market-place, now the site of Mansion House.

69   **hose**: stockings, leggings.

71   **stitched**: embroidered. **trunks**: trunk-hose, baggy trousers covering the hips and upper thighs.

72   **Gascoyne guise**: in the style of gaskins, that is, wide breeches, supposedly worn in Gascony or Spain.

73   **pantables**: pantofles, overshoes.

75   **Cornwall**: a debated site, but probably a printer's error for 'Cornhill', where there was a large market (see Martin, p. 294).

78   **Bow**: the church of St Mary le Bow.

80   **indifferent well**: fairly well.

82   **body-makers**: bodice makers (that is, tailors), but distinguished from those who make breeches; bodices would have been made of more expensive and durable materials.

84   **guards**: ornamental borders, with a pun on weaponry which is taken up in the next line.

86   **dags**: large, heavy pistols.

88   **nigh ... until**: almost as far as the Fleet.

92   **junkets**: sweetmeats, delicacies.

93   **'pothecaries**: apothecaries, who sold sweet foods such as preserves, as well as drugs.

94   **banquets**: the items which would have made up the dessert, that is, sweet foods.

97   **roisters**: riotous swaggerers.

98   **cut it out:** show off.

101   **cunning:** skilful.

111   **Mint:** the Tower of London, where money was officially made.

112   **tell it:** count it.

113   **Steelyard:** Stillyard, a hall on Upper Thames Street where German merchants sold strong Rhenish wines.

115   **men:** the young apprentices, who were not allowed to get married while their apprenticeship ran.

117   **proper:** of good character and social standing.

119   **need ... lures:** emotional and/or sexual need compels, or the desire for economic gain lures, the apprentices into marriage.

122   **repair:** go to.

124   **air:** it was believed that infections could be transmitted through the air.

126   **drug:** drudge.

128   **smug:** smart.

139   **remember me:** in their prayers.

141   **Counter:** the prison for debtors.

142   **wrack:** ruin, but with a pun on the torture instrument, the rack (although the reference is Whitney's ironic exaggeration).

143   **coggers:** cheats.

144   **draw aback:** force to retreat, but with a pun on to 'draw' or 'drag' a criminal, as in 'hanged, drawn and quartered' (see 159–64 below).

147   **Hole:** the worst level of the debtors' prison, which provided no comfort at all.

148   **little ease:** a pun on the name of a form of cell which was so small that prisoners could neither stand nor sit.

149   **Newgate:** the prison for those who were accused of criminal or treasonable offences.

150   **sessions:** the hearings and trials, presided over by a Justice of the Peace.

151   **heaped:** crowded.

154   **burning ... thumb:** convicted criminals were often branded on the hand or face.

155   **fees:** those convicted of a crime were sometimes allowed to become 'professed beggars' so that they could raise the money to pay for their fines.

158   **twelve:** a jury was summoned to judge serious offences.

159   **Holborn:** on the route to Tyburn, where executions took place.

161   **nag:** horse, which would draw the condemned to the gallows; alternatively it might also break the convict's neck if it broke into a gallop.

164   **press:** crowd.

165   **Fleet:** the prisoners of the Court of Chancery, where cases of equity were heard.

167   **ere:** before.

169   **Papist:** Catholics had to pay heavy fines if they failed to conform to the rules of Anglican worship.

171   **box:** a poor box for collecting alms, but with a pun on 'to hit'.

172   **behoof**: benefit.

176   **Ludgate**: another debtor's prison.

177   **in case**: in a position.

182   **debtor**: a pun on being in someone's debt, in terms of honour as well as financially; Whitney suggests that her debts may well mean she will be incarcerated in Ludgate herself.

185   **shroud**: to conceal, but with a pun on a winding-sheet, suggested by 'die' in the next line.

190   **credit**: a pun on credence and borrowing money.

193   **Paul's**: the churchyard at St Paul's Cathedral, which was known for its printers and booksellers.

197   **my printer**: Richard Jones, who published several women authors.

204   **afloat**: in a monetary sense.

209   **plate**: goods plated in precious metal.

211   **bags**: money bags.

212   **see … burst**: ironic comment on how young husbands should use or sell the possessions and money of their elderly wives.

215   **fruit-wives**: female fruit-sellers, who traditionally sat at the city gates, calling to those who passed by in order to sell their wares.

217   **Smithfield**: most commonly a horse-market, but also selling more general goods; an area beyond the city walls.

222   **neat**: oxen.

223   **spital**: St Bartholomew's hospital at Smithfield.

225   **Bedlam**: St Bethlehem's Hospital, which was a lunatic asylum; Whitney is ironic about her own visits to Bedlam and those she left there, referring to the hospital's reputation as a popular source of entertainment as well as implying a lack of mental stability amongst her acquaintances.

229   **Bridewell**: a poor house for women, who would have been made to undertake domestic tasks as part of their upkeep.

231   **chalk … chopped**: probably the production of fuller's earth (known as 'chalk') for the cleaning of cloth.

239   **rut**: rout, a disorderly crowd of young men, with a pun on 'rutting', having sex; perhaps a sixteenth-century comment upon students.

245   **cloyed**: fed up with an excess of work.

248   **fence**: fencing.

250   **make them sport**: to amuse themselves.

251   **players**: actors; the Inns of Court were notorious breeding-grounds for the dramatists and actors of the early modern period.

261   **named have**: have nothing to my name, i.e. that I can call my own.

265   **shrouding sheet**: winding-sheet for wrapping up dead bodies.

267   **oblivion**: debtors were often buried in unmarked graves, since they had no money to pay for a headstone.

269   **Ringings**: the ringing of church bells in memory of the dead; these had to be paid for. In the next line, Whitney prohibits the ringing of bells at her death precisely because of the expense involved.

274 **this vale**: in Christian terms, the valley of human sufferings (i.e. the earth on which we live); a better existence is promised in Heaven after death.

284 **run at large**: run short.

285 **Happy Days and Quiet Times**: like Fortune, these companions represent Whitney's positive experiences of London, and moreover ones which are not designated by their material worth.

286 **her**: Fortune's.

298 **rue**: regret.

301-3 **if ... luck**: a sharp comment suggesting that if her friends had wanted to keep her they would have lent her money.

309 **persuade**: convinced.

316 **descry**: observe.

321 **Standish**: Ink-stand.

324 **hie**: hurry.

325-6 **nearer kin ... vary**: closer relatives, (i.e. Whitney's actual relatives, not the allegorical figures in the poem) who might contest the will.

## Elizabeth I

### Woodstock: the Window Poem
During the reign of Mary I, Elizabeth was under constant suspicion of various treasonable activities, particularly as she was the focus of Protestant hopes of overthrowing her Catholic sister. This poem (and the next, 'Woodstock: The Shutter Poem') was written during her imprisonment in a manor at Woodstock from May 1554 to April 1555 (see Notes on the Authors, pp. 350-52 below); she inscribed it on a window using a diamond.

1 **by me**: about me.

### Woodstock: The Shutter Poem
See note to 'Woodstock: the Window Poem' above; this poem was written upon a shutter and follows the discourse on Fortune in Boethius' *Consolation of Philosophy* (1.5).

4 **quit**: repaid.

### French Psalter Poem
Although this poem cannot be dated officially, it probably belongs to Elizabeth's youth, and deals with doubts and concerns about betrayal.

### The Doubt of Future Foes
The poem relates Elizabeth's concerns about Mary Stuart, Queen of Scotland, who had taken refuge in England in 1568; Mary was the focus of Catholic hopes to overthrow the Protestant Elizabeth, and as such was a constant source of worry to the English queen. The poem's form, poulter's measure, was popular during the period.

1 **doubt of**: fear of.

2 **wit**: intelligence, reason.

6 **Which ... winds**: as policy changes, so belated repentance 'rains' down.

**7–8  The top ... see:** the metaphor is botanical and recalls the garden scene in Shakespeare's *Richard II* (III.iv).

**9–10  dazzled ... finds:** the metaphor refers to falconry: another courtly allusion. **wights:** persons.

**11  daughter of debate:** Mary Stuart. **aye:** always.

**14  brooks not:** does not tolerate.

**16  poll their tops:** prune, but with a pun on beheading. **gape:** desire, wish for.

*On Monsieur's Departure*
Ostensibly written by Elizabeth when the Duke of Alençon (whom she called 'Monsieur'), the last of her formal suitors, left England in 1582, the poem was found with material relating to the Earl of Essex so it is possible that the poem is addressed to him (see Notes on the Authors, pp. 350–2 below). However, the general sense, that love is both inexpressible and inescapable is common to the love poetry of the period.

**4  stark:** completely. **prate:** chatter.

**5  freeze ... burned:** a conventional Petrarchan image.

*An Answer*
This was written in response to Sir Walter Ralegh's 'Fortune Hath Taken Thee Away', which deals with Ralegh's exile from the court in 1587; for a detailed discussion of the various versions of this text, see May (1991).

**1  pug:** a term of endearment.

**2  Wat:** a shortened version of Walter, that is, Sir Walter Ralegh.

**3  Fortune ... blind:** Fortune was traditionally depicted as blind.

**9  Ne:** Nor. **rede:** counsel, advice.

**12  thy mistress:** a double reference, to both Sorrow and Elizabeth herself. **jest with thee:** make yourself an object of ridicule.

**17  brackish:** salty.

**19  bands:** bonds.

**22  her ... blow:** Fortune, who cannot hurt the wise man.

**24  sped:** fare, succeed.

*Now Leave and Let Me Rest*
This poem was originally considered of doubtful authorship, but in recent years has been gradually accepted as part of Elizabeth's canon; although it is not possible to date it, the focus upon youth and age, especially in the last stanza, suggests that the poem was written in the latter years of the queen's reign.

**4  doting:** fond, foolish; with a suggestion of courtship and romance.

**8  asketh:** demands.

**9–10  Nature ... try:** in nature, time is a worry to all things, since as time goes by, all natural things age and die.

**22  trains:** lures.

**26  fain:** gladly.

**37  fancies strange:** extraordinary loves, imaginings.

**38  fond:** foolish.

**45  fleet:** slip away.

*When I Was Fair and Young*
Like the previous poem ('Now Leave and Let Me Rest'), this text has only recently been accredited to Elizabeth's canon; like the former poem too, it is undated but clearly composed in middle or old age.
9  **Venus' son**: Cupid, in classical mythology the god of love, as Venus is the goddess.
11  **pluck your plumes**: humble you.

## Anne Cecil de Vere

### Four Epitaphs
**Lord Bulbeck**: the only son of Anne and her husband, Edward de Vere; he was born in May 1583 and died a few hours later. 1: the first sonnet is indebted to Philippe Desportes's second epitaph to François-Louis de Maugiron (*Cartels et masquarades*), and to Ovid's elegy for Tibullus (*Amores*, III.9). I have regularized the sonnet form.
3  **glutton up**: swallow greedily.
5  **Venus**: goddess of love in Roman mythology, here used in an Ovidian sense.
6  **inveighing**: railing at.
9  **dolour**: grief.
10  **Papheme**: Cupid.
12  **venom**: poison.
13  **Cupid**: god of love and Venus' son, usually depicted as a child.

2: the second sonnet is indebted to Philippe Desportes's 'Regrets funèbres sur la mort de Diane' (*Cartels et masquarades*); I have regularized the sonnet form.
1  **doleful**: sorrowful.
3  **ordinance of the Destin's**: decree of the Fates (in classical mythology three divinities who decided upon human destiny).
4  **seasons ... prime**: the spring.
9  **tane**: taken.
13  **consume**: to be consumed by.

3: the third sonnet shows the general influence of Desportes and Petrarch; I have regularized the sonnet form.
8  **Promet**: Prometheus, who in classical mythology is said to have made human beings from clay.
11  **it**: the child.

4: the fourth sonnet is indebted to Philippe Desportes's epitaph to Jacques de Lévy (*Cartels et masquarades*); I have regularized the sonnet form.
1  **Idal Venus**, goddess of love; from the town Idalium (in Cyprus), which was sacred to Venus (more commonly, Idalia). **Adon**: Adonis, a youth beloved of Venus who died when hunting a boar.
2  **Thet' for Pelid**: Thetis for Pelides (Achilles); in classical mythology the divinity Thetis was the mother of Achilles, the famous warrior who was slain during the Trojan War. **Phoebus for Hyacinthus**: in classical mythology

Phoebus, the sun god, fell in love with the youth Hyacinthus, but the latter was killed by a jealous rival for his affections.

3    Atis ... prophetesses: in classical mythology Atis was a young shepherd with whom Cybele, the mother goddess, fell in love; when he proved unfaithful to her she caused his death.

5    brute: report. Aphroditan queen: Venus.

6    distil: fall.

7    daisies: a reference to Alcestis, who gave her life so that her husband Admetus might live; she was transformed into a daisy (the source is probably Chaucer's *Legend of Good Women*).

9    Charits: Charities; in classical mythology the goddesses of grace and beauty. perugs: perukes, wigs.

10   Muses: in classical mythology the goddesses of the arts. Nymphs: in classical mythology the female spirits of nature, in this case Oreades.

11   Olympus: in classical mythology the dwelling-place of the gods.

12   Laches, Clothon, and Atropos: the Fates, who in classical mythology decided upon human destiny. plain: complain.

4    But ... shadow: these lines are indebted to Philippe Desportes' 'Regrets funèbres sur la mort de Diane' (*Cartels et masquarades*).

1    Amphion's wife: Niobe, who in classical mythology was metamorphosed into a rock by the gods for boasting about her children.

3    sepulchre: tomb.

## Anne Dowriche

*The French History*
(The Biblical references are, to a great extent, provided by Dowriche herself in the printed text. Dowriche's glosses have been added in the notes where they explicate the text.)

Title   broils: tumults. The French ... Christ: the title refers to three events in the persecution of the Protestants in France (the disruption of a prayer meeting in 1557, the execution of Annas Burgeus in 1559, and the murder of Gaspard de Coligny in 1572), which culminated in the massacre on St Bartholomew's Day 1572.

2    I: the English narrator; probably an allusion to the first translator of Dowriche's source, Thomas Tymme.

7    I ... aside: the speaker partly adopts the role of the Good Samaritan in the parable (Luke 10:25–37).

12   wight: person.

15   he: the French exile; probably a reference to the author of Dowriche's source, Jean de Serres. bor'st ... bell: took first place (proverbial).

19   verdant: fresh, flourishing.

22   erst: before.

36   Have ... beware: Have belatedly understood, to their own cost, that they must beware France's faithlessness.

37 **coasts:** regions.

40 **spider's spite:** proverbial allusion to the supposed malice and venom of the spider.

43 **Juda:** Jeremiah 9:12.

48 **gall and wormwood:** Deuteronomy 29:18.

49–50 **And why ... go:** Exodus 7–13.

51 **Saul:** I Samuel 15.

55 **Amalek:** Exodus 17:4.

58 **Egypt:** Numbers 24:20.

59 **file:** cause, with a sense of defilement.

64 **intreat:** treat.

67 **thou with Juda:** the textual gloss points out that in the following passage France is compared to Juda, Egypt and Jerusalem, in that all have at certain times betrayed God's law.

73 **Moses:** in the Bible, Moses helped the Israelites to defeat the Amalekites (Exodus 17); here, an allusion either to one of the Protestant martyrs referred to in the poem's title, or to Henry of Navarre, the Protestant heir to the throne of France.

74 **lap:** wrap.

77 **God's elect:** the Protestants.

89 **sith:** since.

90 **list:** desires.

92 **pleasant isle:** Britain.

97 **of yore:** in the past.

102 **Englishman:** see note to line 2 above; the gloss adds that the Frenchman sees the Englishman and approaches him. This is the first of a series of visualizations which lend dramatic impact to the poem.

126 **Antichrist:** the Pope.

129 **pitch:** lay down, determine.

137–9 **But ... sent:** a reference to the way in which Christ was rejected by the Jews in general and, more specifically, by the scribes and Pharisees (Matthew 12).

143 **Pharaoh ... oppress:** Pharaoh attempted to keep the Jews in captivity in Egypt (Exodus 7–13).

146 **silver sound:** clear and gentle sound.

151 **let:** hindrance.

152 **says Christ:** Matthew 19:24.

155 **fall at square:** get ready to defend themselves.

157 **prophecy:** Matthew 10:34 and Luke 12:31.

166 **states:** officers of state. **as of yore:** as in the past.

169 **knack:** device.

172 **feat:** act, but with a pun on 'feet'. **crush ... head:** possibly an inversion of Genesis 3:15.

174 **quoth he:** by introducing Satan as a speaking character in the text, Dowriche reinforces the Machiavellian aspects of her poem, as well as

contributing to the overall dramatic framework of the text (see Notes on the Authors).

189  **filed:** refined, polished.

200  **meet ... hosts:** waylay the Protestants as they arrived at their destinations.

208  **gleanst:** gather, in the sense of 'harvest'. **sap:** life.

209  **Mother Queen:** Catherine de Medici, wife of Henry II of France, and regent during Charles IX's minority; she was staunchly Catholic, and hated by the Protestants.

210  **gin:** snare.

212  **Lewes of Lorraine town:** Charles de Guise, Cardinal of Lorraine, a renowned Catholic and persecutor of the Protestants.

216  **Guises:** the powerful Catholic family from Lorraine who were involved in the persecution of the French Protestants.

219  **time:** 1557.

222  **last:** Philip defeated the Constable of France in the battle of St Laurence's Day.

225  **pray:** the gloss adds: 'The godly in danger fall to prayer as their last refuge.'

231  **spies:** the gloss adds: 'The wicked cannot abide any good exercise.'

238  **suits:** petitions.

231  **'swage:** assuage, calm.

242  **steed:** stead; helped them.

243  **Peter:** Acts 12:7. **pent:** confined.

245  **passage ... give:** the gloss adds: 'A certain gate in this assault by the providence of God was wonderfully opened for the safeguard of many.'

255  **clink:** prison.

257  **watch and ward:** guard.

260  **thrall:** bondage

261  **fain:** obliged.

265  **noised:** rumoured. **some ... sent:** the gloss adds: 'Commandment was given by the king that some meet [fit] men should be chosen to consider the causes [offences] of these captives.'

268  **vulgar ... book:** the Bible translated into French, rather than the Latin, and therefore Catholic, version.

270-2  **feast ... pain:** I Corinthians 10:16-33.

274  **commons:** the common people.

283  **in post:** in haste.

285  **Lutherans:** followers of Luther, Protestants.

293  **belly cheer:** hospitality for the stomach, i.e. food.

294  **privy:** secret. **Bacchus:** in classical mythology, the god of wine, here used as an adjective, 'drunken'.

299  **monks ... mind:** the gloss adds: 'The devil's ambassadors'; here, Pluto, who in classical mythology is the god of the underworld, is used to represent Satan.

300  **blaze:** proclaim. **wind:** breath as used in speaking, i.e. talk.

305  **silly:** poor, helpless, with a sense of innocence.

309  Prince's: Revelation 12:7.

311  light: insubstantial.

320  pressed: bound.

328  Pharaoh: Exodus 5–12.

334  God's ... best: those chosen by God to be elected to grace accept all injuries in this world as part of God's divine plan; early modern Protestant groups often referred to themselves as 'God's elect'.

337  ure: use.

338  writing: the gloss adds: 'The godly captives write to the king.' assay: try.

344  Sorbonne's: the Sorbonne, the University of Paris, had declared that it only accepted as valid the Catholic faith.

350  pelf: possessions, wealth.

353  So ... ear: the gloss adds: 'This King Henry the 2 was once an enemy to the Pope, and seemed to favour the Gospel.'

355  German: guarantees had been given to the German states that there would be freedom of religious practice in France.

356  priest of Rome: the Pope.

357  a clean ... way: completely wrong.

360  bent: determined.

363  Constable of France: Montmorency, one of the powerful French nobles; he was a Catholic supporter and eventually allied himself with the Guises.

366  Geneva: one of the key centres of the Reformation and home to Luther; Geneva was the main source of Protestant influence in France in the mid-sixteenth century.

375  blood: the gloss adds: 'The blood of the Martyrs is the seed of the church.'

378  ashes ... raise: the gloss adds: 'Truth, the true Phoenix', which alludes to the legendary bird which rose from the ashes of its own funeral pyre.

379  wit: ingenuity, intelligence.

384  Munerius: he who loves wealth, rewards.

388  states: the governing bodies of the city.

394  not to receive: the gloss adds: 'He that has been once false forsworn is not to be received a witness in any matter.'

400  cankered: corrupt, used here as part of the garden metaphor.

402  whelps ... brood: the offspring of the dog Pontius Pilate (the Roman procurator who authorized Christ's crucifixion); in other words, weak judges who are too easily swayed by authority.

418  crown ... flesh: James 1:2 and Job 5:17.

421  Lord: II Chronicles 32:31, Acts 4:28 and Ephesians 1:11.

423  deadly sign: Philippians 1:28.

427  Abel: Genesis 4:10.

431  repent ... thing: Acts 7:60.

440  trash: worthless people and things.

445  draws: approaches.

574  plighted: pledged.

579  crave: desire.

582 doubted: feared. **Annas Burgeus**: a Protestant senator, whose execution is described in the text following.

591 ark: II Samuel 6:11 and Chronicles 15.

593 Hilkiah: II Kings 22:8.

595 Gideon: Judges 6:11 and 37.

597 Balaam's ass: Numbers 22:23–8.

598 flame: Jeremiah 20:9.

599 lively spring: Psalms 42:1.

600 shining lantern: Psalms 119:105.

601 flame: Exodus 13:21. earst: before, as in, earlier times.

603 Elgathe's: Elijah's; I Kings 18:31–8. flake: fire, flash of fire, i.e. lightning. **fume**: burn.

604 blast: II Kings 1:10 and Numbers 16:15.

605 voice: Psalms 29.

606 Liban: Lebanon.

607 wine: Isaiah 55:1.

608 milk: I Peter 2:22.

611 Ashur: Ahaz, II Kings 17; the gloss adds: 'Hoshea the King and all Israel were carried captive to Babylon by the King of the Assyrians for despising the word and commandments of the Lord.'

619 angel: Revelation 10:2.

624 deface: cancel, obliterate.

625 lively faith: Hebrews 4:10.

628 he ... eyes: Luke 24:5 and 45.

629 Popish lies: Catholicism.

630 trades: ways, paths.

635 gall: as bitter as gall.

641 let him in: Revelation 3:20.

643 supper: Luke 14:11.

647 Lamb: Revelation 19:7 and 18:2.

648 whore of Babel: cf. Revelation 17. In Renaissance Protestant ideology, the whore of Babylon was seen to represent the Roman Catholic Church.

651 daunted: subdued. Saul: Acts 9:3–4.

656 prick: spur.

662 Popish ... fall: Rome and Catholicism; the gloss adds a number of Biblical references, all of which focus upon truth (Esther 3:12 and 4:33–40; Matthew 16:18; Luke 21:15; Acts 6:10; Revelation 13:2; Ephesians 4:30; II Peter 1:10; Philippians 1:29; and Romans 3:15).

664 David: Psalms 30:11.

671 truth deny: II Corinthians 13:8.

674 Lutherans: followers of Luther, Protestants.

676 Cain: Genesis 4. fact: deed.

681 wanton: perverse, unrestrained. assay: test, assault.

684 scanned: judged.

688 God ... heart: Romans 3:13–28.

691 Ahab's: I Kings 21.

692   **two wicked men**: Jannes and Jambres (Exodus 7:11–12 and II Timothy 3:6–8).

697   **you ... call**: Proverbs 3.

705   **King**: the gloss adds: 'The King's answer unto Burgeus, wherein he shows his deadly anger and malice against the Truth.'

708   **durst**: dared.

714   **lewd**: wicked.

716   **guerdon**: reward.

721   **moot**: assembly of people.

723   **Luther's sect**: Protestants.

725   **set some stay**: bring to an end.

727   **meed**: reward. **hire**: wages.

957   **fast**: close.

959   **watch and ward**: proverbial, to guard against attack.

969–70   **The ... faith**: the gloss adds: 'Burgeus uses but this short speech to the people for so he had promised before: whereupon the use of his tongue was permitted unto him, which to others was denied.'

973   **oft**: often.

974   **hap**: chance.

975–6   **O ... request**: the gloss adds: 'The last words of Annas Burgeus being tied to the stake.'

980   **elect**: God's chosen people, here the Protestants.

985   **passing**: pre-eminent.

**Heading**   *Dilated ... Word*: the examples are all glossed in the subsequent text. *Dilated*: Set forth.

995   **Eli's sons**: I Samuel 2.

1001   **Ahab**: I Kings 22.

1009   **Amaziah**: II Chronicles 25.

1012   **spoiled**: defeated, destroyed.

1013   **Zedekiah**: Jeremiah: 36:23, 20:2, 32:3, 38:6 and 39:5.

1015   **pent**: confined.

1025   **ruff**: swaggering display, as in 'ruffle'.

1032   **limber**: flexible.

1034   **Montgomery**: Count of Montgomery, captain of the Scottish guard.

1045   **Elymas**: the gloss adds: 'By Elymas is meant the Cardinal of Lorraine', a leading Catholic, who persecuted the Protestants; cf. Acts 13:6–8.

1049   **hap**: chance occurrence.

1056   **eyes ... head**: the gloss adds: 'King Henry died the 10th August 1559.' **Devil**: the subsequent speech (lines 1085–1128) is spoken by Satan, again emphasizing the theatrical nature of the text. **Queen Mother**: Catherine de Medici (see note to line 208).

1085   **cankered**: infected.

1091   **civil wars**: the religious wars in France, 1562, 1567 and 1568–70.

1094   **princes**: including, among others, Gaspard de Coligny and Henry of Navarre. **subvart**: subvert.

1096  **bewray**: betray, disclose.

1101  **rase**: erase.

1112  **Guise**: the powerful Catholic family from Lorraine.

1126  **ure**: use.

1393  **But ... play**: Dowriche self-consciously alludes to the theatrical tone she creates in the poem.

1401  **quoth she**: the queen's speech is couched in dramatic verse and may be compared with the monologues of other Machiavellian characters, such as Marlowe's Barabas and Shakespeare's Richard III, although it may be noted that Dowriche's poem pre-dates both plays and that she chooses a woman to display such consummate villainy. Dowriche's gloss adds specific references to her source, Innocent Gentillet's *Discours ... contre Nicholas Machiavel, Florentin.* The subsequent references may be found in Machiavelli's *The Prince.*

1404  **those**: the Protestant leaders.

1410  **Prince of Condé**: a militant Protestant.

1425  **masters**: those who teach us: here, Machiavelli. **cog**: cheat.

1433  **woman ... kind**: this resembles Lady Macbeth's speeches in *Macbeth* I.v.37–53 and vi.47–59.

1451  **simple**: foolish.

1452  **galled**: bitter, rancorous.

1457  **passing**: extremely.

1462  **perfect years**: experience.

1465  **imps**: children.

1467  **To ... call**: to submit instead of ordering, and to obey rather than command.

1478  **depaint**: depict.

1487  **where**: whether or not.

1492  **lewd**: wicked.

1494  **Turk or devil**: the association of black skins with devils was a commonplace in the period and is not questioned by Dowriche.

1497  **Marcel**: former Provost of the Merchants in Paris; he helped guide the Paris crowd in their persecution of the Protestants.

1503  **Provost Carron**: Provost of the merchants in Paris. **stomach**: courage.

1513  **doubtful**: awful, suspicious.

1515  **trained**: lured.

1516  **she**: the Queen Mother.

1531  **tocsin**: an alarm signal, usually a bell.

1534  **brawn**: fleshy part.

1536  **hap**: occur.

1541  **great and famous**: an ironic comment in this staunchly Protestant account.

1544  **Chevalier**: the illegitimate son of Henry II.

1545  **posting**: hurrying. **Cossin**: captain of the guard, and a Guisian supporter.

1546  **Woe worth**: proverbial, it was unfortunate. **wolf ... sheep**: proverbial.

1555  **false**: betray.

1561  **band**: bond.

1563–4 Queen of England ... Prince of Orange ... Germans came: the Protestant rulers of Europe, Elizabeth I of England, the Prince of Orange, and the heads of state from Saxony and Brandenburg had all signed treaties with France against Spain in which religious freedom in France was guaranteed.

1572 forlorn: abandoned.

1582 partisan: double-edged spear.

1596 rasing: erasing.

1607 retire: withdraw.

1609 traitors: the gloss adds: 'the Queen Mother, the King and the Duke of Guise'. trothless train: faithless troop.

1612 For ... endure: here Dowriche contrasts the Protestants' torments on earth, which are brief, with the unending pains their persecutors will endure in Hell.

1632 vale ... life: the valley of human sufferings (i.e. the earth on which we live); a better existence is promised in Heaven after death.

1641 Lest ... heart: Psalms 79:10.

1646 Benvise ... mates: Benvise was a German follower of the Guise faction, the other two are Cossin and Attin, also Guisians. targets: shields.

1659 Attin: a servant of the Duke of Guise.

1674 vizard-like: as if wearing a visor or mask. imbrued: stained.

1695 no ... old: the gloss adds: 'The right picture of a bloody tyrant'.

1707 larum: alarm.

1711–16 Here ... desired: the gloss indicates that an Italian follower of the Duke of Gonzaga cut off the Admiral's head and sent it to the Pope.

1721 rustic: rough.

1725 Furies frying: in classical mythology the Furies were the goddesses of vengeance; 'frying' suggests the crowding of a mob.

1727 receipt: accommodation.

1736 County Rouchfoucault: Count Rochefoucauld, a well-known Protestant noble.

1741 De Nance: captain of the guard.

1747 a day: Revelation 6:10.

1749 King: Romans 13:1, I Peter 2:13 and Titus 3:1.

1750 hests: commands.

1751 Joab: II Samuel 111:16.

1754 Naboth: I Kings 21.

1755 Doeg: I Samuel 22:18.

1772 Saul: I Samuel 22.

1775 sprite: spirit.

1777 King David: II Samuel 11.

1779 Saul: I Samuel 18–31.

1781–2 Jezebel ... Naboth: II Kings 18–19.

1784 testy: irritating.

1788 attend: wait for and expect.

1789 Auernois: the gloss notes that Laberg, an Auernois agreed to kill

Rouchfoucault in return for being made captain of the horse. **cused**: accused, suspected of a crime.

Theligny: de Coligny's son-in-law.

**1825** imp: youth.

**1826** Papist's oath: the gloss adds a warning: 'Beware of the guileful promises of the Papists.' **affiance**: trust.

Monsieur de Pilles: a leading Protestant.

**1925** posted: hurried.

**1927** in post: in haste.

**1938** Mandelot: the governor of Lyons.

**1950** sheep ... slaughter: Romans 8:36.

**1954** enjoins: binds with an oath.

**1955** hangman: The gloss adds: 'The common hangman of Lyons had more grace and honesty than Mandelot the Governor.'

**1963** didstain: from stain, blemish; not to undertake something unworthy of their status.

**1964** fame: rumours.

**1966** far unmeet: very unfitting.

**1973** bent: inclined.

**1996** sugred: eloquent.

**2006** Francis Collute: a Protestant merchant of the city. **wan**: won.

**2014** accompt: reckoning.

**2025–6** For ... back: this emblem of Truth is pictured and described at the end of the text (see p. 58 below).

**2028** depaints: depicts.

**2030** paws: an odd choice of word, when 'claws' would have been more appropriate for a bird.

**2033** taste this cup: cf. Mark 14:36.

**2047** bands: fetters.

**2052** present: an immediate occurrence, with the overtones of a representation.

Masson de Rivers: a Protestant preacher. *Dilated*: Set forth.

**2174** requite: repay.

**2173–8** Whoso ... die: Genesis 9:6, Exodus 21:14 and Numbers 35:20. The gloss adds: 'The blood of man is of so great price with the Lord, that he will not only require it of men, but also of the very dumb creatures', and goes on to give the example of Joab, who 'was taken from the altar by Solomon and slain (I Kings 2:31)'.

**2180** Abimelech: Judges 9.

**2184** brain ... to-rent: skull was torn.

**2187** Tryphon: from the Apocrypha, I Maccabees 12:41; Dowriche also cites Josephus' *Antiquities*, 13:10; finally she points out that Tryphon represents Charles IX.

**2191** Aristobolus: Dowriche does not give the source where she 'read' of Aristobolus, but it was most probably Josephus.

2201  **corse**: corpse.

2202  **brother's ... call**: Genesis 4:10.

2225  **man**: Christopher Thaune, president of the parliament.

2229  **Lewes**: Louis XI.

2230  **Mithridates**: king of Pontus in Asia, and renowned for his bloody victories over the Romans.

2237  **King of Arragon**: Peter of Aragon, who massacred the French in battle.

2238  **Sicill**: Sicily.

2239  **Philip**: Philip of Macedon, asassinated by Pausanias, who believed that Philip had betrayed his trust.

2248  **Elizabeth ... sheep**: Queen Elizabeth I was head of the English Protestant Church.

2257  **charged**: burdened.

2258  **warping**: pronouncing.

2260  **charge**: burden.

*Verity ... Pilgrim*
Immediately before the verse an emblem is inserted which depicts a naked woman, wearing a crown and bearing a whip on her back.

1  **supernal**: heavenly. **Jove**: in classical mythology the king of the gods, but here an allusion to the Christian God.

2  **weed**: clothes.

## Mary Sidney

*To Queen Elizabeth*
This poem, often entitled 'Even Now That Care', was one of two written to preface the Juel–Jensen manuscript version of the Psalm translations; the other, 'To the Angel Spirit', is included below: see pp. 61–4).

4  **line out goes**: metre is broken.

7  **dispose**: settle.

19  **these the posts**: these two poems ('Even Now' and 'To the Angel Spirit') which carry the letters of the Psalms.

20  **press**: push forward.

21  **once ... go**: once there were two subjects, Mary and Philip Sidney, but when the latter died only the former was left to present the Psalms to the queen.

22  **reft**: snatched.

23  **O ... woe**: alludes to Philip Sidney's *Astrophil and Stella* 33.

27  **web**: the Psalms; the image of weaving is one of Sidney's feminine allusions.

28  **stuff**: matter; that is, the original Biblical text which was authored by David, not the Sidneys. **curious**: skilfully wrought.

29  **Psalmist King**: King David.

30  **denizened**: naturalized.

32  **repining**: complaining.

35  **parcel**: part of. **undischarged**: not paid.

38  **scanted**: limited.

40  till: work in the fields.

43  laurels: laurels were used in wreaths given to denote poetic excellence, but this is also an allusion to the poems themselves.

45  seat: throne.

51  minds: recalls. meet: fitting.

55  president: one who presides; here an allusion to Elizabeth's role as head of the Church of England.

57  square: suitable.

58  His ... ditties: King David's exalted poems/songs.

59  triumphs: festive shows.

63  holy garments: the Psalms. assays: tries on, tries to understand.

64  sorting ... sort: a pun on going through ('sorting') and are fitting consorts ('sort').

65  painted: figured.

66  both ... oppressed: David was attacked by the Philistines, as Elizabeth is confronted by the Spanish; both foes are seen as enemies of the true God, for Mary Sidney, therefore, as enemies of Protestantism.

69  Philistines: the enemies of the Israelites in the Bible.

78  eft: probably a misprint for 'oft', that is, often.

79  pitch: level of tone; Sidney here reminds herself of the appropriate subject-matter for her poem.

77–9  very winds ... love: an allusion to the defeat of the Spanish Armada in 1588 by the English forces and seen here also as a victory of English Protestantism over Catholicism.

81  lay: to give the government of.

85  restitution: restoration.

89  Thy: Mary Sidney's muse.

94  Juda's ... king: David was king of Judaea.

*To the Angel Spirit*
The second of the dedicatory poems appended to the Psalms, here addressed to Mary's dead brother, Philip Sidney. It is found in the Juel–Jensen manuscript and, attributed to Samuel Daniel, in the 1623 collection of Daniel's works; the latter is probably the earlier version of the poem, the former being regarded as a more 'personal' revision. I have chosen the later version of the poem; the first version may be found in Waller (1977). The form follows the 7-line stanzas traditional in Renaissance elegies.

6  stuff: dust.

8–9  transformed ... substance: a pun on the concept of transubstantiation during the Communion service (where the bread and wine are believed to be *trans*formed into the flesh and blood of Christ), and the act of translating the Psalms (where the Hebrew and Latin sources are *trans*formed into an English version); unlike the Catholics, who believed in transubstantiation, the Protestant Philip Sidney did not 'transform' the body of the Psalms.

9  tire: ornament.

16  reft: taken away from.

**29  sith**: since.

**38  Phoenix**: the legendary bird that rises from the ashes of its own funeral pyre; here an allusion to Philip Sidney who is resurrected through the continuation of his literary work by his sister.

**44  reckoning**: Matthew 18:23–4; the language in this stanza shows the influence of the Geneva Bible.

**45  strange passions**: it has been suggested that this phrase, together with the personal nature of the whole poem, point towards an intense and perhaps disturbing love between Mary and Philip Sidney.

**56  sealed above**: a double meaning, which refers both to falconry (cf. note to line 10 of Elizabeth I's 'Doubt') and to the setting of Philip Sidney as a star in the heavens; thus, Mary Sidney offers a suitable courtly image of her brother alongside his idealization in metaphysical terms.

**57  fellow lights**: the stars as well as angels; alluding to Philip Sidney's poetic name 'Astrophil' (star-lover).

*A Dialogue ... of Astraea*

The dialogue between two shepherds, Thenot and Piers, in praise of Elizabeth I was probably written as part of an entertainment planned for the queen on her aborted visit to Wilton House in 1599; the text was published in Francis Davison's *A Poetical Rhapsody* (1602). The names of the shepherds are traditional in early modern pastorals; however, Piers is derived specifically from Spenser's *Shepheard's Calender* (May and October eclogues), where Piers advocates plain speech and Protestant values, as he does in Sidney's version; while Thenot differs from Spenser's version (in the February, April and November eclogues) in that he is given rather than offers good advice in *A Dialogue* ... The name Astraea refers to the goddess of justice in classical mythology; Elizabeth I was commonly addressed as 'Astraea' in literary panegyrics.

**2  Muses**: in classical mythology the nine goddesses who inspired artistic accomplishment.

**4  plainly**: the key to the whole debate, for Piers supports Protestant plain speech and suspects that poetic language is lying, whereas Thenot promotes a Neoplatonic view whereby ideal art may offer access to a perfect truth.

**15  Momus**: in classical mythology the god of satire.

**23  one ... other**: virtue and wisdom.

**36  measure**: a pun on moderation and a regular poetic metre.

**41  clime**: climate; during the golden age when Astraea reigned there was perpetual spring.

**50  manly ... bay**: combining male and female (the bay and palm were both used to denote military victory and poetic skill, hence combining traditional masculine and feminine skills) and thereby suggesting an androgynous ideal.

**51  verdure**: flourishing condition.

**58  conceit**: poetic invention.

**60  silence**: as that which has no material substance, silence represents a mystical and spiritual ideal.

*The Tragedy of Antonie*

Mary Sidney's translation of Robert Garnier's *Marc Antoine*; it was initially published in 1592 under the title *Antonius: A Tragedy*, together with her translation of Philippe de Mornay's *A Discourse of Life and Death*. The text here follows the first single publication of the play as *The Tragedie of Antonie* (1595). There are three extracts, the initial speech by Antonius (I.1–148) and two speeches by Cleopatra, the second of which concludes the play (II.151–81 and V.137–208).

1: the first speech in the play, given by Antonius (I.1–148), it describes the narrative events as well as setting an overall Senecan tone.

2  **round engine**: wheel of Fortune.

7  **meet**: fitting.

9  **sister's ... wife**: Antonie was married to Octavia, Octavius Caesar's sister, whom he has wronged by leaving her for Cleopatra, his 'queen'.

21  **Pelusium**: a city in Egypt lost to Octavius' forces, supposedly with Cleopatra's compliance.

34  **baits**: enticements.

40  **fatal sisters**: the three Fates who in classical mythology determined human destiny.

50  **burial ... wolf**: be eaten by wolves.

53  **Megaera**: one of the three Furies who in classical mythology enacted revenge on human wrongdoers.

55  **Cupid's fire**: since Cupid was the god of love in classical mythology, his 'fire' denotes passionate desire.

57  **Orestes**: in classical mythology Orestes murdered his mother and was pursued by the Furies, who eventually drove him mad.

62  **Stygian**: in classical legend the river Styx conveyed the souls of the dead to the underworld; here, Orestes sees his mother's ghost.

67  **bays**: a bay wreath signified military victory.

68  **Venus' myrtles**: the myrtle tree was sacred to Venus, the goddess of love in classical mythology.

73  **filed**: defiled. **Crassus**: a triumvir (along with Pompey and Julius Caesar), who was known for his wealth and influence. He was slain by the Parthians, and his head was sent to their king, Orodes, who had gold poured into the corpse's mouth to signify Crassus' greed when alive. **foil**: sword.

74  **cuirass**: armour; breast- and back-plates which buckled together.

83  **Recured**: Restored.

85  **Euphrates**: a river in south-west Asia; the subsequent accounts of Antonie's military achievements are mainly taken from Plutarch's *Antonius*.

91  **Parth ... Mede**: the Parths were a semi-nomadic war-like nation in western Asia who had at one time governed the Medes; the Parths particularly were regarded as barbarous in the early modern period.

92  **Hyrcanie**: Hyrcania, an Asian province where the Parths spent their summers.

94  **Phraate**: Phraates, king of Parthia and Media.

96  **engines**: siege machines.

110 **Nilus**: the Nile.

116 **bristled**: parched.

118 **Pharos**: the lighthouse on the island of Pharos at Alexandria was one of the seven wonders of the ancient world.

133–6 **Alas … gain**: Plutarch, in *Antonius*, recounts how Cleopatra bargained with Octavius after Antonie's defeat at Actium; Mary Sidney, however, follows Garnier in denying this betrayal even though Antonie doubts Cleopatra at this point.

145–8 **But … company**: women's fickleness was proverbial in the English Renaissance; here Antonie will be proved wrong, for Cleopatra is constant.

2: the second passage occurs in Act II, where Cleopatra laments that Antonie believes her to be false; as such her speech here is a direct refutation of Antonie's above (1).

7 **'lighten**: flash down upon.

17 **hap**: fortune.

25 **Charon's barge**: in classical mythology Charon ferried the souls of the dead in his barge to the underworld.

29 **'plain**: complain.

3: this speech occurs at the end of the tragedy, when Antonie has died and Cleopatra considers suicide to be united with him in death. At the beginning of the play the two lovers are mutually doubtful, but by the close they are reconciled and united.

2 **Venus of Paphos**: in classical mythology Venus was said to have been born off the coast of Cyprus near the town of Paphos; Julius Caesar had claimed descent from Venus via Aeneas (see Virgil's *Aeneid* I), but Antonie was also able to claim Venus as an ancestor, through his mother, who was Julius Caesar's aunt.

10 **block**: someone who resembles a block of wood; hence, inert, dead.

19 **ruth**: sorrows, pity.

20 **amity**: love.

28 **him … despised**: Cleopatra's brother, Ptolemy, whom she had defeated with the aid of Julius Caesar.

45–6 **Under … moan**: the scene echoes the description of Elysium from Virgil's *Aeneid* VI.

50 **plaints**: complaints.

56 **brinish**: salt-water-like.

*The Psalms*

The translation of the Psalms was begun by Philip Sidney (Psalms 1–43) and completed by Mary Sidney (Psalms 44–150); she worked on the translation from 1593 to 1600. The Psalms existed only in manuscript versions until 1823 and it was not until 1963 that a modern edition appeared; I have primarily used the A MS (De L'Isle, Penshurst Place). The following text provides only a selection of Mary Sidney's Psalm translations; reasons of space have prohibited the inclusion of all 116.

**Psalm 45**: here Mary Sidney is able to combine an adherence to the original text with a commentary upon Elizabeth I and her court; this Psalm uses political allegory to praise Elizabeth in a courtly fashion, as well as to remind her of the Protestant cause.

1   indites: proclaims.

9   gird: worn, attached to.

15  erst: formerly.

18  cast: attempt to challenge or throw off as in wrestling.

19  fain: eager.

22  ensign: insignia.

25  Justice ... wrong: you love justice and hate wrong.

27  flong: flung.

29  Sabean: the territory of Sheba, whose peoples, the Sabeans, were known as traders and are often referred to in the Bible as importers of spices.

30  Myrrh, aloes, cassia: myrrh, aloes and cassia were unguents used in the making of perfume.

36  Ophir: a country renowned for its fine gold in the Bible.

39  enrold: enrolled, i.e. recorded.

45  Tyrus: Tyre, a territory adjacent to Israel known for its seafaring prowess and hence its trading. fain: obliged.

46  moe: more.

54  maids ... attend: as in the court of Elizabeth I, where her maids of honour waited upon her.

62  partadg'd: apportioned.

63  Myself: Mary Sidney as the 'singer' of the Psalms.

Psalm 50: Sidney here adopts a personal voice and conversational tone to emphasize a Protestant, even Calvinist, reading of the Psalm, which stresses that outward obedience to God is insufficient.

3   pursuivant: herald, messenger.

11  bands: laws, covenants.

13  subsigned: signed.

29  brawny flesh: fleshy meat.

32  bearded cattle: goats.

42  prate: speak insolently of.

44  what I relate: God's words; an allusion to the overriding truth of the Gospel, which was a common Protestant concern.

45  consort: company.

51  wink: close my eyes. embrace: take hold of the present circumstances.

57  marking: attentive.

Psalm 52: the Biblical event in which David complains of the tyranny of his adversary Doeg, which led to the persecution of his priests, is transposed by Mary Sidney on to the sixteenth-century repression of the Protestants by the Pope and the Catholic Church.

1-4 Tyrant ... wanting: the direct address of the opening verse is typically Metaphysical in its tone.

1   swell'st: swell with pride.

2   **vaunting**: boasting.

5   **Lewd**: vile, wicked.

14  **gulfs**: voracious appetite, that which consumes everything.

25  **wight**: person.

28  **guard**: protection.

29  **olive tree**: the olive was a symbol of peace and divine blessing.

**Psalm 53**: an attack against the ungodly; here a Protestant commentary upon the Catholic Church.

3   **fancy**: idea, thought. **bewray**: expose.

9   **cankered**: rotten, diseased.

11  **senselessness**: being without reason.

12  **carriage**: conduct.

15  **vain**: foolish.

19  **vile**: evil, base.

24  **Jacob's house**: where God's chosen people dwell; here an allusion to English Protestants.

**Psalm 58**: the enemies of David, who are accused in this Psalm of flattering King Saul, are presented as the enemies of Protestantism at the English court.

2   **You**: the counsellors (of Saul and Elizabeth).

5   **long**: enduring.

7   **balance**: scales.

8   **indifferent**: impartial.

9–10  **in birth ... injuries**: according to the Calvinist theory of election, all humans were predestined to be either good or bad.

13  **aspic**: asp.

16  **self-deaf**: wilfully refusing to hear. According to the bestiaries, the asp stops its ear with its own tail so as not to hear the snake-charmer's music; it thus symbolizes those who refuse to hear the voice of God.

21  **dishoused**: evicted.

22  **vital band**: umbilical cord; usually read as an example of Mary Sidney's stress upon female experience.

25  **thorns**: in the image of the thorn tree Waller (1977) notes that Mary Sidney uses the Coverdale Bible rather than the Geneva.

26  **untimely**: premature, continuing the metaphor of miscarriage/abortion.

32  **God ... own**: another allusion to the theory of election (see note to lines 9–10 above); God creates each individual according to their own level of good and evil.

**Psalm 59**: David prays to God to be saved from the assassins sent by King Saul; the theme of persecution is used here in relation to the martyrdom of Protestants by the Catholic Church, with specific reference to the St Bartholomew Day massacre in Paris in 1572 (also the subject-matter of Anne Dowriche's *The French History*: see pp. 18–55 above).

15  **band**: band together.

28  **amain**: violently.

30  **maw**: stomach.

31  **elder grown:** grown older, and therefore more powerful.

40  **stay:** support.

44  **Prevented hast:** have anticipated.

60  **a-buy:** pay.

63  **forego:** forgone.

75  **trails ... trace:** lays down a scent so that the quarry's path may be followed.

78  **at bay:** baying, barking.

85–6  **My ... sing:** self-referential comment upon Sidney's authoring of the Psalms; however, Martin (1997) notes that she also makes an ironic comment upon her gender, since her source text, the Geneva Bible, refers to the *weakness* of women being used to defeat the enemy (an allusion to I Samuel 19:12).

**Psalm 63:** a Psalm addressed by David to God while he was in the wilderness; here an attack upon Elizabeth's counsellors who are represented as the ungodly who are oppressing the Protestants.

17  **target of:** shield at.

22  **such:** the ungodly.

23  **gulf:** that which swallows all; a continuation of the eating metaphor.

24  **living date:** term of existence.

**Psalm 72:** addressed to King Solomon; Mary Sidney uses this Psalm to appeal to Elizabeth I, whom she both praises and admonishes; a similar approach is found in the dedicatory poem 'Even Now That Care' (see pp. 59–61 above).

11  **th' oppressed relieve:** a request for aid to help the persecuted Protestants of Europe.

19  **meads:** meadows.

21  **ay:** always.

23  **many-formed queen:** Cynthia, the moon goddess in classical mythology, was represented as changeable, since like the moon she waxed and waned; also an allusion to Elizabeth I, who was commonly referred to as Cynthia in the court poetry of the period.

28  **trace:** the line denoting where the territories divide.

29  **Physon's race:** Physon was an alternative name for Ptolemaeus or Ptolemy, one of the kings of Egypt; hence, Egyptians.

33  **Tharsis:** Tarshish; in the Bible, a wealthy territory adjacent to Israel.

34  **Seba, Saba:** the kings of Sheba and Seba; in the Bible, two lands associated with Africa.

45  **sleight:** trickery.

53–4  **Arabia ... scant:** Arabian gold was highly valued ('dearness'), and therefore in short supply, but also expensive ('dear') because of its rarity.

60  **passport:** leave, freedom.

61  **interlaced:** interwoven; this image recalls the pastoral poetry of Philip Sidney and prefigures that of Mary Wroth (see pp. 183–228 above).

69  **numbrous:** abounding.

73  **this ... stain:** will be stained, dimmed, in comparison to his glory.

76  **earthly ball:** the earth.

82  **Jacob's stock:** the chosen people; here a reference to the Protestants.

88  round: the earth.
90  O: a further emphasis upon the round earth.

Psalm 73: this Psalm encourages perseverance in faith despite oppression and, as such, conforms with a common Protestant discourse of the period which stressed that suffering was merely a prelude to salvation (see also Anne Dowriche's *The French History*: pp. 18–55 above). Walker (1996) suggests that the poem is also a witty commentary upon contemporary love-discourses.

1   **It is most true:** lines 1–6 recall Philip Sidney's *Astrophil and Stella* 5.
4   **albe:** although.
5   **conceit:** idea, understanding.
6   **declined:** fell away.
20  **aught:** anything.
22  **wanton:** unrestrained, perverse.
24  **pitch:** height.
29  **horn of plenty:** the cornucopia is classical mythology; also proverbial.
31  **they:** the ungodly, contrasting with 'godly we' at line 34 below.
35  **pine:** starve, waste away.
42  **check:** censure.
43  **bewray:** reveal.
49  **nigh:** completely.
51  **these:** the ungodly.
57  **clean:** completely.
58  **Right as:** just like.
62  **fume:** rage.
73  **O ... skies:** recalls Philip Sidney's *Astrophil and Stella* 31
78  **lot:** fortune, condition.

Psalm 79: the oppression of the Israelites in this Psalm is linked by Mary Sidney to the persecution of the Protestants and especially to the massacre of St Bartholomew's Day in Paris 1572 (see also Anne Dowriche's *The French History*; pp. 18–55 above).

3   **holily:** in a holy fashion.
13  **blood ... street:** an image which corresponds to many of the descriptions of the St Bartholomew's Day massacre, but here more generally applied to Protestant martyrs.
17  **neighbour places:** neighbouring countries.
20  **flout:** mock.
29  **Jacob:** seen as the father of God's chosen people (Genesis 27), here equated with Protestants.
30  **razed:** destroyed.
33  **cumbers:** troubles.
35  **prevent us:** aid us with timely action.
43  **their:** the ungodly.
48  **wreakful:** revenging.
56  **sev'n-fold gain:** seven times as much; seven being the number of wholeness or completion in the Bible.

**Psalm 82**: a complaint against the partiality of judges, both in the original Biblical context and with a reference to the persecution of the Protestants under the reign of Mary I.

1   **bar**: court of justice.

2   **vice regents**: deputies; Hannay (1989) and Martin (1997) suggest that the implication of this stanza, that subjects are not bound by absolute rule but only by the justness of that rule, would have been considered subversive in the late sixteenth century.

3   **pight**: set up, established.

5   **wight**: person.

8   **own**: justice as well as possessions; this begins an extended double metaphor of the individual state and material property.

13   **loose**: set free, redeem. **quiet**: make peaceful.

15   **debate**: discussions, litigation.

16–20   **This ... confound**: Hannay (1989) suggests that the image of the law as a lamp is derived from the Protestant Psalm translations of Théodore de Bèze.

21   **style**: form of address.

**Psalm 88**: a psalm of personal grief and persecution; Brooks-Davies (1992) indicates a parallel with Surrey's translation of the same Psalm as relevant to his own imprisonment and death.

7   **presence**: the royal presence at court.

12   **nigh**: near.

19   **murdered**: Mary Sidney departs from her sources in suggesting a violent death.

37   **My ... away**: I weep.

38   **amain**: suddenly.

48   **lowly lodgings**: burial places.

52   **of mark**: deserving note.

66   **amazed**: stupefied.

**Psalm 93**: the lyrical form of this Psalm denotes its courtly subject-matter.

1   **girt**: girded, braced.

8   **plight**: position, state.

9–11   **Rivers ... shore**: the image of rivers breaking the shore is archetypally Sidneian and refers to the flooding of the River Medway on the Penshurst estate.

10   **sea-billows**: waves.

**Psalm 105**: describes the Biblical events from Abraham to Moses (Genesis 12–Deuteronomy 34); God's promise to his chosen people and the account of their troubles and final salvation may well be an allegory for the persecution and hoped-for triumph of the Protestants.

7   **ark**: a complex set of meanings: the Ark of the Covenant and therefore God's laws (Exodus 25); and with a pun on 'arch', pre-eminent strength and the rainbow.

8   **inquest**: enquiry, again with legal overtones.

11–12   **Abraham's ... sons**: God's chosen people; here an allusion to the Protestants.

14    **All be**: although.
16    **untermed**: without terms, that is, no set period of time.
19    **Isaac's ... son**: Jacob.
21    **in fee**: in fee-simple, that is, in absolute possession.
26    **seatless**: without an estate, without lands.
30    **procure**: cause.
33    **foresent**: gone before.
36    **clog'd**: burdened.
38    **saws**: words.
47-8    **Sem ... Cham**: Shem and Ham, two of the sons of Noah, from whom the Israelites and the Egyptians were descended.
61    **noisome**: unpleasant, harmful.
75    **spoil**: plunder.
82    **bevies**: flocks.
84    **Candies**: Coats, covers as with sugar.
85    **well**: well up.
90    **trains**: leads, entices.

**Psalm 130**: a musical setting for this Psalm has survived (British Library, Add. MS 15117), suggesting that Mary Sidney might well have envisaged her translations as linked to public performance (within her own family) as well as private contemplation.
5-6    **crying ... weighing**: recalls the colloquial power of Metaphysical poetry.
10    **cark**: burden, trouble.
35    **Jacob**: the father of the chosen and therefore representing the Protestant forces in England.

**Psalm 134**: an exhortation to praise God; the form is that of a bird in flight (note the allusions to rising at lines 6 and 20) and recalls Herbert's 'Easter Wings'. See also Psalm 139 below.
2    **watch**: the guard patrolling at night.
19    **embowered**: sheltered, as if in a bower.

**Psalm 139**: a personal Psalm in which the psalmist (David/Mary Sidney) declares his/her faith in and allegiance to God. The form of the stanzas resembles Psalm 134 (see p. 94 above) in that, turned sideways, they resemble wings ascending to heaven; the content echoes the structure with specific references at lines 5, 21, 23-4, 29-33 and 69.
6    **closet**: personal room, a small space.
13    **cast**: send forth.
26    **dead ... stay**: Hell.
28    **assay**: attempt.
34    **he**: God.
35    **western things**: in the west, where the sun sets.
37    **sable**: black.
44    **While ... dwelt**: the image here (44-60) is that of a foetus growing in the womb; the main source is Calvin's commentary, but the gradual growth of the child is her own and may reflect a particularly female perspective.

47  **strangely**: remarkably.
**50–51  black ... ribs**: the image is of a roof, the spine being the central beam and the ribs resembling the rafters.
55  **brave**: fine.
**55–6  embroid'ry ... low**: the child's growth in the womb is described in terms of a small, dark shop where beautiful clothes are embroidered.
73  **cursed brood**: the ungodly.
81  **cankered knot**: corrupt group: again, the ungodly.

**Psalm 148**: towards the end of the Psalms Mary Sidney combines the conventional praises of the Bible with sixteenth-century imagery, such as the harmony of the spheres in stanza 2, to stress a complete and perfect whole.
7  **soldiers**: recalls the militant Protestantism of the Geneva Bible.
12  **spangles**: sequins.
13  **sphere**: in early modern astronomy, a sphere was supposed to be a hollow globe which revolved about the earth and carried heavenly bodies.
14  **emball**: to encompass with a sphere.
22  **utmost**: furthest.
30  **stones**: hailstones.
32  **appast**: food, repast.
52  **Jacob's sons**: the chosen people; hence, here an allusion to the Protestants who are indicated above and beyond all else in the poem.

**Psalm 150**: the final Psalm, which, by returning to the sonnet form, unites the formal styles of Mary Sidney and her brother Philip.
1  **laud**: praise.
7  **tabret**: drum.
9  **timbrels**: tambourines.

## Aemilia Lanyer

### Salve Deus Rex Judaeorum
**Title**: Hail God, King of the Jews. Lanyer adds at the conclusion of the text: 'Gentle reader, if thou desire to be resolved why I gave this title, Salve Deux Rex Judaeorum, know for certain that it was delivered unto me in sleep many years before I had any intent to write in this manner, and was quite out of my memory until I had written the Passion of Christ, when immediately it came into my remembrance, what I had dreamed long before, and thinking it a significant token, that I was appointed to perform this work, I gave the very same words I received in sleep as the fittest title I could devise for this book.'
**Queen's ... Majesty**: Anne of Denmark, queen to James I.
12  **Paris**: in classical mythology, Paris, when judging which goddess was the most beautiful, awarded the prize to Venus, rather than Juno or Diana; he was given the love of Helen of Troy in return.
16  **indued**: endowed.
19  **Muses**: in classical mythology, the nine sisters who offered inspiration in the arts.

21–3  **sylvan gods and satyrs ... Cynthia**: in classical mythology, these may individually be identified as spirits of the woods, mythic beings who were half-man and half-goat, and as the goddess of the moon. However, there is also a general sense of the court masque in this description of the queen.

29  **Phoebe**: moon goddess.

31  **Apollo**: the sun.

33  **estate**: social standing.

37  **mirror**: that is, the poem.

40–1  **glass/steel**: a steel mirror was supposed to give a particularly truthful reflection; the specific reference is to George Gascoigne's *The Steele Glas* (1576).

42  **su'th**: sues.

44  **Monarch**: Christ.

50  **meaner sort**: lower classes.

67  **sith**: since.

73  **Eve's apology**: a section of the main body of the poem, but also a reference to the debate about the virtues and vices of women (see Introduction, pp. xxviii–xxix).

76  **text**: the Bible.

79  **great lady**: Eve.

83  **feast**: the poem, and the beginning of an extended metaphor which envisages the text in terms of the Passover feast with the guests being those women addressed in the dedicatory poems.

85  **paschal lamb**: Passover lamb, that is, Christ.

89  **Passover**: a feast to commemorate the salvation of the Jewish first-born sons (Exodus 12:22–7).

91  **she**: *The Lady Elizabeth's Grace* (in the text); Elizabeth of Bohemia was Anne's daughter, and this reference commences another extended trope, here of mothers and daughters. A short dedicatory poem to Elizabeth follows this in the full version of the poem, but is not included here.

110  **Eliza**: Elizabeth I; Lanyer spent her early adulthood at the court of Elizabeth; from what we know of her history, this was the most successful and glamorous stage in her life.

115  **Lady**: ambiguous reference; possibly alludes to the Duchess of Kent who is celebrated in a separate dedicatory poem (see pp. 106–7 below).

126  **queen**: Queen Anne.

150  **sad**: serious.

153  **Jove's**: God's.

154  **her and hers**: the goddess Nature and those under her protection who are here, as in many seventeenth-century representations, identified as women.

161–2  **To ... less**: a conventional disclaimer, suggesting that while the text should praise the patron, poetry cannot do justice to her merits.

*To All Vertuous Ladies*

6  **queen**: Queen Anne, as in the first dedicatory poem.

9  **Bridegroom**: Christ (Isaiah 62:5 and Matthew 25:1–13).

13  **fill ... zeal**: Matthew 25:1–13.

16    Virtue: Christ. *The robes that Christ wore before his death* (in the text).

17    lilies: Matthew 6:28–9 and Luke 12:27; also a traditional emblem of the Virgin Mary.

19    Solomon: Biblical king renowned for his wisdom and wealth. **dight**: arrayed.

22    Daphne: in classical mythology, the nymph Daphne was transformed into a laurel tree in order to save her from the advances of Apollo (Ovid, *Metamorphoses* 1); Lanyer adds in the text: *In token of Constancy*.

25    Minerva: in classical mythology, the goddess of wisdom.

26    Cynthia: goddess of the moon and chastity. **Venus**: goddess of love.

27    Aesop: Greek author of moral fables, and here invoked as a protector of virtue.

30    Pallas: in classical mythology, the goddess of wisdom; here used to represent and compliment Queen Anne.

36    Aaron's precious oil: Aaron was anointed with sanctifying oil, making him the first priest of Israel (Leviticus 8:12).

41    odours ... frankincense: oils used to sanctify and to anoint the dead.

42    King: Christ.

43    Titan: pre-Olympian god of the sun in classical myth.

45    Age ... Days: gods and goddesses in pre-Olympian myth.

49    simple: innocent. **subtle**: clever.

56    Phoebus: sun god in classical myth.

59    he: Christ.

62    Elizium: Elysium, heaven in classical mythology; spelled with a *z* it also alludes to the idealized reign of Elizabeth I.

64    sensual: material.

66    second birth: after baptism (John 3:3–5).

70    others ... graced: the ladies become saint-like in their ability to confer grace on others.

*To the Lady Susan*

Title    Lady Susan: Susan Bertie, the widow of Reynold Grey of West, Earl of Kent, later married Sir John Wingfield; this second marriage allied her to the Sidney family and thus creates a link to the next poem, which is dedicated to Mary Sidney. Susan Bertie was also the daughter of Catherine Willoughby, Duchess of Suffolk, a renowned Protestant figure who had fled England during the reign of the Catholic Mary I (see lines 19–24 below). From the first two lines of the poem it is probable that Lanyer joined Susan Bertie's retinue when she was first at court.

6    holy feast: the poem.

7    glass: mirror.

23    mother: see note to title of the poem above.

25    prier: prior, that is, the Pope.

28    weeds: clothes.

37    love: Christ.

44    desertless: undeserving.

*The Author's Dream*

**Title   Lady Mary ... Pembroke:** Mary Sidney, Countess of Pembroke, was an important author and a model for women writers of her age; Lanyer refers to Mary Sidney's canon in the poem (see pp. 59–98 for a selection of her poems, and Notes on the Authors for a more complete critical biography). The address takes the form of a dream vision.

1   **Edalyan:** Idalion, from Mount Ida, the home of the Muses.

2   **Graces:** in classical mythology, the goddesses of kindness and good offices.

8   **she:** Mary Sidney.

9   **nine ... virgins:** the nine muses who offered inspiration in the arts.

14   **brazen:** brass.

18   **Morphy:** Morpheus, the god of sleep; Lanyer adds in the text: *The God of Dreams.*

21   **welkin:** sky.

33   **Bellona:** Lanyer adds in the text: *Goddess of War and Wisdom.*

45   **Dictina:** from Diana, goddess of the moon; Lanyer adds in the text: *The Moon.*

61   **Aurora:** goddess of the dawn; Lanyer adds in the text: *The Morning.*

62   **Phoebe:** moon goddess.

63   **Lady May:** goddess of the spring and of flowers, later called Flora (line 75); also a reference to Philip Sidney's (Mary's brother's) pastoral entertainment *The Lady of May.*

104   **anatomy:** a body reduced to skin and bone.

105   **Pallas:** Pallas Athene, another name for Minerva.

108   **Pergusa:** a lake in Sicily where, in classical mythology, Pluto abducted Proserpina to the underworld. **hight:** was called.

110   **sundry:** various.

113   **wanton:** playful.

117   **Israel's king:** David, the Biblical author of the Psalms; Lanyer adds in the text: *The Psalms written newly by the Countesse Dowager of Pembrooke.*

129   **hard:** heard.

138   **Sidney:** Philip Sidney, Mary's brother, was one of the most renowned figures of his age; he excelled at all courtly and political skills and, after his death in the Netherlands campaign, became a model for the ideal Renaissance man.

146   **Bellona:** goddess of war and wisdom.

151   **And ... esteemed:** in contradiction to all other estimations of the time, Lanyer praises Mary before her brother.

176   **Jove's fair queen:** Jove, the ruler of the gods, was married to Juno, who was thus the queen of heaven.

176   **thief:** sleep; Lanyer adds in the text: *To Sleep.*

187   **Actaeon:** in classical myth, Actaeon is a hunter who spies on Diana, the goddess of chastity; in revenge, she turns him into a stag who is slaughtered by his own dogs.

199   **painful:** labouring, taking pains.

206   **feast:** the poem.

212   **glass**: mirror; here, the poem. **steel**: a steel mirror was said to give the most accurate reflection (see note to 'To the Queen's Most Excellent Majesty' line 41 above).

218   **shepherd's weed**: poor clothing, but also a conventional representation of Christ (John 10:11–17).

*To the Lady Anne*

**Title   Lady Anne**: Lady Anne Clifford, Countess of Dorset, was the daughter of Margaret Clifford, Dowager Duchess of Cumberland, to whom Lanyer dedicated her famous country-house poem 'The Description of Cooke-Ham' (see pp. 148–53 below). Anne Clifford was herself a writer, compiling an extensive and fascinating diary; she later married Philip Herbert, Mary Sidney's younger son.

15   **Bridegroom**: Christ (Matthew 25:1–13).

48   **he ... blood**: he is illegitimate.

54   **discharge ... place**: perform those duties.

56   **purpose**: intend.

63   **diadem**: crown.

65   **heir apparent**: although Lanyer's reference is to a spiritual inheritance, she also alludes to the lengthy legal battles undertaken by Anne Clifford and her mother to claim Anne's actual inheritance; Anne Clifford finally gained her titles and estates by default in 1643.

79   **pelf**: riches.

117   **lamb**: Christ.

121–2   **world ... parts**: a common metaphor, best-known from Shakespeare's *As You Like It*, II.vii.139–40.

133   **shepherdess**: Anne is here compared to an apostle (cf. John 21:15–17).

*Salve Deux Rex Judaeorum*

1   **Cynthia**: goddess of the moon; here an allusion to Elizabeth I, who was often depicted as Cynthia.

9   **Countess**: Lanyer adds in the text: *The Lady Margaret, Countess Dowager of Cumberland.*

13   **Muse**: a classical deity who inspired artistic achievement.

18   **delightful place**: Paradise, but also a reference to Cooke-Ham, the country house and garden celebrated by Lanyer in her closing poem (see pp. 148–53 below).

37   **infinite annoys**: the legal difficulties encountered by Margaret Clifford in securing her daughter's inheritance (see note to 'To the Lady Anne, Countess of Dorset', line 65, above).

38   **well-stayed**: firm.

54   **enroll**: keep a record of.

57   **The heavens**: the following ten stanzas draw upon Psalms 18, 84, 89 and 104; Lanyer's use of the Psalms demonstrates her indebtedness to Mary Sidney (see note to 'The Author's Dream to the Lady Mary, the Countess Dowager of Pembroke', line 117, above).

58    vesture: garment.

76    rear: elevate.

77    bridegroom: Christ (Matthew 25:1–13); also see Song of Solomon.

113   Froward: wilful and perverse.

116   pray: prey, with a pun on prayer.

123   mean: lowly.

129   tabernacle: temple; Psalms 15:1.

134   whets: sharpens.

137   Jehovah: God.

139   berth: dwelling-place.

141   dearth: a time of scarcity and famine.

145   good madam: Lanyer adds in the text: *To the Countess of Cumberland*.

156   turtle dove: a symbol of constancy.

165   wantons: those who are pleased with trifles and childish pursuits.

185   beauty: Lanyer adds in the text: *An Invective against outward beauty unaccompanied with virtue*.

192   queen: Helen of Troy, whose renowned beauty was ultimately the cause of Troy's destruction.

208   white: the white part of the target in archery.

210   Helen: Helen was taken from her husband, Menelaus, by Paris of Troy, an act which initiated the Trojan war.

211   Lucrece: Lucretia was commonly depicted as an ideal of virtue, since she chose to commit suicide after being raped by Tarquin rather than to live with the shame; the story was used by Shakespeare in *The Rape of Lucrece*. It is interesting to note that Lanyer as a woman author uses the word 'fact' ('deed') rather than 'rape'.

213–16 Antonius/Cleopatra/Octavia: Antony deserted his wife Octavia for Cleopatra, whose beauty was legendary; the two lovers committed suicide after Antony's defeat by Octavius (Octavia's brother). The story is told by Mary Sidney in her play *The Tragedy of Antonie*, and in Samuel Daniel's *The Tragedy of Cleopatra*.

217   fair ... tree: adultery, but with a reference to Adam and Eve's fall from grace (Genesis 3:1–7).

219   blinded: figuratively, that is deceived by love.

225   Rosamund: mistress of King Henry II, she was reputedly poisoned by Henry's wife, Eleanor of Aquitaine; Rosamund was also the subject of Samuel Daniel's poem *The Complaint of Rosamond*. Lanyer adds in the text: *Of Rosamund*.

233   Matilda: queen of Henry I, renowned for her good works and spiritual faith. Lanyer follows the conventional story and may have drawn upon Michael Drayton's *Matilda*; in the text Lanyer adds: *Of Matilda*.

249   great lady: Lanyer adds in the text: *To the Lady of Cumberland, the Introduction to the Passion of Christ*.

251   control: restrict.

257   dowager: although Margaret Clifford was denied her material inheritance

on the death of her husband, Lanyer here claims that she has gained a spiritual legacy.

**260    Judas-kiss:** Judas' kiss betrayed Christ (Matthew 26:47–9), yet Christ's death redeemed mankind, raising them from spiritual death.

**265    deserts:** deservings: that is, Margaret Clifford's faith and Christ's sacrifice deserve to be celebrated in verse.

**266    him:** Lanyer adds in the text: *A preamble of the Author before the passion.*

**745    Pontius Pilate:** the Roman governor of Jerusalem; Lanyer follows the conventional New Testament narrative.

**751    wife:** Pilate's wife was believed to have been a Christian (Matthew 27:19) and was traditionally depicted as an example of a good woman.

**763    Eve:** Lanyer adds in the text: *Eve's Apology.*

**765    simply:** artlessly.

**770    him:** the serpent.

**776    die ... wise:** Genesis 3:3 and 6.

**777–8    Adam ... blame:** Lanyer here inverts convention by claiming that Adam was most at fault, rather than Eve.

**783–4    For ... breath:** Genesis 2:7–22.

**787    strait:** strict.

**803    prove:** experience.

**810    made of him:** Genesis 2:21–3.

**813    train:** treachery, but with a pun on the use of 'train' to describe a serpent's elongated body.

**826    challenge:** attribute.

**838    Saul:** Acts 9:1–31.

**846    dejection:** humiliation.

**849    Barabbas:** Matthew 27:16–26.

**875    Herod:** Luke 23:12.

**881    his great place:** Herod's kingship.

**890, 897    robes of honour / crown of thorns:** Matthew 27:28–9.

**927–8    All ... away:** Matthew 27:24.

**945    hour:** Lanyer adds in the text: *Christ going to death.*

**951    general doom:** Last Judgement.

**969    women:** Luke 23:27–31; Lanyer adds in the text: *The Tears of the Daughters of Jerusalem.*

**974    Flora:** the goddess of the spring and of flowers.

**991    eagle's eyes:** proverbially eagles were credited with strong eyesight.

**1009    mother:** Lanyer adds in the text: *The Salutation of the Virgin Mary.*

**1021    Jesse ... bud:** a child of the House of Jesse and of David, and therefore prophesied as the Messiah (Isaiah 11:1 and 10).

**1025    Virgin:** the following eight stanzas refer to Luke 1:26–55.

**1061    cheer:** disposition.

**1067    house of Jacob:** Israel.

**1088    curse:** the burden of original sin, brought about by the eating of the apple, which caused Adam and Eve to be expelled from Eden.

1091   approve: prove.

1093   lamb: a symbol of Christ. turtle dove: a symbol of constancy.

1111   scarlet dye: blood.

1289   rise: risen; Ephesians 5:22–3. Lanyer adds in the text: *Christ's resurrection*.

1301   Christ: the following description (1289–1320) alludes to the Song of Solomon; Lanyer adds in the text: *A brief description of his beauty upon the Canticles* (Canticles is another name for the Song of Solomon).

1321   good Lady: Lanyer adds in the text: *To my Lady of Cumberland*.

1335   alms-deeds: acts of charity.

1339   crosses: obstructions, with obvious Christian overtones.

1343   her: the soul's; an allusion back to the Song of Solomon 1:13.

1369   keys ... Peter: Matthew 16:19; the reference to St Peter's keys suggests a Catholic overtone to Lanyer's comments here.

1370   spiritual power: apostolic power.

1371   strangely taken: rendered odd or confused, with the suggestion of spiritual malaise.

1388   place: a position of importance, such as at the head of the table.

1395   stains ... themselves: the sins of others, so that they may redeem themselves.

1397   lost sheep: Matthew 9:36 and 12:11–12.

1407   dross: worthless, impure matter.

1409   Cleopatra's ... Anthony: Cleopatra abandoned Antony during a battle, causing the defeat of their combined forces; see note to lines 213–19 above.

1421   leaden: heavy, earth-bound.

1423   Octavia's wrongs: Antony abandoned his wife Octavia for Cleopatra; see note to lines 213–19 above.

1429   this lady: the Countess of Cumberland.

1447   Rome: under the leadership of Octavius, the Roman forces triumphed over Cleopatra and the Egyptian troops.

1453–4   touch ... eyes: touch is an abbreviation for touch-powder, which was used to ignite a fire; here Lanyer suggests that her own poem lights fires of admiration for the Countess.

1465   famous ... known: the list that follows belongs to the literary convention of praising women (such as Chaucer's *Legend of Good Women*), but Lanyer follows no specific source, and the list is very much her own.

1469   Scythian women: renowned in classical history for their ferocious barbarity.

1481   Deborah: Judges 4–5; one of the Old Testament heroines who helped to save Israel.

1482   Judith: one of the heroines in the Apocrypha; she defeated an army attacking Israel by beguiling and then beheading their commander, Holofernes.

1485   queal: overcome, kill.

1505   Hester: Esther 5–9; an Old Testament heroine who aided her people and hanged their enemy, Haman.

**1529** **Joachim's wife**: Susanna, the wife of Joachim, appears in the Apocrypha as an ideal for married chastity.

**1535** **child**: Daniel.

**1539** **Holy Writ**: Lanyer suggests that Susanna's story is from the Bible, which coincides with the Catholic view at the time. The Protestant tradition from the sixteenth century on, however, places the book as part of the Apocrypha (works not recognized as part of the Old Testament canon, but accepted for private edification).

**1553** **laurel**: traditional symbol of constancy.

**1569** **Ethiopian queen**: the Queen of Sheba; 2 Samuel 10:1–13.

**1593** **affect**: are drawn to one another.

**1603–4** **niceness ... kind**: the fastidiousness and respectability which should keep women at home.

**1610** **figure ... love**: a representation (i.e. not the actual person) of Christ.

**1614** **son**: pun on 'son' of God, and 'sun'.

**1633–8** **Prepared ... eyes**: Revelation 4; allusions to Revelation continue in the following four stanzas.

**1661** **cornerstone**: Matthew 21:42.

**1663** **God's ... pleased**: repeated in each of the Gospels (e.g. Matthew 3:17, Mark 1:11).

**1673** **Lady**: Lanyer adds to the text: *To the Lady dowager of Cumberland.*

**1678** **viols**: possible pun on 'viols', musical instruments, and 'vials', small glass bottles.

**1683** **great judicial day**: Last Judgement.

**1686** **behove**: need.

**1689** **phoenix**: a mythical unique bird, which rose from the ashes of its own funeral pyre; here, the Queen of Sheba, yet also an allusion to Elizabeth I, who was often emblematized by the phoenix.

**1695** **creature**: one who has been created; here, Solomon.

**1705** **affected**: by love.

**1717** **fishermen**: Apostles.

**1725** **characters**: letters.

**1728** **rivers of his grace**: Christ's blood.

**1729** **holy rivers**: Revelation 22:1.

**1746** **Stephen**: one of the Christian Church's first martyrs; Acts 6–8.

**1750** **attaint**: blow.

**1775** **discreteness**: sage and wise discourse.

**1789** **Laurence**: St Lawrence was one of the Christian Church's earliest martyrs; he was a deacon in Rome and was tortured on a red-hot griddle.

**1799** **Andrew**: one of the Apostles, who was supposedly crucified at Patras.

**1801** **princes ... Apostles**: Peter and John the Baptist.

**1815** **gallows**: Peter, who was crucified upside-down; Matthew 14:1–12.

**1816** **sword**: John the Baptist, who was beheaded; Acts 12:2.

**1828** **white and red**: Lanyer adds in the text: *Colours of Confessors and Martyrs.*

**1839** **arctic star**: pole star, used by travellers as a guide.

*The Description of Cooke-Ham*

**Title** **Cooke-Ham**: a manor near Maidenhead, Berkshire, which was tenanted by the Countess's brother, William Russell, between 1605 and 1610.

**2** **Grace/Grace/grace**: favour/her Grace, Margaret Clifford, Countess of Cumberland/virtue. The multiple meanings continue at lines 12 and 19 below.

**5** **indite**: compose.

**6** **sacred ... delight**: the previous poem, *Salve Deus*.

**11** **great Lady**: Margaret Clifford, Countess of Cumberland.

**12** **grace**: spiritual enlightenment.

**19** **grace**: adorn.

**22** **similes**: Lanyer proceeds to construct an extended metaphor which compares the garden to the court; a direct reference to the 'conceit' is made at line 111.

**31** **Philomela**: the nightingale; see note to line 189 below.

**41** **sad**: serious.

**44** **phoenix**: here a complimentary reference to the Countess of Cumberland.

**51-2** **Yet ... stand**: while hunting was an acceptable sport for women of the Renaissance, the allusion is to the classical virgin goddess Diana, who was depicted as a huntress; there is also a link with Elizabeth I, who was often represented as Diana; thus, the image culminates in praise for the Countess of Cumberland, who is like both goddess and queen.

**55, 57, 61** **oak/cedar/palm**: the cedar and palm are referred to in Psalm 92; the oak, however, while common in the Bible is here the ony 'male' figure in the garden and as such takes on a gender signification.

**64** **Defended Phoebus**: protected against the sun.

**70** **prefer**: offer, submit. **suit**: service.

**73** **thirteen shires**: not thirteen counties in the modern sense, but thirteen districts.

**76** **meditation**: Margaret Clifford was known to have been very religious, and her frequent meditations are also mentioned by her daughter (Lady Anne Clifford) in her diary.

**82** **Christ ... apostles**: the New Testament; in other words, the reference is to reading the Bible; the use of a tree as a book-rest is attested by Anne Clifford in her diary.

**85** **Moses**: Exodus 24-34.

**87** **David**: author of the Psalms.

**91** **Joseph**: Genesis 47:12.

**92** **pined**: afflicted.

**93** **sweet lady**: Lady Anne Clifford (1590-1676); this and the following two lines relate her lineage as the daughter of George Clifford, Earl of Cumberland, and Margaret Clifford (the daughter of Francis Russell, Earl of Bedford), and her marriage to Richard Sackville, Earl of Dorset.

**107** **orbs of state**: court circles.

**108** **Parters**: an ambiguous term, meaning both 'sharers' and 'dividers'.

**111** **conceit**: an extended metaphor; see note to line 22 above.

**112** **conster**: construe.

119 **Dorset's former sports**: probably a reference to Anne Clifford's participation in the court masque; the defence offered in the next line could allude to the general censure of ladies participating in these court shows, or to the demands made by Anne's husband that she should remain at home.

138 **pray you**: beg you.

141 **vain**: in vain.

145 **rivelled rine**: wrinkled rind or skin: that is, bark; or perhaps the lines made by frost.

147 **occasions**: circumstances, requirements.

160 **Dorset**: Anne Clifford married Richard Sackville, Earl of Dorset, in 1609.

166 **bereave**: deprive.

167 **senseless**: without feeling.

172 **vouchsafed**: condescended.

178 **consort**: companion; but with a pun on 'concert', that is, a musical performance.

185 **wonted**: accustomed.

189 **Philomela**: the nightingale; in classical mythology Philomela is transformed into a nightingale and her sister Procne into a swallow while fleeing Procne's husband, an allusion which might be foregrounded by Lanyer because of the close relationship she claims existed between herself and Anne Clifford.

199 **Echo**: in classical mythology, a heart-broken wood nymph who is metamorphosed into a vocal repetition; here, again, Lanyer images herself in the role of the forsaken nymph, placing Clifford in the somewhat ambiguous role of Narcissus, Echo's self-absorbed beloved.

207 **her**: the Countess of Cumberland's.

## Rachel Speght

(The Biblical references are, to a great extent, provided by Speght herself in the printed text.)

### A Mouzell for Melastomus
**Title**: a muzzle for the black-mouth (i.e. slanderer): that is, Joseph Swetnam (see Notes on the Authors).

### The Dream
1 **Sol**: the sun.

3 **Phoebus**: the sun, but made female rather than the usual male. **Titan**: Oceanus, the ocean.

7 **Morpheus**: the god of sleep.

13 **Aurora**: goddess of the dawn.

14 **invest**: dress.

19 **supernal**: heavenly.

46 **science**: knowledge.

55 **golden mean**: Aristotelian ideal measure, meaning moderation in all things.

63 **conceive**: understand.

66 **appoint**: direct.

105 **remoraes**: obstacles.

111 **harquebuz**: gun.

124 *labor omnia vincet*: the Virgilian precept that labour overcomes obstacles, but also an inversion of the Ovidian *amor vincet omnia*, which claims that love conquers all; Speght is here inverting the traditional courtly-love ethos of the dream vision into one more suited to a Protestant poet.

128 **Paul**: I Thessalonians 5:23.

133 **talent**: money, but also natural gifts; cf. Luke 19:23.

135 **parts**: abilities.

136 **God of knowledge**: I Samuel 2:3.

137 **Mary's choice**: Luke 10:42.

139 **Cleobulina**: a celebrated authoress of riddles. **Demophila**: poet, and companion of Sappho.

140 **Telesilla**: lyric poet of Argos.

143 **Cornelia**: renowned as the educator of her sons and for the brilliant rhetorical style of her letters.

145 **Hypatia**: a renowned astronomer and philosopher.

146 **Aspatia**: celebrated patron of the arts who is often accused of using her eloquence to tempt King Pericles away from his wife.

148 **Areta**: philosopher. The above list of learned women from the classical ages of Greece and Rome, while drawing upon convention, is entirely Speght's own and demonstrates a knowledge of the classics.

160 **Contemned**: Despised.

173 **purchase**: obtain.

190 **savours**: smells.

205 **God's image**: Colossians 3:10.

210 **not ... good**: Proverbs 19:2.

213 **Hosea**: a prophet from the Bible.

216 **hap**: chance. **as ... crow**: proverbial.

218 **speculate**: observe.

222 **life ... know**: John 17:3.

223 **Alexander**: Alexander the Great was tutored by Aristotle; the exact source of this reference is Plutarch's *Alexander* VIII.

234 **Till ... away**: feminist critics have identified this event as emblematic of Speght's role as a woman: that is, as being 'called away' by marriage or household duties. There is, however, nothing specific mentioned by Speght, and the device of being drawn back to reality was a dream-vision convention.

241 **beast**: Joseph Swetnam (see Notes on the Authors).

244 **falling evil** epilepsy.

246 **Mouzel**: Speght's previous work, *A Mouzell for Melastomus* (see Notes on the Authors). **chaps**: jaws.

248, 251, 252 **self-conceited creature/Haman/Ester**: Ester Sowernam in *Ester Hath Hang'd Haman*, another refutation of Swetnam, denigrated Speght's work: 'I did observe that whereas the Maid [Speght] doth many times excuse the tenderness of her years, I found it to be true in the slenderness of her answer' (see Notes on the Authors).

**252**  pretertense: past tense.

**255**  Prudence: Constantia Munda (see note to line 264 below) refers to her mother as 'Prudentia' (see Notes on the Authors).

**257**  gave ... sop: Cerberus was a dog guarding the entrance to the classical underworld. To 'give Cerberus a sop' (i.e. to stop his mouth) was a common allusion to Virgil, *Aeneid*, VI.417. Here, the allusion is to Joseph Swetnam (see Notes on the Authors).

**261**  artist: medical practitioner.

**264**  Constance: Constantia Munda, author of a further attack upon Swetnam, *The Worming of a Mad Dogge: or, A Soppe for Cerberus the Jaylor of Hell*, is kinder to Speght, calling her 'the first Champion of our sex' (see Notes on the Authors).

**273**  Tophet's flames: Hell.

**274**  Canaan land: Heaven.

**284**  ta'ne: taken.

**292**  lenify: assuage.

**297**  blaze: proclaim.

*Esto Memor Mortis*

**Title**  Here is set forth Mortality's Memorandum.

**1**  Elohim: God.

**2–3**  In ... earth: Genesis 1:1.

**4**  glory's sake: Proverbs 16:4.

**13**  jointly sin: Speght is quite radical in her defence of women and in her claim that Adam was as much to blame for their fall from grace as Eve.

**16**  Death: Genesis 3:17. fact: deed.

**19**  In ... die: I Corinthians 15:22.

**22**  Christ: Romans 5:12.

**25**  Jehovah's: God's.

**32**  Death in sin: Ephesians 2:1.

**35**  Paul: I Timothy 5:6.

**42**  children ... give: Matthew 15:26.

**43**  Death to sin: Romans 6:2–11.

**58–9**  just ... Christ: Romans 8:1.

**60**  Whose ... highest: Colossians 3:3.

**68**  dust ... earth: Ecclesiastes 12:7.

**79–80**  Death ... head: Genesis 15–19.

**86**  God: Romans 8:1.

**94**  labours ... rest: Revelation 14:13.

**103**  bocardo: dungeon.

**105**  sinks: sewers.

**106**  draught: cesspool.

**108**  Egested: thrown out.

**109**  From ... Lord: Psalms 142:7.

**111**  Elijah: I Kings 19:4.

**115, 117, 118**  Argis/Biton and Cleobis/Juno: in classical mythology 'Argis', a priestess of Juno (the mother goddess), asked that her sons, Biton and Cleobis, should be given the 'greatest good', whereupon the goddess rewarded them with instant death. The name Argis is inaccurate (Cydippe is the correct version) but allows us to trace Speght's source to Cicero (*Tusculan Disputations* I.xlvii), who merely mentions that she is a priestess of Argos.

121   Thracians: the source is Herodotus (1.4).

125–6   David's ... meat: II Samuel 12:15–23.

130   Esay: Isaiah 57:1.

131   Jeroboam's son: I Kings 14:13.

145   fine: ending.

148–50   Christ ... relief: Luke 23:40–3.

169–73   The eye ... Father: I Corinthians 2:9.

176–7   bodies ... Christ: Philippians 3:21.

180   cornerstone: Ephesians 2:20.

181   Solomon: Ecclesiastes 7:8.

185   Lazar/Dives: the beggar, Lazarus, goes to heaven but Dives, the rich man, is sent to Hell; Luke 16:20–31.

204   wight: person.

208   *Nunc dimittis*: the prophecies accompanying Christ's advent; Luke 2:29–35.

227   Juventus: youth.

236   pricking: goading.

243   Auditus: Hearing.

244   Visus: Eyesight.

245   Gustus: taste.

246   Olfactus: smell.

247   Tactus: touch.

250   obtrectations: slanders.

258   squats: sudden falls.

266   annoy: suffering.

267   live in office: devote oneself to an official life.

270   traffic: trade.

273   vain: to no purpose.

284   mark: target.

286   anatomise: lay bare.

294   Except ... move: personal love is here accredited with some worth.

304   noisome: unwholesome.

305   liking ... above: Colossians 3:2.

307–8   Which ... die: Philippians 1:23.

309   Job: Job 6:8–9.

325   Dives: the rich man; see note to line 181 above.

329   Hezekiah: II Kings 20:3.

329   David: Psalms 119:175.

333–4   Christ ... will: Luke 22:42.

342   cursed death: Galatians 3:13.

344   nature's: human nature's.

345   spirit ... weak: Matthew 26:41.

349  conscience ... misled: the consciences of those whose lives have been misled in sin.

351  Belshazzar: Daniel 5:6. wonted: usual.

361  Balaam: Numbers 23:10.

363  assimilate: become like.

372  annoy: suffering.

377  Nabal: I Samuel 25:37.

379  weal: prosperity.

380  Joseph: Genesis 40:13–19.

387  favour: pardon.

394  Mors: Death.

397  sting ... sin: I Corinthians 15:56.

399  conquering word: Hosea 13:14.

401  Death ... victory: I Corinthians 15:55.

402  maugre: in spite of.

408  dissolution: ending.

417  exordium: beginning.

429  censures: judges. deserts: actions.

437  pregnantly: compellingly.

441–4  First ... dispense: Psalms 89:48 and Deuteronomy: 31:14.

444  oportet: necessity.

445  speculate: observe.

449  vegetives: plants.

450  Hiems: winter.

451  elements ... heat: II Peter 3:10.

452  pass away: Luke 21:33.

452–3  Macrocosmus ... Microcosmus: the great and the little world; here, the world as a whole, and humankind.

454  Golgotha: the site of Christ's crucifixion.

457–8  Medes ... be: Daniel 6:15.

459  appointment: instruction. all ... die: Hebrews 9:27.

461  need ... lend: II Samuel 14:14.

464  descant: melody.

466  no abiding city: Hebrews 13:14.

467–8  Man's ... run: Job 7:6.

478  sinister: unjust, a term which fits with the extended legal metaphor of this stanza.

481  Absolom: II Samuel 13–18.

482  David: I Kings 2:1–10. Solomon: I Kings 11.

482  Crassus: a Roman infamous for his love of wealth; his full name was M. Licinius Crassus Dives, which allows a certain overlap with the following figure. Dives: Luke 16:20–31.

484  Samson: Judges 13–16.

486  silver thread: in classical mythology the three fates spun out and cut the thread of life.; cf. also Ecclesiastes 12:6.

488  Lazarus ... die: Luke 16:22.

489   **down-bed:** feather bed.

491   **carking:** labouring anxiously.

493   **Like ... heart:** II Kings 9:24.

494   **aweless:** fearless.

495   **David:** I Kings 2:2.

497   **corps:** body.

501   **beesome:** blindness.

502   *Mortuus est*: death, to die; Genesis 5:5 and Psalms 42:3.

505   **Alexander:** Alexander the Great; see note to *The Dream* lines 223–8, above.

511   **Methuselah:** Genesis 5:21–7.

515   **dejects:** throws down.

518   **David/Jonathan:** I Samuel 18–20.

525   **Tully:** Cicero (M. Tullius Cicero), who was executed for defending the Republic.

528   **Death's ... came:** Genesis 3:19.

536   **stork ... know:** Jeremiah 8:7.

543   *punctum*: stop.

547   **preter:** past.

561   **David's young son:** II Samuel 12:28.

574   **surfeit:** too much.

577   **Pope Adrian:** Adrian IV, the only British Pope, choked on a fly as he was drinking a glass of water.

578   **Anacreen:** the Greek poet Anacreon, who was known for his debauchery and excesses, choked on a grape pip.

579   **Fabius:** the famous Roman general, Fabius Maximus, who choked on a horse's hair.

580   **Saphira:** wife of Ananais who, with her husband, tried to conceal the value of their land from God and was struck dead as a punishment; Acts 5:1–10.

591   **Moses:** Deuteronomy 32:50.

609   **meed:** praise, merit.

610   **trump:** the dead are awakened to the Last Judgement with a final trumpet call: I Thessalonians 4:16.

613   **Jehovah ... show:** Deuteronomy 32:29. *utinam*: earnest wish.

623   **tree:** Ecclesiastes 11:3.

629   **Jerusalem:** the holy city.

634   **taken tardy:** taken unawares.

642   **dispense:** give exemption to.

652   **Paul's:** I Corinthians 15:31.

656   **vain:** empty.

657–8   **Into ... again:** I Timothy 6:7.

661   **dove:** Genesis 8:9.

667   **David:** Psalms 42:1–2

669–70   **father ... remain:** Hebrews 11:9.

675   **mortify the flesh:** Galatians 5:24.

681   **material:** essential being.

682   wind: Job 7:7.

684   eagle ... prey: Job 9:26.

685–7   Man ... withering: I Peter 1:24.

691   Our ... smoke: Psalms 102:3.

692   bavin: firewood.

693   ship: Job 9:26.

697   Job: Job 8:9 and 20:8.

701   David's: Psalms 39:5.

707   Moses: Psalms 90:10.

709   Xerxes: King of Persia, the overlord of Haman and husband of Esther; the account is taken from the Book of Esther (Apocrypha). Esther is an appropriate allusion for Speght, since she was seen as a defender of her nation and was an examplar commonly chosen by the defenders of women (see Notes on the Authors).

722   Dives: Luke 12:19; see note to line 185 above.

723   disport: amuse himself.

741   Esay: Isaiah 38:1.


## Mary Wroth

*Sonnet 1 (P1)*

1–4   When ... require: the dream vision of the procession of Venus and Cupid ('her son') is drawn from Petrarch's *Trionfe d'Amore*; it is also used by Wroth in her play, *Love's Victory* I.i.

1   prove: display.

2   hire: engage.

5–6   chariot ... Love: Venus was traditionally represented in a chariot drawn by doves, as in Ovid's *Metamorphoses*, XIV and in Philip Sidney's *Astrophil and Stella* 79.

9   heart: Venus is depicted holding a burning heart on the title-page of Wroth's prose romance *Urania I*; the source is probably Dante's *Vita nuova*, III.

11   shoot: in the Folger MS, Wroth has 'shut', implying a pun on pierce and enclose.

12   martyred: the shooting of the lover's heart was a conventional sonnet trope in the early modern period (see especially the final poem in William Herbert's poetic sequence, in which he claims to have suffered 'Love's Martyrdom'; this initiates a series of direct poetic responses between the lovers/cousins Wroth and Herbert (see Notes on the Authors, p. 362). See also Philip Sidney's *Astrophil and Stella* 20).

*Sonnet 2 (P2)*

4   court: the traditional trope of the court of love, but also an indirect allusion to the court of Elizabeth I, where Wroth would have associated with her cousin William Herbert. Thus, the autobiographical tone of *Pamphilia to Amphilanthus* is made apparent in the second sonnet (see Notes on the Authors, pp. 362–3).

9  **stars**: the image of the eyes as stars is a Petrarchan and Sidneian commonplace, used both by Philip Sidney in *Astrophil and Stella* and by Robert Sidney in his poetry.

*Sonnet 3 (P3)*

3  **Shine**: the idea of Love (that is, Cupid) shining in the eyes of the beloved was used by Philip Sidney in *Astrophil and Stella* 12, a sonnet which influences the whole of P3.

6  **mine**: my breast.

13  **love's crown**: Cupid's sovereignty is re-established later in the sequence (P76, 77–90 and 92).

14  **lie**: rely, but with a pun on untruth.

*Sonnet 4 (P4)*

4  **wane**: decrease.

7  **woes ... fill**: woes take the place of pride.

12  **great Snow**: the capitalization of *Snow* suggests a specific winter; the most famous (1607/8 and 1614/15) are described by Thomas Dekker in *The Great Frost* and *The Cold Year*.

*Sonnet 5 (P5)*

6  **sight's string**: in the early modern period it was thought that the eyes emitted beams (strings); the image is used by Donne in 'The Extasie'.

12–14  **Desire ... love**: the list-like form of line 12, and the correlative patterns of the last two lines, are both stylistic Sidneian commonplaces, as in Philip Sidney's *Astrophil and Stella* 43 and 100, and in Robert Sidney's sonnets and songs.

*Sonnet 6 (P6)*

10  **will**: possibly an allusion to *Will*iam Herbert, Wroth's lover; she often uses 'will' as a pun on Herbert's name in her writing. This use of puns is reciprocated by Herbert in his own poetry, where 'Wroth' becomes 'Worth'.

*Song 1 (P7)*

1–17  **spring ... shepherdess**: echoes Robert Sidney's 'Song 3', except that Wroth, with her usual emphasis upon gender inversion, turns the lover into a shepherdess, rather than her father's choice of a shepherd; the pastoral motif is a common Sidneian device and used by Wroth again in her play *Love's Victory* IV.i.425–30.

23  **willow**: a symbol of disappointed love; see Shakespeare's *Othello* II.iii.39.

33  **bark**: of a tree; a pastoral convention of lovers inscribing poems on trees, used again by Wroth in *Urania I* (1.75–6).

45  **constant**: coupled with 'change' in the last line, the allusion to Wroth/Pamphilia (all-loving) and Herbert/Amphilanthus (lover of two) is made clear. It is noticeable that while Wroth persistently characterizes Herbert/Amphilanthus as fickle, in his own poetry Herbert makes a direct refutation of this: 'Can you suspect a change in me,/And value your own constancy?' (first song in his published poetry sequence).

*Sonnet 7* (P8)
1–4 Love ... persist: echoes Robert Sidney's 'Sonnet 18'.
1 hand: the upper hand.
13 Sir God: a mocking reference to Cupid which recalls Philip Sidney's *Astrophil and Stella* 53.
14 want of eyes: the idea of love being blind is proverbial.

*Sonnet 8* (P9)
2 conceit: wit, imagination; begins the allusion to poetry in the first four lines of the sonnet, continued by 'lines' and 'art'.
9–12 It ... sight: a Petrarchan convention of setting night against day; see Philip Sidney, *Astrophil and Stella* 96.
11 drive: yield.

*Sonnet 9* (P10)
6 crosses: misfortunes.
9–12 Joys ... marry: echoes Robert Sidney's 'Song 3'.
13–14 grief ... wed: similar to Philip Sidney's *Astrophil and Stella* 100, and Robert Sidney's 'Sonnet 7'.

*Sonnet 10* (P11)
1 weary traveller: a commonplace in early modern discourse, although similar to the 'endless alchemist' of Robert Sidney's 'Sonnet 17'.
5 fraught: laden.

*Sonnet 12* (P13)
3 cross: misfortune.
5 Then ... flight: the lover's alternate cries for night and for day are a Petrarchan convention; see Philip Sidney, *Astrophil and Stella* 89, and Robert Sidney, 'Sonnet 19'.
6 Rest: begins a series of personifications of which 'Night' is the foremost.

*Song 2* (P14)
A version of this poem was reprinted anonymously in the anthology *Wit's Recreations* (1645).
5 freeze ... burn: a Petrarchan commonplace which Wroth self-consciously mocks at lines 9–10.
15–17 forest ... Court: a familiar early modern attack upon the court in favour of a pastoral retreat.

*Sonnet 13* (P15)
2 Destroy ... save: recalls Robert Sidney's 'Sonnet 26'.
6 worth: a pun on *Wroth*.
14 chameleon-like: the chameleon was reputed to live on air.

*Sonnet 14* (P16)
9 purblind: quite blind.
10 list: desires.
12 babish: babyish.

14   **farewell liberty**: the loss of the lover's liberty is a Petrarchan convention; see also Philip Sidney's *Astrophil and Stella* 2 and 47.

*Sonnet 15 (P17)*
This sonnet draws upon Philip Sidney's *Astrophil and Stella* 96 and 97.

*Sonnet 16 (P18)*
This draws upon Philip Sidney's address to Night (*Astrophil and Stella* 39), and on Robert Sidney's 'Sonnet 6', as well as upon Petrarchan convention.
3    **vilder**: more vile.
10   **fond**: foolish.

*Sonnet 17 (P19)*
1    **shades**: shadows, phantoms.
2    **vild**: vile.
12–14 **Heat ... be**: a traditional Petrarchan evocation of the opposites of heat and cold.

*Sonnet 18 (P20)*
1    **day or night?**: traditional Petrarchan use of opposites (see Philip Sidney, *Astrophil and Stella* 89, and Robert Sidney, 'Sonnet 19'; however, while both male Sidneys retain the opposition, Wroth insists on a choice).
10   **humours**: moods, feelings.
14   **spill**: destroy.

*Song 3 (P21)*
13   **plain**: complain.

*Sonnet 19 (P22)*
This sonnet is influenced throughout by Robert Sidney's 'Sonnet 31'; see also Shakespeare's 'Sonnet 73'.
11   **vade**: fade.

*Sonnet 20 (P23)*
The association of darkness and absence is conventional; specific references may be found to Philip Sidney, *Astrophil and Stella* 89 and 91, to Robert Sidney, 'Sonnet 30', to William Herbert, poem 28, as well as to Wroth's evocation of her father's verse through the character of Forrester in *Love's Victory* II.i.
10   **desert**: any deserted place.

*Sonnet 21 (P24)*
9–10 **sleep ... thought**: dreaming of the beloved was a conventional love discourse; see Philip Sidney, *Astrophil and Stella* 38.

*Sonnet 22 (P25)*
1    **Indians**: Wroth's use of colonialist discourse is particularly interesting in that it presents the impossibility of being both desired and black in early modern England; a similar point is made by Pamphilia in *Urania I*, 396. William Herbert uses a parallel fair/dark contrast in 'A Paradox, that Beauty Lies not in Women's Faces, but in their Lover's Eyes' (77) in which he accepts blackness as desirable and likens his lady to an 'Ethiope'.

5   **blackness:** Wroth performed in Ben Jonson's *Masque of Blackness* (1605), in which her skin was painted black.

8   **undone:** Wroth's use of the alternative spelling, 'undunn', in the manuscript also suggests that a pun on *dun* as 'dark' is intended.

9   **received's:** is received.

10  **worthless rite:** double pun on *worth/Wroth* and *rite/write*.

13  **Phoebus':** the sun god's.

*Sonnet 23 (P26)*

1   **hies:** hastens.

2   **hunt:** possibly an allusion to Wroth's husband, Sir Robert Wroth, who was renowned for his hunting and hawking, pastimes Wroth always refers to disparagingly.

5   **eyes:** the gaze of others.

7   **void:** lacking.

9   **chase:** pun on pursuing one's thoughts and hunting.

*Sonnet 24 (P27)*

1   **aged father:** the advice from age to youth is proverbial, but see also Philip Sidney, *The Old Arcadia*, the song between Geron, Histor and Philisides in the First Eclogues.

*Song 4 (P28)*

1   **Sweetest ... again:** a direct response to Donne's 'Sweetest love I do not go ...'.

16  **bands:** bonds, fetters.

21  **crossed:** obstructed.

*Sonnet 25 (P29)*

4   **Making ... store:** echoes Robert Sidney's 'Sonnet 20'.

7   **floods:** a common Sidneian allusion; see William Herbert's poetry (41) and notes to P51 below.

12–13   **star ... Mars:** the star is the beloved, whose light is compared favourably with that of the planet Mars, in classical mythology the god of war; hence the other 'star' probably denotes love. However, a more specific allusion is made to Philip Sidney's *Astrophil and Stella*, where the male poet (Sidney) loves the female star (Penelope Rich), and by implication therefore in Wroth's sonnet the female poet's love for the male star signifies Wroth's desire for William Herbert.

*Sonnet 26 (P30)*

1   **this:** the lover's heart; the image of two lovers exchanging hearts was a courtly love convention; see especially Philip Sidney, *Astrophil and Stella*, song 10, and *The Old Arcadia*, the first song in Book III, sung by Dorus. **will:** a pun on *Will*iam Herbert.

8   **spill:** destroy.

13  **vade:** fade.

12–14   **sacrifices ... found:** a Neoplatonic image which combines physical and spiritual love.

*Sonnet 27* (P31)
1–2  **Hope ... me:** close to Philip Sidney's *Astrophil and Stella* 67.
4  **trophies:** those won in battle.

*Sonnet 28* (P32)
1  **Grief:** Wroth's address to grief echoes that of Philip Sidney in *Astrophil and Stella* 94, where the emotion is similarly reviled and then welcomed.

*Sonnet 29* (P33)
5  **heav'n's changing:** the movement of the stars and, hence, the governing of the individual's fate; also an ironic reference to the changing nature of Amphilanthus/William Herbert. Wroth makes a similar accusation in the speech of Philisides/William Herbert in *Love's Victory*, III.ii.1–20.
14  **rests:** halts, ceases.

*Sonnet 30* (P34)
11–14  **But ... grieve:** draws upon Robert Sidney's 'Song 19'.

*Song 5* (P35)
17  **worthy ... worth:** pun on Wroth.
19–24  **Time ... Fame's:** Wroth reverses the traditional Petrarchan order where Time conquers Fame.

*Sonnet 31* (P36)
5  **Fortune ... blinded:** Fortune was traditionally depicted with a blindfold.
14  **move:** initiate, propose.

*Sonnet 32* (P37)
1  **How ... wings:** echoes Robert Sidney's 'Sonnet 35'.
10  **bee:** the selfless endeavours of the bee were proverbial and often used as a Sidneian emblem; see William Herbert, 'A Sonnet' (40–2).
13  **lade:** load.

*Sonnet 33* (P38)
8  **unbarred:** not subject to any restrictions.
9–10  **Art ... find:** echoes Philip Sidney's *Astrophil and Stella* 5.

*Sonnet 34* (P39)
4  **brings ... fast:** starves the lover of the affection he or she desires.
5  **all ... eyes:** the eyes of those who are jealous; see Philip Sidney, *Astrophil and Stella* 78.

*Sonnet 35* (P40)
1–2  **spill... breeds:** the metaphor is of a miscarriage, an interesting comparison with the political discourse of lines 5–10; both imply a violation of trust (see Philip Sidney, *Astrophil and Stella* 1).
4  **dearth:** shortage.
8  **will:** a possible pun on *William* Herbert, an allusion which is strengthened by the fact that Herbert's 'A Sonnet' (75) uses the same idea of romantic love and political favour being short-lived, although he also appears to rebut Wroth's condemnation of his own faithlessness by asserting that he '*will* constant prove'

(my italics).

9   **shadow**: conceal.

10  **show**: appearance.

11  **shows**: spectacle, pageantry.

13  **pride**: peak, with both political and sexual connotations.

*Sonnet 36 (P41)*

1   **witness**: as in a trial (of love); the metaphor of a trial and torture is extended throughout the sonnet.

10  **descried**: perceived.

12  **only one**: the concealment of love was a Petrarchan commonplace, yet there is also an autobiographical allusion since Wroth had to conceal her adulterous love for her cousin William Herbert.

*Song 6 (P42)*

This poem echoes Robert Sidney's 'Song 1', as well as William Herbert's 'A Sonnet' (38–9).

*Sonnet 37 (P43)*

4   **humour**: temperament, referring to the medieval theories of the body's 'humours', in which the four chief fluids of the body (blood, phlegm, choler and melancholy) were thought to determine a person's physical and mental qualities.

7   **hie**: hasten away.

13  **three**: Night, Silence and Grief; these three personifications also appear in Philip Sidney's *Astrophil and Stella* 96.

*Sonnet 38 (P44)*

1   **banished**: Wroth was herself banished from court and includes an autobiographical allusion to this in the Lindamira episode of *Urania I*.

4   **biding**: a place to bide, live.

*Sonnet 39 (P45)*

5   **wits**: fashionable courtiers who displayed their skill in imaginative rhetoric; here they are more specifically court poets who revel in the literary expression of their own grief. Like her uncle, Philip Sidney, in *Astrophil and Stella* (passim, but especially 3, 34 and 50), Wroth mocks such false excesses.

7   **moss**: that which grows externally, not the heart.

12–14  **Grudge ... make**: echoes Robert Sidney's 'Sonnet 1'.

14  **crossed**: a victim of misfortune.

*Sonnet 40 (P46)*

1   **poor fools**: a reference to the 'wits' of the previous sonnet.

3   **toying**: playing with affections. **swearing's gloze**: specious protestations (of love).

8   **beseem**: become.

13  **desert**: an uninhabited place.

*Sonnet 41 (P47)*

This sonnet displays the influence of Robert Sidney's 'Sonnet 1', and Philip Sidney's *Astrophil and Stella* 68.

*Sonnet 42 (P48)*
5  addressed: as in 'to address oneself', to make ready.
7  trunk: human body.
11  he: referring both to the god, Love, and to the beloved.
12  stage: a period of time, but with a pun on the open display of the theatre.

*Song 7 (P49)*
1  miss: fail.
18  miss: be lacking.

*Sonnet 43 (P50)*
2  Cupid: the god of love.
10  poor lost rooms: the 'places' of line 5, but with a suggestion of the lover's body/heart.

*Sonnet 44 (P51)*
1  Spring: the river of the poem recalls the Medway, which ran through the Sidney estate at Penshurst, and which was known for its flooding; the image is recalled by each of the Sidneys (Philip Sidney, *Other Poems* 5; Robert Sidney, 'Pastoral 8'; William Herbert's poetry (41), and Mary Sidney, 'Psalm 50').
4  Ere: before.
13  your way: to your course.

*Sonnet 45 (P52)*
The address to a friend recalls Philip Sidney's *Astrophil and Stella* 14 and 21, as well as Donne's 'The Canonisation'.
6  cross: perversely, but with a pun on the Christian cross.
10  possessed: Wroth presents herself as mad in that she has been possessed by a devil. This association of women with the demonic was common in the Jacobean period (indeed, it also echoes Philip Sidney's description of Stella in *Astrophil and Stella* 74), but Wroth parodies this link, since her show of 'possession' is merely undertaken to 'fright' her friend.

*Sonnet 46 (P53)*
7  obtained: discovered.
13  glass: mirror; the water in the well ('she') reflects back the image of the lover, just as the lover reflects the face of Love in her own visage.

*Sonnet 48 (P55)*
6  will: a pun on *Will*iam Herbert.
12–14  My ... prove: echoes Robert Sidney's 'Sonnet 9'.
Pamphilia: this signature (made on the Folger MS) marks the end of the first series of songs and sonnets (P1–P55).

*Sonnet (P56)*
The next seven poems, consisting of a sonnet and six songs, have no formal numbering system. This group (P56–P62) forms the second section of *Pamphilia to Amphilanthus*, and in it Wroth reverses the traditional Petrarchan pattern (six sonnets and a song) which she has adhered to in the first fifty-five poems.
6  her: as the last two lines of the sonnet make clear, 'her' may well refer to the

speaker; however, the suggestion of a rival complies with the general sense of loss in this central section (see P59, P61 and P62).

*Song* (P57)
17  **witchcrafts**: recalls Philip Sidney's *Astrophil and Stella*, Song 5.

*Song* (P58)
13  **wayward child**: the following allusion to Cupid's wounding of his own mother comes from Ovid, *Metamorphoses* IV and was a common reference in early modern love poetry; see specifically Philip Sidney, *Astrophil and Stella* 17, and Wroth's *Love's Victory*, I.i.
20  **murder**: echoes Philip Sidney, *Astrophil and Stella* 20.

*Song* (P59)
1  **crossed**: thwarted.
8  **another ruler**: the use of political metaphors (ruler/servant) was a common-place in early modern love poetry. There is also a suggestion that the beloved has found a new lady (see P56, P61 and P62).

*Song* (P60)
2  **faithful shepherd's**: the faithful shepherd is a common Sidneian character but is perhaps most closely linked with Robert Sidney, who portrays himself in this guise in 'Pastoral 9', and is similarly depicted as Forrester by Wroth in her play *Love's Victory*.
24  **speed**: fare.

*Song* (P61)
6  **new love**: again referring to the rival lover (see P56, P59 and P62).
12–13  **Then ... still**: an allusion to Amphilanthus (William Herbert), whose name signifies 'lover of two', and Pamphilia (Mary Wroth), whose name means 'all-loving'.
20  **crossed**: thwarted.

*Song* (P62)
6  **jealous**: the poem concludes the central section with an avowal of jealousy caused by the beloved finding a new mistress (see P56, P59 and P61).

*Sonnet* 1 (second series) (P63)
There are ten sonnets in the second series (P63–P72), and the theme shifts from suspecting that a rival exists to fully-fledged jealousy and a recognition of loss.
9  **Fortune**: the goddess Fortune was often depicted with a wheel, which, constantly turning, demanded that all who were successful (at the top of the wheel) should also taste misfortune (revolve to the bottom); Philip Sidney also uses this image, in *Astrophil and Stella* 66.

*Sonnet* 2 (second series) (P64)
1  **juggler**: the theme of change is continued from the previous sonnet with the idea of the god of love as a conjuror or juggler; this depiction of Cupid echoes Philip Sidney, *Astrophil and Stella* 11. **prize**: game.
3  **wanting**: lacking; Cupid was traditionally depicted as blind, or blindfolded.

6  **prettily**: skilfully, attractively.
7  **hire**: serve.
8  **badge and office**: signs and service.
13  **lost will**: pun on *Will*iam Herbert, whose love has been 'lost'.

*Sonnet 3 (second series) (P65)*
6  **god**: Mercury, who in Ovid's *Metamorphoses* 1 lulled the hundred-eyed Argos to sleep by playing on his reed pipe and telling him the story of Syrinx, who spurned the love of Pan and was metamorphosed into the reeds of a stream to avoid his embraces; Pan subsequently turned the reeds into the reed-pipe used by Mercury. Argos is then slain by Mercury at the behest of Jupiter in order to rescue his lover, Io, who had been changed into a cow to protect her from Juno's (Jupiter's wife's) jealousy. The sonnet reworks both narratives in order to present a love that is both fulfilled and denied, as well as retaining the themes of jealousy and the poetic inscription of loss. Philip Sidney uses the same myth in *Astrophil and Stella*, Song 11. **reed**: reed pipe.

*Sonnet 4 (second series) (P67)*
9  **fond child**: a reference to the common image of Cupid as a mischievous, disobedient boy.

*Sonnet 6 (second series) (P68)*
The metaphor of the distressed lover as a ship wrecked at sea is ultimately Petrarchan (*Rime* 189). Wroth has also used her father's similar evocation (Robert Sidney, 'Sonnets 23'); and see her own *Love's Victory*, IV.i.220.
5  **Goodwins**: a treacherous shoal off the Kentish coast which was used in proverbial fashion in early modern England (for an example of such use, see Shakespeare's *The Merchant of Venice*, III.i.4–6).

*Sonnet 7 (second series) (P69)*
13  **will**: pun on *Will*iam Herbert.

*Sonnet 8 (second series) (P70)*
1–2  **Love ... Diana's**: the punishment of Cupid, the boy-god of love, was a common Neoplatonic theme, for physical love had to be disciplined before true spiritual love could be attained; here the chastisement is undertaken by Diana, the goddess of chastity. Within the poetic sequence this punishment occurs appropriately close to (four poems before) the crown of sonnets with its elevation of ideal Neoplatonic love. For similar treatments, see Philip Sidney, *Astrophil and Stella* 17.
6  **slight**: small amount.
8  **chief**: the disdain to his honour was Cupid's chief reason for revenge.

*Sonnet 9 (second series) (P71)*
3  **Let ... tomb**: echoes Robert Sidney, 'Sonnet 30'.
7  **will**: a possible pun on *Will*iam Herbert.

*Sonnet 10 (second series) (P72)*
1  **Folly**: traditionally personified as female (see line 3); however, Wroth's first version of the sonnet introduced Cupid as the 'follifier' with the resulting use of

'he' as the associated pronoun (see Paulissen (1982), p. 139); this sets up a complicated use of pronouns throughout the sonnet; see Wroth's similar use of Folly in her play *Love's Victory*, II.i.93–114.

4   **bands**: fetters, bonds.
7   **vanity**: the illusion of true love.
10  **he**: the god of love, Cupid; the 'wanton boy' of line 14.
14  **he**: the lover, rather than the god, or idea, of love.

### Songs (P73–P76)

These four poems consist of three unnumbered songs and one sonnet; they act as a transition from the second to the third sonnet series and similarly evince a change from bitterness against love to praise for Cupid and all he stands for.

### Song (P73)

1   **spring**: the seasonal metaphor was one commonly applied in early modern love poetry; see John Donne, 'Love's Growth'.
14  **love and reason**: a common Sidneian pairing; see Philip Sidney, the second eclogues of *The Old Arcadia*, William Herbert's 'It is enough, a Master you grant Love' (7–9), and Wroth, *Love's Victory*, II.i.213–24 (see also notes to P86 below).

### Song (P74)

10  **cozen**: cheat; with a possible pun on 'cousin': that is, William Herbert.
11  **gain the hand**: gain the upper hand.

### Sonnet (P76)

1   **Cupid**: Wroth reverses her accusations against love in this sonnet, which heralds the most explicit honouring of love in the next sequence (see also Wroth's *Love's Victory*, III.ii.169–76).
12  **crown**: a reference to the following fourteen poems.

### A Crown of Sonnets Dedicated to Love

A crown or corona of sonnets was a traditional form in which a series of sonnets was linked by the use of the same or similar last and first lines of succeeding pieces; the final line of the sequence usually echoes the first line, thus bringing the whole full-circle to make the 'crown'. Wroth draws upon the sonnet crowns of her uncle Philip Sidney (the poems sung by Strephon and Klaius in the fourth eclogues of *The Old Arcadia*, which consist of ten linked dizains, was the first corona in English), her father Robert Sidney (an incomplete corona, sonnets 11–14), and possibly Samuel Daniel (*Delia*, sonnets 31–5), who was a member of her aunt's, Mary Sidney's, circle. Wroth's own corona (P77–90) is a complex sequence of fourteen sonnets which initially asserts the superiority of spiritual love (with Christian Neoplatonic and chaste variations), only to repudiate this assertion in the final poem, and (unlike the male-authored crowns mentioned above) is centred upon the idea of love rather than the self.

### Sonnet 1 (third series) (P77)

1   **labyrinth**: the trope of love as a labyrinth or maze was common in early modern love discourses (for example, Petrarch, *Rime* 211; Robert Sidney,

'Pastoral 9'; and Wroth herself, *Love's Victory*, IV.i.67); it is a particularly apt metaphor for Wroth after the confusion of love, jealousy and loss in the previous poetic sequences.

5  left: proverbially, the left side was regarded as unlucky.

7  crosses: misfortunes, but also with a sense of the crossing of paths in the maze.

11  allay: lessening.

12  travail: both travel and travail (labour). hire: payment.

14  thread: the thread laid by Ariadne to help her lover Theseus escape from the labyrinth in which he had killed the Minotaur; Wroth uses a similar image in *Urania* (U35).

### Sonnet 2 (third series) (P78)

2  soul's: this sonnet marks the shift from secular to spiritual love; Wroth here echoes her father's, Robert Sidney's, Neoplatonic belief in the inevitable combining of spiritual and bodily love (see especially his 'Sonnet 2'), and William Herbert, who in the first poem of his collection refers to the union of the soul and body (1–3).

4  fancy: love, amorous desire.

8  constant lovers: a reference to the poetic second self of the sonnet sequence, Pamphilia, whose name means 'all-loving'.

9–12  Love ... increase: a series of Biblical, and particularly New Testament, images: the 'star' recalls the star of Bethlehem (Matthew 2:7); the 'fire of zeal' may be found throughout the Bible (for example, Matthew 3:10–11); peace was brought by Christ to earth; the 'lamp' belongs to the wise virgins of Matthew 25:1–13; the image of faith is again Christ; and the womb belongs to Mary, who bore Jesus. Combined, these references initiate a religious interpretation of love, more redolent of Mary Sidney's Psalm translations (see pp. 72–98 above) than the secular love discourses of the male Sidney authors.

### Sonnet 3 (third series) (P79)

A mono-rhymed sonnet which follows Philip Sidney's *The Old Arcadia* (42), which is given by the inconstant Gynecia; Wroth contrasts this sharply with the constant Pamphilia, offering a very different view of female love and loyalty. She also draws upon Robert Sidney's 'Sonnet 3' of the corona, but again comments upon the male/female roles, for whereas her father accepts that the male 'I' of the sonnet is fickle, Wroth's female 'I' complains of the inconstancy of the male beloved.

1  His: the god of love here acquires both Christian and secular significance; the images of purity suggest Christ, while the idea of a 'court' (line 14) implies the adult Cupid and his 'Court of Love' popular in courtly love discourse.

8  requite: repay.

### Sonnet 4 (third series) (P80)

7  chaos: in Neoplatonic theory, the world would ultimately be destroyed with a reversion to original chaos.

*Sonnet* 5 (third series) (P81)
8   his: Cupid's, but with strong spiritual overtones.
14   prophet: as Wroth uses an alternative spelling of *profit* (in one of the versions of the poem) a pun is surely intended.

*Sonnet* 6 (third series) (P82)
1   prove: become.
3–4   To ... mind: the uniting of the bodies of the two lovers in one heart and soul is a Neoplatonic image recalling the hermaphrodite; it is also used by William Herbert in 'On One Heart Made of Two' (43).
14   prove: experience.

*Sonnet* 7 (third series) (P83)
4   Cupid: here a mature and spiritual force rather than the naughty child of the earlier poetic sequences.
9   painter: a common Sidneian comparison; see Philip Sidney, *Astrophil and Stella* 1 and 45; Robert Sidney, 'Sonnet 11'. This is more specifically a reference to Herbert's own artistic skills in depicting Wroth in his own poetry, which is particularly important in a sequence which allows the cousins/lovers to enact poetic exchanges; In his first poem (3) Herbert returns the compliment when he refers to Wroth as 'singing'.
11   true: a pun on 'accurate' and 'honest'.

*Sonnet* 8 (third series) (P84)
3   worth: here and at line 6 a rather arch pun on *Wroth*; this line also finds echoes in Robert Sidney's 'Sonnet 4'.
11   chastely: this sonnet subtly alters the focus of the corona, since the spiritual love lauded in sonnets 1–7 is turned to the lover's own advantage, in that she may now 'chastely' deny the overtures which were previously welcome.
13   fancies: amorous desires.

*Sonnet* 9 (third series) (P85)
2   Venus: the goddess of love is here contrasted in traditional courtly love fashion as the representation of physical love, with Cupid as the god of spiritual love.
3   worthless: a pun on *Wroth*: that is, 'without Wroth'.
5   son: Cupid. Wroth has a variant spelling, 'sun', which underlines the Neoplatonic idealism of Cupid in this sonnet.
9   lust ... love: a conventional comparison.
10   gloss: interpretation.
12   the own: their own.
12–13   beget ... love: echoes Philip Sidney, *Astrophil and Stella* 1.

*Sonnet* 10 (third series) (P86)
1   Love and Reason: a typically Sidneian juxtaposition: see Philip Sidney, the second eclogues of *The Old Arcadia*; Wroth, *Love's Victory*, II.i.213–24, and P73 (above); as well as William Herbert, 'It is enough, a Master you grant Love' (7–9).
3   Desert: merit.

13   sour: wet and cold.

*Sonnet 11* (third series) (P87)
2   **heaven**: Genesis 1:11–12.
4   **dearth**: value.
7   **hemlock**: a plant which yields a deadly poison; Robert Sidney makes a similar reference in 'Song 22'; Wroth continues the allusion in the next sonnet (P88).   **sick-wit**: the ailing imagination of those who love excessively or without moral worth.
8   **vapours**: according to early modern medical understanding, these were exhalations produced within the body which were injurious to the health.

*Sonnet 13* (third series) (P89)
4   **will**: pun on *Will*iam Herbert.
5   **fill**: fulfilled.
9   **Lord**: Cupid, but with a Christian connotation as suggested by the other religious vocabulary of the sonnet.
11   **feigned**: a pun, both necessary (fained) and false (feigned).
13   **crown**: the crown of sonnets.

*Sonnet 14* (third series) (P90)
3   **worthless**: a pun on *Wroth*. **choice store**: a valuable or select storehouse, treasury.
4   **one**: the beloved, who is able to leave the 'labyrinth', unlike the speaker of the sonnet.
6   **score**: debt.
7   **Constancy**: a reference to Wroth's poetic second self, Pamphilia, whose name means 'all-loving'.
11   **Jealousy**: the personification reappears at the end of the corona, despite the earlier avowals of a chaste and spiritual love.
14   **In ... turn**: the crown of sonnets completes itself with a return to the first line; the self-contained form thus echoes the sense of the speaker's entrapment, in that she cannot free herself from the bonds of love and jealousy. Wroth repeats this line in her prose romance *Urania* 1 (II.ii.61).

*Song 1* (second series) (P91)
The next sequence in *Pamphilia to Amphilanthus* consists of four songs (P91–P94) which all convey a darker and more cynical tone. The first song echoes Robert Sidney's 'Song 20'.

*Song 2* (second series) (P92)
1   **Silvia**: a traditional pastoral name.
3   **Cupid**: the Neoplatonic god of the corona is once more depicted as a naughty child (as in the Greek poet Anacreon's amatory and erotic verse); he is mocked at lines 7–8 below.
4   **crown**: a reference to the previous sequence of sonnets.
6   **myrtle**: a tree sacred to Venus, and hence a symbol of love.
12   **will's**: possibly a pun on *Will*iam Herbert.
17   **dart**: Cupid is traditionally depicted with a bow and arrows.

18    'lighting: alighting.
28    want his eyes: Cupid was usually depicted with a blindfold.

*Song* 3 (second series) (P93)
14    Philomel: in Ovid's *Metamorphoses* VI Philomel was transformed into a
nightingale after being raped by Tereus; the light tone of the song's first verse is
therefore questioned by the sadness of the conclusion (see also Philip Sidney,
'Certain Sonnets' 4).

*Song* 4 (second series) (P94)
12    worth: a pun on *Wroth* which is repeated at line 21 and is coupled with a
double pun on 'will'.
16    will: a pun on *Will*iam Herbert, repeated at line 22.
26    fashion: echoes speech in Wroth's *Love's Victory*, IV.i.320.
32    Popish law: a sharp attack upon the Catholic rule of Papal absolutism,
which aligns well with the strong English Protestant tradition of the Sidney
family; however, the association of the beloved/Amphilanthus/William Herbert
with the Pope provides a hostile and bitter conclusion to this penultimate section
of poems.
35    martyrs: repeating the religious theme.

*Sonnet* 1 (fourth series) (P95)
This sonnet heralds the last section of *Pamphila to Amphilanthus* (P95–P103)
and takes as its main theme the use of poetry to define and represent love.
3    fancy: imagination.
4    mourning: in the manuscript version, Wroth uses 'morning' which parallels
the 'ev'ning' of line 2; a pun is certainly intended.
9    Cupid ... mother: in this sonnet the idealization of Cupid from the crown
(P77–P90) is reactivated, and he is seen as associated with love (line 13), in
contrast to Venus, who is referred to as the goddess of 'lust' (line 13), and whose
unrequited passion for Adonis (Ovid, *Metamorphoses* X) is alluded to at line 10.
This contrast between love and lust is a Neoplatonic assertion and similar to
that used by William Herbert in 'That Lust Is Not His Aim' (33).

*Sonnet* 2 (fourth series) (P96)
10    Cupid: here depicted as a child (the Anacreontic Cupid); the subsequent
description of him as a cold and starving beggar was extremely common in early
modern sonnets (see Philip Sidney, *Astrophil and Stella* 17 and 65).
6    stay: being stopped.
12    myrtle: the myrtle was sacred to Venus, and hence a symbol of love.

*Sonnet* 3 (fourth series) (P97)
1    Juno ... Jove: the infidelities of Jove/Jupiter to his wife Juno were numerous,
many being described by Ovid in *Metamorphoses* (Wroth alludes to Jupiter's
liaison with Io in P65); the mythological reference is used here to reassert the
themes of male inconstancy and female jealousy.
7    hie: hurry.

*Sonnet* 4 (fourth series) (P98)

1   **image**: the power of the lover's image was often cited in early modern love poetry; see Philip Sidney, *Astrophil and Stella* 32, and John Donne, 'The Dream'.

7   **Genius**: a tutelary spirit, here one particularly associated with love.

14   **lie**: a pun on 'to take its place' and 'to tell an untruth'.

*Sonnet* 5 (fourth series) (P99)

3   **wrong ... me**: Wroth might well be making an autobiographical point (particularly given the pun on her own name at line 7) about her banishment from court.

8   **crosses**: misfortunes.

*Sonnet* 6 (fourth series) (P100)

11   **stage play like**: Wroth sets up a comparison between fictional love (re-emphasized with the reference to 'ancient fictions', line 12) and true love, the metaphor of dark mists shifting into the veiling devices of art; the use of such a trope is ironic since the sonneteer's 'thoughts' (line 14) are only accessible through the sonnet itself.

*Sonnet* 7 (fourth series) (P101)

1   **room**: space. **writing**: a self-conscious reference to the 'art' of poetic writing which is sustained throughout the sonnet; as in the previous sonnet, Wroth denies that poetry can truly represent her love, although the poetic expression of this sentiment leads to an inevitable conundrum.

3–4   **fancy ... measure**: imagination able to comprehend the extent; but also with a pun upon literary form, imagination able to analyse the poetic metre.

7   **art**: the beloved (Amphilanthus/William Herbert) is accredited with the poetic skill the author denies for herself, the 'seems' of the next line again implying an ironic tone.

10   **travail**: work, but also with a pun on 'travel' (the spelling used in the manuscript version).

12–14   **glory ... discern**: an ironic comment upon the claim of sonneteers to immortalize their subject (and themselves) in their verses.

*Sonnet* 8 (fourth series) (P102)

4   **time**: echoes John Donne's 'A Nocturnal Upon St Lucy's Day'.

6   **north**: recalls Philip Sidney's *Astrophil and Stella* 8.

12   **that sight**: a reference to the absence of the lover, whose departure is likened to the colds of winter and the remoteness of the north.

*Sonnet* 9 (fourth series) (P103)

3   **Write**: this sonnet, like the others in the final sequence, makes a self-referential comment upon the author's act of writing, which must now be passed to others to continue.   **fancies**: imaginative thoughts, both of love and of poetic inspiration.

9   **Venus ... son**: there is a pun on 'sun' implied by the manuscript spelling.

13   **leave off**: stop loving, stop writing poetry.

14   **constancy**: a reference to Pamphilia, who represents that virtue in Wroth's prose romance *Urania I*. There is considerable dispute as to the meaning of the

last couplet, some critics suggesting that it moves towards a Christian and
spiritual version of love, as in the crown of sonnets (P77–P90), while others
interpret the lines as a statement of independence and a focus upon the self
which undercuts the usual male self-abnegating conclusion of sonnet sequences,
where a combination of love and frustration is perpetuated (see Philip Sidney,
*Astrophil and Stella* 70, and *Certain Sonnets* 32).

## Diana Primrose

### A Chain of Pearl
The title refers both to the text itself, where each separate 'pearl' or poem forms
part of the whole 'chain' or book, and to the trope of a necklace, which
ornaments the memory of Elizabeth I in the same way that the poem eulogizes
the dead queen.
**Dat ... virus:** The Rose gives honey to bees, and thus puts to flight the venom of
spiders.

### TO ALL NOBLE LADIES
1   **our ... sex:** the work is specifically directed towards a female readership, and
immediately the poem begins a complicity is initiated with other women through
the use of pronouns.
3   **her:** Elizabeth I.
5   **trophy:** monument or memorial.

### TO THE EXCELLENT LADY
1   **Diana:** in classical mythology, the goddess of the moon and chastity; during
her reign Elizabeth I was often compared to Diana. **golden rays:** as the moon,
Diana would have had silver rays, the golden rays belonging to Phoebus, the god
of the sun, who is alluded to in 'The Induction' (line 1); here the goddess, and by
implication Elizabeth I and Primrose, are seen to acquire masculine attributes.
2   **her:** Elizabeth I's.
3   **quill:** a pen made from a feather.
5   **golden days:** soon after her death in 1603, Elizabeth's reign began to be
described as a 'golden age', and this nostalgia, combined with criticism of the
Stuart monarchies, persisted well into the seventeenth century (see also Anne
Bradstreet's 'In Honour of Queen Elizabeth', pp. 260–63).
9   **Prime-Rose:** a pun on the author's name, Primrose. **Muses nine:** in classical
mythology, the nine Muses were the divinities who presided over the arts and
sciences.
12   **native:** natural, own.
13   **peerless-orient:** a pun on orient 'pearls' which were thought to be
particularly precious, and on 'peerless', that is, without equal.
15   **censure:** judgement. **royal chain:** the poem itself.
**Dorothy Berry:** nothing is known of this author, but the fact that the only
dedicatory piece is written by another woman adds to the overall female-centred
tone of the book.

## THE INDUCTION

**Title:** the introductory poem.

1  **Phoebus:** the comparison with Elizabeth I (at lines 7–9) contributes to the shift from male to female power structures within the text as a whole.

3  **asterisms:** constellations of stars.

10  **damp:** restrain and depress their glorious achievements.

12  **verge:** limit.

13  **empress of our sex:** the empress of women.

16  **blazon:** proclaim and, with a specific literary connotation, set forth honourably in words; most commonly used by male authors in their descriptions of women. **parts:** attributes; but with 'blazon' the word also suggests 'parts of the body', since male sonneteers 'blazoned' their ladies' physical beauties more often than their inner qualities. Primrose in the subsequent poems praises Elizabeth's moral virtues, which suggests that the allusion to the sonnet tradition here is ironic.

18  **Apollo:** in classical mythology, Apollo is the god of song and music.

21  **pearly rows:** a pun on 'rows of pearls' (in a necklace), and the 'rows' or lines of the poem.

23  **black and impolite:** the poems are 'black' since they form an elegy, and 'impolite' because Primrose, in a common disclaimer, suggests that her poetry is 'unpolished'.

24  **lustre:** sheen, but also splendour and renown.

**Votary:** a devoted admirer, with spiritual overtones, endowing Elizabeth I with a quasi-divinity.

## RELIGION

The choice of religion as the first 'pearl' determines the Protestant tenor of the whole book; it also suggests that Spenser's *The Faerie Queene* is one of the key influences on Primrose's work, since Spenser also chose religion as the first moral virtue to be depicted; she might also have been influenced by Aristotle's *Nicomachean Ethics*, which was one of Spenser's sources.

1  **Chain:** the book of poems.

2  **true religion:** Protestantism, as opposed to Catholicism. **gain:** acquire.

4  **Mary:** Mary I, Queen of England, who died in 1558; she was Elizabeth's half-sister and a devout Catholic, who had tried to impose her religion upon the country.

8–9  **domestic ... Spain and France:** rebellion from Catholic groups in Britain, and resistance from the Catholic countries, Spain and France.

11  **ensign:** military banner. **maugre:** in spite of.

12  **ten years:** from the Act of Uniformity in 1559 to the suppression of the Northern Uprising in 1569, which had attempted to depose Elizabeth and put the Catholic Mary Stuart in her place.

14  **Romist:** Catholic.

15–16  **edicts ... sacrament:** the Act of Uniformity ('edicts') of 1559 made going to church ('temple') compulsory for all laymen, but failure to do so was merely punished with a fine of one shilling, and no one was compelled to take Communion ('holy sacrament').

17 **factious**: rebellious.

18 **holy father**: Pope.

19 **bull**: Papal edict.

18–20 **holy ... heretic**: in 1570 Pope Pius V issued a bull which excommunicated Elizabeth and allowed her subjects to choose another monarch.

22 **masking**: as acting in a mask; commonly used in this period to suggest the deceiving nature of the Catholic priests who administered the mass.

23 **evangelical profession**: the Protestant ministers.

26 **leaden**: dull and ineffectual.

27 **By which**: probably a printer's error; the correct reading should be 'Which by'. **Felton**: John Felton, who nailed a copy of the Pope's bull to the garden gate of the Bishop's Palace in London in 1570; he was convicted of high treason and hanged.

31 **wild-fire**: gunpowder; an allusion to the gathering of rebellious forces in the north.

34 **idolatry**: the worship of idols; here, practising Roman Catholics. **range**: go about.

35 **Northumberland**: Thomas Percy, 7th Earl of Northumberland, and one of the key instigators of the Northern Rebellion of 1569; he was defeated and executed.

36 **Westmoreland**: Charles Neville, 6th Earl of Westmoreland, was another of the Northern rebels, but escaped to the Continent.

37 **mo**: more.

39 **Sussex**: Thomas Radcliffe, 3rd Earl of Sussex, who commanded Elizabeth's troops in their victory over the rebels.

44 **stricter laws**: the two anti-Catholic bills of 1571 were the immediate consequences of the Northern Rebellion, but further measures, for example the Act of Obedience (1581), were passed as the Counter-Reformation gathered force in the mid-1570s.

45 **recusants**: Catholics who refused to attend the services of the Protestant Church of England.

46 **bang'd**: defeated. **gospel's part**: the use of an English Bible rather than the Latin version prescribed by the Catholic Church.

47 **bated**: weakened.

48 **rude sort**: violent manner.

49–50 **Spain ... nation**: the Pope requested the aid of Catholic Spain, which made repeated attempts between 1586 and 1588 to invade England. A note in the text adds: 'In ultimam rabiem furoremque conversi' (turned to extreme anger and fury).

## CHASTITY

This second moral was commonly associated with Elizabeth I and is one of the 'female' virtues in the poem. Primrose draws upon Book III of Spenser's *The Faerie Queene*, which similarly focuses upon chastity.

1   **Pearl**: a reference to the poem.

4   **anadem**: a wreath or ceremonial garland for the head.

8   **rarely**: splendidly.

10   **vestal**: virginal; the votaries of the goddess Vesta, who kept the temple flame alight, vowed to remain chaste.

12   **Hymen's rites**: marriage; in classical mythology, Hymen was the god of marriage.

13   **French Monsieur**: the Duke of Alençon, who wooed Elizabeth unsuccessfully between 1579 and 1581, although of all her royal suitors he appears to have been her preferred choice, and she mourned his departure in her own verse (see pp. 12–13 above).

14   **golden fleece**: in classical mythology, the precious and beautiful golden fleece is obtained by Jason; here Alençon is compared to Jason, and Elizabeth I to the golden fleece.

15   **Spanish Philip**: Philip II of Spain, who had been married to Mary I, Elizabeth's half-sister; he wooed Elizabeth unsuccessfully in 1559.

17–18   **Pope … it**: it was suggested that Philip would be able to obtain a bull (Papal dispensation) allowing the marriage between himself and Elizabeth, which would otherwise have been prohibited by the Bible.

18   **gull**: trick.

19   **Pope**: in traditional Protestant fashion, Primrose sets the law of God against and above the authority of the Catholic Church; it was unsurprising that Elizabeth herself chose to refute the Pope's power to pronounce conclusively upon marriage settlements, since such an acceptance would have questioned her own right to the throne. A note in the text adds: 'Yet his canonists say; Bené dispensat Dominus Papa contra Apostolum. Extra de Renune. Ca post translationem' (The Pope may well give a dispensation against the Acts taken from the Apostles; from the official report. Against the translation.)

29   **vidual**: as befitting a widow.

30   **affects**: loves.

31   **noble lady**: a note in the text gives the source: 'Related by the Honourable Knight and Baronet, Sir Richard Houghton of Houghton Tower.'

33   **Taxis**: the source of the whole narrative was Sir Richard Houghton, who presumably supplied the names of the individuals involved.

34   **she**: Elizabeth I; after her death (a note in the text adds, 'Primo Jacobi' (James I)).

40   **horned**: cuckolded.

42   **trophy**: a token of victory.

44   **Pearl**: a reference to the poem.


PRUDENCE

This virtue is not found either in Spenser's *The Faerie Queene* or in Camden's *Annales*, Primrose's two source texts, but it was a moral quality often associated with women and, as such, a suitable one for this female-centred text.

12   **pensions**: payments or benefices. **move**: persuade (to give); in her praise of Elizabeth's reliance upon unpaid loyalty, Primrose is condemning the Stuart

monarchs, especially Charles I, who were known for their extravagant gifts and for purchasing allegiance.

14 **Argus-eyes**: in classical mythology, Argos had a hundred eyes and was proverbially used to suggest 'all-seeing'.

16 **arts or arms**: stratagems or warfare.

17–19 **gift ... sex**: Primrose suggests that Elizabeth's skill in government was exceptional in a woman, rather than seeing the queen as proving all women were capable rulers; a discussion of women as exceptions and/or examples may be found in the Introduction (see pp. xxiv–xxv above).

20 **than alone**: than when alone.

27 **Pearl of Prudence**: a reference to the poem.

30 **president**: sovereign.

## TEMPERANCE

Primrose draws upon Spenser's *The Faerie Queene*, where the second book focuses upon the virtue temperance.

1 **golden ... Bellerophon**: in classical mythology, the goddess Athena gave Bellerophon a golden bridle with which to harness the winged horse Pegasus; in the early modern period the bridling of a horse came to represent the controlling of animal passions, especially the sexual ones.

4–6 **else ... events**: the 'we' and 'our' clearly indicate a female readership who must protect their chastity from men, since yielding will lead to 'foul events', perhaps an allusion to unwanted pregnancy and thereby disgrace. Primrose interestingly inverts the traditional image of sirens (mermaids) luring men to their doom, by suggesting that it is the persuasive words of men that entice women and cause their downfall.

7 **this Pearl**: chastity.

8 **King**: Edward VI, Elizabeth's half-brother.

9 **Sister Temperance**: the source for this name is Camden's *Annales*, and it suggests that Primrose used either the Latin original or the French translation, since the English translation that retains 'Sister Temperance' was not published until 1630. Greer suggests that, given Primrose's use of Latin tags in her own text, she used the Latin version (p. 87).

13 **tenor**: movement, manner of proceeding.

15 **rock of temperance**: a note in the text adds: 'Semper eadem' (always the same), which was one of Elizabeth's mottoes.

16 **mazed**: bewildered. **chance**: (unfortunate) event.

17–18 **empty ... fed**: proverbial.

18 **cast ... moon**: proverbial: to go to extravagant lengths.

20 **fond to love**: foolishly eager to fall in love.

21 **siren-songs**: see note to line 5 above.

21–4 **Not charmed ... villainy**: by praising Elizabeth's lack of susceptibility to court flattery, Primrose is, in fact, condemning Charles I for his lack of discernment and for allowing his favourites to dominate the court.

22 **sugred**: sugared; sweetened with eloquence.

29 **subjects' love**: a note in the text adds: 'Omnibus incutiens blandum per

pectora amorem' (for all, thrusting seductive love into the heart); the quotation comes from the invocation to Venus in Lucretius' *De rerum natura*, which is also used as a source in Spenser's *The Faerie Queene* (IV.x.44–66). The comment by Primrose is again intended to compare Charles I unfavourably with Elizabeth, suggesting that Charles cannot command the 'true' love of his subjects as did Elizabeth.

**34 music ... spheres**: the movement of the stars in heaven was thought to produce perfectly harmonious music.

## CLEMENCY

In this virtue, as with prudence (see p. 233 above), Primrose does not follow her main source authors, Spenser and Camden, but could be referring to Book IV of Aristotle's *Nicomachean Ethics*, which focuses on 'Liberality'.

**3 maker**: God. **that**: clemency.

**4–5 commiserate ... rebels**: in the Bible generally, God extends his mercy over all that he has made, including the rebel angels who have fallen from heaven.

**6 diamonds bright**: stars.

**8–10 those ... combine**: the Catholic rebels who approached Spain in order to overthrow both Elizabeth ('state') and the Protestant faith ('church'); although Elizabeth's punishment of these dissidents was hardly clement by twentieth-century standards, during her own day she was considered, especially by her counsellors, to be dangerously lenient towards the committed Catholics, especially those at court. A note in the text adds: 'Monstra, terrima monstra' (Monsters, most foul monsters).

**19 auri**: golden.

## JUSTICE

Influenced by Spenser's *The Faerie Queene*, where the fifth book concentrates upon justice.

**4 malefactors**: wrong-doers.

**9 putrid ... away**: cut off as infected parts of the body should be; in the early modern period a diseased body was commonly used as a metaphor for rebellion in the state.

**13 feminine hands**: a woman writer; hence, a reference to her own poem, where Primrose eschews 'feminine' subjects in order to encompass the whole political history of Elizabeth's reign.

**17–19 Pope ... martyrs**: Pope Urban VIII reissued the 1584 *Roman Martyrology* in 1630; the following descriptions, however, refer instead to William Allen's *Briefe Historie of the Glorious Martyrdom of xii Reverand Priests*, which was a sixteenth-century account of the execution of Catholic priests in England. Such martyrologies were popular amongst recusant groups in Britain; Greer suggests (p. 89) that Primrose would have had a specific dislike of these Jesuit-authored texts, since it was the Jesuits who had caused Gilbert Primrose to be expelled from France (see Notes on the Authors, pp. 365–6).

**24 phantasms**: nightmares, dreams. **bables**: baubles; children's toys.

**26 oft**: often.

**28   Golden Legend**: William Caxton published an illustrated translation of Jacobus de Voragine's *The Golden Legend*, a collection of fantastical tales, which formed saints' legends, in 1483.

**29   he**: a note in the text adds: 'Vappa Voraginesa' (worthless Voragine), confirming that Primrose had specific knowledge of the text.

## FORTITUDE

In the seventh virtue, Primrose again moves away from her sources; however, the inclusion of fortitude, not a quality commonly associated with women during the period, might well have been to facilitate a description of Elizabeth's speech at Tilbury (see note to line 14 below).

**2   endued**: endowed.

**3   Parry**: Dr William Parry, who was executed for plotting to assassinate Elizabeth I in 1584.

**10   her paragon**: compare with her.

**14   Tilbury**: on 9 August 1588, Elizabeth travelled to Tilbury to address her troops as they prepared to do battle with the Spanish forces which threatened to invade England; the speech made by the queen on this occasion became her most famous, and remains a popular inclusion in her canon (see Notes on the Authors below, p. 350).

**19   sort**: manner.

**23   Henry**: Henry VIII, Elizabeth's father, who had won acclaim for his valour at the Field of Cloth of Gold in 1520.

**26   Enthronized ... diadem**: set on the throne and crowned (monarchs).

## SCIENCE

An unusual inclusion in a list of moral virtues directed at either a male or a female audience, but a particularly important one since it concerns Elizabeth's eloquence and thereby affirms the ability of women in general, and Primrose in particular, to display rhetorical excellence.

**2   van**: the foremost division of a procession, often of a military force.

**3   Pearl**: pearls were often dissolved in wine, as they were believed to have a restorative effect.

**3-4   Egyptian Queen ... Anthony**: Cleopatra and Antony. In early modern literature, Cleopatra was most commonly used to represent the dangers of unbridled sexual desire in women; however, Primrose may have been aware of the more positive depiction of the queen in Mary Sidney's *The Tragedy of Antonie* (see pp. 66–72 above). Nevertheless, the association of Elizabeth I and Cleopatra is a fraught one in a poem that claims to eulogize the Tudor monarch.

**4   Quaffed**: Drank deeply.

**5   Indian gold**: gold and gems from the East were considered particularly valuable, but in conjunction with the reference to Cleopatra (line 3) and the use of 'ravish' in the next line (6) the allusion to the East takes on an exotic and sensual signification.

**6   ravish**: entrance, but with sexual overtones.

**7   deck**: adorn, beautify.

8   heroina: heroine. beck: her command.

9   **Muses and the Graces**: in classical mythology, the Muses were deities who governed the arts and the sciences, while the Graces were goddesses who bestowed charm and beauty.

12   **Apollo ... lyre**: in classical mythology, Apollo, the god of song and music, is often credited with the invention of the lyre with which he is depicted; here Apollo's 'song' is compared unfavourably with Elizabeth's speech, as in the 'Induction' the god's skills are said to excel those of Primrose (see pp. 229–30 above).

13   Ne'er: Never.

14   manna: divine nourishment.

15   **nectar-flowing vein**: a vein carrying sweet nectar is here used as a metaphor for the sweet sound of the queen's voice which flows about those who listen to her.

17   men: Elizabeth's rhetorical skills are described as affecting men only (the following list, lines 19–30, includes no female audiences); partly this describes an accurate historical situation in which women would have been denied access to political activities, but it also suggests, especially in conjunction with the reference to Cleopatra (line 3), that the female voice always carries threatening erotic overtones.

19   **Alasco**: Albertus Alasco, a Polish Palatine (a palace official with royal privileges) who visited England in 1583 and attended an entertainment prepared for him at Oxford University. **Polonian**: Polish.

20   **perorated**: was versed in rhetorical skills. **Slavonian**: the Slavs were considered to be a rough and barbaric race.

21   rude: uneducated. roll: speak.

22   Attic: Greek; in the early modern period, classical learning was held in high esteem.

23   **Academians**: university scholars; Elizabeth I was often entertained at Oxford and Cambridge, where she replied with ease to speeches in Latin and Greek.

24   **Athenians**: dwellers in the ancient Greek city renowned during the early modern period as the centre for arts and eloquence; here, members of the universities.

26   **punctually accords**: agrees with careful attention to every detail.

27   ravishments: entrancing speeches, with a sexual overtone, as at line 6 above.

28   parliaments: Elizabeth's speeches to Parliament were highly regarded during her own lifetime and in the early seventeenth century; in the late twentieth century the speeches are once more the focus of critical attention (see Notes on the Authors, pp. 350–52).

29–32   **last ... grace**: the 'Golden Speech' of 1601 which is Elizabeth I's most famous address to the House of Commons, and in which she moved from an acceptance of Parliament's monetary controls to a powerful assertion of her own love for the people.

## PATIENCE

Primrose departs from her sources in her choice of patience; indeed, although patience was a virtue considered appropriate for women, Elizabeth's biographies suggest it was not an attribute she herself possessed.

3    **sister**: Mary I.

5    **mot**: motto. *Tanquam Ovis*: Like a Fool.

9    **pent**: imprisoned; Elizabeth was confined in the Tower of London in 1554 and then removed to a country house at Woodstock (for Elizabeth's own poetic response to this situation, see p. 11 above).

15   **Bonner**: Edmund Bonner, Catholic Bishop of London. **beck**: command. **Gardiner**: Stephen Gardiner, Catholic Bishop of Winchester, one of Elizabeth's most stringent opponents.

17   **Susanna**: the story of Susanna is derived from the Apocrypha, where the beautiful and chaste Susanna is watched bathing by some church elders, and when she fails to submit to their sexual approaches is accused falsely by them of being an adulteress; Susanna is finally saved by God's intervention, through the child Daniel.

19   **cross**: misfortune; but, in its depiction of Elizabeth in a Christ-like state, Primrose reveals vehemently Protestant and anti-Catholic sentiments.

## BOUNTY

Primrose chooses a concluding virtue which allows her to commend Elizabeth's international renown.

1–2  **rose ... grace**: the rose and lily, together with the colours white and purple, were commonly associated with the Virgin Mary; Primrose here enacts a common Protestant shift in allowing Elizabeth to appropriate the Mariological iconography.

2    **lustre**: sheen, but also glorious renown.

7–8  **France ... Belgia**: all countries which could be seen to have received some sort of aid from Elizabeth during her reign. In 1562 Elizabeth sent a small number of troops to aid the French Protestants (for another poetic depiction of these events see Anne Dowriche, pp. 18–58); in 1589 English troops had unsuccessfully attempted to free Portugal from Spanish rule; in 1584 Walter Ralegh began to develop the colony of Virginia in the Americas (the settlement which grew up there, however, was uninhabited when in 1590 Elizabeth sent a relief ship to aid the settlers); the reference to Germany is an allusion to the Netherlands campaign of 1585–6 in which the Germanic Protestant states were involved; by imprisoning the Catholic Mary Queen of Scots Elizabeth could be interpreted as having aided the Protestant cause in Scotland; the colonization of Ireland and the repression of the Irish 'rebels' could only be interpreted as 'aid' by a staunch supporter of English Protestantism such as Primrose; line 8 contains another reference to the Netherlands campaign, since Belgium was one of the states that comprised the Protestant alliance of the Low Countries.

11   **Spain's king**: Philip II, whose pro-Catholic stance and territorial acquisitions ran directly against English interests and hence Elizabeth's policy in all the cases mentioned above (lines 7–8).

13   **distaff**: a cleft stick used for spinning; here Primrose mocks Philip II by suggesting that Elizabeth was able to defeat him even though she was a woman armed only with a 'distaff'.

14   **By**: a note in the text adds: 'Elisabetha suit Terra Regina Marisque Primo Jacobi (Elizabeth was queen of land and sea. James I).

16   **he**: a note in the text adds: 'James I'.

**At nos ... asternumqué**: But you, who have been reduced to ashes on the funeral pyre, we shall incessantly and perpetually mourn.

## Alice Sutcliffe

**Acrostic**: a short poem in which the first letter of each line goes to make up a word or phrase.

**Katherine, Duchess of Buckingham**: the widow of George Villiers, 1st Duke of Buckingham; she was the sister-in-law of Susan, Countess of Denbigh, and her daughter married Philip Herbert's son. Hence, the dedicatees of Sutcliffe's poem are all directly related, as well as being part of the Buckingham faction at court.

4   **moul**: mould.

9   **prowess**: excellence.

10   **RUTLAND**: see the note on the title above.

13   **'reaved**: bereft. **turtle**: the turtle dove was considered to be especially faithful to its mate.

15   **e'er ... date**: ever become out of date, forgotten.

**Susanna, Countess of Denbeigh**: Susan, Countess of Denbeigh, was the sister of George Villiers, 1st Duke of Buckingham; she was a well-known patron.

3   **Susanna**: one of the heroines of the Apocrypha, a collection of books which were not approved as part of the Bible, but were acceptable for private study.

**PHILIP, Earl of Pembroke and Montgomery**: Philip Herbert, Earl of Montgomery, and 4th Earl of Pembroke, associated with the Buckingham faction, although his political independence probably means that the dedication was familial (his son married Buckingham's daughter) rather than partisan; he too was a well-known patron of the arts.

2   **guerdon**: reward.

8   **Minerva's infant muse**: in classical mythology, Minerva was the goddess of wisdom, and is therefore fitting inspiration for a spiritual text.

13   **our sex's**: women's; female authors often followed convention by denigrating women's, and therefore their own, ability to write.

15   **coeliac**: of the stomach; i.e. bodily, material.

23   **Deborah**: a prophetess from the Old Testament whose 'song' is preserved in Judges 5:2–31.

*Of our loss ...*

**I Corinthians 15**: full reference, I Corinthians 15:22.

1   **God**: the first eighty lines of the poem refer to Genesis.

6   **sore**: the first in a series of disease images.

38   sorrow ... forth: Genesis 3:16.

51   amiss: error.

79   courage, woman: although Sutcliffe follows convention in blaming women for the fall from grace, she also offers them special encouragement.

81   Be ... head: Genesis 3:15.

83   Lion of Judea: one of Christ's Messianic titles; see Revelation 5:5.

86   mortal wight: human being.

97   amain: with full force.

103   Furies: in classical mythology, avenging deities; Satan appropriately calls upon pagan deities to help him.

108   compass even: steady measure; also a mariner's compass used to plot one's course.

121   Bacchus: in classical mythology, the god of wine.

125   Isaiah: Isaiah 5:22.

131   Paul: I Timothy 5:23.

137   Lot: Genesis 19:30–8.

138   Noah: Genesis 9:20–9.

141   Stolen ... slake: Proverbs 9:17.

151   David: II Samuel 11.

158   tills: lures.

170   Satan ... Hell: Isaiah 14:12–14, and Luke 10:18.

172   Eve: Genesis 3:5.

180   hermaphrodite: a mythical being with both male and female properties; hence pride is equally applicable to both men and women.

181   Judas: John 13:2 and 27, and Mark 14:43.

182   hail: greeting.

185   siren: in classical mythology, a creature, half-woman, half-fish, whose singing lured sailors to their death.

193   Nature ... brothers: Sutcliffe explains the union in the following two stanzas; nature is seen as bodily rather than spiritual, and therefore base like Satan.

204   Pharisee: Mark 7.

212   David's: I Chronicles 21.

219   Samuel: lines 220–8 draw upon I Samuel 15:12–23.

243   dive: penetrate, perceive.

249   Ehud: an Old Testament hero whose slaying of his enemy relied upon deception (Judges 3:15–30).

251–2   In ... live: the Tree of Knowledge and the Cross.

264   herb: a plant useful and attractive to humans; here with the sense of concealment.

271   panther's skin: black was the proverbial colour of the Devil.

274   chaps: mouth, jaws.

279   Benhadad's: lines 279–86 draw upon I Kings 20.

288   Jael ... Sisera: Jael broke the laws of hospitality by killing Sisera, an enemy, within her tent; her actions, however, saved the Israelites, and she was

accorded the role of heroine (Judges 4:21 and 5:24–7). Sutcliffe here contrasts a woman (Jael) favourably with a man (Ahab).

293 **Joab-like:** treacherously; from Joab, who betrayed Abner and killed him (II Samuel 3:26–7).

302 **train:** trick.

315 **Esau:** Genesis 33:1–16.

320 **present:** present way of living.

337 **pared:** cut back, diminished.

354 **operation:** effect; i.e. becoming ill from the poison; i.e. although the taste is bitter, there are no ill effects from Death's potion, as to die means to go to Heaven.

355 **glass:** hour glass.

356 **span:** the duration of human life.

379 **Abraham:** Luke 16:23–6.

396 **bootless:** unavailing.

402 **betime:** in good time.

403 **Belshazzar:** Daniel 5.

407 **endite:** indite, written down.

408 **Thou'rt ... light:** Daniel 5:25.

426 **Ixion:** in classical mythology, Ixion, although indebted to Zeus, attempted to woo his wife, Hera. Zeus retaliated by creating a phantom Hera, who fooled Ixion.

432 **prorogue:** defer.

465 **Hyena-like:** the Hyena was proverbially deceptive.

473 **guerdon:** reward.

## Jane and Elizabeth Cavendish

### The Concealed Fancies

The following verses are taken from *The Concealed Fancies*, a play jointly composed by the two elder Cavendish sisters when they were besieged in Welbeck Abbey during the Civil War. The two extracts (which consist of two complementary 'songs' each) are set pieces of poetry in which the two characters in the play who represent Jane and Elizabeth (Luceny and Tattiney) perform formal elegiac complaints. The first extracts (IV.i.44–56 and 65–8) are sung by Luceny (Jane Cavendish) and Tattiney (Elizabeth Cavendish) when they retire from society in order to grieve for their friends who are involved in the Civil War; their lovers, Courtley and Presumption pursue them, but are spurned in the subsequent verses. The second pieces (V.ii.1–28) mark the ending of the sisters' seclusion, when they begin to acknowledge the darker side of their confinement, both in the play, as nuns, and in reality, as imprisoned by Parliamentary troops. At the close of their songs they are rescued by Courtley and Presumption.

44 **I ... go:** sung by Luceny to Courtley.

45 **profane ... priesthood:** Luceny and Tattiney are dressed as nuns in this

scene, but the whole tone is romantic rather than spiritual, and the sisters quickly shed their disguises at the end of the play when they decide to marry their suitors.

**46  wantonly**: frivolously, with the sense of sexual freedom immediately denied by Luceny.

**49  sacred church**: Luceny's spiritual and sexual roles are here combined so that Courtley's attempts to follow her become both a failure to respect her grief and an assault upon her chastity.

**50  honest**: true to their friends (and therefore the Royalist cause) and chaste.

**51  votes**: votive offerings, prayers.

**52  love ... friends**: a biographical reference, since Jane and Elizabeth's father, William, Duke of Newcastle, and their two brothers were 'absent' fighting for the king.

**54  bay**: another term for 'laurel', symbolizing victory.

**65  Bless ... you**: Tattiney's corresponding response to Presumption.

**1  When ... think**: the first verse is sung by Luceny (v.ii.1–18).

**2  wink**: closing of the eyes.

**6  swound**: swoon, faint.

**13  white ... pray**: white symbolizes innocence; the sheet is both the winding-sheet worn by a corpse, which corresponds with the intimations of death in the previous lines, and the sheet commonly ascribed to ghosts – an allusion which is taken up in the subsequent lines of the song.

**19  My ... look**: the second verse is sung by Tattiney (v.ii.19–28).

**21  delitive**: delightful, pleasant.

## Jane Cavendish

The two subsequent poems were written by Jane alone.

*An Answer to my Lady Alice Egerton's Song*
A note in the text adds: 'Of I prethy send mee back my Hart'. Alice Egerton was the sister of John Egerton, Elizabeth Cavendish's husband, and the daughter of the Earl of Bridgewater; she is best known for having played the part of the Lady in Milton's *Comus*. The poem referred to by Jane Cavendish was included in Henry Lawes's *Ayres and Dialogues ... The Third Book* (1658) but wrongly attributed to Henry Hughes; Egerton's text is worth including here since it also has associations with Elizabeth's verse 'Spoken Upon Receiving ... a Heart' (see p. 259 above).

I prithee send me back my heart,
    Since I cannot have thine;
For if from yours you will not part,
    Why then should you keep mine?

Yet, now I think 'n't, let it lie,
    To send it me were vain;
For th'hast a thief in either eye
    Will steal it back again.

Why should two hearts in one breast lie,
    And yet not lodge together?
Oh Love, where is thy sympathy
    If thus our hearts thou sever?

3   **sentry:** a guard; this commences an extended military metaphor which is notable in that it envisages a full-scale war rather than the more usual association of love with chivalry, thereby reflecting a historical reality rather than a nostalgic evocation of courtly love.

4   **watchman:** a lookout, also a spy.

7   **scouts:** spies. **allay:** means of abatement, help.

8   **face:** oppose (my troops).

12   **net:** capture, entrapment.

*On the Death of My Dear Sister*
The full title is: 'On the Death of My Dear Sister the Countess of Bridgewater, Dying in Childbed, Delivered of a Dead Infant, a Son, the 14th Day of June 1663'. The elegy's title is self-explanatory; the poem was written by Jane when Elizabeth died.

3   **heaven:** a conventional elegiac image, but one that appears to have been based on fact; Elizabeth's piety is evidenced in her manuscript book, *True Copies of Certain Loose Papers Left by the Right Honourable Elizabeth Countess of Bridgewater*.

9   **ere:** ever.

17   **vale:** farewell, address.

## Elizabeth Cavendish

The two final poems were written by Elizabeth.

*On My Boy Henry*
In June 1656 Elizabeth gave birth to a boy, named Henry, who died twenty-nine days later; Elizabeth's manuscript book, *True Copies of Certain Loose Papers Left by the Right Honourable Elizabeth Countess of Bridgewater*, also contains prose accounts of the deaths of two other children, Frances and Catherine.

5   **It:** the child.

9   **high:** in heaven.

10   **cry:** the cry which denoted the baby's death.

*Spoken Upon Receiving a Cake of Perfume Made up in the Shape of a Heart*
The most likely donor of this gift is Elizabeth's husband, John Egerton, since his love for her was clearly recorded on his tomb, where he asserted that she was the 'Best of Wives'. The cake of perfume was most probably made of wax (for burning and perfuming a room) or, less likely of soap.

1   **it:** the perfume heart, but also the idea of the heart and therefore their love (also at lines 4 and 6 below.)

## Anne Bradstreet

*In Honour of ... Elizabeth*

**Title Elizabeth**: Elizabeth I, a choice of subject-matter which indicates Bradstreet's allegiance to English literary subjects as well as her focus upon female characters and historical personages.

**Memory**: an elegy, aligning Bradstreet with several other women poets in this anthology (Anne Cecil de Vere, Mary Sidney and Jane Cavendish).

*Proem*: this short introductory poem includes a traditional disclaimer in which Bradstreet declares that her verse is not as worthy or fine as that which is written by other poets; interestingly, however, she does not make her sex an excuse.

**3 every clime**: every region or country: that is, in the Americas as well as England.

**6 rapts**: holds the attention of.

**9 out of date**: Elizabeth I died in 1603, while Bradstreet first published this poem in 1650.

**11 hecatombs**: great public sacrifices.

**15 erst**: formerly.

**19 Phoenix**: Elizabeth I was often compared to the phoenix, the mythological bird which arose from the ashes of its own funeral pyre; here Bradstreet claims that no literary work can raise the memory of Elizabeth in a way that equals her achievements in life. **Spenser**: Edmund Spenser, the author of *The Faerie Queene*, an allegorical epic dedicated to Elizabeth I; Spenser was one of the key poetic influences on Bradstreet.

**20 Speed's nor Camden's**: John Speed, *The History of Great Britain*, and William Camden, *Annales*, recorded the life of Elizabeth I.

**21 e'er compact**: ever summarize.

**24 'leven Olympiads**: a reference to the four-year gap between the Olympic games; hence the forty-four years of Elizabeth's reign.

**26 kings**: monarchs, but with a gendered overtone.

**30 rex**: king; Bradstreet continues the theatre metaphor begun at line 22 above.

**29 She ... sex**: Elizabeth has proved that women are not inadequate rulers as many (male) scholars suggest; Bradstreet continues this defence of women throughout the poem.

**31-2 Spain's ... cost**: Philip II of Spain attempted to invade Britain with a fleet of ships, the Spanish Armada, in 1588; his defeat was considered one of the highlights of Elizabeth's reign.

**33-4 Salic ... queen**: the Salic Law forbade women to inherit the crown in France; here Bradstreet suggests that the French would have evaded such a law if they could have had a monarch as great as Elizabeth I.

**35 doctors**: scholars, especially those who attacked the idea of a woman monarch, and perhaps a covert attack upon John Knox, whose *The First Blast of the Trumpet Against the Monstrous Regiment of Women* (1558) was the most renowned denunciation of early modern female rulership.

**37-9 Sun ... man**: a series of seemingly impossible opposites. The sun must perpetually move through the skies, running a 'race' that can never be finished ('run'); at New Year the earth is simultaneously at the end of the 'old' year and at the start of the 'new' year; while the 'unmanly man' probably refers to the hermaphrodite, a mythological being who was half-man, half-woman, and was supposed to have inhabited earth at the start of time (Spenser draws upon this myth in *The Faerie Queene*, II.xii; 1590 edition).

**42**    stirs: wars.

**44–6**    Her … Armado: the description of the sea battles begins with a reference to the rivalry of England and Spain for the wealth of the Americas and concludes with a reference to the sinking of the Spanish Armada (see note to lines 31–2 above).

**46**    wracked: destroyed.

**47–8**    Her … install: the Portuguese expedition of 1589, which was condoned by Elizabeth I, was intended finally to destroy the Spanish fleet, to liberate Portugal from Spanish control, and to install Don Anthony on the Portuguese throne; the action proved futile and the advance on Lisbon ended in a demoralized withdrawal.

**48**    in's: in his.

**49**    She … king: Elizabeth's aid given to the Protestant King Henry IV of France; again this support proved fruitless, since Henry ultimately converted to Catholicism.

**50**    states: of the Protestant Netherlands, which were sent aid by Elizabeth I in their battle against the Catholic powers of Spain.

**51**    protectrix: a female protector.

**52**    dread virago: a revered, or feared, female warrior, an Amazon.

**53**    nobles: a general reference to those who lost their life in the Netherlands campaign of the mid-1580s, but more specifically to Sir Philip Sidney, who died at the battle of Zutphen in 1586; Sidney had considerable poetic influence on Bradstreet, and she wrote 'An Elegy Upon Sir Philip Sidney' in his memory (see Notes on the Authors, pp. 370–3).

**55**    Irish … quell: the continual attempts by the Elizabethan state to colonize Ireland; more specifically, the Irish campaigns of the 1590s led by the Earl of Essex.

**56**    Tyrone: Hugh O'Neill, Earl of Tyrone, the Irish nobleman (or 'rebel' to the English) who fought against British troops in the Ulster rebellion of 1595, and afterwards against the forces of the Earl of Essex.

**58**    Minerva: in Roman mythology, the goddess of wisdom; connected to the Greek goddess Athene (see line 60 below) and often used to figure Elizabeth I.

**60**    Pallas: Pallas Athene, the Greek goddess of wisdom; she was also associated with virginity and as such was commonly used to represent Elizabeth I.

**61**    world did round: a reference to Sir Francis Drake, whose circumnavigation of the globe in 1577–80 passed through the Straits of Magellan.

**62**    *Terra incognita*: unknown or unexplored land (Latin); in the early modern period this term was most commonly used to describe the Americas.

**63**    Drake: Sir Francis Drake, one of the most popular and successful seamen of Elizabeth I's reign.

**64**    Essex: Robert Devereux, Earl of Essex, who had mixed success in his military endeavours; he was triumphant in the 1587 sacking of Cadiz and destruction of the Spanish fleet, but failed miserably in the Irish campaign of the late 1590s. **Herculean hold**: Hercules was a celebrated hero in Greek mythology and renowned for his strength; hence, 'a strong and powerful hold'.

67 **Semiramis**: a legendary Syrian queen who was renowned for her power, beauty and wealth; Bradstreet also focuses on her in *The Four Monarchies*, and the source for both is Walter Ralegh's *The History of the World*. Semiramis is the first of a series of famous women, all of whom Bradstreet claims cannot compare with Elizabeth I.

69 **Babel's**: Bradstreet here amalgamates two characteristics of the ancient Assyrian city of Babel; she undoubtedly refers to the infamous Tower of Babel (Genesis 11:1–11), which was considered a symbol of worldly pride and meaningless discourse, but she also suggests, through the word 'walls', the material luxury of the Hanging Gardens of Babylon, one of the seven wonders of the ancient world. In both cases Bradstreet stresses the insubstantial nature of worldly fame.

71 **Tomris**: Tomyris, the Amazon warrior queen of the Scythians, who killed Cyrus, the Persian commander, in battle.

73 **Amazon ... Tilbury**: Elizabeth I made a powerful and well-known speech to her troops before their battle against the Spanish Armada; in it she proclaimed herself a warrior queen, and this led to numerous representations of her, both literary and pictorial, in Amazon mode.

77 **Dido**: the queen of Carthage whose abandonment by Aeneas and subsequent suicide are recounted in Virgil's *Aeneid*; she was also called 'Elissa', hence the reference to 'Eliza' at line 79 below.

81 **Cleopatra**: the legendary queen of Egypt, who was best-known in the early modern period for her adultery with Mark Antony; Bradstreet follows this negative interpretation by referring to the meaning of Cleopatra's name, 'glory to the father/fatherland'. However, several women authors of this period, such as Mary Sidney in *The Tragedy of Antonie* (1595), chose to defend Cleopatra.

85 **Zenobya**: Zenobia, queen of Palmyra, whose ambition caused her to claim the title 'Queen of the East'; she was defeated by the Roman emperor Aurelian.

89–90 **She ... she**: a complex use of pronouns, meaning: Zenobia was a phoenix-like queen as was Elizabeth I, but Zenobia did not rise phoenix-like from the ashes in verse, or spiritually, as did Elizabeth.

92 **Heleconian well**: Mount Helicon, on which stood the fountains of the Muses, classical deities of poetic inspiration.

93 **I may not**: an ironic disclaimer of literary activity, since the line is in itself found in a poem praising Elizabeth I; the key may be found in the 'his' of the previous line (92), suggesting that poets are all men, and in the next but one line (95) which proclaims the worth of women: here, both Elizabeth I as ruler and Bradstreet as poet.

97 **taxed**: accused.

99 **such**: the debate about women is a common theme for the women poets represented in this anthology; probably the most outspoken against such 'slander' was Rachel Speght (see pp. 154–82 above).

105   **Full fraught**: completely laden, replete.

106   **Titan**: the sun in classical mythology.

106–7   **set ... set ... set**: threefold pun, meaning 'the days she set (ordained, ruled over) were replete with riches and honour, as she set (descended) on the earth with a glory like the sun's, but no more will such a sun rise or set (as in sunset)'.

108   **heaven's ... revolution**: the Day of Judgement, when it is thought that all those true Christians saved by God would be resurrected in the body as well as the spirit: in other words, would regain their 'old forms'.

110   **Albion**: Britain; however, in the millenarian version of the last four lines of the poem, Britain becomes the new earth of the righteous, and, by implication, Eliza takes on a Messianic role as its ruler. Thus, in a startling shift, Bradstreet moves from a political poem replete with classical allusion, to a spiritual vindication of English Protestantism as embodied by a woman ruler and described by a woman poet.

*The Vanity of All Worldly Things*

6   **they**: those who have gained honour on earth.

7   **turn their fate**: an allusion to the Wheel of Fortune, which, constantly turning, brings those down who were formally elevated.

23   **wisest ... men**: see Ecclesiastes 1:2.

27   **stoics**: those who followed the philosophy of patient endurance and the repression of emotion; stoicism was particularly popular as a dominant principle in early modern drama, but failed to appeal to the mid-seventeenth century Protestant authors such as Bradstreet and Milton.

29   **stocks**: blockheads, with a pun on 'stoics'.

33   **sound**: investigate.

34   *summum bonum*: supreme good. **stay**: compose.

37   **living crystal fount**: the waters of eternal life in Biblical tradition (Jeremiah 17:13, and Psalms 36:9).

47   **conceit**: fancy or imagination.

51   **pearl ... tree ... spring**: all Biblical references denoting spiritual rather than material worth; see Matthew 13:45–6, Genesis 3:22, and Psalms 36:9.

52   **king**: in heaven, rather than on earth.

54   **his**: Christ's, the crown of grace that was given to Christians on the Day of Judgement (II Timothy 4:8).

*The Author to Her Book*

A reference to Bradstreet's *The Tenth Muse*, which was published in 1650 without her knowledge (see Notes on the Authors, pp. 370–3 below); the present poem was probably written in 1666, when a new edition of her works was first thought of, but was not published until 1678.

15   **feet**: a pun on feet as parts of the body, and the metrical feet of poetry.

16   **meet**: appropriate.

19   **vulgars**: common people who like popular writing, rather than the sophisticated critics of the next line.

*Before the Birth of One of her Children*
This poem appears, with twelve others, under the heading 'Several Other Poems Made by the Author upon Diverse Occasions, were found among her Papers after her Death, which she never meant should come to public view; amongst which, these following (at the desire of some friends that knew her well) are here inserted'. The theme of the poem was not uncommon: see, for example, Elizabeth Joceline's *The Mother's Legacie to her unborne Childe* (1624), although Bradstreet addresses her husband, not the baby.

13   half ... due: proverbially, the allotted life span was 70 years; Bradstreet implies here that she is not yet 35.

22   dear: precious; the 'Dear' of line 7 above refers to her husband.

24   step-dame's: stepmother's.

*A Letter to Her Husband, Absent Upon Public Employment*
Simon Bradstreet was frequently involved in the new colony's business affairs.

2   magazine: storehouse.

4   Ipswich: Ipswich, Massachusetts, where the Bradstreets lived from 1635/6 until 1646.

8   My ... zodiac: in astrology the sun moves through the signs of the zodiac determining one's fortune; here 'My sun' is Bradstreet's husband, as at line 12 below.

12   Sol: sun, a reference to Bradstreet's husband. Capricorn: the sign of the zodiac running from 22 December to 20 January, therefore signifying winter and the emotional chill of separation.

14   fruits: children.

17   southward: towards Boston, where most of the new colony's official business took place.

21   Cancer: the sign of the zodiac running from 22 June to 23 July, hence signifying summer and the warmth of reconciliation.

24   nature's sad decree: death.

25   Flesh ... bone: see Genesis 2:23.

*On My Dear Grandchild*
Title   Simon Bradstreet: Anne Bradstreet's grandson by her oldest son, Samuel, and his wife, Mercy Tyng.

3   Three flowers: three children; the first two sisters had died and Simon, the third child, is 'the last i' th' bud'. Of the other two children born to Samuel and Mercy, only one, Mercy, survived.

4   yet: the assertion of God's goodness in the face of misfortune was conventional, but is perhaps tacitly questioned by the word 'yet'.

10   crosses: misfortunes.

*Here Follows Some Verses Upon the Burning of Our House*
This poem was first published in John Harvard Ellis's 1867 edition of Bradstreet's works; before that it existed only in a family notebook which contains holograph poems by Bradstreet herself and copies made of her works by her husband (the present poem belongs to the latter category). I have followed the convention set by Jeannine Hensley in her standard 1967 edition of

Bradstreet's works in placing this after the 1650 and 1678 poems; in Hensley's text the 1867 poems are identified as the 'Andover Manuscripts'. The poem exemplifies the later 'domestic' poems, but at the same time presents an archetypal representation of pioneer life in the Americas and, as such, demonstrates Bradstreet's movement away from the scholarly influences of the Old World to the personal immediacy of New World writing.

14  blest His name: the ambivalence felt by Bradstreet about the trials which beset her (ill-health, the death of her close relatives, and the burning of her house) is demonstrated in this poem through the close conjunction of a stated acceptance of God's will and a powerful evocation of the previous domestic harmony of her material life.

26  store: accumulation of goods (see also line 52 below).

36  vanity: insubstantial, an illusion; for a formal and less personal treatment of this theme, see the 1650 poem 'The Vanity of All Worldly Things' (pp. 263–4 above).

37  gin: begin.

39  mold'ring: crumbling.

44  mighty Architect: God.

47  purchased and paid for: the beginning of eight lines of material imagery which, by its very presence, undercuts the overall dismissal of worldly goods in the rest of the poem.

52  pelf: property.

# NOTES ON THE AUTHORS

ISABELLA WHITNEY (fl. 1567–78) is unusual in any collection of early modern women authors, particularly those of the sixteenth century, in that she did not come from a noble family and, as she makes perfectly clear in her work, had very little economic security; in other words, she did not possess the 'room of one's own' and regular income deemed by Virginia Woolf to be essential to female literary production. Yet this penniless young woman, who left her home in Cheshire to enter service in London, demonstrated an acute awareness of public taste which, combined with a sharp satirical tone, allowed her to become one of the earliest professional women writers in Europe, and the first English-woman to publish a book of poems. Indeed, Whitney's canon seems to be expanding: her two best-known works, *The Copy of a Letter, lately written in metre, by a young Gentlewoman to her unconstant Lover* (1567) and *A Sweet Nosegay, or Plesant Posy* (1573), have been augmented by *The Lamentation of a Gentlewoman upon the Death of her Late-Deceased Friend, William Gruffith, Gentleman* (1578), and it is likely that she contributed to further anthologies and collections which have not yet been identified. If we accept, as most critics do, that her work contains a certain degree of autobiographical material, then the reason for these literary forays was primarily to supplement her meagre income, and this would certainly correspond to her choice of the popular ballad metre and her lively reworkings of popular themes and genres. The two connected poems included in this collection, *A Communication Which the Author had to London Before She Made Her Will* and *The Manner of Her Will, and What She Left to London and to All Those in it, of Her Departing* (included in *A Sweet Nosegay*), both comply with the need to attract a popular readership with their animated and witty descriptions of everyday life. Moreover, it was this evocation of the hectic and festive life in sixteenth-century London that first captivated feminist critics such as Betty Travitsky (in 'The "Wyll and Testament" of Isabella Whitney' (1980) and *The Paradise of Women* (1981)) and that brought Whitney's work back into the canon. However, more recent research has suggested that the *Will* poems, together with her other writings, are far more complex than was originally supposed.

Investigation into Whitney's identity has revealed that her brother, Geoffrey Whitney, also published poetry (*Whitney's Choice of Emblems* (1586)) and that her family was reformist, allowing the daughters as well as sons access to a certain degree of humanist education. This recognition of her scholarship throws Whitney's self-conscious manipulation of genres, such as elegy, complaint and satire, into sharp relief and enables us to see her reworking of other texts, such as Hugh Plat's *The Floures of Philosophie* (1572), as ironic commentary rather than derivative imitation (as is suggested by Fehrenbach (1983)). Indeed, although *The Manner of Her Will* begins with a mock inversion of the formal testament (it turns out Whitney has nothing to leave London but what it already owns) and with a sprightly panoply of materialism, a third of the way through, the poem turns into a darker comment upon the profligacy, immorality and social injustice of the city it initially appears to celebrate. The tone shifts to an even blacker key as the city satire develops into a powerful evocation of, and implicit attack upon, London's prisons, public punishments (including hanging) and insane asylums. Then, in a final twist back upon its own social focus, the poem reclaims both its literary identity and its emblematic status as the poet brings the text to a moment of closure and a recognition of absence. The complex movement of the poems, together with their stylistic sophistication, has allowed recent criticism to locate several diverse discourses. The social realism identified early on by Betty Travitsky has been expanded by Elaine V. Beilin in 'Writing Public Poetry: Humanism and the Woman Writer' (1990), Krontiris (1992) and Martin (1997) to reveal a powerful political invective against the disparity of wealth between upper and lower classes, and an acute grasp of commercial and economic structures. Beilin also identifies a strong Christian tradition of Protestant teaching, and this is followed by Schleiner (1994). By contrast, Martin suggests that Whitney continually identifies with the marginalized and dispossessed groups in society (the poor, the imprisoned and the insane). Finally, the literary radicalism of the texts is explored by Jones (1990) and by Wall (1991); both critics demonstrate how Whitney took the dominant male love discourses of the period (Ovidian and Petrarchan respectively) and succeeded in inverting and undercutting them in order to privilege a female perspective. Isabella Whitney was therefore a pioneer in more ways than one; she wrote and published her poetry when it was neither fashionable nor expected for a woman, especially one from the middle classes, to do so. In addition, she produced popular material that would have been accessible to her own class as well as to the literary elite, and this same class-consciousness pervaded her work, making for stringent political comment as well as for witty and lively verse satire. Finally, she was acutely aware of her own gender role and consistently challenged and overcame male domination of the foremost literary discourses of her day. Given such a wealth of material it is hardly surprising that since the first modern edition of the *Will* poems appeared in Travitsky (1980), and a facsimile edition of her works was edited by Panofsky (1982), Whitney has become a popular early modern woman poet for editors and critics alike. Moreover, as there is still much to be uncovered in her work, this interest is certain to continue.

The poems included here are taken from *A Sweet Nosegay, or Pleasant Posy* (1573).

ELIZABETH I (1533–1603) is unique amongst the women poets collected in this anthology since she was pre-eminent in her own period and has been equally lauded through the subsequent centuries. When she was alive her every movement was recorded and subjected to scrutiny, at first to police her political ambitions and later, once she had acceded to the throne, to analyse the complex interweaving of court stratagems. After her death, her biography became well charted, and in recent times it has been the subject of numerous media representations, from Hollywood movies to BBC 'heritage' serials. By comparison with poets like Diana Primrose, about whom nothing is known, there is almost too much information on Elizabeth I to be included in a brief note such as this. However, while there has been a veritable industry and/or 'cult' built about the queen's image, her personality, her court and her reign, very little attention has been given to her writings. Indeed, while her speeches were applauded and her poems anthologized during her lifetime, in later years her authorship was increasingly questioned, so that it is only recently, thanks to the work of critics such as Frances Teague, Steven W. May and Carole Levin, that Elizabeth I is once more being credited with a canon of literary and political texts. The eight poems collected here are now regarded as her original poems, although it is expected that this number will increase as further research into the queen as an independent author continues.

The number of excellent biographies available, such as Somerset (1991), render a full account of the queen's life obsolete; however, it is important to note several key events in her life as they relate strongly to her literary concerns. There are roughly three relevant discourses: political, romantic and temporal. The first four poems collected here, 'Woodstock: the Window Poem', 'Woodstock: the Shutter Poem', 'French Psalter Poem' and 'The Doubt of Future Foes', all focus upon Elizabeth's concerns for her political safety. Of these the first two were written during Elizabeth's imprisonment in Woodstock on the orders of Mary I, her sister. Both refer to the injustice of her punishment and, while complaining about fate, clearly also complain about her sister's sense of fairness. The Psalter poem cannot be firmly dated, but the similarity of tone and theme confirm that it too was written before Elizabeth became queen. The final poem in this group, 'The Doubt of Future Foes', was most probably written when Mary Stuart, Queen of Scotland, took refuge in England in 1568. Mary became the focus of Catholic plots to overthrow Elizabeth, and in an ironic echo of her sister's caution, Elizabeth chose to imprison Mary in a series of castles and manors until her eventual execution in 1587. Although Elizabeth was by this time firmly established, the poem betrays doubts about the stability of her reign as well as real fears concerning Mary's threat to the throne.

The second group of poems consists of two texts, 'On Monsieur's Departure' and 'An Answer'. The occasion of the first's composition is uncertain, for while the name 'Monsieur' was given by Elizabeth to the last of her formal suitors, Francis, Duke of Alençon, the text was found amongst papers which relate to the Earl of Essex, the ambitious young courtier who wooed the queen in her old age. The second poem was written in answer to one by Sir Walter Ralegh on the occasion of his banishment from court and affirms the queen's affection for her court favourite. Whichever of these men is addressed in the poems, all comply with the discourse of courtly love used between the ageing queen and her youthful male courtiers, and as such they must be read not as statements of personal desire, but as part of a formal literary code.

Finally, the last two poems, 'Now Leave and Let Me Rest' and 'When I Was Fair and Young', are both undated but their predominant concerns – mortality, time and age – suggest that they were composed late in Elizabeth's reign. Both regret the passing of youth and of the joys of love, but both acknowledge the inevitability of ageing, the former with a turning to moral truths and the latter with a wry self-parody. This last group may clearly be read as autobiographical, in the same manner as the other five poems collected here. However, this is a key issue, for although it is easy to allow Elizabeth I's amply documented life to dominate any interpretation of her verse, at the same time her writing participates in common early modern discourses. The themes of politics, love and time found in her poetry were dominant concepts of the period and affirm that Elizabeth I should not only be read as exceptional, but as a Renaissance woman poet whose verse cannot be separated from the works by the lesser-known authors represented in this collection.

Of the numerous editings of Elizabeth's verse, the most useful editions are Bradner (1964) and the selections in May (1991); both have been consulted in the preparation of this anthology.

ANNE CECIL DE VERE (1556–88) belonged to the learned and illustrious Cooke family through her mother, Mildred Cooke; her father was William Cecil, Lord Burleigh. While it is readily accepted that Anne's father scaled the heights of political success, becoming Elizabeth I's trusted advisor for over forty years, the particular achievement of her mother has only recently been re-excavated. Mildred Cooke was one of the four daughters of Sir Anthony Cooke, who in good, but not common, humanist fashion provided his progeny with an excellent education regardless of their sex. Each woman became an author in her own right, being particularly skilled in translation. Moreover, each sister bequeathed her literary interest to her own family, again to male and female heirs alike. As such, Anne Cecil could count amongst her family eight women writers: her mother; three aunts (Anne Bacon, Elizabeth Hoby and Katherine Killigrew); through marriage, Margaret Hoby and Margaret Russell; and, in the subsequent generation, Anne Clifford and Lucy Harrington. It would, therefore, have been perfectly acceptable, even expected, for Anne Cecil to write poetry, or perhaps to follow her mother in translating verses, and it is from this sense of her background that we must approach the recent disputes about the authorship of her sonnets.

Anne de Vere's sonnets were first published in John Soowthern's (or Southern's) poetry collection *Pandora* (1584), which is dedicated to Anne's husband, Edward de Vere, Seventeenth Earl of Oxford (they had married in 1571), and which provides a clear and undisputed attribution to the countess. In subsequent editions and compilations the poems were consistently ascribed to Anne de Vere, and a modern edition of the text was provided by Ellen Moody in 1989. Following this, a debate about authorship has arisen, initiated by May (1992), where he argues that the stylistic similarities with Soowthern's own work suggest that he had written the sonnets himself and, in an act of prosopopoeia, attributed them to his patron's wife (another poem is said to be by Elizabeth I, and May offers a similar argument for this piece). Smith (1994) follows May and traces a number of similarities with the sonnets of the French poet Philippe Desportes in *Cartels de masquarades, épitaphes* (1573). On the other hand, Schleiner (1994) challenges May's hypothesis, offering a number of stylistic variants between the verses of Soowthern and those of de Vere, a biographical reading of the disputed texts, and a number of other sources which suggest an author versed in the discourses of the English court. These last two points need further explication: first, Edward de Vere appears to have married Anne partly on the understanding that her father would clear his debts, and when this failed to happen, he falsely accused her of adultery and disowned her for the next six years. On their reconciliation in the early 1580s, Anne attempted to embrace the Euphuistic, quasi-Catholic style adopted by her husband, who was himself a poet, and by those writers to whom he offered patronage, including John Lyly, Thomas Watson and, of course, Soowthern. It is from this milieu that Schleiner traces the influence of Ovid's *Metamorphoses* and *Amores*, and Lyly's *Euphues*, as well as the sonnets of Ronsard and Petrarch. In 1583 Anne gave birth to a son, the Lord Bulbeck of the sonnets; as the male heir he would have been valued far more highly than any daughters, and his death in 1584 would have signified not only the demise of a much-loved child, but also the failure of Anne's hopes for a permanent reconciliation with her husband. The poignancy of the poems can thus be read as a personal statement and not merely as a complex reworking of early modern poetic discourses. These arguments are also offered by Walker (1996), who links Anne's elegies into a whole tradition of elegiac writing by Renaissance women poets, and particularly to that of her mother and aunts.

While it is important to investigate attributions to all writers, not only female authors, of the early modern period, the stylistic and historical evidence suggests that Anne de Vere did compose the sonnets; indeed, considering there was no disclaimer made at the time of their publication, which was a commonplace for female authors even when they *had* written the text in question, it seems somewhat overscrupulous to challenge the ascription four hundred years later. The importance of such debate, however, cannot be questioned, and in this instance has resulted in a range of evidence which allows us to draw important conclusions about Anne de Vere's writing. Her indebtedness to her familial literary inheritance is clear from the tendency to translate from Latin, Italian and French sources, although here, as with Mary Sidney's Psalms (some of which are edited in this volume), translation should be interpreted as a loose reworking, rather than a close rendition. The sonnets also, by way of their personal tone, align Anne de Vere with the autobiographical mode favoured by early modern women writers, not least in her own extended family. Finally, the Euphuistic and Ovidian references in her poetry allow us to reread the dominant court discourses of the Elizabethan age from a female perspective. It is, therefore, unfortunate that we have so few of Anne de Vere's poems extant, and, rather than questioning the authorship of those we do possess, perhaps we should be investigating manuscript material to find more.

The poems included here may be found in John Soowthern's *Pandora, the Musique of the Beautie, of his Mistresse Diana* (1584).

ANNE DOWRICHE (d. 1638) is one of the first English women writers to adopt a political topic and tone, although, in common with her male peers, she tended to conceal her historical message within a spiritual discourse. As such, her major work, *The French History* (1589), must be read as one of the important contributions to that particularly hybrid form of discourse, English Protestantism, with its combination of religious fervour, Biblical allusion, national pride and overt praise for Elizabeth I, herself a symbol of the singular union between Church and State. Dowriche sets out to record the events in France which led up to the massacre of 30–50,000 Protestants on St Bartholomew's Day 1572, focusing upon three key episodes in the persecution of the reformists: the slaughter of those attending a prayer meeting in 1557, the execution of Annas Burgeus in 1559, and the murder of Gaspard de Coligny in 1572. The reason Dowriche chose this topic in the late 1580s was that after years of oppression the European Protestants appeared to be gaining ascendancy; England had defeated the Spanish Armada; the Catholic Duke of Guise, the prime instigator of the Bartholomew's Day outrage, had been assassinated; and the heir to the French throne was at that point a Protestant, Henry of Navarre. For her sources she chose more contemporary accounts: Jean de Serres's *The Three Parts of Commentaries containing the whole and perfect discourse of the Civil Wars of France* (1573), the tenth book of which, *True and Plain Report of the Furious Outrages of France*, was written by François Hotman, and the translation of the whole of this work into English by Thomas Tymme in 1574. Intriguingly, the framing device Dowriche adopts for her poem depicts a Frenchman explaining to an Englishman (who is noted as 'the author') what has happened in France, and considering her open acknowledgement of sources throughout the text, it is highly likely that these 'characters' represent de Serres and Tymme respectively. However, the device also serves to protect Dowriche's sex, for she is acutely aware that female authorship was neither common nor admired, commenting defensively in her dedication 'that it is a woman's doing'. But it is essential to realize that *The French History* is not a translation, nor even heavily indebted to the male-authored commentaries Dowriche draws upon, for, along with the assertion of her sex, she defends her choice of the poetic form: 'to restore again some credit ... unto Poetry' and to ensure that 'the matter [is] framed to the better liking of some men's fantasies'. In other words, Dowriche follows the precepts of that other English Protestant family, the Sidneys, by choosing a serious subject for her poetic composition, and by self-consciously aiming both to teach and to delight her readership. It is therefore important to recognize, in conjunction with the more obvious historical material, the text's indebtedness to the providential narrative of the early modern Protestant tradition, the influence of Foxe in the construction of the martyrs' characters, and the use of Biblical exemplars. Finally, and most significantly, Dowriche chooses to 'delight' her readership not with the complex verse forms of the Sidneys (as evidenced in Mary Sidney's Psalm translations in this collection), but with the dramatic poetry and powerful characterization of the public stage. For example, the monologue by Catherine de Medici, who encapsulates the English version of Machiavellian villainy, may easily be placed alongside the prologue to Marlowe's *The Jew of Malta* (1589) and the speeches by Lady Macbeth in Shakespeare's tragedy. Indeed, Marlowe drew on the same sources as Dowriche in his *Massacre at Paris* (c. 1592). This theatrical resonance is aided by the fast-moving verse form (poulter's measure) and the bloodthirsty descriptions common in revenge tragedy.

Considering the complexity and power of *The French History*, it is unfortunate that we know so little of Dowriche's life; she was the daughter of Sir Richard Edgecombe and Margaret Lutterall, and married Hugh Dowriche c. 1580. Her husband, who became the rector of Honiton, Devon, in 1587, also had literary inclinations, and his one extant work, *The Gaoler's Conversion* (1596), contains some dedicatory verses by Anne.

Criticism on Dowriche, and editions of her work, are still very limited, although the renewed interest in female authorship and political discourses of the early modern period should ensure a rapid growth in material available on her. Some of *The French History* was excerpted in Travitsky (1981), although she wrongly ascribes the text to Anne Trefusis (Anne Dowriche's niece). A short piece appears in *The Penguin Book of Renaissance Verse* (1992), edited by H. R. Woudhuysen, and much longer and more carefully edited passages are included in *Women Writers in Renaissance England* (1997), edited by Randall Martin. Beilin (1987 and 1990) has contributed two critical pieces on Dowriche which locate her firmly within the major discourses of the period: humanism, English Protestantism, political intrigue, and the language of the public theatre. Finally Walker (1996) comprehensively covers similar ground to Beilin, but also looks at specifically literary formulations such as metre and metaphor.

The text included here is taken from *The French History. That is, a lamentable discourse of three of the chief and most famous bloody broils that have happened in France for the gospel of Jesus Christ* (1589).

MARY SIDNEY (1561–1621) is most commonly known by her maiden name 'Sidney', but occasionally references to her work are found under her married name 'Herbert' or under her title, the 'Countess of Pembroke'. The cause of this variation developed in her own lifetime, for Mary Sidney retained and emphasized her connections with the culturally elite Sidney family, particularly stressing the links with her renowned brother Sir Philip Sidney, while at court she was known primarily by her married name and title. Thus, like her niece Mary Wroth, who is also anthologized in this collection, Mary Sidney cultivated a double identity, which allowed her both to evade the strictures placed upon women of the period, and thereby to assert a certain literary independence, and at the same time to conform to the early modern ideal of womanhood by being chaste, obedient and devout. This combination of compliance and radicalism is likewise evident in her work, for Mary Sidney's canon comprises mainly translations (her play *The Tragedy of Antonie* is translated from Robert Garnier's *Marc Antoine*, while her major work is a translation of the Psalms), but translations which depart so considerably from their original that they clearly lay claim to originality. In addition, although her ideas appear primarily to further the concerns of her dead brother, when examined closely they also exhibit a marked individualism. It is this split allegiance that enabled the more conservative critics of her own age and throughout the centuries to praise Mary Sidney for her familial duty and spiritual piety, while, more recently, allowing feminist critics to claim her as the first woman to forge an undisputed place in the English canon. These divergences inevitably raise the question of how we are to approach Mary Sidney's poetry, and of how we should interpret material which seems to have divided readers and critics for over four hundred years.

A useful starting-point is Sidney's biography. She was born into the most culturally accomplished family of her age: her brothers Philip and Robert were both writers, the former recognized as one of the key authors of the European Renaissance, while her son and her niece continued the tradition into the subsequent generation. Yet it is unlikely that she began to write until 1586, after her marriage and the birth of her four children, and in the year her parents and Philip died. This seems to have proved a watershed for Sidney, for she began to cultivate her role as one of the greatest literary patrons of the time, to invite writers and artists to her home, Wilton House, although the idea of a formal 'academy' has recently been questioned, and to continue work on Philip's literary projects. Her editing of Philip's *Arcadia*, and her continuation of the Psalm translations (Philip translated the first 43 and Mary the remaining 107) are perhaps her best-known works of this period, but already she was beginning to depart from her brother's original formulations. The Psalms, which she reworked continually over the next thirteen years unmistakably displayed her own concerns. Their metrical innovations, conversational tone and material imagery all served to transform the spiritual verse of the period into a secularized discourse which was to be adopted by the Metaphysical poets, especially Donne, Herbert and Vaughan. Moreover, rather than restricting her sources to the works of her brother, she seems to have read most of the Protestant versions of, and commentaries on, the Psalms written in English, French and Latin, and, as such, her work exhibits that distinctive combination of spiritualism and politics peculiar to early modern English Protestantism. Thus, while Mary Sidney's Psalm translations initially appear mere appendages to her brother's pre-eminent accomplishments, they are now acknowledged as innovative and influential in their own right.

Mary Sidney's other translations have benefited from similar re-evaluations. For example, *The Tragedy of Antonie* is no longer seen as derivative from Garnier's original and as complying with Philip's attempts to restore classical conventions to the English stage; instead, the metrical changes and contemporary allegory adopted by Sidney are seen to echo the dominant dramatic discourses of Marlowe and Shakespeare, with their powerful soliloquies and acute political commentary. The dramatic speeches included in this collection demonstrate the ease with which the play could have been performed on the public stage had not their author been prohibited from such a venture by her sex and class. The two further translations in her canon, Petrarch's *The Triumph of Death* (c. 1600) and Philippe de Mornay's *A Discourse of Life and Death* (1592), have both been re-examined in light of their focus upon death and a female specificity. However, although it is highly likely that Mary Sidney also produced a considerable quantity of her own original verse, her extant canon consists of only three clearly attributable poems, all of which are included in this collection. Like the Psalms, they combine politics and religion, as well as participating in the dominant literary discourses of their day. There is a final disputed poem,

'The Dolefull Lay of Chlorinda', which was originally included in Edmund Spenser's *Astrophil* (1595), a collection of elegies to Philip Sidney. The unresolved debate about authorship focuses upon whether Mary Sidney authored the poem, or whether Spenser assumed her persona in penning the verses himself. The evidence available does not merit inclusion of 'Chlorinda' in this collection, but it may be found in Betty Travitsky (1981).

The body of critical material on Mary Sidney is considerable, and it would be impossible to mention all the important works in this brief note; therefore, while naming a few key works, I should also like to point readers towards the excellent bibliographies produced by the late Josephine Roberts, which have been updated recently by Georgianna Ziegler, in *English Literary Renaissance*. Hannay's excellent biography of Mary Sidney (1990) is a good source of initial information, while accounts focused specifically upon her literary works may be found in Waller (1979), Beilin (1987), Brennan (1988), Lamb (1990), and Walker (1996).

The texts of the original poems derive from MS J, Bent Juel-Jensen, Headington, Oxford ('Even Now ...' and 'To the Angel Spirit ...'); Samuel Daniel, *The Whole Works of Samuel Daniel* (1623; 'To the Angel Spirit ...'); Francis Davison, *A Poetical Rhapsody* (1602; 'A Dialogue'). For the play I have used *The Tragedie of Antonie* (1595). There is a full discussion of the 16/17 manuscript versions of the Psalms in John Rathmell's 1963 edition; I have primarily used MS A (the Penshurst MS). The Psalms were first published in *The Psalms of David ... by Sir Philip Sidney ... and ... The Countess of Pembroke* (1823), but the first critical edition was *The Psalms of Sir Philip Sidney and the Countess of Pembroke*, ed. J. A. Rathmell (1963); while more recent editorial work includes Gary Waller's *The Triumph of Death and Other Unpublished and Uncollected Poems by Mary Sidney, Countess of Pembroke* (1977) and S. P. Cerasano and Marion Wynne-Davies's *The Tragedy of Antonie* in *Renaissance Drama by Women: Texts and Contexts* (1996); these works have been consulted in the preparation of the poems included here. Unfortunately, I have not been able to refer to the critical edition of Mary Sidney's works edited by Margaret P. Hannay and Noel Kinnamon, since it has not yet been published.

AEMILIA LANYER (1569–1645) must be one of the most fascinating and interesting women writers of the early modern period. She first emerges on to the written page in the casebooks of her contemporary, the astrologer Simon Forman, whom she consulted about her husband's preferment at court and her own frequent miscarriages. Forman, however, soon became enamoured of Lanyer and attempted to seduce her. It appears that she was to a certain extent obliging, since he writes: 'Yet he [Forman] tolde all parts of her body wilingly. & kyssed her often but she wold not doe [have intercourse] in any wise.' But when these fruitless episodes persisted, Forman became angry and began to refer to Lanyer somewhat unjustly as a 'hore'. This, however, was not the first time that Lanyer had become exposed to scandalous taunts. She had begun life respectably enough as the daughter of Baptist Bassano, one of Henry VIII's musicians, and, although he died when she was seven, had gained entry into the court world as part of the retinue of Susan Bertie, the dowager Countess of Kent (Susan Bertie is referred to with affection and respect in the dedications to *Salve Deus*). Nevertheless, by the time Aemilia was eighteen she had become the mistress of Henry Cary, a renowned and well-established courtier, and when she became pregnant by him in 1592, she was hastily married off to Alfonso Lanyer, another musician. It was, perhaps, her subsequent exile from court society that drove Lanyer to Forman, for she consistently evokes a poignant nostalgia for the heady days of her youth in her poetry.

The sensual and tumultuous life described here hardly prepares the reader for Lanyer's only known work, *Salve Deus Rex Judaeorum* (1611), a religious complaint poem which sets out to repudiate all fleshly desires and specifically defends women against slanderous attacks on their virtue. The clue to this transformation may be found in the central text's framing devices: at the start Lanyer includes a series of nine dedications to women (including the Queen and 'All Vertuous Ladies in General'), while at the close she appends a country-house poem, 'To Cooke-Ham', which creates a particularly female version of the pastoral ideal. These representations of female communities draw explicitly upon Lanyer's experience in the early 1600s when she joined the circle of Margaret, Countess of Cumberland, and her daughter, Lady Anne Clifford. Margaret's piety and her Biblical learning, coupled with the predominantly female nature of her coterie, seems to have had an enormous impact upon Lanyer. Moreover, in addition to the general inspiration of her circumstances with the Countess of Cumberland, Lanyer appears to have received active encouragement from her patron to write both spiritual text and country-house poem. Yet, after this moment of intense creativity Lanyer sank back into relative obscurity; after the death of her husband in 1613, she attempted to set up a school, which failed in 1620, and subsequently she returned to family life. Certainly, when she died at the age of seventy-six it was as a respectable, financially independent woman surrounded by her grandchildren, who was, coincidentally, one of the most innovative poets of her age.

Like the other women poets in this volume Lanyer's work was largely neglected until the late twentieth century, but she first gained attention through A. L. Rowse and his unfounded claims that she was the Dark Lady of Shakespeare's sonnets (1978). Fortunately, her writing has since benefited from more serious application in the excellent edition by Susanne Woods, *The Poems of Aemilia Lanyer: Salve Deux Rex Judaeorum* (1993), and in numerous anthologies of early modern poetry. Similarly, criticism on Lanyer has been prolific and discerning. Lewalski (1985 and 1993) focuses upon Lanyer's feminization of the Christian narrative and her emphasis upon female communities, and these themes are also dealt with by Beilin (1987); both women stress Lanyer's 'feminist' bias and her clear originality. Hutson (1992) and Pearson (1996) both place Lanyer's writing in its literary context, while Krontiris (1992) lays emphasis upon the discourse of patronage. Perhaps one of the key debates about Lanyer's writing concerns 'To Cooke-Ham', for it is very possibly the first English country-house poem (pre-dating Ben Jonson's 'To Penshurst') and is, moreover, a very fine example of that genre. Lanyer's poetry has come to be acknowledged to rank amongst the most fascinating and interesting literary productions of its day.

There are only nine extant copies of *Salve Deus Rex Judaeorum* (1611), and only five of these retain the complete set of dedications. The poems included in this volume are all taken from *Salve Deus*.

RACHEL SPEGHT (b. 1597) is best known for her contribution to the debate about women, *A Mouzell for Melastomus* (1617), in which she defended her sex against the attack made by Joseph Swetnam in his *Arraignment of Women* (1617). Speght's was the first response to be published and the only one which may be securely attributed to a woman (Esther Sowernam's *Esther hath hanged Haman* (1617) and Constantia Munda's *The Worming of a Mad Dog* (1617) are pseudonymous and may be written by men). However, it seems from the introductory letter to Speght's second work, *Mortality's Memorandum* (1621), that the authorship of the prose tract *Mouzell* had been attributed to her father, and these later poems, with their literary and spiritual affiliations, set out to prove her ability to write. The learned tone of Speght's poetry has allowed *Mortality's Memorandum* to become neglected by comparison with the sharp polemicism of her prose, but her concerns are no less 'feminist' because couched in metaphors and rhetorical flourishes. The dream vision is re-sexed to display a woman's point of view, while her account of death commences with a vigorous defence of Eve. From Speght's adept use of the classics and the Geneva Bible, it is possible to detect the influence of a Protestant and humanist upbringing, and this fits well with what little we know of her life. Rachel Speght was the daughter of James Speght, a rector in London, and the author of *A Brief Demonstration* (1613) and *The Christian's Comfort* (1616); it is possible that she was also related to Thomas Speght, the editor of Chaucer. Speght dedicated *Mortality's Memorandum* to her godmother, Marie Moundford, who was the wife of Thomas Moundford the physician and author. In 1621 Speght married William Proctor and it is probable that they had two children, Rachel (1627) and William (1630); Proctor was himself a writer, publishing *The Watchman Warning* in 1625; Rachel, however, appears to have written nothing after her marriage. The overall impression is of a scholarly atmosphere which encouraged women to express themselves within the limits of certain humanist and Protestant conventions; it is, perhaps not surprising, therefore, that, while Speght is regarded as a staunch defender of women, her 'feminism' has often appeared luke-warm to late twentieth-century critics.

There was little interest in Rachel Speght's writing until the 1980s, when Betty Travitsky excerpted her writing in *The Paradise of Women: Writings by Englishwomen of the Renaissance* (1981) and Simon Shepherd produced a comprehensive edition of *Mouzell* in *The Woman's Sharp Revenge* (1985). More recent selections have appeared in Greer (1988) and in *The Penguin Book of Renaissance Verse* (1992). Criticism has tended to focus on the prose polemic, but Beilin (1987 and 1990) comments upon Speght's rewriting of the garden narrative in *Mortality's* dream vision, while Jones (1990), Purkiss (1992), and Lewalski (1993) all defend Speght's 'feminism' in both works.

The texts included here are taken from *A Mouzell for Melastomus, The Cynical Bayter of, and foul mouthed Barker against Evah's Sex* (1617) and *Mortalities Memorandum, With A Dream Prefixed, imaginarie in manner; reall in matter* (1621).

MARY WROTH (*c.* 1587–*c.* 1651) has come to be acknowledged not only as one of the foremost women writers of the early modern period, but as one of the finest and most versatile authors of her age, comparing favourably with poets such as Jonson, Donne and her uncle, Philip Sidney. The fact that Mary Wroth's poetry has been neglected over the past four hundred years is proof, if proof be needed, that female authors have been dismissed and abandoned because of a prejudice against their sex and not because of the inherent literary value of their texts. Indeed, although Wroth could lay claim to a valuable cultural inheritance through her Sidney family ties (she was Robert Sidney's daughter, the niece of Philip and Mary Sidney, and William Herbert's cousin), at the same time her radical divergence from accepted codes of female behaviour, in both personal and literary terms, led to her exclusion from court and to ultimate obscurity during her own lifetime. In literary terms Mary Wroth was one of the most innovative and revolutionary writers of the Jacobean court; she was the first Englishwoman to write a sonnet sequence, *Pamphilia to Amphilanthus* (which is reproduced here), a prose romance, *The Countess of Montgomery's Urania 1 and 2*, and a dramatic comedy, *Love's Victory*. Similarly, in her personal life she challenged social convention through her prolonged love affair with her cousin, William Herbert, and through her continued support of their two illegitimate children. It is perhaps this very complex interweaving of tradition (the Sidneian inheritance) with fresh and unique insights (as a woman author) that endows her poetry with the rich individualism and vibrancy of language that characterizes the most powerful poetry of the period.

There are excerpts of poetry in all Wroth's work, woven into the narrative strands of her prose romance and included in the dramatic speeches of her play, but her most consistent poetic work, and the one chosen for inclusion in this collection, is *Pamphilia to Amphilanthus*, a mixture of sonnets and songs which was published in 1621 as part of the *Urania*. The poems were in circulation as early as 1613, as is evidenced from an earlier version of the text in manuscript form (Folger MS V.a.104), but were re-ordered and edited for inclusion with the romance, since they are supposedly composed by Pamphilia for her lover Amphilanthus, these two being the protagonists of *Urania*. As such, the poems have a discrete identity as well as forming part of an ongoing romantic discourse between the two lovers, who are fictional characters as well as representing the real-life couple Mary Wroth and William Herbert. The autobiographical element in the text was quickly established by the late Josephine Roberts in her extensive researches on Wroth, and this, together with the mutual poetic indebtedness of the cousins, is an important aspect of interpreting the material. For example, the theme of constancy, represented by Pamphilia/Wroth, is set against the fickleness of the male beloved denoted by Amphilanthus/Herbert (a good analysis of this contrast may be found in Beilin (1981)).

For Wroth, however, the personal element in her writing extends beyond the immediate love relationship to a reworking of the whole Sidneian poetic tradition: the influence of Philip Sidney's *Astrophil and Stella*, Robert Sidney's Neoplatonism and Mary Sidney's Calvinism are all apparent. This has led to several critical defences of *Pamphilia to Amphilanthus* against a presumed attack of plagiarism. In her path-breaking edition of Wroth's poetry (1983), Josephine Roberts identifies many of the parallels between the Sidney authors and also points out that even to attempt a sonnet sequence in 1613 was somewhat old-fashioned, but she also points out that Wroth uses dramatic, Donne-like language, as well as inverting the traditional gender patterns of the sonnet. Similarly, Waller (1986) argues that Wroth challenges the patriarchy of the male sonneteers and provides a transition from the 'drab' Elizabethan age to the Metaphysical writing of the Jacobean era. These defences of Wroth's innovative gendered approach have been echoed or expanded by, among others, Miller (1990), Lewalski (1993), and again Waller (1993). What has become increasingly apparent is that Wroth is adept at reworking the discourses of other, usually male, authors, from Petrarch, through Philip Sidney, to John Donne, and that in each instance she inverts the gender identities and expectations to produce a radically new female-centred commentary upon the interpretation of love in the early modern period.

While there is a general consensus upon the quality of Wroth's poetry, there has been considerable disagreement about the structure and cohesion of *Pamphilia to Amphilanthus* itself. The divisions within the whole have been numbered at two (McLaren (1978)), at four (in three different groupings by Paulissen (1982), Roberts (1983), and Lewalski (1993)) and up to five by Martin (1997), while Masten (1991) suggests that there is no apparent arrangement at all. This edition has identified seven separate groups, although some of these may be classified together: (1) P1–P55 depicts the commencement of love and the confused feelings it arouses in a series of six sonnets followed by a single song; (2) P56–P62 gives the first intimation of loss in an inversion of the first sequence, being composed of six songs followed by a single sonnet; (3) P63–P72 explores the sonneteer's jealousy in a central sequence of ten sonnets; (4) P73–P76 is a group which could easily be linked to the previous one, but also acts as a transitional section from personal animosity to a more philosophical view of love; (5) P77–P90 is the key focal point of the poetic sequence, consisting of a 'crown' of sonnets which elevates the love of the sonneteer to a Neoplatonic and spiritual level; (6) P91–P95 returns the sequence to a darker and more cynical perspective with a series of four songs; (7) P96–P103 invokes nature imagery to contribute to an overall sense of a melancholic culmination and overall closure, the final sonnet concluding both text and romance with the abdication of the poetic self. Thus, the collection as a whole charts the narrative of a romance, explores key themes in early modern love discourses, and traces a Neoplatonic movement from physical to spiritual love. This overall process of transmutation and regeneration is underlined by the text's self-conscious gender inversions and the use of a transitional mood, shifting the language from the drab to the Metaphysical, and the tone from a courtly distance to personal immediacy. It is not surprising, therefore, that Wroth's poetry, which was neglected for so long, should appeal to a late twentieth-century readership, with its welcoming of a gendered awareness and its postmodern acceptance of reworkings and multiple discourses, and it seems equally predictable that Wroth studies should continue to flourish into the twenty-first century.

The poems included here are taken from *The Countesse of Montgomeries Urania* (London, 1621), while additional notes have referred to the manuscript version of *Pamphilia to Amphilanthus* (Folger Ms V.a.104). Three modern editions of the text are well worth consulting: Gary Waller, *Pamphilia to Amphilanthus* (1977), Josephine Roberts, *The Poems of Lady Mary Wroth* (1983), and R. E. Pritchard, *Lady Mary Wroth, Poems: A Modernized Edition* (1996).

DIANA PRIMROSE (fl. 1630) is one of the most obscure women poets of her age, since nothing certain can be ascertained about her except that in 1630 she published her only known work, *A Chain of Pearl*. It is likely, however, that 'Primrose' is a genuine surname, since it belonged to a well-known Scottish family which included Gilbert Primrose, a minister in the French Protestant Church, and Archibald Primrose, from whom the Earls of Rosebery were descended. There are several reasons for arguing that Diana was the wife of the former: there is a close resemblance in their statements of faith and in their criticism of Charles I; they both published their own writings; and 'Diana' was a popular name in France at the time but almost unheard of in England or Scotland (none of the recorded Primrose women are called Diana). Greer (1988) suggests that she could have been one of the daughters or the wife of James Primrose (cousin to Gilbert), who was an Edinburgh printer, but this seems less likely, as *A Chain of Pearl* demonstrates a knowledge of the court and was printed in London by Thomas Paine. It seems probable therefore that Diana was in some way connected (as wife or daughter) with Gilbert Primrose and that she left France with him in 1622/3 after a ban on foreign ministers had been imposed, probably as a result of Jesuit activity. Gilbert was promised support by Charles I but, since nothing was forthcoming, he moved to Oxford and in 1637 married again.

The short hypothetical Primrose biography is, however, substantive when compared to the total lack of information on Dorothy Berry, who wrote a dedicatory poem to Diana Primrose which prefaces the main text. It is, nevertheless, important to include Berry's short verse since it contributes substantially to the overall tone of the book, which is succinctly women-centred. In one of the few criticisms available on Primrose's work, Walker (1996: 68–9) points out that: 'written by a woman on the subject of a female monarch, dedicated to "All Noble Ladies, and Gentle-women," and prefaced by a woman's commendatory verse, *A Chaine of Pearl* advertises itself as a specifically female text.' Indeed, Primrose makes quite clear that the intended readers of the book are women, and she warns them, in a pointed inversion of the more usual condemnation of female wiles, against 'men's siren-blandishments, / Which are attended with so foul events.' (IV.5–6; see p. 233 above). Still, while Primrose may appear to defend women against accusations of immorality and to caution them against unwanted pregnancies, *A Chain of Pearl* cannot be considered pro-women either in a twentieth-century or in an early modern understanding of that term (for example, compare Primrose's poems with those of Lanyer, Speght and Bradstreet included in this collection). This somewhat conservative stance may be seen in Primrose's depiction of Elizabeth I as an exception to her sex rather than as proof that all women could be able rulers and rhetoricians given the opportunity. Similarly, Elizabeth's articulacy and skilled use of languages are depicted in an ambiguous moral light, for, while Primrose lauds the queen's 'Attic eloquence' and her speeches to Parliament, at the same time Elizabeth is compared to Cleopatra (a symbol for uncontrolled female sexuality) and is described as being able to 'ravish' and 'drown' the men who heard her speak (VIII.22, 3, 6, 27 and 17). In a text which constantly demonstrates a literary self-awareness through frequent use of puns on the title, such an equivocal presentation of female eloquence not only undermines the overt praise for Elizabeth I, but also introduces an element of self-doubt on behalf of the poet. Thus, although *A Chain of Pearl* initially appears to be woman-centred, it is fraught with doubts, questions, uncertainties and contradictions about female ability, which positions the author, her text, and all women at the margins of public life.

If we accept that Diana was connected with Gilbert Primrose, then this complex combination of self-defence and self-doubt in terms of gender would be explicable through the marginalized position that the Primroses found themselves in through their religious affiliations and their relationship with the court. Gilbert's treatment by Charles I offers a personal reason for Diana's condemnation of the king, particularly with regard to Charles's penchant for favourites and the unwise awarding of pensions, which she achieves through her praise of Elizabeth; although such attacks were commonplace outside the royal circle. In addition, *A Chain of Pearl* adheres to a stringent form of English Protestantism more redolent of Elizabeth's actual reign rather than the period in which Primrose was actually writing (twenty-seven years after Elizabeth's death), and it is not surprising that her two key source texts are Edmund Spenser's *The Faerie Queene* (1596) and the nostalgic *Annales* (1615) of William Camden. As a staunch Protestant woman writer excluded from the inner court circles, it is not surprising that Primrose combined a bitter self-doubt together with a longing for a past age in which she might assume that she would not have been marginalized because of her faith, sex and class.

At present little is known about Diana Primrose, and critical attention is at present confined to the short piece by Walker mentioned above, excerpts from the text in Germaine Greer's *Kissing the Rod*, and reproduction by the Brown Women Writers Project, and there is thus clearly scope for more research on her life and her writing.

The text used here is *A Chaine of Pearl* (London, 1630).

ALICE SUTCLIFFE (fl. 1628–34) remains an obscure figure in the history of English literature; she is known only for a single text, *Meditations of Man's Mortality, or a Way to True Blessedness* (1634) which comprises a Biblical prose treatise and a spiritual poem, the latter of which is included in his book. Initial researches into her background were undertaken by Ruth Hughey in 'Forgotten Verses By Ben Jonson, George Wither and Others to Alice Sutcliffe' (1934), where she concluded that Sutcliffe was the daughter of Luke Woodhouse of Norfolk, a family which was linked to the court through Prince Henry, and that by 1624 she was married to John Sutcliffe of Yorkshire, a squire to James I and Groom of the Privy Chamber to Charles I. Sutcliffe's contacts with the court world seem, however, to have been primarily through the Buckingham faction, for her dedicatory poems are directed towards Katherine, Duchess of Buckingham, the widow of George Villiers, First Duke of Buckingham; Susan, Countess of Denbeigh, Buckingham's sister; and Philip Herbert, Earl of Pembroke and Montgomery, whose son had married Buckingham's daughter. Indeed, as Hughey indicates, Sutcliffe must at one point have resided in the Duchess's household under her protection, as she is referred to as 'a *Mother* to me' in the text's dedicatory letter. This connection could have important political significations, since the female members of the Buckingham circle were linked to the resurgence of Catholicism at court under the auspices of Queen Henrietta Maria. Indeed, Sutcliffe specifically thanks the Duchess of Buckingham and her sister for the '*Spiritual* blessings' they have bestowed upon her, and she concludes her carefully worded prose treatise with a prayer to God for knowledge of 'the Glory of the inheritance of his Saints'. Any open statement of Catholicism would have been unwise: for example, another early modern woman writer, also associated with the Buckingham faction, Elizabeth Cary, was estranged from her husband, isolated from her children and left penniless because she became a Catholic convert. Nevertheless, Sutcliffe's connections allow us to interpret the warnings in her text as carrying a double meaning, so that their spiritual significance falls into a curious vacuum between an ostracized Catholicism and the dominant discourses of radical English Protestantism.

*Meditations of Man's Mortality* sets out to warn the reader of the omnipresence of death, initially painting a darkly gothic picture of human sin and damnation, but then turning in the final stanzas to welcome death as a way to salvation and eternal life. The poem demonstrates Sutcliffe's Biblical knowledge as well as her classical learning, but she seems to be torn between an open demonstration of her literary skill and scholarship, and the disavowal of expertise on the grounds of her sex. Thus, she denigrates her 'sex's act' in writing to Philip Herbert, but simultaneously praises female intelligence to Katherine, Duchess of Buckingham: 'Nor is there aught that lives in woman kind / Exceeding the rare prowess of her mind.' Similarly, while the poem attacks Eve as a 'Wicked woman' (line 30) Sutcliffe is able to turn fifty lines later to a defence of her sex: 'courage, woman' (line 79). This balancing act between a defence of women and an acceptance of female vilification parallels that of the central theme of the poem, a fear and a welcoming of death, and of the religious subtext of Catholicism and Protestantism. In each case Sutcliffe evades open confrontation between the opposing discourses, but the resulting tensions inevitably thread through the poetry, leaving the reader with a sense of unsettling ambiguity. It is therefore unfortunate that there has been so little criticism on Sutcliffe's work: after Hughey the only two contributions to scholarship in relation to this text have been excerpts from the verse in Greer (1988) and the three-and-a-half-page commentary in Walker (1996). As with so many women poets of the early modern period, more research needs to be undertaken to allow the works the full understanding they deserve.

The text used here is *Meditations of Man's Mortality or, A Way To True Blessedness* (1634).

JANE CAVENDISH (1621–69) and ELIZABETH CAVENDISH (1626–63) were the two elder daughters of William Cavendish, Duke of Newcastle, by his first wife, Elizabeth Bassett; their stepmother (William's second wife) was Margaret Cavendish, who was a prolific author in her own right. In a period in which women's writing was discouraged, it is unusual to find at least three female members of the Newcastle family producing a considerable body of literary works, from plays, through philosophical treatises, to courtly poetry. Indeed, if the familial associations are expanded beyond the immediate group, Alice Egerton, Elizabeth's sister-in-law, also wrote poems (one of which is included in the notes to the Cavendish poems; see p. 340 above); while two of their father's first cousins, Arabella Stuart and Elizabeth Grey, also produced extant works. Thus, in addition to William Cavendish, whose plays were published after the Restoration, Jane and Elizabeth may be linked to at least four further women writers. Although not widely recognized today, this prolificness means that the Cavendish family must rank alongside the Sidneys (Mary Sidney's and Mary Wroth's poems are included in this collection; see pp. 59–98 and 183–228 above) as one of the key groups of women writers in the early modern period. One of the reasons for this relative obscurity is that Jane's and Elizabeth's writing remained in manuscript during their own lifetimes and, even now, little of the material has been published. Unlike the Sidney women, the two Cavendish sisters began to write during the Civil War and continued their literary activities primarily during the Interregnum, when the opportunity for the circulation of manuscripts amongst their peers had been terminated by the overthrow of the court. Moreover, the publication of their writings became a more remote possibility than in the earlier part of the century, since all the nobility, male and female alike, found it difficult to find English publishers who would accept their works. Interestingly, however, it is these very restraints that seem to have spurred the two sisters into their initial literary activity, as well as to have instilled into their writings ideas which show a marked shift from the courtly ideals of the late sixteenth and early seventeenth centuries. While the other late poets in this collection show a distinct nostalgia for the past, Jane and Elizabeth Cavendish provide a link with the writing of the Restoration, and women such as Aphra Behn.

When the Civil War broke out, Jane and Elizabeth were living at the family home, Welbeck Abbey, even though Jane was already married; she became the wife of John Egerton, Viscount Brackley, in 1636 but was deemed too young to live with him at that point, although this explains her use of the initials 'E.B.' on the manuscript material from the 1640s. While William Cavendish and his two sons were fighting for the Royalist cause, the sisters (Jane and Elizabeth were accompanied by their younger sister, Frances) defended Welbeck against the Parliamentary troops and attempted to aid the king in whatever way they could.

Welbeck, however, was captured in 1644 and, despite a brief period when the Royalists regained control, was finally relinquished in 1645. During this period Jane and Elizabeth composed their play *The Concealed Fancies*, as well as several verses and a pastoral drama (they are all contained in the Bodleian MS). These works focus upon the events of the Civil War; for example, the two sections excerpted in this collection demonstrate the grief and despair felt by the Royalist women whose male relatives were involved in the war. Indeed, the works from this period are replete with military imagery, drawn not from the idealized chivalric skirmishes of the first part of the early modern age, but from the darker realities of actual warfare, with its desolation, betrayals and bloodshed. The courtly discourses used by the other women poets collected here are thereby undercut and mocked by the Cavendish sisters, for whom familial safety and personal liberty are more important goals.

With the victory of the Parliamentarians and the exile of many Royalists, including William Cavendish, the two sisters became involved in their separate families. Elizabeth, whose marriage seems to have been intensely happy, retired from London and devoted herself to her children and to an increasingly spiritual life. Her writings after her marriage were collected together by her husband in a small manuscript volume (now in the British Library) which contains mostly prose meditations in addition to three poems, two of which are included here. Jane married Charles Cheney in 1654 and, like her sister, appears to have been very happy, although her nuptial ideal was more romantic and socially polished than was Elizabeth's. Jane too continued to write and is reported in an elegy upon her death to have completed several manuscript volumes of verse, although only one poem, 'On the Death of My Dear Sister' (at present in the Huntington Library, and reproduced here) remains extant. It is particularly unfortunate that Jane's *oeuvre* is incomplete, since her writing displays a rhetorical skill and literary self-awareness that Elizabeth's does not, and it is to be hoped that more of her writing will come to light in the wake of increased critical interest.

At present, criticism on the writings of the Cavendish sisters has focused mainly on *The Concealed Fancies*, partly because of the availability of a modern edition since 1996; for example Ezell (1988) provides an introduction to the text, and recent essays by Chalmers (forthcoming) and Findlay (1998) offer a more complex analysis of the text. Finally, Travitsky's pioneering essay (1990) and some excerpts in Greer (1988) have opened up research on the Cavendish's other manuscript work. However, it is to be hoped that a comprehensive edition of Jane's and Elizabeth's writings, together with associated critical material, will soon be forthcoming.

The texts used here are Bodleian Library, MS Rawlinson Poet. 16 (for *The Concealed Fancies* and 'An Answer to my Lady Alice Egerton's Song'), Huntington Library, MS Ellesmere 8353 (for 'On the Death of My Dear Sister'), and British Library, MS Egerton 607 (for 'On My Boy Henry' and 'Spoken Upon Receiving a Cake of Perfume Made Up in the Shape of a Heart').

ANNE BRADSTREET (*c.* 1612–72) is rarely included in anthologies or criticisms of early modern women's writing (Germaine Greer's edition, *Kissing the Rod*, being a notable exception), because she is classified as an 'American' author and lauded, quite rightly, as one of the first published poets of the New World. However, it is often distorting to police the divide between European and North American writing so rigorously, particularly when discussing the works of the first colonizers, who had been born in England and were often dependent upon English literary discourses. An examination of Anne Bradstreet's poems reveals that many of her concerns and influences echo those of the other women authors in this collection. Thus, it is important to recognize Anne Bradstreet as one of the most prolific and interesting of early modern women poets: both within the context of the European tradition and in her ability to exemplify the changes between Old and New World sensibilities.

Anne Bradstreet was born in Northamptonshire, England, the daughter of Thomas Dudley and Elizabeth Yorke. At the time of Anne's birth Dudley was a legal clerk, but in 1619 he became steward to the Earl of Lincoln, and the family, although staunch Puritans, adopted a genteel lifestyle which gave the children access to a humanist education and to the wealth of Lincoln's library. Anne certainly benefited both from her father's liberal views about educating daughters and from the scholarly resources that were to underpin her first works. In 1622 Dudley was joined by Simon Bradstreet, who became Lincoln's assistant steward for a year until he moved to become a steward in his own right, to the Countess of Warwick. During Simon Bradstreet's association with Dudley a closeness must have developed with Anne, for in 1628 she and Bradstreet were married. Difficulties, however, had already begun to emerge for the English Puritans: in 1627 Lincoln was arrested, and Dudley himself was threatened with imprisonment and decided to emigrate, along with others of his faith, to the New World. Consequently, in March 1630 the Dudleys and Bradstreets set sail for America in the *Arbella*, arriving at Salem in the June of that year. The life of the first colonists was filled with hardhips and recurrent ill-health, and Anne at first bitterly regretted leaving England, even though her family must have been one of the most prosperous in the district; both her father and her husband served as governor of Massachusetts, and their library alone amounted to over 800 books. The Bradstreets moved several times before Anne's death: they initially settled in Cambridge, but moved after five years to Ipswich, and in 1644 again relocated, this time to Andover. It was here that Anne had the last three of her eight children and composed most of her poetry, from the scholarly works in the first edition of *The Tenth Muse* (1650), to the personal domestic poems of *Several Poems* (1678), and the Andover MSS. She died in 1672 and was buried in Andover, Massachusetts.

Anne Bradstreet's work is commonly divided into the two groupings indicated above: the formal, political and public poems of 1650 and the intimate, personal, autobiographical works that followed. The first poems are intensely learned, drawing extensively upon European sources, such as Joshua Sylvester's 1641 translation of Guillaume du Bartas's religious epic *Divine Weeks and Works*; specifically Protestant texts, such as John Foxe's *Actes and Monuments*; historical treatises, such as Walter Ralegh's *History of the World*; and sophisticated English court poetry, such as Edmund Spenser's *The Faerie Queene*, and the writings of Philip Sidney. These works were published in London without Anne's consent by her brother-in-law John Woodbridge. Despite the commonplace nature of disclaimers by women authors of the period, there is no reason to doubt Anne's ignorance of Woodbridge's activities on her behalf; he makes it clear in his prefatory epistle that she knew nothing of the enterprise, and circumstances in the New World would have certainly militated against her publishing her writings.

The New England community was distinctly opposed to its female members pursuing any scholarly activity; for example, in 1637–8 the radical Puritan Anne Hutchinson had been banished for preaching against the dominant patriarchy, and in 1645 John Winthrop, the then governor of Massachusetts, described how a young woman had lost 'her understanding and reason' because she had given 'herself wholly to reading and writing, and had written many books'. It is not surprising, therefore, that Anne, while protected within her own home by both husband and father, chose not to brave public censure by actively pursuing the publication of her works. Even before *The Tenth Muse* was published, she was aware that 'I am obnoxious to each carping tongue / Who says my hand a needle better fits' ('The Prologue', 1650), and in 'In Honour of that High and Mighty Princess Queen Elizabeth of Happy

Memory' (see pp. 260–63 above) she attacks the 'slander' of 'masculines [who] ... have thus taxed us long'. Thus the 1650 edition of her works, with their scholarly erudition, their evocation of a European inheritance, their self-conscious defence of women, and even their publication and popularity in London rather than New England, allows us to perceive a poet who struggled against the dominant discourses of time and place in order to assert the independence of her role as a woman poet.

The later poems, those published in the 1678 edition, *Several Poems*, and those collected in the Andover MSS (not published before 1867, in *Works of Anne Bradstreet*, edited by John Harvard Ellis) are, perhaps surprisingly, a direct shift away from the tone, content and form of the earlier works. Gone are the concerns with politics, either European or those of the New World, the studious references, the sharp responses to male criticism, and in their place are found the personal poems which have since established Bradstreet as a popular poet. As her poem 'The Author to Her Book' (see p. 264 above) makes clear, Bradstreet began correcting her poems after their initial publication in 1650, and she also added more material; these were published posthumously in *Several Poems* (1678), while extra poems were appended in Ellis's 1867 edition. These poems focus upon the private emotions of Anne Bradstreet, her love for her husband and children, her grief at the death of her grandchildren, her fear of death, and her innermost spiritual doubts. Moreover, the poetry becomes more immediate, more representative of her real existence and less dependent upon scholarly exemplar, and, as such, more attuned to a burgeoning New World discourse than to the Old World rhetoric she had left behind. Indeed, it is this second phase of her literary career that has secured Bradstreet's critical reputation.

It is important to note that Bradstreet was a popular author until the nineteenth century, when the quality of her writing was consistently questioned and she was seen as a derivative (1650 poems) or over-personal (later works) writer. It was not until the advent of feminist criticism in the mid-twentieth century that Bradstreet was rediscovered and hailed as one of the 'mothers' of American poetry. One of the key texts in this process of revaluation was *The Works of Anne Bradstreet* (1967) edited by Jeannine Hensley with its feminist foreword by Adrienne Rich, which was followed by *The Complete Works of Anne Bradstreet* (1981), edited by John McElrath and Allan Robb. Critical commentaries began to appear, such as White (1971). Anne Bradstreet has thus been fully reintegrated into the American canon, and it is now time to ensure that her reputation as an 'English' author, which once made *The Tenth Muse* one of the 'most vendible books in London' (Hensley 1967:xxxii) is likewise restored.

The texts drawn upon for this edition are *The Tenth Muse Lately Sprung Up in America* (1650), *Several Poems* (1678), and *Works of Anne Bradstreet* edited by John Harvard Ellis (1867).

# SELECT BIBLIOGRAPHY

## A. *Primary Materials*

Allen, William, *Briefe Historie of the Glorious Martyrdom of xii Reverend Priests* (1582; repr. London: Burns and Oates, 1908).

Anon., *Wit's Recreations* (London, 1645).

Aristotle, *The Nicomachean Ethics of Aristotle*, trans. D. P. Chase (London: Dent, 1933).

Bèze, Théodore de, and Clément Marot, *Les Pseaumes mis en rime francoise* (Geneva, 1577).

*Bible. Authorized King James Version*, ed. Robert Carroll and Stephen Prickett (Oxford: Oxford University Press, 1997).

Boethius, *Consolation of Philosophy*, trans. George Colville (London, 1556).

Bradstreet, Anne, *Several Poems Compiled with great variety of Wit and learning, full of Delight; Wherein especially is contained a compleat Discourse and Description of the four Elements, Constitutions, Ages of Man, Seasons of the Year. Together with an Exact Epitome of the three first Monarchyes, Viz. the Assyrian, Persian, Grecian. And the Beginning of the Romane Commonwealth to the end of their last King: with diverse other pleasant and serious Poems. The second Edition, Corrected by the Author, and enlarged by an Addition of several other Poems found amongst her Papers after her death* (Boston, Mass., 1678).

—— *The Tenth Muse Lately Sprung up in America. Or Severall Poems, compiled with great variety of Wit and Learning, full of delight. Wherein is especially contained a compleat discourse and description of The Four Elements, Constitutions, Ages of Man, Seasons of the Year. Together with an Exact Epitomie of The Four Monarchies, viz. The Assyrian, Persian, Grecian, Roman. Also a Dialogue between Old England and new, concerning the late troubles. With divers other pleasant and serious Poems. By a Gentlewoman in those parts.* (London: Stephen Botwell, 1650).

—— *The Works of Anne Bradstreet*, ed. John Harvard Ellis (Charlestown, Mass.: A. E. Cutter, 1867).

—— *The Works of Anne Bradstreet*, ed. Jeannine Hensley (Cambridge, Mass.: Harvard University Press, 1967).

—— *The Complete Works of Anne Bradstreet*, ed. Joseph McElrath and Allan Robb (Boston, Mass.: Twayne, 1981).

Brooks-Davies, Douglas, ed., *Silver Poets of the Sixteenth Century* (London: Dent, 1992).

Calvin, John, *The Psalmes of David and Others. With M. John Calvin's Commentaries*, trans. Arthur Golding (London, 1571).

Camden, William, *Annales rerum Anglicarum et Hibernicarum, regnante Elizabetha, ad annum salutis M.D. LXXXIX* (London, 1615).

—— *Annales. The True and Royall History of Elizabeth Queen of England* (London, 1625–9).

Cavendish, Elizabeth, *True Copies of Certain Loose Papers left by the Right Honourable Elizabeth Countess of Bridgewater, Collected and Transcribed together here since her death AD 1663* (British Library, MS Egerton 607).

Cavendish, Jane, 'On the Death of My Dear Sister' (Huntington Library, MS Ellesmere 8353).

Cavendish, Elizabeth and Jane, *The Concealed Fancies* (Bodleian Library, MS Rawlinson Poet. 16).

—— *The Concealed Fancies*, in *Renaissance Drama by Women: Texts and Documents*, ed. S. P. Cerasano and Marion Wynne-Davies (London: Routledge, 1996).

Caxton, William, *The Golden Legend* (London, 1483).

Chaucer, Geoffrey, *The Works of Geoffrey Chaucer*, ed. F. N. Robinson, 2nd edn (London, Oxford University Press, 1974).

Cicero, Marcus Tullius, *Tusculan Disputations*, trans. J. E. King (London: Heinemann, 1927).

Clifford, Anne, *The Diaries of Lady Anne Clifford*, ed. D. J. H. Clifford (Stroud: Alan Sutton, 1990).

Coverdale, Miles, *The Bible in Englyshe* (London, 1539).

Daniel, Samuel, *The Complaint of Rosamond* (London, 1594).

—— *Delia* (London, 1592).

—— *The Tragedie of Cleopatra*, ed. M. Lederer (London: David Nutt, 1911).

—— *The Whole Works of Samuel Daniel* (London, 1623).

Dante Alighieri, *The New Life: La vita nuova*, trans. William Anderson (Baltimore, Md: Penguin, 1964).

Davison, Francis, *A Poetical Rhapsody* (London, 1602).

Dekker, John, *The Cold Year, 1614, a Deep Snow: in which Men and Cattell have Perished* (London, 1615).

—— *The Great Frost: Cold Doings in London* (London, 1608).

Desportes, Philippe, *Cartels et masquarades, épitaphes*, in *Les Premières Oeuvres* (1573), ed. V. E. Graham (Geneva: Droz, 1958).

Donne, John, *The Elegies and the Songs and Sonnets*, ed. Helen Gardner (Oxford: Clarendon Press, 1965).

Dowriche, Anne, *The French History* (London, 1598).

Dowriche, Hugh, *The Gaoler's Conversion* (London, 1596).

Drayton, Michael, *Matilda* (London, 1594).

du Bartas, Guillaume, *Weeks and Works*, trans. Joshua Sylvester (London, 1641).

Elizabeth I, *The Poems of Queen Elizabeth I*, ed. Leicester Bradner (Providence, RI: Brown University Press, 1964).

Forman, Simon, *Casebooks* (Bodleian Library, MS Ashmole 226).

Foxe, John, *The Acts and Monuments of John Foxe*, ed. George Townshend (London: Burnside & Seeley, 1849).

Garnier, Robert, *Two Tragedies*, ed. C. M. Hill and M. G. Morrison (London: Athlone Press, 1975).

Gascoigne, George, *The Steele Glas* (London, 1576).

*Geneva Bible* (Geneva, 1560).

Gentillet, Innocent, *Discours ... contre Nicholas Machiavel, Florentin* (Paris, 1576).

Greer, Germaine, ed., *Kissing the Rod: An Anthology of Seventeenth-Century British Women's Verse* (London: Virago, 1988).

Herbert, George, *The Poems of George Herbert* (London: Oxford University Press, 1913).

Herbert, William, *Poems* (London, 1660).

Herodotus, *The History*, trans. David Grene (Chicago: University of Chicago Press, 1987).

Joceline, Elizabeth, *The Mothers Legacie, To her unborne Childe* (London, 1624).

Jonson, Ben, *Works*, ed. C. H. Herford and Percy Simpson (Oxford: Clarendon Press, 1937).

Josephus, Flavius, *The Works of Flavius Josephus*, ed. W. Whiston (London: William Baynes and Son, 1825).

Knox, John, *The First Blast of the Trumpet Against the Monstrous Regiment of Women* (Geneva, 1558).

Lanyer, Aemilia, *Salve Deus Rex Judaeorum* (London, 1611).

—— *The Poems of Shakespeare's Dark Lady*, ed. A. L. Rowse (London: Jonathan Cape, 1978).

—— *The Poems of Aemilia Lanyer*, ed. Susanne Woods (Oxford: Oxford University Press, 1993).

Lawes, Henry, *Ayres, and Dialogues, For One, Two, and Three Voyces: The Third Book* (London, 1658).

Lucretius, Titus Caius, *On the Nature of the Universe*, trans. John Godwin (Harmondsworth: Penguin, 1994).

Lyly, John, *Euphues, the Anatomy of Wit* (London, 1578).

Machiavelli, Niccolò, *The Prince*, trans. George Bull (Harmondsworth: Penguin, 1961).

Marlowe, Christopher, *The Works of Christopher Marlowe*, ed. C. F. Tucker Brooke (Oxford: Clarendon Press, 1910).

Martin, Randall, ed., *Women Writers of Renaissance England* (London: Longman, 1997).

May, Steven M., *The Elizabethan Courtier Poets: The Poems and Their Contexts* (Columbia: University of Missouri Press, 1991).

Milton, John, *The Poems of John Milton*, ed. John Carey and Alastair Fowler (Harlow: Longman, 1968).

Munda, Constantia, *The Worming of a Mad Dogge: or, A Soppe for Cerberus the Jaylor of Hell* (London, 1617).

Ovid, *Heroides and Amores*, trans. Grant Showerman (London: William Heinemann, 1985).

—— *Metamorphoses*, trans. Rolfe Humphries (London: John Calder, 1957).

Petrarch, Francis, *Petrarch's Lyric Poems*, trans. Robert M. Durling (Cambridge, Mass.: Harvard University Press, 1976).

—— *Trionfi e poesie latine* (Milano: Riccardo Ricciardi, 1951).

Plat, Hugh, *The Floures of Philosophie* (London, 1572).

Plutarch, *Plutarch's Lives*, trans. A. Steward and G. Long (London: Bell and Sons, 1904).

Primrose, Diana, *A Chaine of Pearl: or, A Memoriall of the peerles Graces and Heroick Vertues of Queene Elizabeth, of Glorious Memory* (London: Thomas Paine, 1630).

Proctor, William, *The Watchman Warning* (London, 1625).

Ralegh, Walter, *The Historie of the World* (London, 1614).

*Roman Martyrology* (St Omer, 1627).

Ronsard, Pierre, *Poèmes de Ronsard*, ed. Francis Poulenc (Paris: Heugel, 1925).

Shakespeare, William, *The Riverside Shakespeare*, ed. G. Blakemore Evans (Boston, Mass.: Houghton Mifflin, 1974).

Shepherd, Simon, ed., *The Women's Sharp Revenge: Five Women's Pamphlets from the Renaissance* (London: Fourth Estate, 1985).

Sidney, Mary, *The Countess of Pembroke's Translation of Philippe de Mornay's Discourse of Life and Death*, ed. Diane Bornstein (Detroit, Mich.: Consortium for Medieval and Early Modern Studies, 1983).

—— *The Psalms*, MS A (Penshurst, Lord De L'Isle), MS J (Headington, Oxford, Juel-Jensen) British Library, MS Add. 15117.

—— *The Psalms of Philip Sidney and the Countess of Pembroke*, ed. J. C. A. Rathmell (New York: New York University Press, 1963).

—— *The Tragedy of Antonie*, in *Renaissance Drama by Women: Texts and Documents*, ed. S. P. Cerasano and Marion Wynne-Davies (London: Routledge, 1996).

—— *The Triumph of Death and Other Unpublished and Uncollected Poems*, ed. Gary F. Waller (Salzburg: Institut für Anglistik und Amerikanistik, Universität Salzburg, 1977).

—— *Two Poems by the Countess of Pembroke*, ed. Bent Juel-Jensen (Oxford, 1963).

Sidney, Philip, *An Apology for Poetry*, ed. Geoffrey Shepherd (Manchester: Manchester University Press, 1973).

—— *Certain Sonnets* (Cambridge, Mass.: Riverside Press, 1904).

—— 'The Lady of May', in *The Last Part of the Countesse of Pembroke's Arcadia ...*, ed. Albert Feuillerat (Cambridge: Cambridge University Press, 1922).

—— *The Old Arcadia*, ed. Jean Robertson (Oxford: Clarendon Press, 1973).

—— *The Poems of Sir Philip Sidney*, ed. W. A. Ringler (Oxford: Clarendon Press, 1962).

Sidney, Robert, *The Poems of Robert Sidney*, ed. P. J. Croft (Oxford: Clarendon Press, 1984).

Sowernam, Ester, *Ester hath hang'd Haman: or, An Answere to a lewd Pamphlet, entituled 'The Arraignment of Women'* (London, 1617).

Speed, John, *The History of Great Britain* (London, 1611).

Speght, James, *A Brief Demonstration, who have, and of the certainty of their salvation, that have the Spirit of Christ* (London, 1613).

—— *The Christian's Comfort* (London, 1616).

Speght, Rachel, *A Mouzell for Melastomus, The Cynical Bayter of, and foul mouthed Barker against Evah's Sex. Or an Apologeticall Answere to that Irreligious and Illiterate Pamphlet made by Jo. Sw. and by him Intitled 'The Arraignment of Women'* (London, 1617).

—— *Mortalities Memorandum, with a Dreame prefixed, imaginarie in manner; reall in matter* (London, 1621).

Spenser, Edmund, *The Faerie Queene* (London, 1590 and 1596).

—— *The Poetical Works of Edmund Spenser*, ed. J. C. Smith (Oxford: Clarendon Press, 1909).

Swetnam, Joseph, *The Arraignment of Lewde, idle, froward, and unconstant women* (London, 1615).

Soowthern, John, *Pandora, The Musyque of the beautie of his Mistresse Diana* (London, 1584).

Travitsky, Betty, ed., *The Paradise of Women: Writings by Englishwomen of the Renaissance* (London: Greenwood Press, 1981).

Tymme, Thomas, trans., *The Three Parts of Commentaries, containing the whole and perfect discourse of the Civil Wars of France* (London, 1574).

Virgil, *The Aeneid of Virgil*, trans. Rolfe Humphries (New York: Charles Scribner, 1951).

Whitney, Geoffrey, *Whitney's Choice of Emblems* (London, 1586).

Whitney, Isabella, *The Copy of a Letter, lately written in metre, by a young gentlewoman to her unconstant Lover* (London, 1567).

—— *The Lamentation of a Gentlewoman Upon the Death of her late Deceased Friend, William Gruffith, Gentleman*, in Thomas Proctor, *A Gorgeous Gallery of Gallant Inventions* (London, 1578).

—— *A Sweet Nosegay, or Pleasant Posy* (London, 1573).

—— *A Sweet Nosegay and The Copy of a Letter*, ed. Richard J. Panofsky (New York: Scholars' Facsimiles and Reprints, 1982).

—— 'The "Wyll and testament" of Isabella Whitney', ed. Betty Travitsky, *English Literary Renaissance*, 10 (1980), 76–94.

Woolf, Virginia, *A Room of One's Own* (London: Hogarth Press, 1929).

Woudhuysen, H. R., ed., *The Penguin Book of Renaissance Verse* (London: Penguin, 1992).

Wroth, Mary, *Lady Mary Wroth, Poems: A Modernized Edition*, ed. R. E. Pritchard (Keele: Keele University Press, 1996).

—— *Love's Victory*, in *Renaissance Drama by Women: Texts and Documents*, ed. S. P. Cerasano and Marion Wynne-Davies (London: Routledge, 1996).

—— *Pamphilia to Amphilanthus*, ed. Gary Waller (Salzburg: Institut für Anglistik und Amerikanistik, Universität Salzburg, 1977).

—— *The Poems of Lady Mary Wroth*, ed. J. A. Roberts (Baton Rouge: Louisiana State University Press, 1983).

—— *Sonnets and Songs* (Folger Shakespeare Library, MS v.a.104).

—— *The Countesse of Montgomeries Urania* (London, 1621).

—— *The First Part of the Countess of Montgomery's Urania*, ed. J. A. Roberts (Binghamton, NY: Medieval & Renaissance Texts & Studies, 1995).

—— *The Secound Part of the Countess of Montgomerys Urania* (Newberry Library, MS fy 1565. W.95).

## B. *Secondary Materials*

Ballard, George, *Memoirs of Several Ladies of Great Britain* (Oxford: privately printed, 1752).

Beilin, Elaine V., ' "The onely perfect vertue": constancy in Mary Wroth's *Pamphilia to Amphilanthus*', *Spenser Studies*, 2 (1981), 229–45.

—— *Redeeming Eve: Women Writers of the English Renaissance* (Princeton, NJ: Princeton University Press, 1987).

—— 'Writing public poetry, humanism and the woman writer', *Modern Language Quarterly*, 51 (1990), 249–71.

Brennan, Michael, *Literary Patronage in the English Renaissance: The Pembroke Family* (London: Routledge, 1988).

Chalmers, Hero, 'The politics of feminine retreat in Margaret Cavendish's "The Female Academy" and "The Convent of Pleasure" ', *Women's Writing* (forthcoming).

Ezell, Margaret J. M., ' "To be your daughter in your pen": the social functions of literature in the writings of Lady Elizabeth Brackley and Lady Jane Cavendish', *Huntington Library Quarterly*, 51 (1988), 281–96.

Fehrenbach, R. J., 'Isabella Whitney and the popular miscellanies of Richard Jones', *Cahiers elisabéthains*, 19 (1981), 85–7.

—— 'Isabella Whitney, Sir Hugh Plat, Geoffrey Whitney, and "Sister Eldershae" ', *English Language Notes*, 21 (1983), 7–11.

Findlay, Alison, 'Playing the "scene self": power and performance in *The Concealed Fancies*', in *Renaissance Drama by Women: A Reader*, ed. S. P. Cerasano and M. Wynne-Davies (London: Routledge, 1998).

Fisken, Beth Wynne, ' "To the Angell Spirit …": Mary Sidney's entry into the "world of words" ', in *The Renaissance Englishwoman in Print: Counterbalancing the Canon*, ed. Anne M. Haselkorn and Betty S. Travitsky (Amherst: University of Massachusetts Press, 1990).

Hall, Kim F., ' "I rather would wish to be a Black Moor": beauty, race, and rank in Lady Mary Wroth's *Urania*', in *Women 'Race', and Writing in the Early Modern Period*, ed. Mary O. Hendricks and Patricia Parker (London: Routledge, 1994).

Hannay, Margaret P., *Philip's Phoenix: Mary Sidney, Countess of Pembroke* (Oxford: Oxford University Press, 1990).

—— ' "Princes you as men must dy": Genevan advice to monarchs in the *Psalmes* of Mary Sidney', *English Literary Renaissance*, 19 (1989), 22–41.

Haselkorn, Anne M., and Betty S. Travitsky, eds, *The Renaissance English-woman in Print: Counterbalancing the Canon* (Amherst: University of Massachusetts Press, 1990).

Hughey, Ruth, 'Forgotten verses by Ben Jonson, George Wither, and others to Alice Sutcliffe', *Review of English Studies*, 10 (1934) 156–64.

Hutson, Lorna, 'Why the lady's eyes are nothing like the sun', in *Women, Texts and Histories, 1575–1760*, ed. Clare Brant and Diane Purkiss (London: Routledge, 1992).

Jones, Ann Rosalind, 'Counterattacks on "the bayter of women": three pamphleteers of the early seventeenth century', in *The Renaissance English-woman in Print: Counterbalancing the Canon*, ed. Anne M. Haselkorn and Betty S. Travitsky (Amherst: University of Massachusetts Press, 1990).

—— *The Currency of Eros: Women's Love Lyrics in Europe, 1540–1620* (Bloomington: Indiana University Press, 1990).

Krontiris, Tina, *Oppositional Voices: Women as Writers and Translators of Literature in the English Renaissance* (London: Routledge, 1992).

Lamb, Mary Ellen, *Gender and Authorship in the Sidney Circle* (Madison: University of Wisconsin Press, 1990).

Levin, Carole, ' "We princes, I tell you, are set on stages": Elizabeth I and dramatic self-representation', in *Renaissance Drama by Women: A Reader*, ed. S. P. Cerasano and Marion Wynne-Davies (London: Routledge, 1998).

Lewalski, Barbara Kiefer, 'Of God and good women: the poems of Aemilia Lanyer', in *Tudor Women as Patrons, Translators, and Writers of Religious Works*, ed. Margaret Hannay (Kent, Ohio: Kent State University Press, 1985).

—— *Writing Women in Jacobean England* (Cambridge, Mass.: Harvard University Press, 1993).

McLaren, Margaret, 'Lady Mary Wroth's *Urania*: The Work and the Tradition' (unpublished doct. diss., University of Auckland, 1978).

Martin, Randall, 'Anne Dowriche's *The French History* and Innocent Gentillet's *Contre-Machival*', *Notes and Queries*, 242 (1997), 40–2.

Masten, Jeff, ' "Shall I turne blabb?": circulation, gender, and subjectivity in Mary Wroth's sonnets', in *Reading Mary Wroth: Representing Alternatives in Early Modern England*, ed. Naomi J. Miller and Gary Waller (Knoxville: University of Tennessee Press, 1991).

May, Steven W., 'The Countess of Oxford's sonnets: a caveat', *English Language Notes*, 29 (1992), 9–19.

Miller, Naomi J., and Gary Waller, eds, *Reading Mary Wroth: Representing Alternatives in Early Modern England* (Knoxville: University of Tennessee Press, 1991).

—— ' "Rewriting lyric fictions: the role of the lady in Lady Mary Wroth's *Pamphilia to Amphilanthus*', in *The Renaissance Englishwoman in Print:*

*Counterbalancing the Canon*, ed. Anne M. Haselkorn and Betty S. Travitsky (Amherst: University of Massachusetts Press, 1990).

Moody, Ellen, 'Six elegiac poems, possibly by Anne Cecil de Vere, Countess of Oxford', *English Literary Renaissance*, 19 (1989), 152–70.

Paulissen, May Nelson, *The Love Sonnets of Lady Mary Wroth* (Salzburg: Institut für Anglistik und Amerikanistik, Universität Salzburg, 1982).

Pearson, Jacqueline, 'Women writers and women readers: the case of Aemilia Lanyer', in *Voicing Women: Gender and Sexuality in Early Modern Writing*, ed. Kate Chedgzoy, Melanie Hansen and Suzanne Trill (Keele: Keele University Press, 1996).

Purkiss, Diane, 'Material girls: the seventeenth-century woman debate', in *Women, Texts and Histories, 1575–1760*, ed. Clare Brant and Diane Purkiss (London: Routledge, 1992).

Roberts, Josephine A., 'The biographical problem of *Pamphilia to Amphilanthus*', *Tulsa Studies in Women's Literature*, 1 (1982), 43–53.

—— 'Lady Mary Wroth's sonnets: a labyrinth of the mind', *Journal of Women's Studies in Literature*, 1 (1979), 319–29.

—— 'Recent studies in women writers of Tudor England, part II: Mary Sidney, Countess of Pembroke', in *Women in the Renaissance: Selections From English Literary Renaissance*, ed. Kirby Farrell, Elizabeth H. Hageman and Arthur F. Kinney (Amherst: University of Massachusetts Press, 1990).

Schleiner, Louise, *Tudor and Stuart Women Writers* (Bloomington: Indiana University Press, 1994).

Smith, Rosalind, 'The sonnets of the Countess of Oxford and Elizabeth I: translations from Desportes', *Notes and Queries*, 239 (1994), 446–50.

Somerset, Anne, *Elizabeth I* (London: Weidenfeld and Nicolson, 1991).

Teague, Frances, 'Queen Elizabeth in her speeches', in *Gloriana's Face: Women, Public and Private, in the English Renaissance*, ed. S. P. Cerasano and Marion Wynne-Davies (Hemel Hempstead: Harvester, 1992).

Travitsky, Betty, S., ' "His Wife's Prayers and Meditations": MS Egerton 607', in *The Renaissance Englishwoman in Print: Counterbalancing the Canon*, ed. Anne M. Haselkorn and Betty S. Travitsky (Amherst: University of Massachusetts Press, 1990).

—— ed., *The Paradise of Women: Writings by Englishwomen of the Renaissance* (Westport, Conn.: Greenwood Press, 1981).

—— 'The "Wyll and Testament" of Isabella Whitney', *English Literary Renaissance*, 10 (1980), 76–94.

Turberville, A. S., *A History of Welbeck Abbey and Its Owners* (London: Faber and Faber, 1937).

Walker, Kim, *Women Writers of the Engish Renaissance* (London: Twayne, 1996).

Wall, Wendy, 'Isabella Whitney and the female legacy', *English Literary History*, 58 (1991), 35–62.

Waller, Gary, *English Poetry of the Sixteenth Century* (London: Longman, 1986).

—— *Mary Sidney, Countess of Pembroke: A Critical Study of Her Writings and*

*Literary Milieu* (Salzburg: Institut für Anglistik and Amerikanistik, Universität Salzburg, 1979).

—— *The Sidney Family Romance: Mary Wroth, William Herbert, and the Early Modern Construction of Gender* (Detroit, Mich.: Wayne State University Press, 1993).

White, Elizabeth Wade, *Anne Bradstreet: The Tenth Muse* (New York: Oxford University Press, 1971).

Ziegler, Georgianna, 'Recent studies in women writers of Tudor England, 1485–1603', *English Literary Renaissance*, 24 (1994), 229–42.